A Short Guide to Writing about Literature

A Short Guide to Writing about Literature

SEVENTH EDITION

SYLVAN BARNET
Tufts University

HarperCollins*CollegePublishers*

Acquisitions Editor: Lisa Moore
Development Editor: Judith Leet
Project Editor: Bob Ginsberg
Design Manager/Cover Designer: Wendy Ann Fredericks
Cover Art: Henri Matisse, Canvas, 1939/The Granger Collection
Electronic Production Manager: Valerie A. Sawyer
Desktop Administrator: Hilda Koparanian
Manufacturing Manager: Helene G. Landers
Electronic Page Makeup: RR Donnelley Barbados
Printer and Binder: RR Donnelley & Sons Company
Cover Printer: The Lehigh Press, Inc.

For permission to use copyrighted material, grateful acknowledgment is made to the copyright holders on p. 381, which is hereby made part of this copyright page.

A Short Guide to Writing about Literature, 7th Edition

Library of Congress Cataloging-in-Publication Data
Barnet, Sylvan
    A Short Guide to writing about literature / Sylvan Barnet. — 7th ed.
      p. cm.
    Includes index.
    ISBN 0-673-52395-0
    1. English language—Rhetoric. 2. Criticism—Authorship. 3. Exposition (Rhetoric)
4. Report Writing. I. Title.
PE1479.C7B3   1995
808'.0668—dc20
                                          95-9732
                                          CIP

96 97 98 9 8 7 6 5 4 3

Contents

PART 2

Standing Back: Thinking Critically about Literature   75

PART 3

*Up Close: Thinking Critically
about Literary Forms* 147

PART 4

*Inside: Style, Format,
and Special Assignments 293*

Preface

Favorable response to the sixth edition has allowed me to revise the book again. Many changes have been made throughout, but the most obvious are:

- The increased amount of writing by students—annotations, preliminary notes, entries in journals, drafts, and complete essays
- Amplified checklists with questions that writers can ask themselves in order to generate ideas for essays
- Amplified discussions of current critical approaches, for example, Gender (Feminist, Gay and Lesbian) Criticism, Myth Criticism, New Historicism
- Chapters on What Is Literature?, What Is Interpretation?, and What Is Evaluation?
- Bibliographic suggestions concerning criticism and interpretation
- Suggestions about writing with a word processor

Part One (four chapters emphasizing the close connection between reading and writing) assumes that we can't write well unless we can read well. If nothing else, we must be able to read *our own* prose thoughtfully. Reading, after all, is a way of getting ideas for writing. These early chapters emphasize the importance in the writing process of such activities as annotating a text, brainstorming, keeping a journal, and (especially) asking oneself questions in order to generate ideas. (Oddly, these activities are often called "pre-writing," but in fact they are part of the process of writing.) Explication and analysis are discussed and illustrated with examples.

Part Two, on thinking critically about literature, is almost entirely new to the book. It looks at some definitions of literature, considers the relationships among interpretation, meaning, and evaluation, and then offers a survey of some of the chief critical approaches.

Part Three, on writing about essays, fiction, poetry, drama, and film, introduces the reader to the elements of each genre, but looks back to Part One and provides some drafts and essays by students on representative works. In accordance with the assumption in Part One that asking questions is an invaluable way of getting ideas, each chapter on writing about a genre concludes with a checklist of questions that readers may ask themselves as they read, reread, and think about a work.

Part Four contains three chapters. The first of these, "Style and Format," is a fairly short and direct approach to the elements of clear writing. It treats such matters as denotation, connotation, subordination, paragraphing, and so forth. The latter part of the chapter, devoted to manuscript form, is concerned chiefly with mechanical matters, ranging from the form of the title of an essay to advice on how to introduce quotations. The second chapter in this section, "Writing a Research Paper," includes material on discovering a topic and thesis, on finding material (not only through printed bibliographic guides but also through materials on line and on disc), on using a word processor in writing a research paper, and on the MLA system of documentation. The third chapter briefly discusses essay examinations.

Three appendixes conclude the book: The first includes two stories ("Araby" and "The Lottery") that are the subjects of student essays, the second provides a glossary of literary terms, and the third offers a checklist for writing with a word processor.

I hope that the preceding remarks adequately describe the scope of the book, but some further words must be added. Dr. Johnson said,

> There is not so poor a book in the world that would not be a prodigious effort were it wrought out entirely by a single mind, without the air of previous investigators.

I cannot name all of the previous investigators who have helped shape my ideas about literature, about writing about literature, and about teaching writing, but I must acknowledge my indebtedness to Morton Berman, William Burto, and Marcia Stubbs, who never tire of improving my pages, to Lee Edelman, who contributed part of the discussion of gay and lesbian criticism, and (at HarperCollins) to Robert Ginsberg, Judith Leet, and Lisa Moore. Others, who offered valuable help when I revised earlier editions, include Rebecca Argall, James Blake, Randall Brune, David Cavitch, Warren Chelline, Charles Christensen, William Evans, Shearle Furnish, Bruce Golden, Okey Goode, Patricia Graves, Dean Hall, James Heldman, Deena Linnett, William T. Liston, Janet Madden, Gratia Murphy, J. M. Pair, Diane Quantic, Virginia Shale, Isabel Bonnyman Stanley, and Tom Zaniello.

When I thought that the manuscript for this edition was in satisfactory shape, the publisher sent it to the following reviewers, all of whom offered valuable suggestions that I have now incorporated into the text: Ann Andrews, Mississippi State University; Robert Evans, Auburn University at

Montgomery; Sarah Favors, South Carolina State University; Anita Obermeier, Arizona State University; Judy Stokes, Southside Virginia Community College; Juanita Smart, Washington State University; Christopher Thaiss, George Mason University; and Susan Wing, University of Nebraska, Lincoln. One other reader of the manuscript must be singled out for special mention, William Cain of Wellesley College, once my student and now my teacher. His abundant and penetrating annotations of the manuscript have amply repaid me for whatever annotations I put, years ago, on his undergraduate essays.

SYLVAN BARNET

A Key to Types
of Writing Assignments

The index is the best guide if you want to draw together all references to a given topic, such as references to "character" or "theme," but the following key may be useful if you want to locate material—especially a sample essay—that will be of assistance in writing a particular kind of essay. Because the topics are not mutually exclusive, most of the sample essays are listed more than once.

Analysis (*for specific topics, see all other headings*)
    Defined   42–43
    Sample analytic essays   29–30, 97–104, 157–58, 175–78, 183–86, 191–92, 193–98, 205–09, 248

Annotations
    Examples   7, 38, 155, 246, 254

Atmosphere (*see* Setting)

Character
    In fiction   161–68
    In drama   223–24
    In poetry   222–38
    Student essay, "Holden's Kid Sister," 166–68

Comparison and Contrast
    Sample patterns of organization   48–49
    In essay examinations   351
    Student essay, "A Japanese *Macbeth*"   284–88

Critical Approaches
    Summarized   119–40

A Short Guide to Writing about Literature

PART 1

Jumping In

1

The Writer as Reader: Reading and Responding

INTERVIEWER: Did you know as a child you wanted to be a writer?

TONI MORRISON: No. I wanted to be a reader.

Learning to write is in large measure learning to read. The text you must read most carefully is the one you write, an essay you will ask someone else to read. It may start as a jotting in the margin of a book you are reading or as a brief note in a journal, and it will go through several drafts before it becomes an essay. To produce something that another person will find worth reading, you yourself must read each draft with care, trying to imagine the effect your words are likely to have on your reader. In writing about literature, you will apply some of the same critical skills to your reading; that is, you will examine your responses to what you are reading and will try to account for them.

Let's begin by looking at a very short story by Kate Chopin (1851–1904). (The name is pronounced in the French way, something like "show pan.") Kate O'Flaherty, born into a prosperous family in St. Louis, in 1870 married Oscar Chopin, a French-Creole businessman from Louisiana. They lived in New Orleans, where they had six children. Oscar died of malaria in 1882, and in 1884 Kate returned to St. Louis, where, living with her mother and children, she began to write fiction.

Kate Chopin
RIPE FIGS

Maman-Nainaine said that when the figs were ripe Babette might go to visit her cousins down on the Bayou-Lafourche where the sugar cane grows. Not that the ripening of figs had the least thing to do with it, but that is the way Maman-Nainaine was.

It seemed to Babette a very long time to wait; for the leaves upon the trees were tender yet, and the figs were like little hard, green marbles.

But warm rains came along and plenty of strong sunshine, and though Maman-Nainaine was as patient as the statue of la Madone, and Babette as

3

restless as a humming-bird, the first thing they both knew it was hot summer-time. Every day Babette danced out to where the fig-trees were in a long line against the fence. She walked slowly beneath them, carefully peering between the gnarled, spreading branches. But each time she came disconsolate away again. What she saw there finally was something that made her sing and dance the whole long day.

When Maman-Nainaine sat down in her stately way to breakfast, the following morning, her muslin cap standing like an aureole about her white, placid face, Babette approached. She bore a dainty porcelain platter, which she set down before her godmother. It contained a dozen purple figs, fringed around with their rich, green leaves.

"Ah," said Maman-Nainaine arching her eyebrows, "how early the figs have ripened this year!"

"Oh," said Babette. "I think they have ripened very late."

"Babette," continued Maman-Nainaine, as she peeled the very plumpest figs with her pointed silver fruit-knife, "you will carry my love to them all down on Bayou-Lafourche. And tell your Tante Frosine I shall look for her at Toussaint—when the chrysanthemums are in bloom."

READING AS RE-CREATION

If we had been Chopin's contemporaries, we might have read this sketch in *Vogue* in 1893 or in an early collection of her works, *A Night in Acadie* (1897). But we are not Chopin's original readers, and, since we live in the late twentieth century, we inevitably read "Ripe Figs" in a somewhat different way. This difference gets us to an important point about writing and reading. A writer writes, sets forth his or her meaning, and attempts to guide the reader's responses, as we all do when we write a letter home saying that we are thinking of dropping a course or asking for news or money or whatever. To this extent, the writer creates the written work and puts a meaning in it.

The reader, whether reading as an assignment or for recreation, re-creates it according to his or her experience and understanding. For instance, if the letter writer's appeal for money is indirect, the reader may miss it entirely or may sense it but feel that the need is not urgent. If, on the other hand, the appeal is direct or demanding, the reader may feel irritated or imposed on, even assaulted. "Oh, but I didn't mean it that way," the writer later protests. Still, that's the way the reader took it. The letter is "out there," between the writer and the reader, but the *meaning* is something the reader, as well as the writer, makes.

Since all readers bring themselves to a written work, they bring something individual. For instance, although many of Chopin's original readers knew that she wrote chiefly about the people of Louisiana, especially

Creoles (descendants of the early French and Spanish settlers), Cajuns (descendants of the French whom the British had expelled from Canada in the eighteenth century), blacks, and mulattoes, they must have varied in their attitudes about such people. Many of today's readers do not (before they read a work by Chopin) know anything about her subject. Some readers may know where Bayou-Lafourche is, and they may have notions about what it looks like, but other readers will not; indeed, many readers will not know that a bayou is a sluggish, marshy inlet or outlet of a river or lake. Moreover, even if a present-day reader in Chicago, Seattle, or Juneau knows what a bayou is, he or she may assume that "Ripe Figs" depicts a way of life still current; a reader from Louisiana may see in the work a depiction of a lost way of life, a depiction of the good old days (or perhaps of the bad old days, depending on the reader's point of view). Much depends, we can say, on the reader's storehouse of experience.

To repeat: Our reading is a *re*-creation; the author has tried to guide our responses, but inevitably our own experiences, including our ethnic background and our education, contribute to our responses. You may find useful a distinction that E. D. Hirsch makes in *Validity in Interpretation* (1967). For Hirsch, the *meaning* in a text is the author's intended meaning; the *significance* is the particular relevance for each reader. In this view, when you think about meaning you are thinking about what the author was trying to say and to do—for instance, to take an old theme and treat it in a new way. When you think about significance, you are thinking about what the work does for you—enlarges your mind, offends you by its depiction of women, or whatever.

MAKING REASONABLE INFERENCES

If when we read and especially when we speak of significance we are re-creating, is there really no use in talking (or in writing) about literature since all of us perceive it in our relatively private ways, rather like the seven blind men in the fable? One man, you will recall, touched the elephant's tail (or was it his trunk?) and said that the elephant is like a snake; another touched the elephant's side and said the elephant is like a wall; a third touched the elephant's leg and said the elephant is like a tree, and so on. Notice that each of the blind men *did* perceive an aspect of the elephant—an elephant is massive, like a wall or a tree, and an elephant is (in its way) remarkably supple, as you know if you have given peanuts to one.

As readers we can and should make an effort to understand what the author seems to be getting at; that is, we should make an effort to understand the words in their context. Perhaps we shouldn't look up every word we don't know, at least on the first reading, but if certain unfamiliar words are repeated and thus seem especially important, we will probably want to look them up. It happens that in "Ripe Figs" a French word appears: "*Tante Frosine*" means "*Aunt* Frosine." Fortunately, the word is not crucial, and the context probably makes it clear that Frosine is an adult, which is all that we really need to know about her. The point is this: The writer is pitching, and she expects the reader to catch. A reader who does not know that chrysanthemums bloom in the late summer or early autumn, for instance, will miss part of Chopin's meaning.

Although writers tell us a good deal, they do not tell us everything. We know that Maman-Nainaine is Babette's godmother, but we don't know exactly how old Maman-Nainaine and Babette are. Further, Chopin tells us nothing of Babette's parents. It rather *sounds* as though Babette and her godmother live alone, but readers may differ. One reader may argue that Babette's parents must be dead or ill; another may say that the status of her parents is irrelevant and that what counts is that Babette is supervised by only one person, a mature woman. In short, a text includes **indeterminacies** (passages that careful readers agree are open to various interpretations) and **gaps** (things left unsaid in the story, such as why a godmother rather than a mother takes care of Babette). As we work our way through a text, we keep reevaluating what we have read, pulling the details together to make sense of them in a process called **consistency building.**

Whatever the gaps, careful readers are able to draw many reasonable inferences about Maman-Nainaine. We can list some of them:

> She is older than Babette.
> She has a "stately way," and she is "patient as the statue of la Madone."
> She has an odd way (is it exasperating or engaging or a little of each?) of connecting actions with the seasons.
> Given this last point, she seems to act slowly, to be very patient.
> She apparently is used to being obeyed.

You may at this point want to go back and reread "Ripe Figs" to see what else you can say about Maman-Nainaine.

And now, what of Babette?

> She is young.
> She is active and impatient ("restless as a hummingbird").
> She is obedient.

And at this point too you may want to add to the list.

READING WITH A PEN IN HAND

Perhaps the best way to read attentively is to mark the text, underlining or highlighting passages that seem especially interesting, and to jot notes or queries in the margins. Here is the work once more, this time with the marks that a student added after a second reading.

Kate Chopin
RIPE FIGS

Maman-Nainaine said that when the (figs) were ripe Babette might go to visit her cousins down on the Bayou- **?**
Lafourche where the sugar cane grows. Not that the ripening of figs had the least thing to do with it, but that is
odd the way Maman-Nainaine was.

It seemed to Babette a very long time to wait; for the leaves upon the trees were tender yet, and the figs were like little hard, (green marbles.)

But warm rains came along and plenty of strong sunshine, and though Maman-Nainaine was as <u>patient as the</u> *contrast*
<u>statue</u> of la Madone, and Babette as <u>restless as a humming-</u> *between*
<u>bird,</u> the first thing they both knew it was hot summer- *M-N and*
time. Every day Babette danced out to where the fig-trees *B*
were in a long line against the fence. She walked slowly beneath them, carefully peering between the gnarled, spreading branches. But each time she came disconsolate away again. What she saw there finally was something that made her sing and dance the whole long day.

When Maman-Nainaine (sat) down in her stately way *another*
to breakfast, the following morning, her muslin cap stand- *contrast*
check ?ing like an (aureole) about her white, placid face, Babette
this approached. She bore a dainty porcelain platter, which *ceremonious?*
she set down before her godmother. It contained a dozen
(purple figs) fringed around with their rich, green leaves.

nice echo; ("Ah,") said Maman-Nainaine arching her eyebrows, *time passes*
contrast; "how (early) the figs have ripened this year!" *fast for M-N*
like a song ("Oh,") said Babette. "I think they have ripened very *slowly for B*
(late.)

"Babette," continued (Maman-Nainaine) as she peeled *is M-N*
the very plumpest figs with her pointed silver fruit-knife, *herself like*
B entrusted "you will carry my love to them all down on Bayou- *a plump fig?*
with a Lafourche. And tell your Tante Frosine I shall look for her
message at Toussaint—when the (chrysanthemums) are in bloom."
of love *opens with figs.*
ends with chrys. (autumn) *fulfillment?*
Equivalent to figs ripening

RECORDING YOUR FIRST RESPONSES

After you annotate your text, another useful way of getting at meanings is to write down your initial responses to the story, jotting down your impressions as they come to you in any order—almost as though you are talking to yourself. Since no one else is going to read your notes, you can be entirely free and at ease. You can write in sentences or not; it's up to you. Write whatever comes into your mind, whatever the story triggers in your own imagination, whatever rings true or reminds you of your own experiences.

Here is the response of the student who annotated the text.

```
I like the way the "green marbles" turn into "purple
figs." And I like the way Babette and M-N are sort of
opposite. B sings and dances and is restless. On the
other hand, M-N is "patient" and like a statue and she
sits "in a stately way." A young girl and a mature
woman. But, come to think of it, B can also be
dignified--she serves M-N the figs in a fancy dish. I
feel I can see these people, I almost know them. And
I'd like to see Aunt Frosine in the fall, in
chrysanthemum time. She's probably a mature woman, like
M-N, with lots of dignity.
```

Here is another student's first response to "Ripe Figs."

```
This is a very short story. I didn't know stories were
this short, but I like it because you can get it all
quickly and it's no trouble to reread it carefully. The
shortness, though, leaves a lot of gaps for the reader
to fill in. So much is not said. Your imagination is
put to work.
    But I can see Maman-N sitting at her table--
pleasantly powerful--no one you would want to argue
with. She's formal and distant--and definitely has
quirks. She wants to postpone Babette's trip, but we
don't know why. And you can sense B's frustration. But
maybe she's teaching her that something really good is
worth waiting for and that anticipation is as much fun
as the trip. Maybe I can develop this idea.
```

```
      Another thing.  I can tell they are not poor--from
two things.  The pointed silver fruit knife and the
porcelain platter, and the fact that Maman sits down to
breakfast in a "stately" way.  They are the leisure
class.  But I don't know enough about life on the bayous
to go into this.  Their life is different from mine; no
one I know has that kind of peaceful rural life.
```

AUDIENCE AND PURPOSE

Suppose you are beginning the process of writing about "Ripe Figs" for someone else, not for yourself. The first question to ask yourself is: For whom am I writing? In other words, Who is my *audience?* (Of course, you probably are writing because an instructor has asked you to do so, but you still must imagine an audience. Your instructor may tell you, for instance, to write for your classmates or for the readers of the college newspaper.) If you are writing for people who are familiar with some of Chopin's work, you will not have to say much about the author. If you are writing for an audience that perhaps has never heard of Chopin, you may want to include a brief biographical note of the sort given in this book. If you are writing for an audience that (you have reason to believe) has read several works by Chopin, you may want to make some comparisons, explaining how "Ripe Figs" resembles or differs from Chopin's other work.

In a sense, the audience is your collaborator; it helps you decide what you will say. You are helped also by your sense of *purpose:* If your aim is to introduce readers to Chopin, you will make certain points; if your aim is to tell people what you think "Ripe Figs" means about human relationships or about time, you will say some different things; if your aim is to have a little fun and to entertain an audience that is familiar with "Ripe Figs," you may write a parody (a humorous imitation).

A WRITING ASSIGNMENT ON "RIPE FIGS"

The Assignment

Let's assume that you are trying to describe "Ripe Figs" to someone who has not read it. You probably will briefly summarize the action, such as it is, will mention where it takes place and who the characters are (including their relationship), and what, if anything, happens to them. Beyond that, you will probably try to explain as honestly as you can what makes "Ripe Figs" appealing or interesting or trifling or boring or whatever.

Here is an essay that a student, Marilyn Brown, wrote for this assignment.

A Sample Essay

Ripening

Kate Chopin's "Ripe Figs" describes a growing season in a young girl's life. Maman-Nainaine agrees to allow young Babette to visit relatives away from home, but Babette must delay her trip until the figs ripen. Babette watches the signs of the natural world, impatiently observing, straining to have time pass at her own speed. At last, Babette finds that the figs have ripened and she presents them to her godmother, Maman-Nainaine, who gives Babette her leave to go on the journey to Bayou-Lafourche.

Chopin sets the action within the context of the natural world. Babette, young and tender as the fig leaves, can't wait to "ripen." Her visit to Bayou-Lafourche is no mere pleasure trip but represents Babette's coming into her own season of maturity. Babette's desire to rush this process is tempered by a condition that Maman-Nainaine sets: Babette must wait until the figs ripen, since everything comes in its own season. Maman recognizes in the patterns of the natural world the rhythms of life. By asking Babette to await the ripening, the young girl is made to pay attention to these patterns as well.

In this work, Chopin asks her readers to see the relationship of human time to nature's seasons. Try as we may to push the process of maturity, growth or ripening happens in its own time. If we pay attention and wait with patience, the fruits of our own growth will be sweet, plump, and bountiful. Chopin uses natural imagery effectively, interweaving the young girl's growth with the rhythms of the seasons. In this way, the reader is connected with both processes in a very intimate and inviting way.

Other Possibilities for Writing

Of course, one might write a paper of a very different sort. Consider the following possibilities:

1. Write a sequel, moving from fall to spring.
2. Write a letter from Babette, at Bayou-Lafourche, to Maman-Nainaine.
3. Imagine that Babette is now an old woman, writing her memoirs. What does she say about Maman-Nainaine?
4. Write a narrative based on your own experience of learning a lesson in patience.

2

The Reader as Writer: Drafting and Writing

All there is to writing is having ideas. To learn to write is to learn to have ideas.

—Robert Frost

PRE-WRITING: GETTING IDEAS

How does one "learn to have ideas"? Among the methods are the following: reading with a pen or pencil in hand so that (as we have already seen) one can annotate the text; keeping a journal in which one jots down reflections about one's reading; and talking with others about the reading. Let's take another look at the first method, annotating.

Annotating a Text

In reading, if you own the book do not hesitate to mark it up, indicating (by highlighting or underlining, or by marginal notes) what puzzles you, what pleases or interests you, and what displeases or bores you. Of course, later you'll want to think further about these responses, asking yourself if, on rereading, you still feel this way, and if not, why not, but these first responses will get you started.

Annotations of the sort given on page 7, which chiefly call attention to contrasts, indicate that the student is thinking about writing some sort of analysis of the story, an essay in which the parts are examined to see how they relate to each other or in which a part is examined to see how it relates to the whole.

More about Getting Ideas: A Second Story by Kate Chopin, "The Story of an Hour"

Let's look at a story that is a little longer than "Ripe Figs," and then we'll discuss how, in addition to annotating, one might get ideas for writing about it.

12

Kate Chopin
THE STORY OF AN HOUR

Knowing that Mrs. Mallard was afflicted with a heart trouble, great care was taken to break to her as gently as possible the news of her husband's death.

It was her sister Josephine who told her, in broken sentences, veiled hints that revealed in half concealing. Her husband's friend Richards was there, too, near her. It was he who had been in the newspaper office when intelligence of the railroad disaster was received, with Brently Mallard's name leading the list of "killed." He had only taken the time to assure himself of its truth by a second telegram, and had hastened to forestall any less careful, less tender friend in bearing the sad message.

She did not hear the story as many women have heard the same, with a paralyzed inability to accept its significance. She wept at once with sudden, wild abandonment, in her sister's arms. When the storm of grief had spent itself she went away to her room alone. She would have no one follow her.

There stood, facing the open window, a comfortable, roomy armchair. Into this she sank, pressed down by a physical exhaustion that haunted her body and seemed to reach into her soul.

She could see in the open square before her house the tops of trees that were all aquiver with the new spring life. The delicious breath of rain was in the air. In the street below a peddler was crying his wares. The notes of a distant song which some one was singing reached her faintly, and countless sparrows were twittering in the eaves.

There were patches of blue sky showing here and there through the clouds that had met and piled above the other in the west facing her window.

She sat with her head thrown back upon the cushion of the chair quite motionless, except when a sob came up into her throat and shook her, as a child who has cried itself to sleep continues to sob in its dreams.

She was young, with a fair, calm face, whose lines bespoke repression and even a certain strength. But now there was a dull stare in her eyes, whose gaze was fixed away off yonder on one of those patches of blue sky. It was not a glance of reflection, but rather indicated a suspension of intelligent thought.

There was something coming to her and she was waiting for it, fearfully. What was it? She did not know; it was too subtle and elusive to name. But she felt it creeping out of the sky, reaching toward her through the sounds, the scents, the color that filled the air.

Now her bosom rose and fell tumultuously. She was beginning to recognize this thing that was approaching to possess her, and she was striving to beat it back with her will—as powerless as her two white slender hands would have been.

When she abandoned herself a little whispered word escaped her slightly parted lips. She said it over and over under her breath: "Free, free, free!" The vacant stare and the look of terror that had followed it went from her eyes. They stayed keen and bright. Her pulses beat fast, and the coursing blood warmed and relaxed every inch of her body.

She did not stop to ask if it were not a monstrous joy that held her. A clear and exalted perception enabled her to dismiss the suggestion as trivial.

She knew that she would weep again when she saw the kind, tender hands folded in death; the face that had never looked save with love upon her, fixed and gray and dead. But she saw beyond that bitter moment a long procession of years to come that would belong to her absolutely. And she opened and spread her arms out to them in welcome.

There would be no one to live for her during those coming years; she would live for herself. There would be no powerful will bending her in the blind persistence with which men and women believe they have a right to impose a private will upon a fellow creature. A kind intention or a cruel intention made the act seem no less a crime as she looked upon it in that brief moment of illumination.

And yet she had loved him—sometimes. Often she had not. What did it matter! What could love, the unsolved mystery, count for in face of this possession of self-assertion which she suddenly recognized as the strongest impulse of her being.

"Free! Body and soul free!" she kept whispering.

Josephine was kneeling before the closed door with her lips to the keyhole, imploring for admission. "Louise, open the door! I beg; open the door—you will make yourself ill. What are you doing, Louise? For heaven's sake open the door."

"Go away. I am not making myself ill." No; she was drinking in the very elixir of life through that open window.

Her fancy was running riot along those days ahead of her. Spring days, and summer days, and all sorts of days that would be her own. She breathed a quick prayer that life might be long. It was only yesterday she had thought with a shudder that life might be long.

She arose at length and opened the door to her sister's importunities. There was a feverish triumph in her eyes, and she carried herself unwittingly like a goddess of Victory. She clasped her sister's waist and together they descended the stairs. Richards stood waiting for them at the bottom.

Some one was opening the front door with a latchkey. It was Brently Mallard who entered, a little travel-stained, composedly carrying his grip-sack and umbrella. He had been far from the scene of accident, and did not even know there had been one. He stood amazed at Josephine's piercing cry; at Richards' quick motion to screen him from the view of his wife.

But Richards was too late.

When the doctors came they said she had died of heart disease—of joy that kills.

Brainstorming for Ideas for Writing

Unlike annotating, which consists of making brief notes and small marks on the printed page, *brainstorming*—the free jotting down of ideas—requires that you jot down whatever comes to mind, without inhibition. Don't worry about spelling, about writing complete sentences, or about unifying your thoughts; just let one thought lead to another. Later, you will review your jottings, deleting some, connecting with arrows others that are related, amplifying still others. For now, you want to get going, and so there is no reason to look back. Thus, you might jot down something about the title:

```
Title speaks of an hour, and story covers an hour, but
maybe takes five minutes to read
```

And then, perhaps prompted by "an hour," you might happen to add something to this effect:

```
Doubt that a woman who got news of the death of her
husband could move from grief to joy within an hour.
```

Your next jotting might have little or nothing to do with this issue; it might simply say:

```
Enjoyed "Hour" more than "Ripe Figs" partly because
"Hour" is so shocking
```

And then you might ask yourself:

```
By shocking, do I mean "improbable," or what? come to
think of it, maybe it's not so improbable.  A lot
depends on what the marriage was like.
```

Focused Free Writing

Focused free writing, or directed free writing, is a related method that some writers use to uncover ideas they want to write about. Concentrating on one issue, such as a question that strikes them as worth puzzling over (What kind of person is Mrs. Mallard?), they write at length, nonstop, for perhaps five or ten minutes.

Writers who find free writing helpful put down everything that has bearing on the one issue or question they are examining. They do not stop at this stage to evaluate the results, and they do not worry about niceties of sentence structure or of spelling. They just explore ideas in a steady stream of writing, using whatever associations come to mind. If they pause in their writing, it is only to refer to the text, to search for more detail—perhaps a quotation—that will help them answer their question.

After the free-writing session, these writers usually go back and reread what they have written, highlighting or underlining what seems to be of value. Of course, they find much that is of little or no use, but they also usually find that some strong ideas have surfaced and have received some development. At this point the writers are often able to make a scratch outline and then begin a draft.

Here is an example of one student's focused free writing:

```
What do I know about Mrs. Mallard? Let me put everything
down here I know about her or can figure out from what
Kate Chopin tells me.  When she finds herself alone
after the death of her husband, she says, "Free. Body
and soul free" and before that she said "free, free,
free."  Three times.  So she has suddenly perceived that
she has not been free; she has been under the influence
of a "powerful will."  In this case it has been her
husband, but she says no one, man nor woman, should
impose their will on anyone else.  So it's not a
feminist issue--it's a power issue.  No one should push
anyone else around is what I guess Chopin means, force
someone to do what the other person wants.  I used to
have a friend that did that to me all the time; he had
to run everything.  They say that fathers--before the
women's movement--used to run things, with the father in
charge of all the decisions, so maybe this is an honest
reaction to having been pushed around by a husband.  I
think Mrs. Mallard is a believable character, even if
the plot is not all that believable--all those things
happening in such quick succession.
```

Listing

In your preliminary thinking you may find it useful to make lists. In the previous chapter we saw that listing the traits of characters was helpful in thinking about Chopin's "Ripe Figs":

```
Maman-Nainaine
     older than Babette
     "stately way"
```

```
         "patient as the statue of la Madone"
         expects to be obeyed
         connects actions with seasons
     Babette
         young
         active
         obedient
```

For "The Story of an Hour" you might list Mrs. Mallard's traits, or you might list the stages in her development. (Such a list is not the same as a summary of the plot. The list helps the writer see the sequence of psychological changes.)

```
     weeps (when she gets the news)
     goes to room, alone
     "pressed down by a physical exhaustion"
     "dull stare"
     "something coming to her"
     strives to beat back "this thing"
     "Free, free, free!" The "vacant stare went from her
       eyes"
     "A clear and exalted perception"
     Rejects Josephine
     "She was drinking in the very elixir of life"
     Gets up, opens door, "A feverish triumph in her eyes"
     Sees B, and dies
```

Of course, unlike brainstorming and annotating, which let you go in all directions, listing requires that you first make a decision about what you will be listing—traits of character, images, puns, or whatever. Once you make the decision you can then construct the list, and, with a list in front of you, you will probably see patterns that you were not fully conscious of earlier.

Asking Questions

If you feel stuck, ask yourself questions. (You'll recall that the assignment on "Ripe Figs" in effect asked you to ask yourself questions about the work—for instance, a question about the relationship between the characters—and about your responses to it: "You will probably try to explain as

honestly as you can what makes 'Ripe Figs' appealing or interesting or trifling or boring or whatever.")

If you are thinking about a work of fiction, ask yourself questions about
the plot and the characters: Are they believable? Are they interesting?
What does it all add up to? What does the story mean *to you?* (The chapters on the essay, fiction, drama, poetry, and film include questions on each
form.) One student found it helpful to jot down the following questions:

```
Plot
      Ending false? Unconvincing? Or prepared for?
Character
      Mrs. M. unfeeling? Immoral?
      Mrs. M. unbelievable character?
      What might her marriage have been like? Many gaps.
      (Can we tell what her husband was like?)
      "And yet she loved him--sometimes." Fickle?
        Realistic?
      What is "this thing that was approaching to possess
        her?"
Symbolism
      Set on spring day = symbolic of new life?
```

You don't have to be as tidy as this student. You may begin by jotting down
notes and queries about what you like or dislike and about what puzzles or
amuses you. What follows are the jottings of another student, Janet Vong.
They are, obviously, in no particular order—the student is brainstorming,
putting down whatever occurs to her—though it is equally obvious that one
note sometimes led to the next:

```
Title nothing special. What might be a better title?
Could a woman who loved her husband be so heartless?
Is she heartless? Did she love him?
What are (were) Louise's feelings about her husband?
Did she want too much? What did she want?
Could this story happen today? Feminist
    interpretation?
Sister (Josephine)--a busybody?
Tricky ending--but maybe it could be true
"And yet she had loved him--sometimes. Often she had
    not." Why does one love someone "sometimes"?
Irony: plot has reversal. Are characters ironic too?
```

These jottings will help the reader-writer think about the story, find a special point of interest, and develop a thoughtful argument about it.

Keeping a Journal

A journal is not a diary, a record of what the writer did during the day ("today I read Chopin's 'Hour'"). Rather, a journal is a place to store some of the thoughts you may have inscribed on a scrap of paper or in the margin of the text, such as your initial response to the title of a work or to the ending. It is also a place to jot down further reflections, such as thoughts about what the work means to you, and what was said in the classroom about writing in general or specific works.

You will get something out of your journal if you write an entry at least once a week, but you will get much more if you write entries after reading each assignment and after each class meeting. You may, for instance, want to reflect on why your opinion is so different from that of another student, or you may want to apply a concept such as "character" or "irony" or "plausibility" to a story that later you may write about in an essay. Comparisons are especially helpful: How does this work (or this character, or this rhyme scheme) differ from last week's reading?

You might even make an entry in the form of a letter to the author or from one character to another. You might write a dialogue between characters in two works or between two authors, or you might record an experience of your own that is comparable to something in the work.

A student who wrote about "The Story of an Hour" began with the following entry in his journal. In reading this entry, notice that one idea stimulates another. The student was, quite rightly, concerned with getting and exploring ideas, not with writing a unified paragraph.

> Apparently a "well-made" story, but seems clever rather than moving or real. Doesn't seem plausible. Mrs. M's change comes out of the blue--maybe some women might respond like this, but probably not most.
>
> Does literature deal with unusual people, or ßwith usual (typical?) people? Shouldn't it deal with typical? Maybe not. (Anyway, how can I know?) Is "typical" same as "plausible"? Come to think of it, prob. not.
>
> Anyway, whether Mrs. M is typical or not, is her change plausible, believable? Think more about this.
>
> Why did she change? Her husband dominated her life and controlled her actions; he did "impose a private

```
will upon a fellow creature." She calls this a crime,
even if well-intentioned. Is it a crime.
```

Critical Thinking: Arguing with Yourself

In our discussion of annotating, brainstorming, free writing, listing, asking questions, and writing entries in a journal, the emphasis has been on responding freely rather than in any highly systematic or disciplined way. Something strikes us (perhaps an idea, perhaps an uncertainty), and we jot it down. Maybe even before we finish jotting it down we go on to question it, but probably not; at this early stage it is enough to put down on paper some thoughts, rooted in our first responses, and to keep going on.

The almost random play of mind that is evident in brainstorming and in the other activities already discussed is of course a kind of thinking, but the term **critical thinking** is reserved for something different. When we think critically, we skeptically scrutinize our own ideas, for example by searching out our underlying assumptions, or by evaluating what we have quickly jotted down as evidence. We have already seen some examples of this sort of analysis of one's own thinking in the journal entries, where, for instance, a student wrote that literature should probably deal with "typical" people, and then wondered if "typical" and "plausible" were the same, and then added "prob[ably] not."

Speaking broadly, critical thinking is rational, logical thinking. In thinking critically,

- one scrutinizes one's assumptions, and
- one tests the evidence one has collected, even to the extent of looking for counterevidence.

Let's start with assumptions. If, for instance, I say that a story is weak because it is improbable, I ought at least to think about my assumption that improbability is a fault. I can begin by asking myself if all good stories—or all of the stories that I value highly—are probable. I may recall that among my favorites is *Alice in Wonderland* (or *Gulliver's Travels* or *Animal Farm*)—and so I probably have to withdraw my assumption that improbability in itself makes a story less than good. I may of course go on to refine the idea, and decide that improbability is not a fault in satiric stories but is a fault in other kinds, but that is not the same as saying bluntly that improbability is a fault.

The other aspect of critical thinking that we have isolated—searching for counterevidence within the literary work—especially involves rereading the work to see if we have overlooked material, or have taken a particular detail out of context. If, for instance, we say that in "The Story of an Hour" Josephine is a busybody, we should reexamine the work in order to make sure that she indeed is meddling needlessly and is not offering welcome or necessary assistance. Perhaps the original observation will stand up, but perhaps on rereading the story we may come to feel, as we examine each of Josephine's actions, that she cannot reasonably be characterized as a busybody.

Of course different readers may come to different conclusions; the important thing is that all readers should subject their initial responses to critical thinking, testing their responses against all of the evidence. Remember, your instructor probably expects you to hand in an essay that is essentially an *argument,* a paper that advances a thesis of your own. The thesis might be that the story is improbable, or is typical of Chopin, or is anti-woman, or is a remarkable anticipation of contemporary feminist thinking. Whatever your thesis, it should be able to withstand scrutiny. You may not convince every reader that you are unquestionably right, but you should make every reader feel that your argument is thoughtful. If you read your notes and then your drafts critically, you probably will write a paper that meets this standard.

One last point, or maybe it's two. Just as your first jottings probably won't be the products of critical thinking, your first reading of the literary work probably won't be a critical reading. It is entirely appropriate to begin by reading simply for enjoyment. After all, the reason we read literature (or listen to music, or look at art in a museum, or watch dancers) is to derive pleasure. It happens, however, that in this course you are trying (among other things) to deepen your understanding of literature, and therefore you are *studying* literature. On subsequent readings, therefore, you will read the work critically, taking careful note of (for instance) the writer's view of human nature, and of the writer's ways of achieving certain effects.

This business of critical thinking is important, and we will discuss it again, on pages 95–96, in talking about interpretations of literature.

Arriving at a Thesis, and Arguing It

If you think critically about your early jottings and about the literary work itself, you probably will find that some of your jottings lead to dead ends, but some will lead to further ideas that hold up under scrutiny. What the thesis of the essay will be—the idea that will be asserted and argued (supported with evidence)—is still in doubt, but there is no doubt about one thing: A good essay will have a thesis, a point, an argument. You ought to be able to state your point in a **thesis sentence.**

Consider these candidates as possible thesis sentences:

1. Mrs. Mallard dies soon after hearing that her husband has died.

True, but scarcely a point that can be argued or even developed. About the most the essayist can do with this sentence is amplify it by summarizing the plot of the story, a task not worth doing unless the plot is unusually obscure. An essay may include a sentence or two of summary to give readers their bearings, but a summary is not an essay.

2. The story is a libel on women.

In contrast to the first statement, this one can be developed into an argument. Probably the writer will try to demonstrate that Mrs. Mallard's behavior is despicable. Whether this point can be convincingly argued is another matter; the thesis may be untenable, but it is a thesis. A second problem, however, is this: Even if the writer demonstrates that Mrs. Mallard's behavior is despicable, he or she will have to go on to demonstrate that the presentation of one despicable woman constitutes a libel on women in general. That's a pretty big order.

3. The story is clever but superficial because it is based on an unreal character.

Here, too, is a thesis, a point of view that can be argued. Whether this thesis is true is another matter. The writer's job will be to support it by presenting evidence. Probably the writer will have no difficulty in finding evidence that the story is "clever"; the difficulty probably will be in establishing a case that the characterization of Mrs. Mallard is "unreal." The writer will have to set forth some ideas about what makes a character real and then will have to show that Mrs. Mallard is an "unreal" (unbelievable) figure.

4. The irony of the ending is believable partly because it is consistent with earlier ironies in the story.

It happens that the student who wrote the essay printed on page 29 began by drafting an essay based on the third of these thesis topics, but as she worked on a draft she found that she could not support her assertion that the character was unconvincing. In fact, she came to believe that although Mrs. Mallard's joy was the reverse of what a reader might expect, several early reversals in the story helped make Mrs. Mallard's shift from grief to joy acceptable.

Remember: It's not likely that you will quickly find a thesis. Annotating, making entries in a journal, and writing a first draft are *ways of finding* a thesis.

WRITING A DRAFT

After jotting down notes, and further notes stimulated by rereading and further thinking, you probably will be able to formulate a tentative thesis. At this point most writers find it useful to clear the air by glancing over their preliminary notes and by jotting down the thesis and a few especially promising notes—brief statements of what they think their key points may be, such as key quotations that may help support the thesis.

Here are the selected notes (not the original brainstorming notes, but a later selection from them, with additions) and a draft (page 24) that makes use of them:

```
title? Ironies in an Hour (?) An Hour of Irony (?) Kate
  Chopin's Irony (?)
thesis: irony at end is prepared for by earlier ironies
chief irony: Mrs. M. dies just as she is beginning to
  enjoy life
smaller ironies:
    1. "sad message" brings her joy
    2. Richards is "too late" at end;
    3. Richards is too early at start
```

These notes are in effect a very brief **outline.** Some writers at this point like to develop a fuller outline, but probably most writers begin with only a brief outline, knowing that in the process of developing a draft from these few notes additional ideas will arise. For these writers, the time to jot down a detailed outline is *after* they have written a first or second draft. The outline of the written draft will, as we shall see, help them to make sure that their draft has an adequate organization, and that main points are developed.

A Sample Draft: "Ironies in an Hour"

Now for the student's draft—not the first version, but a revised draft with some of the irrelevancies of the first draft omitted and some evidence added.

The digits within the parentheses refer to the page numbers from which the quotations are drawn, though with so short a work as "The Story of an Hour," page references are hardly necessary. Check with your instructor to find out if you must always give citations. (Detailed information about how to document a paper is given on pages 326–38.)

Ironies in an Hour

After we know how the story turns out, if we reread it we find irony at the very start, as is true of many other stories. Mrs. Mallard's friends assume, mistakenly, that Mrs. Mallard was deeply in love with her husband, Brently Mallard. They take great care to tell her gently of his death. The friends mean well, and in fact they do well. They bring her an hour of life, an hour of freedom. They think their news is sad. Mrs. Mallard at first expresses grief when she hears the news, but soon she finds joy in it. So Richards's "sad message" (12) though sad in Richards's eyes, is in fact a happy message.

Among the ironic details is the statement that when Mallard entered the house, Richards tried to conceal him from Mrs. Mallard, but "Richards was too late" (13). This is ironic because earlier Richards "hastened" (12) to bring his sad message; if he had at the start been "too late" (13), Brently Mallard would have arrived at home first, and Mrs. Mallard's life would not have ended an hour later but would simply have gone on as it had been. Yet another irony at the end of the story is the diagnosis of the doctors. The doctors say she died of "heart disease--of joy that kills" (14). In one sense the doctors are right: Mrs. Mallard has experienced a great joy. But of course the doctors totally misunderstand the joy that kills her.

The central irony resides not in the well-intentioned but ironic actions of Richards, or in the unconsciously ironic words of the doctors, but in her own life. In a way she has been dead. She "sometimes" (13) loved her husband, but in a way she has been dead. Now, his apparent death brings her new life. This new life comes to her at the season of the year when "the tops of trees . . . were all aquiver with the new spring life" (12). But, ironically, her new life will last only an hour. She looks forward to "summer days" (13) but she will not see even the end of this spring day. Her years of marriage were ironic. They brought her a sort of

living death instead of joy. Her new life is ironic too.
It grows out of her moment of grief for her supposedly
dead husband, and her vision of a new life is cut short.

Work Cited

Chopin, Kate. "The Story of an Hour." Literature for
    Composition. 3rd ed. Ed. Sylvan Barnet et al. New
    York: HarperCollins, 1992. 12-13.

Revising a Draft

The draft, though excellent, is not yet a finished essay. The student went on
to improve it in many small but important ways.

First, the draft needs a good paragraph that will let the **audience**—the
readers—know where the writer will be taking them. (Pages 305–06 discuss
introductory paragraphs.) Doubtless you know, from your own experience
as a reader, that readers can follow an argument more easily and with more
pleasure if early in the discussion the writer alerts them to the gist of the
argument. (The title, too, can strongly suggest the thesis.) Second, some of
the paragraphs could be clearer.

In revising paragraphs—or, for that matter, in revising an entire draft—
writers unify, organize, clarify, and polish. Writers are assisted in revising if
they imagine that they are readers. They try to put themselves into the
mind of the imagined audience, asking themselves, "Is this clear?" "Will a
reader need another example?" Or, on the other hand, "Will a reader feel
that I am talking down, giving more examples than are needed?"

1. **Unity** is achieved partly by eliminating irrelevancies. Notice that in the
   final version, printed on page 29, the writer has deleted "as is true of
   many other stories."
2. **Organization** is largely a matter of arranging material into a sequence
   that will help the reader grasp the point.
3. **Clarity** is achieved largely by providing concrete details and quotations
   to support generalizations and by providing helpful transitions ("for instance," "furthermore," "on the other hand," "however").
4. **Polish** is small-scale revision. For instance, one deletes unnecessary
   repetitions. (In the second paragraph of the draft the phrase "the doctors" appears three times, but it appears only once in the final version of
   the paragraph.) Similarly, in polishing, a writer combines choppy sentences into longer sentences and breaks overly long sentences into
   shorter sentences.

Later, after producing a draft that seems close to a finished essay, writers engage in yet another activity. They edit.

5. **Editing** is concerned with such matters as checking the accuracy of quotations by comparing them with the original, checking a dictionary for the spelling of doubtful words, and checking a handbook for doubtful punctuation—for instance, whether a comma or a semicolon is needed in a particular sentence.

Outlining a Draft

Whether or not you draw up an outline as a preliminary guide to writing a draft, you will be able to improve your draft if you prepare an outline of what you have written. (If you write on a word processor it is probably especially important that you make an outline of your written draft. Writing on a word processor is—or seems—so easy, so effortless, that you just tap away, filling screen after screen with loosely structured material.) For each paragraph in your draft, jot down the gist of the topic sentence or topic idea, and under each of these sentences, indented, jot down key words for the idea(s) developed in the paragraph. Thus, in an outline of the draft we have just looked at, for the first two paragraphs the writer might make these jottings:

```
story ironic from start
     friends think news is sad
     Ms. M. finds joy

some ironic details
     Richards hastened, but "too late"
     doctors right and also wrong
```

An outline of what you have written will help you to see if your draft is adequate in three important ways. The outline will show you

1. the sequence of major topics
2. the degree of development of these topics
3. the argument, the thesis

By studying your outline you may see (for instance) that your first major point (probably after an introductory paragraph) would be more effective as your third point, and that your second point needs to be further developed.

An outline of this sort, perhaps even using some phrases from the draft, is essentially a brief version of your draft. But consider making yet another sort of outline, an outline indicating not what each paragraph says but what each paragraph *does*. A first attempt at such an outline of the three-paragraph draft of the essay on " The Story of an Hour" might look like something like this:

1. action of the friends is ironic
2. gives some specific (minor) details about ironies
3. explains "central irony"

One ought to see a red flag here. The aim of this sort of outline is to indicate what each paragraph *does,* but the jotting for the first paragraph does not tell us what the paragraph does; rather, it more or less summarizes the content of the paragraph. Why? Because the paragraph does not *do* much of anything. Certainly it does not (for example) clearly introduce the thesis, or define a crucial term, or set the story in the context of Chopin's other work. An outline indicating the function of each paragraph will force you to see if your essay has an effective structure. We will see that the student later wrote a new opening paragraph for the essay on "The Story of an Hour."

Peer Review

Your instructor may encourage (or even require) you to discuss your draft with another student or with a small group of students; that is, you may be asked to get a review from your peers. Such a procedure is helpful in several ways. First, it gives the writer a real audience, readers who can point to what pleases or puzzles them, who make suggestions, who may disagree (with the writer or with each other), and who frequently, though not intentionally, *misread.* Though writers don't necessarily like everything they hear (they seldom hear "This is perfect. Don't change a word!"), reading and discussing their work with others almost always gives them a fresh perspective on their work, and a fresh perspective may stimulate thoughtful revision. (Having your intentions *misread* because your writing isn't clear enough can be particularly stimulating.)

The writer whose work is being reviewed is not the sole beneficiary. When students regularly serve as readers for each other, they become better readers of their own work and consequently better revisers. As was said in Chapter 1, learning to write is in large measure learning to read.

If peer review is a part of the writing process in your course, the instructor may distribute a sheet with some suggestions and questions. An example of such a sheet follows.

QUESTIONS FOR PEER REVIEW   ENGLISH 125a

Read each draft once, quickly. Then read it again, with
the following questions in mind.

1. What is the essay's topic? Is it one of the assigned
   topics, or a variation from it? Does the draft show
   promise of fulfilling the assignment?
2. Looking at the essay as a whole, what thesis (main
   idea) is stated or implied? If implied, try to state
   it in your own words.
3. Is the thesis reasonable? How might it be
   strengthened?
4. Looking at each paragraph separately:
   a. What is the basic point? (If it isn't clear to you,
      ask for clarification.)
   b. How does the paragraph relate to the essay's main
      idea or to the previous paragraph?
   c. Should some paragraphs be deleted? Be divided into
      two or more paragraphs? Be combined? Be put
      elsewhere? (If you outline the essay by jotting
      down the gist of each paragraph, you will get help
      in answering these questions.)
   d. Is each sentence clearly related to the sentence
      that precedes and to the sentence that follows?
   e. Is each paragraph adequately developed?
   f. Are there sufficient details, perhaps brief
      supporting quotations from the text?
5. What are the paper's chief strengths?
6. Make at least two specific suggestions that you think
   will assist the author to improve the paper.

THE FINAL VERSION

Here is the final version of the student's essay. The essay that was submitted to the instructor was typed, but here, so that you can easily see how the draft has been revised, we print the draft with the final changes written in, by hand.

Ironies of Life in Kate Chopin's
"The Story of an Hour"

~~Ironies in an Hour~~

Kate Chopin's "The Story of an Hour"—which takes only a few minutes to read—turns out to have an ironic ending. On rereading it, however, one sees that the irony is not concentrated only in the outcome of the plot—Mrs. Mallard dies just when she is beginning to live—but is also present in many details.

After we know how the story turns out, if we reread it we find irony at the very start / ~~as is true of many other stories.~~ **because** Mrs. Mallard's friends **and her sister** assume, mistakenly, that ~~Mrs. Mallard~~ **she** was deeply in love with her husband, Brently Mallard /. ~~They~~ **They** take great care to tell her gently of his death. ~~The friends~~ **They** mean well, and in fact they do well /, ~~they~~ bring**ing** her an hour of life, an hour of **joyous** freedom /. ~~They~~ **but it is ironic that They** think their news is sad. **True,** Mrs. Mallard at first expresses grief when she hears the news, but soon **(unknown to her friends)** she finds joy in it. So Richards's "sad message" (12), though sad in Richards's eyes, is in fact a happy message.

Among the **small but significant** ironic details is the statement **near the end of the story** that when Mallard entered the house, Richards tried to conceal him from Mrs. Mallard, but "Richards was too late" (13). This is ironic because **almost at the start of the story, in the second paragraph** ~~earlier~~ Richards "hastened" (12) to bring his sad message; if he had at the start been "too late" (13), Brently Mallard would have arrived at

home first, and Mrs. Mallard's life would not have ended
an hour later but would simply have gone on as it had
been. Yet another irony at the end of the story is the
diagnosis of the doctors. ~~The doctors~~ *They* say she died of
"heart disease—-of joy that kills" (14). In one sense
~~the doctors~~ *they* are right: Mrs. Mallard has *for the last hour* experienced a
great joy. But of course the doctors totally
misunderstand the joy that kills her. *It is not joy at seeing
her husband alive, but her realization that the great joy she
experienced during the last hour is over.*

All of these ironic details add richness to the story, but
The central irony resides not in the well-
intentioned but ironic actions of Richards, or in the
unconsciously ironic words of the doctors, but in *Mrs. Mallard's* ~~her~~
own life. ~~In a way she has been dead.~~ She "sometimes"
(13) loved her husband, but in a way she has been dead *,*
a body subjected to her husband's will.
Now, his apparent death brings her new life. *Appropriately,* This new
life comes to her at the season of the year when "the
tops of trees . . . were all aquiver with the new spring
life" (12). But, ironically, her new life will last only
She is free, free, free - but only until her husband walks through
an hour. She looks forward to "summer days" (13) but she *the*
doorway
will not see even the end of this spring day. *If* Her years
bringing
of marriage were ironic *,* ~~They brought~~ her a sort of
living death instead of joy *,* Her new life is ironic too *,*
not only because
It grows out of her moment of grief for her supposedly
but also because her vision of a long progression of years."
dead husband, ~~and her vision of a new life~~ is cut short *,*
within an hour on a spring day.

[New page]

Work Cited

Chopin, Kate. "The Story of an Hour." <u>Literature for
Composition</u>. 3rd ed. Ed. Sylvan Barnet et al. New
York: HarperCollins, 1992. 12-13.

A Brief Overview of the Final Version

Finally, as a quick review, let us look at several principles illustrated by this essay.

- The **title of the essay** is not merely the title of the work discussed; rather, it gives the reader a clue, a small idea of the essayist's topic. Because your title will create a crucial first impression, make sure that it is interesting.
- The **opening or introductory paragraph** does not begin by saying "In this story. . . ." Rather, by naming the author and the title it lets the reader know exactly what story is being discussed. It also develops the writer's thesis a bit so that readers know where they will be going.
- The **organization** is effective. The smaller ironies are discussed in the second and third paragraphs, the central (chief) irony in the last paragraph; that is, the essay does not dwindle or become anticlimactic—rather, it builds up. (Again, if you outline your draft you will see if it has an effective organization.)
- Some **brief quotations** are used, both to provide evidence and to let the reader hear—even if only fleetingly—Kate Chopin's writing.
- The essay is chiefly **devoted to analysis, not to summary.** The writer, properly assuming that the reader has read the work, does not tell the plot in great detail. But, aware that the reader has not memorized the story, the writer gives helpful reminders.
- The **present tense** is used in narrating the action: "Mrs. Mallard dies"; "Mrs. Mallard's friends and relatives all assume."
- Although a **concluding paragraph** is often useful—if it does more than merely summarize what has already been clearly said—it is not essential in a short analysis. In this essay, the last sentence explains the chief irony and, therefore, makes an acceptable ending.
- **Documentation** is given according to the form set forth in Chapter 15.
- There are no typographical errors. The author has **proofread** the paper carefully.

THE ADVANTAGES OF WRITING WITH A WORD PROCESSOR

If possible, write your paper on a word processor. Writing a first draft on a word processor is physically somewhat easier than writing by hand or by typewriter, and revising the draft is incomparably easier. (You can almost effortlessly move material around or insert new material.) Further, for many people the screen is less intimidating than a sheet of paper, and when you do put words down, they look a lot better than handwritten or typed material. And if your paper includes footnotes or endnotes and a list of works cited your software probably will automatically format them.

A word processor probably will not save you time, but it will allow you to use your time efficiently. In the past, writers had to spend a great deal of time on the tedious job of typing a clean copy. The more they revised, the more they doomed themselves to hours of retyping. With a word processor, you can spend all of your time reading, writing, and rewriting, and you can virtually leave to the printer the job of typing.

Pre-writing

Your first notes probably will be in the margins of your text, but once you go beyond these, you can use a word processor, for instance to brainstorm. By means of *free association*—writing down whatever comes to mind, without fretting about spelling, punctuation, or logic—you will probably find that you can generate ideas, at least some of which will lead to something. Or you can try *listing*, jotting down key terms (for instance the names of characters in a play, or technical terms such as "meter," "imagery," "stanza" for a poem) and then inserting further thoughts about each of these. Produce a printout, and then start *linking* or *clustering* (with circles and connecting lines) related items. Then return to your screen and reorganize the material, moving *this* word or phrase over to connect it with *that* one.

Many students find *dialoguing* helpful. After writing a sentence or two, they imagine a somewhat skeptical critic who asks questions such as: "What examples can you give?" "What counterevidence might be offered?" and "Have you defined your terms?" In answering such questions writers get further ideas.

Back up your material. Don't run the risk of losing your work. Write on a hard drive (it's faster), and keep a floppy disk nearby for making backups at the close of each work session.

Taking Notes

Write into one file all of your notes for a paper. If the notes are for a paper on (say) Kate Chopin, you will probably name the file *Chopin*. The name does not matter, so long as you remember it.

Put all bibliographic references in one place. If you are using written sources, you will want to keep a record of each source. Some programs, for instance *Fifty-Third Street Writer*, will automatically alphabetize each entry. But even if your program does not alphabetize bibliographic entries, you can easily insert a new entry by scrolling down through the existing references to the appropriate alphabetic place where you can then insert the new reference, last name first.

When taking notes, be sure to check the accuracy of your transcription. If you quote directly, make certain that you have quoted exactly. Use three periods to indicate any omissions within a quotation, and use square brackets to enclose any addition that you make within a quotation. (See pages 312–13.) As we will see in a moment, when you are drafting your paper you may want to block some of this material and move it into the draft.

It's a good idea to print out all of your notes before you prepare a first draft. Because the screen shows you very little of the material that constitutes your notes, print it all out, so that you can survey it as a whole. Cut apart the various notes, and discard material that no longer seems helpful. Next, arrange the surviving material into a tentative sequence, just as you would arrange index cards with handwritten notes. (The word processor is a great help, but don't hesitate to produce hard copy at various stages, and to work with the printed material. The screen is too small to give you a feel of the whole.)

Many writers find it helpful to put this selection of material, now in a sequence, back into the computer. They do this by *blocking* and moving the useful material. Do *not* delete the unused material; as you work on the essay you may realize that you can use some of this material in the final version. It's advisable to copy this selected and arranged material into a new file, named *draft* or some such thing. If you simply add it to the end of the file containing all of the notes, you may sometimes find yourself working with the unselected notes when you meant to be working with the selected notes.

Writing a First Draft

Even if you did not take notes on a computer, you can of course write your drafts and ultimately the final paper on a word processor. Set the line spacing at double-spacing, to allow space for handwritten additions on a printed version of the draft, and start writing.

Some writers find it useful to start writing on the computer by setting down a rough outline—perhaps phrases, in a sequence that at least for the moment seems reasonable. They then go back and fill in the outline, expanding words or phrases into detailed sentences and paragraphs. Of course, as they write they may find that they want to rearrange some of the material, which they can easily do by blocking commands.

Let's assume, however, that you do have notes in the word processor, and that you have arranged them in a sequence. You may want to begin by looking at the first note and writing an opening paragraph that will lead into it, and then go on to the next note. Of course, as you work you will find that some of the notes are unneeded. Don't delete them, since they may come in handy later. Just block them and move them to the end of the file.

Because it is so easy to produce a clean final copy—with a keystroke or two you can tell the printer to print the file—don't hesitate in your draft to incorporate comments that you know you won't retain in the final version, such as CHECK QUOTATION or GET BETTER EXAMPLE. (Use capitals or boldface for such comments, so that you will focus on them when you read the draft, and so you cannot overlook them when the time comes to delete them.)

When you think you have come to the end of your draft, you will probably want to read it on the screen, from the beginning, to correct typos and to make other obvious corrections. Fine, but remember that because the screen is small you cannot get a good sense of the whole. You won't be able to see, for instance, if a paragraph is much too long; even when you scroll through the draft you will not experience the material in the way that the reader of a printed copy will experience it. What you need to do at this stage is to print your draft.

Revising a Draft

Read the printed draft, making necessary revisions in pen or pencil. Probably you will find that some of the material that you have quoted can be abridged, or even deleted, and that in some places better transitions are needed. It is also likely that you will see the need to add details and to reorganize some of the material. Try to read the draft from the point of view of someone new to the material. Keep asking yourself, "Will my reader understand *why* I am making this point at this stage in the essay?" If you ask this question, you probably will find yourself not only adding helpful transitions ("An apparent exception is. . . ") but also occasionally reorganizing. Make these changes on the printed copy, and then incorporate them into the computer and print the revised version.

Read the revised version with a critical eye; you probably will find that you can extensively revise even this version. You may get some help from a computer program. For instance, if you are using *Fifty-Third Street Writer*, which includes the *Scott, Foresman Handbook*, and you are uncertain about, say, the use of the semicolon, you can consult the index to the *Handbook*, and then bring up the material on semicolons. Similarly, if you are writing a book review, you can find the material on reviews by consulting the index, and can then bring to the screen the discussion of the qualities that make for a good review. Among other software programs that many writers find useful are *Grammatik, Word Plus, Right Writer,* and *Writer's Workbench.* Some of these will alert you to such matters as spelling errors, clichés, split infinitives, overuse of the passive voice, and certain kinds of grammatical errors. For instance, *Writer's Workbench* (and some of the others) will let you check troublesome pairs of words (*affect/effect*), will flag words and phrases that are potentially sexist, will detect most split infinitives and misspellings, and will (among other things) give you help with transitions. You cannot rely entirely on these programs, but they do offer considerable help.

When you get a version that seems to you the best that you can do without further assistance, ask a friend to read it. **Prepare a copy for peer review.** Print your text—double-spaced and letter-quality, of course—and give it to your reader, along with a copy of the sample peer review sheet on page 28, or with a comparable sheet issued by your instructor.

When the paper is returned to you, respond to the suggestions appropriately and then print out this new version. Do not rely on reading the paper on the screen.

The Final Version

After you print out the version you have prepared in response to the comments by your reviewer, read it to see if you can make any further improvements. (Even at this late date you may think of a better title, or you may sense that a quotation doesn't sound quite right.) You can make small changes by hand, in ink, but if you make a substantial number of changes, print out a clean copy. Your paper will be neater—and there is little labor involved.

3

Two Forms of Criticism: Explication and Analysis

EXPLICATION

A line-by-line or episode-by-episode commentary on what is going on in a text is an **explication** (literally, unfolding or spreading out). It takes some skill to work one's way along without saying, "In line one . . . , in the second line . . . , in the third line . . . " One must sometimes boldly say something like, "The next stanza begins with . . . and then introduces. . . ." And, of course, one can discuss the second line before the first line if that seems to be the best way of handling the passage.

An explication does not deal with the writer's life or times, and it is not a paraphrase, a rewording— though it may include paraphrase. Rather, an explication is a commentary revealing your sense of the meaning of the work. To this end it calls attention, as it proceeds, to the implications of words, the function of rhymes, the shifts in point of view, the development of contrasts, and any other contributions to the meaning.

A Sample Explication: Langston Hughes's "Harlem"

The following short poem is by Langston Hughes (1902–67), an African-American writer who was born in Joplin, Mississippi; lived part of his youth in Mexico; spent a year at Columbia University; served as a merchant seaman; and worked in a Paris nightclub, where he showed some of his poems to Dr. Alain Locke, a strong advocate of African-American literature. When he returned to the United States, Hughes went on to publish fiction, plays, essays, and biographies; he also founded theaters, gave public readings, and was, in short, an important force.

HARLEM

What happens to a dream deferred?

>   Does it dry up
>   like a raisin in the sun?
>   Or fester like a sore—
>   And then run?
>   Does it stink like rotten meat?
>   Or crust and sugar over—
>   like a syrupy sweet?
>
>   Maybe it just sags
>   like a heavy load.

Or does it explode?

Different readers will respond at least somewhat differently to any work. On the other hand, since writers want to communicate, they try to control their readers' responses, and they count on their readers to understand the denotations of words as they understand them. Thus, Hughes assumed that his readers knew that Harlem was the site of a large African-American community in New York City. A reader who confuses the title of the poem with Harlem in the Netherlands will wonder what this poem is saying about the tulip-growing center in northern Holland. Explication is based on the assumption that the poem contains a meaning and that by studying the work thoughtfully we can unfold the meaning or meanings. (The point—which has been disputed—will be brought up again at the end of this discussion of explication.)

Let us assume that the reader understands Hughes is talking about Harlem, New York, and that the "dream deferred" refers to the unfulfilled hopes of African-Americans who live in a dominant white society. But Hughes does not say "hopes," he says "dream," and he does not say "unfulfilled," he says "deferred." You might ask yourself exactly what differences there are between these words. Next, after you have read the poem several times, you might think about which expression is better in the context, "unfulfilled hopes" or "dream deferred," and why.

Working toward an Explication of "Harlem"

In preparing to write an explication, write on a computer, or type, or handwrite the complete text of the work—usually a poem but sometimes a short passage of prose—that you will explicate. *Don't* photocopy it; the act of typing or writing it will help you to get into the piece, word by word, comma by comma. Type or write it *double-spaced,* so that you will have plenty of room for annotations as you study the piece. It's advisable to make a few photocopies (or to print a few copies, if you are using a word processor) before you start annotating, so that if one page gets too cluttered you can continue working on a clean copy. Or you may want to use one copy for certain kinds of annotations—let's say those concerning imagery—and other copies for other kinds of notes—let's say those concerning meter, or wordplay. If you are writing on a word processor, you can highlight words, boldface them, put them in capitals (for instance to indicate accented syllables), and so forth.

Let's turn to an explication of the poem, a detailed examination of the whole. Here are the preliminary jottings.

in all the dreams is weakened

images are mostly of "good" things that spoil.

HARLEM

Odd-does not begin by describing Harlem

Set off, sticks out

What happens to a dream deferred?

Black hopes?

all are spoiled.

Does it dry up
like a raisin in the sun?
Or fester like a sore—
And then run?

ugh— Does it stink like rotten meat?
Or crust and sugar over
—like a syrupy sweet?

4 comparisons

contrasts : same sound makes comparison striking.

not so bad?

rhymed sound points to dy. neental p dy. Power m bed

Maybe it just sags
like a heavy load.

Not a question. Strange.

Note italics; emphasis; also, a line by itself. Very emphatic

Or does it explode?

rhyme
Ends with a question. (Begins with a question, too.)

But does the question mark make the ending not so emphatic?

NO LOSS of dream's power m these two images.

These annotations chiefly get at the structure of the poem, the relationship of the parts. The student notices that the poem begins with a line set off by itself and ends with a line set off by itself, and he also notices that each of these lines is a question. Further, he indicates that each of these two lines is emphasized in other ways: The first begins farther to the left than any of the other lines—as though the other lines are subheadings or are in some way subordinate—and the last is italicized.

Some Journal Entries

The student who made these annotations later wrote an entry in his journal:

<u>Feb. 18</u>. Since the title is "Harlem," it's obvious that
the "dream" is by African-American people. Also,
obvious that Hughes thinks that if the "dream" doesn't
become real there may be riots ("explode"). I like
"raisin in the sun" (maybe because I like the play), and
I like the business about "a syrupy sweet"--much more
pleasant than the festering sore and the rotten meat.
But if the dream becomes "sweet," what's wrong with
that? Why should something "sweet" explode?

<u>Feb. 21</u>. Prof. McCabe said to think of structure or form
of a poem as a sort of architecture, a building with a
foundation, floors, etc., topped by a roof--but since we
read a poem from top to bottom, it's like a building
upside down. Title is foundation (even though it's at
top); last line is roof, capping the whole. As you
read, you add layers. Foundation of "Harlem" is a
question (first line). Then, set back a bit from
foundation, or built on it by white space, a tall room
(7 lines high, with 4 questions); then, on top of this
room, another room (2 lines, one statement, not a
question). Funny; I thought that in poems all stanzas
are the same number of lines. Then--more white space,
so another unit--the roof. Man, this roof is going to
fall in--"explodes." Not just the roof, maybe the whole
house.

<u>Feb. 21, pm</u>. I get it; one line at start, one line at
end; both are questions, but the last sort of says
(because it is <u>in italics</u>) that it is the <u>most likely</u>
answer to the question of the first line. The last line
is also a question, but it's still an answer. The big
stanza (7 lines) has 4 questions: 2 lines, 2 lines, 1
line, 2 lines. Maybe the switch to 1 line is to give
some variety, so as not to be dull? It's exactly in the

middle of the poem. I get the progress from raisin in the sun (dried, but not so terrible), to festering sore and to stinking meat, but I still don't see what's so bad about "a syrupy sweet." Is Hughes saying that after things are very bad they will get better? But why, then, the explosion at the end?

Feb 23. "Heavy load" and "sags" in next-to-last stanza seems to me to suggest slaves with bales of cotton, or maybe poor cotton pickers dragging big sacks of cotton. Or maybe people doing heavy labor in Harlem. Anyway, very tired. Different from running sore and stinking meat earlier; not disgusting, but pressing down, deadening. Maybe <u>worse</u> than a sore or rotten meat--a hard, hopeless life. And then the last line. Just one line, no fancy (and disgusting) simile. Boom! Not just pressed down and tired, like maybe some racist whites think (hope?) blacks will be? Bang! Will there be survivors?

Drawing chiefly on these notes, the student jotted down some key ideas to guide him through a draft of an explication of the poem. (The organization of the draft posed no problem; the student simply followed the organization of the poem.

11 lines; short, but powerful; explosive
Question (first line)
Answers (set off by space and also indented)
"raisin in the sun": shrinking
"sore"
"rotten meat"
} disgusting
"syrupy sweet": relief from disgusting comparisons
final question (last line): explosion?
    explosive (powerful) because:
        short, condensed, packed
        in italics
        stands by self—like first line
        no fancy comparison; very direct

The Final Draft

Here is the final essay:

Langston Hughes's "Harlem"

"Harlem" is a poem that is only 11 lines long, but it is charged with power. It explodes. Hughes sets the stage, so to speak, by telling us in the title that he is talking about Harlem, and then he begins by asking "What happens to a dream deferred?" The rest of the poem is set off by being indented, as though it is the answer to his question. This answer is in three parts (three stanzas, of different lengths).

In a way, it's wrong to speak of the answer, since the rest of the poem consists of questions, but I think Hughes means that each question (for instance, does a "deferred" hope "dry up / like a raisin in the sun?") really is an answer, something that really has happened and that will happen again. The first question, "Does it dry up / like a raisin in the sun?" is a famous line. To compare hope to a raisin dried in the sun is to suggest a terrible shrinking. The next two comparisons are to a "sore" and to "rotten meat." These comparisons are less clever, but they are very effective because they are disgusting. Then, maybe because of the disgusting comparisons, he gives a comparison that is not at all disgusting. In this comparison he says that maybe the "dream deferred" will "crust over-- / like a syrupy sweet."

The seven lines with four comparisons are followed by a stanza of two lines with just one comparison:

> Maybe it just sags
> like a heavy load.

So if we thought that this postponed dream might finally turn into something "sweet," we were kidding ourselves. Hughes comes down to earth, in a short stanza, with an image of a heavy load, which probably also calls to mind images of people bent under heavy loads, maybe of cotton, or maybe just any sort of heavy load carried by African-Americans in Harlem and elsewhere.

The opening question ("What happens to a dream deferred?") was followed by four questions in seven lines, but now, with "Maybe it just sags / like a heavy load" we get a statement, as though the poet at last has found an answer. But at the end we get one more question, set off by itself and in italics: "<u>Or does it explode?</u>" This line itself is explosive for three reasons: it is short, it is italicized, and it is a stanza in itself. It's also interesting that this line, unlike the earlier lines, does <u>not</u> use a simile. It's almost as though Hughes is saying, "O.K. we've had enough fancy ways of talking about this terrible situation; here it is, straight."

Topic for Discussion

The student's explication suggests that the comparison with "a syrupy sweet" deliberately misleads the reader into thinking the ending will be happy, and it thus serves to make the real ending even more powerful. In class another student suggested that Hughes may be referring to African-Americans who play Uncle Tom, people who adopt a smiling manner in order to cope with an oppressive society. Which explanation do you prefer, and why? What do you think of combining the two?

Does some method or principle help us decide which interpretation is correct? Can one, in fact, talk about a "correct" interpretation, or only about a plausible or implausible interpretation and an interesting or uninteresting interpretation?

Note: Another explication (of W. B. Yeats's "The Balloon of the Mind") appears in Chapter 12.

ANALYSIS: THE JUDGMENT OF SOLOMON

Explication is a method used chiefly in the study of fairly short poems or brief extracts from essays, stories, novels, and plays. Of course, if one has world enough and time one can set out to explicate all of *The Color Purple* or *Hamlet;* more likely, one will explicate only a paragraph or at most a page of the novel, and a speech or two of the play. In writing about works longer than a page or two, a more common approach than explicating is **analyzing** (literally, separating into parts in order better to understand the whole). An analysis of, say, *The Color Purple,* may consider the functions of the setting, or the uses that certain minor characters serve; an analysis of *Hamlet* may consider the comic passages, or the reasons for Hamlet's delay; an analysis of *Death of a Salesman* may consider the depiction of women, or the causes of Willy Loman's failure.

Analysis, of course, is not a process used only in talking about literature. It is commonly applied in thinking about almost any complex matter. Steffi Graf plays a deadly game of tennis. What does her serve do to her opponent? How does her backhand contribute? And so it makes sense, if you are writing about literature, to try to examine one or more of the components of the work, in order to see how they contribute to the whole, either as part of an esthetic pattern or as part of the meaning. In Chapter 5 we will see, for example, how the meter of Frost's "The Span of Life" contributes to the meaning—heavy stresses for the line about the tired old dog, fewer and lighter stresses for the line about the puppy.

Although other chapters of this book include brief specimens of analytic criticism, for instance of a proverb ("A rolling stone gathers no moss") and of short poems by Robert Frost, Pat Mora, Eugene Field, and X. J. Kennedy, a brief analysis of a very short story about King Solomon, from the Hebrew Bible, may be useful here. Because the story is short, the analysis can consider all or almost all of the story's parts, and therefore the analysis can seem relatively complete. ("*Seem* relatively complete" because the analysis will in fact be far from complete, since the number of reasonable things that can be said about a work is almost as great as the number of readers. And a given reader might, at a later date, offer a rather different reading from what the reader offers today.)

The following story about King Solomon, customarily called "The Judgment of Solomon," appears in the Hebrew Bible, in the latter part of the third chapter of the book called 1 Kings or First Kings, probably written in the mid-sixth century BCE. The translation is from the King James Version of the Bible (1611). Two expressions in the story need clarification. (1) The woman who "overlaid" her child in her sleep rolled over on the child and suffocated it; (2) it is said of a woman that her "bowels yearned upon her son," that is, her heart longed for her son. (Among the early Hebrews, the bowels were thought to be the seat of emotion.)

Then came there two women, that were harlots, unto the king, and stood before him. And the one woman said, "O my lord, I and this woman dwell in one house, and I was delivered of a child with her in the house. And it came to pass the third day after that I was delivered, that this woman was delivered also, and we were together; there was no stranger in the house, save we two in the house. And this woman's child died in the night, because she overlaid it. And she rose at midnight, and took my son from beside me, while thine handmaid slept, and laid it in her bosom, and laid her dead child in my bosom. And when I rose in the morning to give my child suck, behold, it was dead; but when I considered it in the morning, behold, it was not my son, which I did bear."

And the other woman said, "Nay, but the living son is my son, and the dead is thy son." And this said, "No, but the dead is thy son, and the living is my son." Thus they spoke before the king.

Then said the king, "The one said, 'This is my son that liveth, and thy son is dead.' And the other said, 'Nay, but thy son is the dead, and my son is the living.'" And the king said, "Bring me a sword." And they brought a sword before the king. And the king said, "Divide the living child in two and give half to the one, and half to the other."

Then spake the woman whose the living child was unto the king, for her bowels yearned upon her son, and she said, "O my lord, give her the living child, and in no wise slay it." But the other said, "Let it be neither mine nor thine, but divide it."

Then the king answered and said, "Give her the living child, and in no wise slay it. She is the mother thereof."

And all Israel heard of the judgment which the king had judged, and they feared the king, for they saw that the wisdom of God was in him, to do judgment.

Let's begin by analyzing the *form,* or the shape, of the story. One form or shape that we notice is this: The story moves from a problem to a solution. We can also say, still speaking of the overall form, that the story moves from quarreling and talk of death to unity and talk of life. In short, it has a happy ending, a form that (because it provides an optimistic view of life and also a sense of completeness) gives pleasure to most people.

In thinking about a work of literature, it is always useful to take notice of the basic form of the whole, the overall structural pattern. Doubtless you are already familiar with many basic patterns, for example tragedy (joy yielding to sorrow) and romantic comedy (angry conflict yielding to joyful union). If you think even briefly about verbal works, you'll notice the structures or patterns that govern songs, episodes in soap operas, political speeches (beginning with the candidate's expression of pleasure at being in Duluth, and ending with "God bless you all"), detective stories, westerns, and so on. And just as viewers of a western film inevitably experience one western in the context of others, so readers inevitably experience one story in the context of similar stories, and one poem in the context of others.

Second, we can say that "The Judgment of Solomon" is a sort of detective story: There is a death, followed by a conflict in the testimony of the witnesses, and a solution by a shrewd outsider. Consider Solomon's predicament. Ordinarily in literature characters are sharply defined and individualized, yet the essence of a detective story is that the culprit should not be easily recognized as wicked, and here nothing seems to distinguish the two petitioners. Solomon is confronted by "two women, that were harlots." Until late in the story—that is, up to the time Solomon suggests dividing the child—they are described only as "the one woman," "the other woman," "the one," "the other."

Does the story suffer from weak characterization? If we think analytically about this issue, we realize that the point surely is to make the women as alike as possible, so that we cannot tell which of the two is speaking the truth. Like Solomon, we have nothing to go on; neither witness is known to be more honest than the other, and there are no other witnesses to support or refute either woman.

Analysis is concerned with seeing the relationships between the parts of a work, but analysis also may take note of what is *not* in the work. A witness would destroy the story, or at least turn it into an utterly different story. Another thing missing from this story is an explicit editorial comment or interpretation, except for the brief remark at the end, that the people "feared the king." If we had read the story in the so-called Geneva Bible (1557-60), which is the translation of the Bible that Shakespeare was familiar with, we would have found a marginal comment: "Her motherly affection herein appeareth that she had rather endure the rigour of the lawe, than see her child cruelly slaine." Would you agree that it is better, at least in this story, for the reader to draw conclusions than for the storyteller explicitly to point them out?

Solomon wisely contrives a situation in which these two claimants, who seem so similar, will reveal their true natures: The mother will reveal her love, and the liar will reveal her hard heart. The early symmetry (the identity of the two women) pleases a reader, and so does the device by which we can at last distinguish between the two women.

But even near the end there is a further symmetry. In order to save the child's life, the true mother gives up her claim, crying out, "Give her the living child, and in no wise slay it." The author (or, rather, the translator who produced this part of the King James Version) takes these very words, with no change whatsoever, and puts them into Solomon's mouth as the king's final judgment. Solomon too says, "Give her the living child, and in no wise slay it," but now the sentence takes on a new meaning. In the first sentence, "her" refers to the liar (the true mother will give the child to "her"); in Solomon's sentence, "her" refers to the true mother: "Give her the living child. . . ." Surely we take pleasure in the fact that the very words by which the mother renounces her child (1) are the words that reveal to Solomon the truth and (2) are the words Solomon uses to restore the child to its mother.

This analysis has chiefly talked about the relations of parts, and especially it has tried to explain why the two women in this story are *not* distinct, until Solomon finds a way to reveal their distinctive natures: If the story is to demonstrate Solomon's wisdom, the women must seem identical until Solomon can show that they differ. But the analysis could have gone into some other topic. Let's consider several possibilities.

A student might begin by asking this question: "Although it is important for the women to be highly similar, why are they harlots?" (It is too simple to say that the women in the story are harlots because the author is faithfully reporting an historical episode in Solomon's career. The story is widely recognized as a folktale, found also in other ancient cultures.) One possible reason for making the women harlots is that the story demands that there be no witnesses; by using harlots, the author disposed of husbands, parents, and siblings who might otherwise be expected to live with the women. A second possible reason is that the author wanted to show that Solomon's justice extended to all, not only to respectable folk. Third, perhaps the author wished to reject or at least to complicate the stereotype of the harlot as a thoroughly disreputable person. He did this by introducing another (and truer?) stereotype, the mother as motivated by overwhelming maternal love.

Other Possible Topics for Analysis

Another possible kind of analytic essay might go beyond the structure of the individual work, to the relation of the work to some larger whole. For instance, one might approach "The Judgment of Solomon" from the point of view of gender criticism (discussed in Chapter 8): In this story, one might argue, wisdom is an attribute only of a male; women are either deceitful or emotional. From this point one might set out to write a research essay on gender in a larger whole, certain books of the Hebrew Bible.

We might also analyze the story in the context of other examples of what scholars call Wisdom Literature (the Book of Proverbs and Ecclesiastes, for instance). Notice that Solomon's judgment leads the people to *fear* him—because his wisdom is great, formidable, and God-inspired.

It happens that we do not know who wrote "The Judgment of Solomon," but the authors of most later works of literature are known, and therefore some critics seek to analyze a given work within the context of the author's life. For some other critics, the larger context would be the reading process, which includes the psychology of the reader. (Biographical criticism and reader-response criticism are discussed in Chapter 8.)

Still another analysis—again, remember that a work can be analyzed from many points of view—might examine two or more translations of the story. You do not need to know Hebrew in order to compare this early seventeenth-century translation with a twentieth-century version such as the New Jerusalem Bible or the Revised English Bible. One might seek to find which version is, on literary grounds, more effective. Such an essay might include an attempt, by means of a comparison, to analyze the effect of the archaic language of the King James Version. Does the somewhat unfamiliar language turn a reader off, or does it add mystery or dignity or authority to the tale, valuable qualities perhaps not found in the modern version? (By the way, in the New Revised English Bible, Solomon does *not* exactly repeat the mother's plea. The mother says, "Give her the living child," and Solomon then says, "Give the living child to the first woman." In the New Jerusalem Bible, after the mother says "Let them give her the live child," Solomon says, "Give the live child to the first woman." If you prefer one version to the other two, why not try to analyze your preference?)

Finally, it should be mentioned (or, to be more truthful, it must be confessed) that an analysis of the structure of a work, in which the relationships of the parts to the whole are considered, allows the work to be regarded as independent of the external world ("autonomous," to use a word common in criticism). If we insist, say, that literature should in all respects reflect life, and we want to analyze the work against reality as we see it, we may find ourselves severely judging "The Judgment of Solomon." We might ask, for instance, if it is likely that a great king would bother to hear the case of two prostitutes quarreling over a child, or if it is likely that the false claimant would really call for the killing of the child. Similarly, to take an absurd example, an analysis of this story in terms of its ability to evoke laughter would be laughable. The point: An analysis will be interesting and useful to a reader only insofar as the aim of the analysis seems reasonable.

Comparison: An Analytic Tool

Analysis frequently involves comparing: Things are examined for their resemblances to and differences from other things. Strictly speaking, if one emphasizes the differences rather than the similarities, one is contrasting rather than comparing, but we need not preserve this distinction; we can call both processes *comparing*.

Although your instructor may ask you to write a comparison of two works of literature, the *subject* of the essay is the works; comparison is simply an effective analytic technique to show some of the qualities in the works. You might compare Chopin's use of nature in "The Story of an

Hour" (page 13) with the use of nature in another story, in order to reveal the subtle differences between the stories, but a comparison of works utterly unlike can hardly tell the reader or the writer anything.

Something should be said about organizing a comparison, say between the settings in two stories, between two characters in a novel (or even between a character at the end of a novel and the same character at the beginning), or between the symbolism of two poems. Probably, a student's first thought after making some jottings is to discuss one half of the comparison and then go on to the second half. Instructors and textbooks (though not this one) usually condemn such an organization, arguing that the essay breaks into two parts and that the second part involves a good deal of repetition of categories set up in the first part. Usually, they recommend that the students organize their thoughts differently, somewhat along these lines:

1. First similarity
   a. first work (or character, or characteristic)
   b. second work
2. Second similarity
   a. first work
   b. second work
3. First difference
   a. first work
   b. second work
4. Second difference
   a. first work
   b. second work

and so on, for as many additional differences as seem relevant. If one wishes to compare *Huckleberry Finn* with *The Catcher in the Rye*, one may organize the material thus:

1. First similarity: the narrator and his quest
   a. Huck
   b. Holden
2. Second similarity: the corrupt world surrounding the narrator
   a. society in *Huck*
   b. society in *Catcher*
3. First difference: degree to which the narrator fulfills his quest and escapes from society
   a. Huck's plan to "light out" to the frontier
   b. Holden's breakdown

Another way of organizing a comparison and contrast:

1. First point: the narrator and his quest
   a. similarities between Huck and Holden
   b. differences between Huck and Holden
2. Second point: the corrupt world
   a. similarities between the worlds in *Huck* and *Catcher*
   b. differences between the worlds in *Huck* and *Catcher*
3. Third point: degree of success
   a. similarities between Huck and Holden
   b. differences between Huck and Holden

A comparison need not employ either of these structures. There is even the danger that an essay employing either of them may not come into focus until the essayist stands back from the seven-layer cake and announces in the concluding paragraph that the odd layers taste better. In one's preparatory thinking, one may want to make comparisons in pairs (good-natured humor: the clown in *Othello,* the clownish grave-digger in *Hamlet;* social satire: the clown in *Othello,* the grave-digger in *Hamlet;* relevance to main theme:. . . ; length of role:. . . ; comments by other characters:. . .), but one must come to some conclusions about what these add up to before writing the final version. This final version should not duplicate the thought processes; rather, it should be organized so as to make the point—the thesis—clearly and effectively. After reflection, one may believe that although there are superficial similarities between the clown in *Othello* and the clownish grave-digger in *Hamlet,* there are essential differences; then in the finished essay one probably will not wish to obscure the main point by jumping back and forth from play to play, working through a series of similarities and differences. It may be better to discuss the clown in *Othello* and then to point out that, although the grave-digger in *Hamlet* resembles him in A, B, and C, the grave-digger also has other functions (D, E, and F) and is of greater consequence to *Hamlet* than the clown is to *Othello.* Some repetition in the second half of the essay ("The grave-digger's puns come even faster than the clown's. . . .") will bind the two halves into a meaningful whole, making clear the degree of similarity or difference. The point of the essay presumably is not to list pairs of similarities or differences but to illuminate a work or works by making thoughtful comparisons.

Although in a long essay one cannot postpone until page 30 a discussion of the second half of the comparison, in an essay of, say, fewer than ten pages nothing is wrong with setting forth one half of the comparison and then, in light of it, the second half. The essay will break into two unrelated parts if the second half makes no use of the first or if it fails to modify the first half, but not if the second half looks back to the first half and calls attention to differences that the new material reveals. Students ought to learn how to write an essay with interwoven comparisons, but they ought also to know that a comparison may be written in another, simpler and clearer way.

Finally, a reminder: The purpose of a comparison is to call attention to the unique features of something by holding it up against something similar but significantly different. You can compare Macbeth with Banquo (two men who hear a prophecy but who respond differently), or Macbeth with Lady Macbeth (a husband and wife, both eager to be monarchs but differing in their sense of the consequences), or Hamlet and Holden Caulfield (two people who see themselves as surrounded by a corrupt world), but you can hardly compare Holden with Macbeth or with Lady Macbeth—there simply are not enough points of resemblance to make it worth your effort to call attention to subtle differences. If the differences are great and apparent, a comparison is a waste of effort. ("Blueberries are different from elephants. Blueberries do not have trunks. And elephants do not grow on bushes.") Indeed, a comparison between essentially and evidently unlike things can only obscure, for by making the comparison the writer implies that significant similarities do exist, and readers can only wonder why they do not see them. The essays that do break into two halves are essays that make uninstructive comparisons: The first half tells the reader about five qualities in Kate Chopin, and the second half tells the reader about five different qualities in Toni Morrison.

FINDING A TOPIC

All literary works afford their own topics for analysis, and all essayists must set forth their own theses, but a few useful generalizations may be made. You can often find a thesis by asking one of two questions:

1. **What is this doing?** That is, why is this scene in the novel or play? Why is Beckett's *Waiting for Godot* in two acts, rather than one or three? Why the biblical allusions in *Waiting for Godot*? Why does Hamlet delay? Why are these lines unrhymed? Why is this stanza form employed? What is the significance of the parts of the work.?

If you don't know where to begin, think about the title, the first part of a work. Titles are often highly significant parts of the work: Ibsen explained that he called his play *Hedda Gabler* rather than *Hedda Tesman* because "She is to be regarded as her father's daughter rather than as her husband's wife." But of course there are other ways of beginning. If the work is a poem without a title, and you don't know where to begin, you may be able to get a start by considering the stanza form, or the chief images. If the work is a story or play, you may get a start by considering the relation between the chief character and the second most important character.

2. **Why do I have this response?** Why do I find this poem clever or moving or puzzling? How did the author make this character funny or dignified or pathetic? How did he or she communicate the idea that this character is a bore without boring me? Why am I troubled by the representation of women in this story? Why do I regard as sexist this lover's expression of his love?

The first of these questions, "What is this doing?" requires that you identify yourself with the author, wondering, for example, whether this opening scene is the best possible for this story. The second question, "Why do I have this response?" requires that you trust your feelings. If you are amused or bored or puzzled or annoyed, assume that these responses are appropriate and follow them up, at least until a rereading of the work provides other responses.

CONSIDERING THE EVIDENCE

Once your responses have led you to a topic ("The Clown in *Othello*") and then to a thesis ("The clown is relevant"), be certain that you have all the evidence. Usually this means that you should study the context of the material you are discussing. For example, if you are writing about *The Catcher in the Rye,* before you argue that because Holden distrusts the adult world, "old" is his ultimate word of condemnation, remember that he speaks of "old Phoebe" and of "old Thomas Hardy," both of whom he values greatly.

ORGANIZING THE MATERIAL

"Begin at the beginning," the King of Hearts in *Alice in Wonderland* said very gravely, "and go on till you come to the end: then stop." This is how your paper should seem to the reader, but it need not have been drafted thus. In fact, unless you are supremely gifted, you will (like the rest of us) have to work very hard to make things easy for the reader.

After locating a topic, converting it into a thesis, and weighing the evidence, a writer has the job of organizing the material into a coherent whole, a sequence of paragraphs that holds the reader's interest (partly because it sets forth material clearly) and that steadily builds up an effective argument. Notice that in the essay on irony (pp. 29–30) in Kate Chopin's "The Story of an Hour," the student wisely moves from the lesser ironies to the chief irony. To begin with the chief irony and end with the lesser ironies would almost surely be anticlimactic.

The organization of an essay will, of course, depend on the nature of the essay: An essay on foreshadowing in *Macbeth* probably will be organized chronologically (material in the first act will be discussed before material in the second act), but an essay on the character of Macbeth may conceivably begin with the end of the play, discussing Macbeth as he is in the fifth act, and then may work backward through the play, arriving at last at the original Macbeth, so to speak, of the beginning of the play. (This is not to suggest that such an organization be regularly employed in writing about a character—only that it might be employed effectively.) Or suppose one is writing about whether Macbeth is a victim of fate. The problem might be stated, and the essayist might go on to take up one view and then the other. Which view should be set forth first? Probably it will be best to let the reader first hear the view that will be refuted, so that you can build to a climax.

The important point is not that there is only one way to organize an essay, but that you find the way that seems best for the particular topic and argument. Once you think you know more or less what you want to say, you will usually, after trial and error, find what seems the best way of communicating it to a reader. A scratch outline (see p. 23) will help you find your way, but don't assume that once you have settled on an outline the organization of your essay finally is established. After you read the draft that you base on your outline, you may realize that a more effective organization will be more helpful to your reader—which means that you must move paragraphs around, revise your transitions, and, in short, produce another draft.

If you look at your draft and you outline it, as suggested on page 26, you will quickly see whether the draft needs to be reorganized.

COMMUNICATING JUDGMENTS

Because a critical essay is a judicious attempt to help a reader see what is going on in a work or in a part of a work, the voice of the critic usually sounds, on first hearing, impartial; but good criticism includes—at least implicitly—evaluation. The critic may say not only that the setting changes (a neutral expression) but also that "the novelist aptly shifts the setting" or "unconvincingly describes. . ." or "effectively juxtaposes. . . ." These evaluations are supported with evidence. The critic has feelings about the work under discussion and reveals them, not by continually saying "I feel" and "this moves me," but by calling attention to the degree of success or failure perceived. Nothing is wrong with occasionally using "I," and noticeable avoidances of it—"it is seen that," "this writer," "the present writer," "we," and the like—suggest an offensive sham modesty; but too much talk of "I" makes a writer sound like an egomaniac.

Consider this sentence from the opening paragraph in a review of George Orwell's *1984*.

> I do not think I have ever read a novel more frightening and depressing; and yet, such are the originality, the suspense, the speed of writing and withering indignation that it is impossible to put the book down.

Fine—provided that the reviewer goes on to offer evidence that enables readers to share his or her evaluation of *1984*.

One final remark on communicating judgments: Write sincerely. Any attempt to neglect your own thoughtful responses and replace them with fabrications designed to please an instructor will surely fail. It is hard enough to find the words that clearly communicate your responses; it is almost impossible to find the words that express your hunch about what your instructor expects your responses to be. George Orwell shrewdly commented on the obvious signs of insincere writing: "When there is a gap between one's real and one's declared aims, one turns as it were instinctively to long words and exhausted idioms, like a cuttlefish squirting out ink."

REVIEW: HOW TO WRITE AN EFFECTIVE ESSAY

All writers must work out their own procedures and rituals (John C. Calhoun liked to plow his farm before writing), but the following suggestions may provide some help. The writing process may be divided into four stages—Pre-writing, Drafting, Revising, and Editing—though as the following discussion admits, the stages are not always neatly separate.

1. Pre-writing

Read the work carefully. You may, on this first reading, want to highlight or annotate certain things, such as passages that please or that puzzle, or you may prefer simply to read it through. In any case, on a second reading you will certainly want to annotate the text and to jot down notes either in the margins or in a journal. You probably are not focusing on a specific topic, but rather are taking account of your early responses to the work.

If you have a feeling or an idea, jot it down; don't assume that you will remember it when you get around to drafting your essay. Write it down so that you will be sure to remember it and so that in the act of writing it down you can improve it. Later, after reviewing your notes (whether in the margins or in a journal) you'll probably find that it's a good idea to transfer your best points to three-by-five inch cards, writing on one side only. By putting the material on cards, you can easily group related points later.

2. Drafting

After reviewing your notes and sorting them out, you will probably find that you have not only a topic (a subject to write about) but a thesis (a point to be made, an argument). Get it down on paper. Perhaps begin by jotting down your thesis and under it a tentative outline. (If you have transferred your preliminary notes to index cards, you can easily arrange the cards into a tentative organization.)

If you are writing an explication, the order probably is essentially the order of the lines or of the episodes. If you are writing an analysis, you may wish to organize your essay from the lesser material to the greater (to avoid anticlimax) or from the simple to the complex (to ensure intelligibility). If you are discussing the roles of three characters in a story, it may be best to build up to the one of the three that you think the most important. If you are comparing two characters, it may be best to move from the most obvious contrasts to the least obvious.

At this stage, however, don't worry about whether the organization is unquestionably the best possible organization for your topic. A page of paper with some ideas in some sort of sequence, however rough, will encourage you that you do have something to say. If you have doubts, by all means record them. By writing down your uncertainties, you will probably begin to feel your way toward tentative explanations of them.

Almost any organization will help you get going on your draft; that is, it will help you start writing an essay. The process of writing will itself clarify and improve your preliminary ideas. If you are like most people, you can't do much precise thinking until you have committed to paper at least a rough sketch of your initial ideas. Later, you can push and polish your ideas into shape, perhaps even deleting all of them and starting over, but it's a lot easier to improve your ideas once you see them in front of you than it is to do the job in your head. On paper, one word leads to another; in your head, one word often blocks another.

Just keep going; you may realize, as you near the end of a sentence, that you no longer believe it. Okay; be glad that your first idea led you to a better one, and pick up your better one and keep going with it. What you are doing is, in a sense, by trial and error pushing your way not only toward clear expression but toward sharper ideas and richer responses.

Although we have been talking about drafting, most teachers rightly regard this first effort at organizing one's notes and turning them into an essay not as a first draft but as a zero draft, really a part of pre-writing. When you reread it, you will doubtless find passages that need further support, passages that seem out of place, and passages that need clarification. You will also find passages that are better than you thought at the outset you could produce. In any case, on rereading the zero draft you will find things that will require you to go back and check the work of literature and to think further about what you have said about it. After rereading the literary work and your draft, you are in a position to write something that can rightly be called a first draft.

3. Revising

Try to allow at least a day to elapse before you start to revise your zero draft and another day before you revise your first draft. If you come to the material with a relatively fresh eye, you may see, for example, that the thesis needs to be announced earlier or more clearly or that certain points need to be supported by concrete references—perhaps by brief quotations from the literary work. A review by your peers will give you a good sense of which things need clarification and of whether your discussion is adequately organized.

At this stage, pay special attention to the following matters.

The Title   If you haven't already jotted down a tentative title for your essay, now is the time to do so. Make sure that the title is interesting and informative. There is nothing interesting and there is very little that is informative in a title such as "On a Play by Arthur Miller," or even in "On *Death of a Salesman*." Such titles are adequate to get you going, but try, as you think about your draft, to come up with something more focused, such as "The Women in *Death of a Salesman*" (this title announces the topic) or "A Feminist Reading of *Death of a Salesman*" (this title announces the approach). Because you are still drafting your essay, of course you will not yet settle on a final version of the title, but thinking about the title will help you to write an essay that is focused.

The Opening   Try to make sure that your introductory sentences or paragraphs engage the reader's interest. It's usually desirable also to give the reader the necessary information concerning which work you are writing about, to indicate your thesis (this information itself may get the reader's interest), and to indicate what your organization will be. Here is a sample that does all of these things:

```
Arthur Miller's Death of a Salesman is so much a play
about a salesman that one hardly thinks about the other
characters, except perhaps for his wife, Linda.  But there
are other women in the play, too, and this essay will
examine Miller's depiction of them, beginning with the
```

briefest sketches and going to Miller's fullest picture of a
woman, Linda Loman. Given that the play is chiefly about
Willy Loman, and given that Miller wrote it nearly fifty
years ago, we might not expect the representation of women
to be as insightful as in fact it is.

Again, this opening paragraph identifies the author and the work (Miller's
Death of a Salesman), and it also indicates the topic (women), the thesis
(Miller's depiction is surprisingly insightful), and the structure (from minor
characters to a major character). Perhaps because it is so informative it is at
least moderately interesting.

Of course an opening need not do all of these things, and perhaps this
example is a bit overloaded, but in revising your draft, be sure to ask yourself *what* your opening does, and if it does enough. Here is another possible opening, again for an essay on the women in *Death of a Salesman*. This
passage does less than the previous example, but it seeks to interest the
reader by means of brief quotations from the play and by means of a question that hints at the thesis.

In Arthur Miller's Death of a Salesman, one
character, Happy, characterizes women as "strudel"--
things created for men to consume--and another
character, Stanley, describes two women in a bar as
"chippies," that is, as prostitutes. Does Arthur Miller
share these chauvinistic views of women, or does he
imply, in the actions of his female characters, that
women are persons of no less worth than men?

(For further discussion of introductory paragraphs, see page 305–06).

The Thesis and the Organization.   In addition to announcing your
thesis early—perhaps in the title, or in the opening paragraph—be sure to
keep the thesis in view throughout the essay. For instance, if you are
arguing that Miller's depiction of women is surprisingly sympathetic, you
will say so, and you will reaffirm the point during the essay, when you
present supporting evidence. Similarly, even if you have announced the
organization, you will keep the reader posted by occasionally saying such
things as "One other minor character must be looked at," and "the last
minor character that we will look at," and "With Linda Loman, the most
important woman in the play," and so on. And of course you will make the
organization clear to your readers by using the appropriate lead-ins and

transitions, such as "Furthermore," "On the other hand," "The final example. . . ."

The Closing.   Say something more interesting than "Thus we see," followed by a repetition of the thesis sentence. Among the tested and effective ways of ending effectively are these: (1) glance back to something from the opening paragraph, thus giving your essay a sense of closure, (2) offer a new bit of evidence, thus driving the point home; (3) indicate that the thesis, now established, can be used in other investigations of comparable material, for instance in a discussion of Miller's later plays. (For further discussion of concluding paragraphs see page 306–07.)

4. Editing

Small-scale revision, such as checking the spelling, punctuation, and accuracy of quotations, is usually called *editing*. Even when you get to this stage, you may unexpectedly find that you must make larger revisions. In checking a quotation, for instance, you may find that it doesn't really support the point you are making, so you may have to do some substantial revising.

Time has run out. Type or write a clean copy, following the principles concerning margins, pagination, and documentation set forth later in this book. If you have borrowed any ideas, be sure to give credit to your sources. Finally, proofread and make corrections as explained on page 311.

The whole process of writing about literature, then, is really a process of responding and of revising one's responses—not only one's responses to the work of literature but also to one's own writing about those responses. When you jot down a note and then jot down a further thought (perhaps even rejecting the earlier note) and then turn this material into a paragraph and then revise the paragraph, you are in the company of Picasso, who said that in painting a picture he advanced by a series of destructions. You are also following Mrs. Beeton's famous recipe:

First catch your hare, then cook it.

Learning from Duke Ellington

When someone asked Duke Ellington why he had not found time to complete a promised piece of music, Ellington replied, "I don't need time. I need a deadline!"

When your instructors give you deadlines they are doing you a favor. But they assume that you will take the deadlines seriously *and* that you will begin reading, thinking, drafting, and revising several days—perhaps a week or more—before the deadline. Even a genius like Duke Ellington found that a deadline was a stimulus to creativity. But unless you are a genius, don't count on being able to produce excellent—or even good—work at the last minute. When instructors set deadlines, they assume that students will apportion their work over a period of days. They assume, that is, a process involving the stages outlined, and they will evaluate the final product in terms of that process, not in terms of a last-minute frenzy to meet the deadline.

A Word about Technical Language

Literature, like, say, the law, medicine, the dance, and, for that matter, cooking and baseball, has given rise to technical terminology. A cookbook will tell you to boil, or bake, or blend, and it will speak of a "slow" oven (300 degrees), a "moderate" oven (350 degrees), or a "hot" oven (400 degrees). These are technical terms in the world of cookery. In watching a baseball game we find ourselves saying, "I think the hit-and-run is on," or "He'll probably bunt." We use these terms because they convey a good deal in a few words; they are clear and precise. Further, although we don't use them in order to impress our hearer, in fact they do indicate that we have more than a superficial acquaintance with the game. That is, the better we know our subject, the more likely we are to use the technical language of the subject. Why? *Because such language enables us to talk precisely and in considerable depth about the subject.* Technical language, unlike jargon (pretentious diction that needlessly complicates or obscures), is illuminating—provided that the reader is familiar with the terms.

In writing about literature you will, for the most part, use the same language that you use in your other courses, and you will not needlessly introduce the technical vocabulary of literary study—but you *will* use this vocabulary when it enables you to be clear, concise, and accurate.

✓ Editing Checklist: Questions to Ask Yourself

1. Is the title of my essay at least moderately informative and interesting?
2. Do I identify the subject of my essay (author and title) early?
3. What is my thesis? Do I state it soon enough (perhaps even in the title) and keep it in view?
4. Is the organization reasonable? Does each point lead into the next without irrelevancies and without anticlimaxes?

5. Is each paragraph unified by a topic sentence or a topic idea? Are there adequate transitions from one paragraph to the next?

6. Are generalizations supported by appropriate concrete details, especially by brief quotations from the text?

7. Is the opening paragraph interesting and, by its end, focused on the topic? Is the final paragraph conclusive without being repetitive?

8. Is the tone appropriate? No sarcasm, no apologies, no condescension?

9. If there is a summary, is it as brief as possible, given its purpose?

10. Are the quotations adequately introduced, and are they accurate? Do they provide evidence and let the reader hear the author's voice, or do they merely add words to the essay?

11. Is the present tense used to describe the author's work and the action of the work ("Shakespeare *shows*," "Hamlet *dies*")?

12. Have I kept in mind the needs of my audience, for instance by defining unfamiliar terms, or by briefly summarizing works or opinions that the reader may be unfamiliar with?

13. Is documentation provided where necessary?

14. Are the spelling and punctuation correct? Are other mechanical matters (such as margins, spacing, and citations) in correct form? Have I proofread carefully?

15. Is the paper properly identified—author's name, instructor's name, course number, and date?

4

Other Kinds of Writing about Literature

A SUMMARY

The essay on "The Story of an Hour" in Chapter 2 does not include a *summary* because the writer knew that all of her readers were thoroughly familiar with Chopin's story. Sometimes, however, it is advisable to summarize the work you are writing about, thus reminding a reader who has not read the work recently, or even informing a reader who may never have read the work. A review of a new work of literature or of a new film, for instance, usually includes a summary, on the assumption that readers are unfamiliar with it.

A summary is a brief restatement or condensation of the plot. Consider this summary of Chopin's "The Story of an Hour."

A newspaper office reports that Brently Mallard has been killed in a railroad accident. When the news is gently broken to Mrs. Mallard by her sister Josephine, Mrs. Mallard weeps wildly and then shuts herself up in her room, where she sinks into an armchair. Staring dully through the window, she sees the signs of spring, and then an unnameable sensation possesses her. She tries to reject it but finally abandons herself to it. Renewed, she exults in her freedom, in the thought that at last the days will be her own. She finally comes out of the

room, embraces her sister, and descends the stairs. A
moment later her husband--who in fact had not been in
the accident--enters. Mrs. Mallard dies--of the joy that
kills, according to the doctors' diagnosis.

Here are a few principles that govern summaries:

1. A summary is **much briefer than the original.** It is not a paraphrase—a word-by-word translation of someone's words into your own. A
paraphrase is usually at least as long as the original, whereas a summary is
rarely longer than one-fourth of the original and is usually much shorter. A
novel may be summarized in a few paragraphs, or even in one paragraph.

2. A summary **usually achieves its brevity by omitting almost all
of the concrete details of the original** and by omitting minor characters
and episodes. Notice that the summary of "The Story of an Hour" omits the
friend of the family, omits specifying the signs of spring, and omits the business of the sister imploring Mrs. Mallard to open the door.

3. A summary is **as accurate as possible,** given the limits of space.

4. A summary is **normally written in the present tense.** Thus "A
newspaper office reports . . . , Mrs. Mallard weeps.. . . "

5. If the summary is brief (say, fewer than 250 words), it **may be given
as a single paragraph.** If you are summarizing a long work, you may feel
that a longer summary is needed. In this case your reader will be grateful to
you if you divide the summary into paragraphs. As you draft your summary,
you may find **natural divisions.** For instance, the scene of the story may
change midway, providing you with the opportunity to use two paragraphs.
Or you may want to summarize a five-act play in five paragraphs.

Summaries have their place in essays, but remember that a summary is not
an analysis; it is only a summary.

A PARAPHRASE

A paraphrase is a restatement—a sort of translation into the same language—of material that may in its original form be somewhat obscure to a
reader. A native speaker of English will not need a paraphrase of "Thirty
days hath September," though a non-native speaker might be puzzled by
two things, the meaning of *hath* and the inverted word order. For such a
reader, "September has thirty days" would be a helpful paraphrase.

Although a paraphrase seeks to make clear the gist of the original, if the
original is even a little more complex than "Thirty days hath September"

the paraphrase will—in the process of clarifying something—lose something, since the substitution of one word for another will change the meaning. For instance, "Shut up" and "Be quiet" do not say exactly the same thing; the former (in addition to asking for quiet) says that the speaker is rude, or perhaps it says that the speaker feels he can treat his listener contemptuously, but the paraphrase loses all of this.

Still, a paraphrase can be helpful as a first step in helping a reader to understand a line that includes an obsolete word or phrase, or a word or phrase that is current only in one region. For instance, in a poem by Emily Dickinson (1830–86), the following line appears

The sun engrossed the East. . . .

"Engrossed" here has (perhaps among other meanings) a special commercial meaning, "to acquire most or all of a commodity; to monopolize the market," and so a paraphrase of the line might go thus:

The sun took over all of the east.

(It's worth mentioning, parenthetically, that you should have at your elbow a good desk dictionary, such as *The American Heritage Dictionary of the English Language,* 3rd edition. Writers—especially poets—expect you to pay close attention to every word. If a word puzzles you, look it up.)

Idioms, as well as words, may puzzle a reader. The Anglo-Irish poet William Butler Yeats (1865–1939) begins one poem with

The friends that have it I do wrong. . . .

Because the idiom "to have it" (meaning "to believe that," "to think that") is unfamiliar to many American readers today, a discussion of the poem might include a paraphrase—a rewording, a translation into more familiar language, such as

The friends who think that I am doing the wrong thing. . . .

Perhaps the rest of the poem is immediately clear, but in any case here is the entire poem, followed by a paraphrase:

The friends that have it I do wrong
When ever I remake a song,
Should know what issue is at stake:
It is myself that I remake.

Now for the paraphrase:

The friends who think that I am doing the wrong thing when I revise one of my poems should be informed what the important issue is; I'm not just revising a poem; rather, I am revising myself (my thoughts, feelings).

Here, as with any paraphrase, the meaning is not translated exactly; there is some distortion. For instance, if "song" in the original is clarified by "poem" in the paraphrase, it is also altered; the paraphrase loses the sense of lyricism that is implicit in "song." Further, "Should know what issue is at stake" (in the original), is ambiguous. Does "should" mean "ought," as in (for instance) "You should know better than to speak so rudely," or does it mean "deserve to be informed," as in "You deserve to know that I am thinking about quitting"?

Granted that a paraphrase may miss a great deal, a paraphrase often helps you, or your reader, to understand at least the surface meaning, and the act of paraphrasing will usually help you to understand at least some of the implicit meaning. Furthermore, a paraphrase makes you see that the original writer's words (if the work is a good one) are exactly right, better than any words we might substitute. It becomes clear that the thing said in the original—not only the rough "idea" expressed but the precise tone with which it is expressed—is a sharply defined experience.

A LITERARY RESPONSE

Of course anything that you write about a work of literature is a response, even if it seems to be as matter-of-fact as a summary. It's sometimes useful to compare your summary with that of a classmate. You may be surprised to find that the two summaries differ considerably—though when you think about it, it is not really surprising. Two different people are saying what they think is the gist of the work, and their views are inevitably shaped, at least to some degree, by such things as their gender, their ethnicity, and their experience (including, of course, their *literary* experience).

But when we talk about writing a response, we usually mean something more avowedly personal, something (for instance) like an entry in a journal, wherein the writer may set forth an emotional response, perhaps relating the work to one of his or her own experiences. (On journals, see pages 19–20.)

Writing a Literary Response

You may want to rewrite a literary work, for instance by giving it a different ending, or by writing an epilogue in which you show the characters 20 years later. (We have already talked about the possibility of writing a sequel to Chopin's "Ripe Figs," or of writing a letter from Babette to Mama-Nainaine, or of writing Babette's memoirs). Or you might want to rewrite a literary work, presenting the characters from a somewhat different point of view. A student who in an essay on Thurber's "The Secret Life of Walter Mitty" argues that Mitty *needs* someone very much like Mrs. Mitty might well rewrite Thurber's story along those lines. The fun for the reader would of course rest largely in hearing the story reinterpreted, in (so to speak) seeing the story turned inside out.

A Story Based on a Story

Here is an example, written by Lola Lee Loveall for a course taught by Diana Muir at Solano Community College. Ms. Loveall's story is a response to Kate Chopin's "The Story of an Hour" (p. 13). Notice that Loveall's first sentence is close to her source—a good way to get started, but by no means the only way; notice, too, that elsewhere in her story she occasionally echoes Chopin—for instance, in the references to the treetops, the sparrows, and the latchkey. A reader enjoys detecting these echoes.

What is especially interesting, however, is that before she conceived her story Loveall presumably said to herself something like, "Well, Chopin's story is superb, but suppose we shift the focus a bit. Suppose we think about what it would be like, *from the husband's point of view,* to live with a woman who suffered from 'heart trouble,' a person whom one had to treat with 'great care'" (Chopin's words, in the first sentence of "The Story of an Hour"). "And what about Mrs. Mallard's sister, Josephine—so considerate of Mrs. Mallard? What, exactly, would *Mr.* Mallard think of her? Wouldn't he see her as a pain in the neck? And what might he be prompted to do? That is, how might this character in this situation respond?" And so Loveall's characters and her plot began to take shape. As part of the game, she committed herself to writing a plot that, in its broad outline, resembled Chopin's by being highly ironic. But read it yourself.

```
Lola Lee Loveall
English 6
                    The Ticket
     (A Different View of "The Story of an Hour")
     Knowing full well his wife was afflicted with heart
trouble, Brently Mallard wondered how he was going to
break the news about the jacket. As he strode along his
boots broke through the shallow crust from the recent
rain, and dust kicked up from the well--worn wagon road
came up to flavor his breathing. At least, the gentle
spring rain had settled the dusty powder even as it had
sprinkled his stiffly starched shirt which was already
```

dampened from the exertion of stamping along. The
strenuous pace he set himself to cover the intervening
miles home helped him regain his composure. Mr. Brently
Mallard was always calm, cool, and confident.

However, he hadn't been this morning when he stepped
aboard the train, took off his jacket and folded it
neatly beside him, and settled in his seat on the
westbound train. He had been wildly excited. Freedom was
his. He was Free! He was off for California, devil take
the consequences! He would be his old self again, let
the chips fall where they may. And he would have been
well on his way, too, if that accursed ticket agent
hadn't come bawling out, "Mr. Mallard, you left your
ticket on the counter!" just when Mallard himself had
spied that nosy Jan Ardan bidding her sister goodbye
several car lengths down the depot. How could he be so
unfortunate to run into them both twice this morning?
Earlier, they had come into the bank just as the banker
had extended the thick envelope.

"You understand, this is just an advance against the
estate for a while?"

Only Mallard's persuasiveness could have extracted
that amount from the cagey old moneybags.

Mallard had carefully tucked it into his inside
pocket.

This was the kind of spring day to fall in love--or
lure an adventurer to the top of the next hill. Sparrows
hovered about making happy sounds. Something about their
movements reminded Mallard of his wife--quick,
fluttering, then darting away.

He had loved her at first for her delicate ways.
They had made a dashing pair--he so dark and worldly,
she so fragile and fair--but her delicacy was a trap,
for it disguised the heart trouble, bane of his life.
Oh, he still took her a sip of brandy in bed in the
morning as the doctor had suggested, although, of
course, it wasn't his bed anymore. He had moved farther
down the hall not long after her sister, Josephine, came
to help, quick to come when Mrs. Mallard called, even in

the middle of the night. After one such sudden
appearance one night--"I thought I heard you call"--he
had given up even sharing the same bed with his wife,
although there had been little real sharing there for
some time.

"No children!" the doctor had cautioned.

Mallard concentrated harder on the problem of the
missing jacket. What to say? She would notice. Maybe not
right away, but she would be aware. Oh, he knew Louise's
reaction. She would apparently take the news calmly,
then make a sudden stab toward her side with her
delicate hands, then straighten and walk away--but not
before he observed. A new jacket would cost money.
Discussing money made the little drama happen more
often, so now Mr. Mallard handled all the financial
affairs, protecting her the best he could. After all, it
was her inheritance, and he took great care with it, but
there were the added costs: doctors, Josephine living
with them, the medications, even his wife's brandy. Why,
he checked it daily to be sure it was the proper
strength. Of course, a man had to have a few pleasures,
even if the cards did seem to fall against him more
often than not. He manfully kept trying.

Everyone has a limit, though, and Mr. Mallard had
reached his several days ago when the doctor had
cautioned him again.

"She may go on like she is for years, or she may
just keel over any time. However, the chances are she
will gradually go downhill and need continual care. It
is impossible to tell."

Mallard could not face "gradually go downhill." His
manhood revolted against it. He was young, full of life.
Let Josephine carry the chamber pot! After Louise's
demise (whenever that occurred!) the simple estate which
she had inherited reverted to Josephine. Let her earn
it. Also, good old friend Richards was always about with
a suggestion here or a word of comfort there for Louise.
They'd really not care too much if Mallard were a long
time absent.

As he drew nearer his home, Mallard continued to try to calm his composure, which was difficult for he kept hearing the sound of the train wheels as it pulled away, jacket, envelope, and all, right before his panic-- stricken eyes: CALIFORNIA; California; california; california.

DUTY! It was his duty not to excite Louise. As he thought of duty he unconsciously squared his drooping shoulders, and the image of Sir Galahad flitted across his mind.

The treetops were aglow in the strange afterlight of the storm. A shaft of sunlight shot through the leaves and fell upon his face. He had come home.

He opened the front door with the latchkey. Fortunately, it had been in his pants pocket.

Later, the doctors did not think Mr. Mallard's reaction unusual, even when a slight smile appeared on the bereaved husband's face. Grief causes strange reactions.

"He took it like a man," they said.

Only later, when the full significance of his loss reached him, did he weep.

A PARODY

One special kind of response is the **parody,** a comic form that imitates the original in a humorous way. It is a caricature in words. For instance, a parody may imitate the style of the original—let's say, short, punchy sentences—but apply this style to a subject that the original author would not be concerned with. Thus, because Ernest Hemingway often wrote short, simple sentences about tough guys engaged in butch activities such as hunting, fishing, and boxing, parodists of Hemingway are likely to use the same style but for their subject they may choose something like opening the mail, or preparing a cup of tea.

We once heard on the radio a parody of an announcer doing a baseball game. It went something like this:

Well, here's Bill Shakespeare now, approaching the desk. Like so many other writers, Bill likes to work at a desk. In fact, just about every writer we know writes at a desk, but every writer has his own way of approaching the desk and sitting at it. Bill is sitting down now; now he's adjusting the chair, moving it forward a little. Oh, he's just pushed the chair back an inch or two. He likes his chair to be just right. Now he's picking up a pen. It's a gray quill. I think it's the pen he uses when he writes a tragedy, and he's due for a tragedy—of his last five plays, only one was a tragedy, and two were comedies and two were history plays. But you never can tell with Bill, or "The Bard" as his fans call him. Some people call him "The Swan of Avon," but I'm told that he really hates that. Well, he's at the desk, and, you know, in circumstances like these, he might even sneak in a sonnet or two. Oh, he's put down the gray quill, and now he's trying a white one. Oh boy, oh boy, he's written a *word*. NO, he's going for *a whole sentence!*

Parodies are, in a way, critical, but they are usually affectionate too. In the best parodies one feels that the writer admires the author being parodied. The distinguished sociologist Daniel Bell wrote a deliberate parody of sociological writing. It begins thus:

> The purpose of this scene is to present a taxonomic dichotomization which would allow for unilinear comparison. In this fashion we could hope to distinguish the relevant variables which determine the functional specifities of social movements.

H. L. Mencken, who had a love-hate relationship with what he called the Great American Booboisie, wrote a parody in which he set forth the Declaration of Independence as it might have been written (or spoken) by Joe Sixpack in the mid-twentieth century. Here the target is not the original document, but the twentieth-century American. The original document, you will remember, begins in this way:

> When in the course of human events it becomes necessary for one people to dissolve the political bonds which have connected them with another, and to assume among the powers of the earth the separate and equal station to which the laws of nature and of nature's God entitle them, a decent respect to the opinions of mankind requires that they should declare the causes which impel them to the separation.

Now for Mencken's version:

> When things get so balled up that the people of a country got to cut loose from some other country, and go it on their own hook, without asking no permission from nobody, excepting maybe God Almighty, then they ought to let everybody know why they done it, so that everybody can see they are not trying to put nothing over on nobody.

A REVIEW

A review, for instance of a play or of a novel, also is a response, since it normally includes an evaluation of the work, but at least at first glance it may seem to be an analytic essay. Here we will consider a review of a production of a play, but you can easily adapt this discussion to a review of a book.

A Review of a Dramatic Production

Your instructor may ask you to write a review of a local production. A review requires analytic skill, but it is not identical with an analysis. First, a reviewer normally assumes that the reader is unfamiliar with the production being reviewed and also with the play if the play is not a classic. Thus, the first paragraph usually provides a helpful introduction along these lines:

> Marsha Norman's recent play, 'night, Mother, a tragedy with only two actors and one set, shows us a woman's preparation for suicide. Jessie has concluded that she no longer wishes to live, and so she tries to put her affairs in order, which chiefly means preparing her rather uncomprehending mother to get along without her.

Inevitably some retelling of the plot is necessary if the play is new, and a summary of a sentence or two is acceptable even for a familiar play. The review will, however, chiefly be concerned with

describing,
analyzing, and
evaluating.

If the play is new, much of the evaluation may center on the play itself, but if the play is a classic, the evaluation probably will chiefly be devoted to the acting, the set, and the direction. Other points:

1. **Save the program;** it will give you the names of the actors, and perhaps a brief biography of the author, a synopsis of the plot, and a photograph of the set, all of which may be helpful.
2. **Draft your review as soon as possible,** while the performance is still fresh in your mind. If you cannot draft it immediately after seeing the play, at least jot down some notes about the setting and the staging, the acting, and the audience's response.
3. **If possible, read the play**—ideally, before the performance and again after it.
4. **In your first draft, don't worry about limitations of space;** write as long a review as you can, putting down everything that comes to mind. Later you can cut it to the required length, retaining only the chief points and the necessary supporting details, but in your first draft try to produce a fairly full record of the performance and your response to it, so that a day or two later, when you revise, you won't have to trust a fading memory for details.

A Sample Review: "An Effective Macbeth"

If you read reviews of plays in *Time, Newsweek,* or a newspaper, you will soon develop a sense of what reviews normally do. The following example, an undergraduate's review of a production of *Macbeth,* is typical except in one respect: As has been mentioned, reviews of new plays customarily include a few sentences summarizing the plot and classifying the play (a tragedy, a farce, a rock musical, or whatever), perhaps briefly putting it into the context of the author's other works, but because *Macbeth* is so widely known, the reviewer has chosen not to insult her readers by telling them that *Macbeth* is a tragedy by Shakespeare.

Preliminary Jottings

During the two intermissions and immediately after the end of the performance, the reviewer made a few jottings, which the next day she rewrote thus:

Compare with last year's Midsummer Night's Dream
Set: barren;
        pipe framework at rear. Duncan exits on it.
•   Useful?
witches: powerful, not funny
stage: battlefield? barren land?
    costume: earth-colored rags
        they seduce--even caress--Mac.
Macbeth
        ~~witches caress him?~~
        strong; also gentle (with Lady M)
Lady Macb.
        sexy in speech about unsexing her
        too attractive? Prob. ok
Banquo's ghost: naturalistic; covered with blood
Duncan: terrible; worst actor except for Lady Macduff's
    boy
costumes: leather, metal; only Duncan in robes
pipe framework used for D, and murder of Lady
    Macduff
forest: branches unrealistic; stylized? or cheesy?

The Finished Version

The published review follows, accompanied by some marginal notes commenting on its strengths .

Sandra Santiago

Title conveys information about thesis.

An Effective <u>Macbeth</u>

<u>Macbeth</u> at the University Theater is a thoughtful and occasionally exciting production, partly because the director, Mark Urice, has trusted Shakespeare and has not imposed a gimmick on the play. The characters do not wear cowboy costumes as they did in last year's production of <u>A Midsummer Night's Dream</u>.

Opening paragraph is informative, letting the reader know the reviewer's overall attitude.

Reviewer promptly turns to a major issue.

Probably the chief problem confronting a director of <u>Macbeth</u> is how to present the witches so that they are powerful supernatural forces and not silly things that look as though they came from a Halloween party. Urice gives us ugly but not absurdly grotesque witches, and he introduces them most effectively. The stage seems to be a bombed-out battlefield littered with rocks and great chunks of earth, but some of these begin to stir--the earth seems to come alive--and the clods move, unfold, and become the witches, dressed in brown and dark gray rags. The suggestion is that the witches are a part of nature, elemental forces that can hardly be escaped. This effect is increased by the moans and creaking noises that they make, all of which could be comic but which in this production are impressive.

First sentence provides an effective transition.

The witches' power over Macbeth is further emphasized by their actions. When the witches first meet Macbeth, they encircle him, touch him, caress him, even embrace him, and he seems helpless, almost their plaything. Moreover, in the scene in which he imagines that he sees a dagger, the director has arranged for one of the witches to appear, stand near Macbeth, and guide his hand toward the invisible dagger. This is, of course, not in the text, but the interpretation is reasonable rather than intrusive. Finally, near the end of the play, just before Macduff kills Macbeth, a witch appears and laughs at Macbeth as Macduff explains that he was not "born of woman." There is no doubt that throughout the tragedy Macbeth has been a puppet of the witches.

Paragraph begins with a broad assertion and then offers supporting details.

Macbeth (Stephen Beers) and Lady Macbeth (Tina Peters) are excellent. Beers is sufficiently brawny to be convincing as a battlefield hero, but he also speaks the lines sensitively, and so the audience feels that in addition to being a hero he is a man of insight and imagination, and even a man of gentleness. One can believe Lady Macbeth when she says that she fears he is "too full of the milk of human kindness" to murder Duncan. Lady

Reference to a particular scene.

Macbeth is especially effective in the scene in which she asks the spirits to "unsex her." During this speech she is reclining on a bed and as she delivers the lines she becomes increasingly sexual in her bodily motions, deriving excitement from her own stimulating words. Her attachment to Macbeth is strongly sexual, and so too is his attraction to her. The scene when she persuades him to kill

Duncan ends with them passionately embracing. The strong attraction of each for the other, so evident in the early part of the play, disappears after the murder, when Macbeth keeps his distance from Lady Macbeth and does not allow her to touch him. The acting of the other performers is effective, except for Duncan (John Berens), who recites the lines mechanically and seems not to take much account of their meaning.

Description, but also analysis.

The set consists of a barren plot at the rear on which stands a spidery framework of piping, of the sort used by construction companies, supporting a catwalk. This framework

Concrete details.

fits with the costumes (lots of armor, leather, heavy boots), suggesting a sort of elemental, primitive, and somewhat sadistic world. The catwalk, though effectively used when Macbeth goes off to murder Duncan (whose room is presumably upstairs and offstage) is not much used in later scenes. For the most part it is an interesting piece of scenery but it is not otherwise helpful. For instance, there is no

Concrete details to support evaluation.

reason why the scene with Macduff's wife and children is staged on it. The costumes are not in any way Scottish--no plaids--but in several scenes the sound of a bagpipe is heard, adding another weird or primitive tone to the production.

Summary

This Macbeth appeals to the eye, the ear, and the mind. The director has given us a unified production that makes sense and that is faithful to the spirit of Shakespeare's play.

[New page]

Documentation
Work Cited

<u>Macbeth</u>. By William Shakespeare. Dir. Mark

    Urice. With Stephen Beers, Tina Peters,

    and John Berens. University Theater,

    Medford, MA. 3 Mar. 1990.

The marginal notes call attention to certain qualities in the review, but three additional points should be made:

1. The reviewer's feelings and evaluations are clearly expressed, not in such expressions as "furthermore I feel," and "it is also my opinion," but in such expressions as "a thoughtful and occasionally exciting production," "excellent," and "appeals to the eye, the ear, and the mind."
2. The evaluations are supported by details. For instance, the evaluation that the witches are effectively presented is supported by a brief description of their appearance.
3. The reviewer is courteous, even when (as in the discussion of the cat-walk, in the next-to-last paragraph) she is talking about aspects of the production she doesn't care for.

PART 2

*Standing Back:
Thinking Critically
about Literature*

5

What Is Literature?

Perhaps the first thing to say is that it is impossible to define *literature* in a way that will satisfy everyone. And perhaps the second thing to say is that in the last 20 years or so, some serious thinkers have argued that it is impossible to set off certain verbal works from all others, and on some basis or other to designate them as *literature*. For one thing, it is argued, a work is just marks on paper or sounds in the air. The audience (reader or listener) turns these marks or sounds into something with meaning, and different audiences will construct different meanings out of what they read or hear. There are *texts* (birthday cards, sermons, political speeches, magazines, novels that sell by the millions and novels that don't sell at all, poems, popular songs, editorials, and so forth), but nothing that should be given the special title of *literature*. John M. Ellis, a literary critic, argues in *The Theory of Literary Criticism* (1974) that the word *literature* is something like the word *weed*. A weed is just a plant that gardeners for one reason or another don't want in the garden, but no plant has characteristics that clearly make it a weed and not merely a plant.

An important school of criticism known as *cultural materialism* argues that what is commonly called literature and is regarded with some awe as embodying eternal truths is in fact only a "cultural construct," like, say, the film industry. According to cultural materialism, the writers of literature are the products of their age, and they are producing a product for a market, and the critic therefore ought to be concerned chiefly not with whether the text is beautiful or true—these ideas themselves are only social constructions—but, rather, with how writers are shaped by their times (for instance, how the physical conditions of the Elizabethan playhouse and how the attitudes of the Elizabethan playgoer influenced Shakespeare), and how writings work upon the readers and thus help to shape the times.

Although there is something to be said for the idea that *literature* is just an honorific word and not a body of work embodying eternal truths and eternal beauty, let's make the opposite assumption, at least for a start. Let's assume that certain verbal works are of a distinct sort—whether because the author shapes them, or because a reader perceives them a certain way—and that we can call these works *literature*. But what are these works like?

LITERATURE AND FORM

We all know why we value a newspaper (for instance) or a textbook or an atlas, but why do we value a verbal work that doesn't give us the latest news or important information about business cycles or the names of the capitals of nations? About a thousand years ago a Japanese woman, Lady Murasaki, offered an answer in *The Tale of Genji*, a book often called the world's first novel. During a discussion about reading fiction, one of the characters offers an opinion as to why a writer tells a story:

> Again and again something in one's own life, or in the life around one, will seem so important that one cannot bear to let it pass into oblivion. There must never come a time, the writer feels, when people do not know about this.

Literature is about human experiences, but the experiences embodied in literature are not simply the shapeless experiences—the chaotic passing scene—captured by a mindless, unselective camcorder. Poets, dramatists, and storytellers find or impose a shape on scenes (for instance, the history of two lovers), giving readers things to value—written or spoken accounts that are memorable not only for their content but also for their *form*—the shape of the speeches, of the scenes, of the plots. (In a little while we will see that form and content are inseparable, but for the moment, for textbook purposes, we can talk about them separately.)

Ezra Pound said that literature is "news that *stays* news." Now, "John loves Mary," written on a wall, or on the front page of a newspaper, is news, but it is not news that stays news. It may be of momentary interest to the friends of John and Mary, but it's not much more than simple information and there is no particular reason to value it. Literature is something else. The Johns and Marys in poems, plays, and stories—even though they usually are fairly ordinary individuals, in many ways often rather like us—somehow become significant as we perceive them through the writer's eye and ear. The writer selects what is essential, and makes us care about the characters. Their doings stay in our mind.

To say that their doings stay in our mind is *not* to deny that works of literature show signs of being the products of particular ages and environments. It is only to say that these works are not exclusively about those ages and environments; they speak to later readers. The love affairs that we read about in the newspaper are of no interest a day later, but the love of Romeo and Juliet, with its joys and sorrows, has interested people for 400 years.

Those who know the play may feel, with Lady Murasaki's spokesman, that there must never come a time when these things are not known. It should be mentioned, too, that readers find, on rereading a work, that the works are still of great interest but often for new reasons. That is, when as adolescents we read *Romeo and Juliet* we may value it for certain reasons, and when in maturity we reread it we may see it differently and we may value it for new reasons. It is news that remains news.

As the example of *Romeo and Juliet* indicates, literature need not be rooted in historical fact. Although guides in Verona find it profitable to pcint out Juliet's house, the play is not based on historical characters. Literature is about life, but it may be fictional, dealing with invented characters. In fact, almost all of the characters in literature are imaginary—though they *seem* real. In the words of Picasso,

> Art is not truth. Art is a lie that makes us realize truth. . . . The artist must know the manner whereby to convince others of the truthfulness of his lies.

We can put it this way: Literature shows *what happens*, rather than what happened. It may indeed be accurate history, but the fact that it is factual is unimportant.

One reason that literary works endure (whether they show us what we are or what we long for) is that their *form* makes their content memorable. In Picasso's terms, the artist knows how to shape lies (fictions, imagined happenings) into enduring forms. Because this discussion of literature is brief, we will illustrate the point by looking at one of the briefest literary forms, the proverb. (Our definition of literature is not limited to the grand forms of the novel, tragedy, and so on. It is wide enough, and democratic enough, to include brief, popular, spoken texts.) Consider this statement:

> A rolling stone gathers no moss.

Now let's compare it with a **paraphrase** (a restatement, a translation into other words), for instance "If a stone is always moving around, vegetation won't have a chance to grow on it." What makes the original version more powerful, more memorable? Surely much of the answer is that the original is more concrete and its form is more shapely. At the risk of being heavy-handed, we can analyze the shapeliness thus: *Stone* and *moss* (the two nouns in the sentence) each contain one syllable; *rolling* and *gathers* (the two words of motion) each contain two syllables, each with the accent on the first of the two syllables. Notice, too, the nice contrast between stone (hard) and moss (soft).

The reader probably *feels* this shapeliness unconsciously, rather than perceives it consciously. That is, these connections become apparent when one starts to analyze, but the literary work can make its effect on a reader even before the reader analyzes. As T. S. Eliot said in his essay on Dante (1929), "Genuine poetry can communicate before it is understood." Indeed, our *first* reading of a work, when, so to speak, we are all eyes and ears (and the mind is highly receptive rather than sifting for evidence) is sometimes the most important reading. Experience proves that we can feel the effects of a work without yet understanding *how* the effects are achieved.

Probably most readers will agree that the words in the proverb are paired interestingly and meaningfully. And perhaps they will agree, too, that the sentence is not simply some information but is also (to quote one of Robert Frost's definitions of literature) "a performance in words." What the sentence *is,* we might say, is no less significant than what the sentence *says.* The sentence as a whole forms a memorable picture, a small but complete world, hard and soft, inorganic and organic, inert and moving. The idea set forth is simple—partly because it is highly focused and therefore it leaves out a lot—but it is also complex. By virtue of the contrasts, and, again, even by the pairing of monosyllabic nouns and of disyllabic words of motion, it is unified into a pleasing whole. For all of its specificity and its compactness—the proverb contains only six words—it expands our minds.

At this point it must be said that many contemporary critics, for one reason or another, deny that unity is a meaningful concept. For instance, they may insist that because each reader reads a text in his or her own way—in effect, each reader constructs or creates the text—it is absurd to talk about unity. Unity, it is said, is illusory. Or, on the other hand, if unity is real it is unwanted, a repressive cultural convention. We will discuss the point later, in Chapter 8, especially in conjunction with deconstruction and reader-response theory, but here we will cite one example. Terry Eagleton, a Marxist critic, in *Literary Theory* (1983) says, "There is absolutely no need to suppose that works of literature either do or should constitute harmonious wholes, and many suggestive frictions and collisions of meaning must be blandly 'processed' by literary criticism to induce them to do so" (81). Like other Marxists, Eagleton assumes that our society is riven with contradictions and that therefore the art it produces is also contradictory, fissured, fractured. Since the works are produced by a particular society and are consumed by that society, therefore they are in effect propaganda for the present economic system, whether the authors know it or not. According to this view, critics who look for artistic unity falsify the works.

It should be mentioned, too, that some critics have no difficulty in finding contradictions. If contradictions are not evident, the critic may point out "absences" or "silences" or "omissions." That is, the critic may argue that certain material indeed is not in the text, but its absence shows that the author has sought to repress the contradiction. Thus, a poem, story, or play about heterosexual romantic love may be seen as embodying a contradiction because it does *not* include any reference to, say, prostitution, or to gay or lesbian love, or to marriage as a patriarchal construction that oppresses women. If one operates this way, it is easy to deny that any work is unified.

On the other hand, it is entirely legitimate to think about the choices a writer makes, and to wonder why *this* is included in the work whereas *that* is not. Shakespeare chose, in his *King Lear*, to alter his source (*King Leir*) essentially; he dropped the happy ending (in the source, Leir is restored to the throne, and his beloved daughter Cordelia does not die). An examination of this sort of choice—which ending is more suitable?—is often far more useful than an examination aimed at chastising a writer for committing an ideological sin.

A Brief Exercise: Take a minute to think about some other proverb, for instance "Look before you leap," "Finders keepers," "Haste makes waste," "Absence makes the heart grow fonder," or whatever. Paraphrase it, and then ask yourself why the original is more interesting, more memorable, than your paraphrase.

Literature and Meaning

We have seen that the form of the proverb pleases the mind and the tongue, but what about **content** or **meaning?** We may enjoy the images and the sounds, but surely the words add up to something. After all, they are not just "tra la la." Probably most people would agree that the content or the meaning of "A rolling stone gathers no moss" is something like this: "If you are always on the move—if, for instance, you don't stick to one thing but you keep switching schools, or jobs—you won't accomplish much."

Now, if this statement approximates the meaning of the proverb, we can say two things: (1) the proverb contains a good deal of truth, and (2) it certainly is not always true. Indeed this proverb is more or less contradicted by a another proverb, "Nothing ventured, nothing gained." Many proverbs, in fact, contradict other proverbs. "Too many cooks spoil the broth," yes, but "Many hands make light the work"; "Absence makes the heart grow fonder," yes, but "Out of sight, out of mind"; "He who hesitates is lost," yes, but "Look before you leap." The claim that literature offers insights, or illuminates experience, is not a claim that it offers irrefutable and unvarying truths, covering the whole of our experience. Of course literature does not give us *the* truth; rather it wakes us up, makes us see, helps us feel intensely some aspect of our experience, and perhaps evaluate it. The novelist Franz Kafka said something to this effect, very strongly, in a letter of 1904:

If the book we are reading does not wake us, as with a fist hammering on our skull, why then do we read it?. . . What we must have are those books which come upon us like ill-fortune, and distress us deeply, like the death of one we love better than ourselves. . . . A book must be an ice-axe to break the sea frozen inside us.

Arguing about Meaning

In Chapter 6 we will discuss at length the question of whether one interpretation—one statement of the meaning of a work—is better than another, but a word should be said about it now. Suppose that while discussing "A rolling stone gathers no moss" someone said to you,

> I don't think it means that if you are always on the move you won't accomplish anything. I think the meaning is something like the saying, "There are no flies on him." First of all, what's so great about moss developing? Why do you say that the moss more or less represents worthwhile accomplishments? And why do you say that the implication is that someone should settle down? The way I see it is just the opposite: The proverb says that active people don't let stuff accumulate on them, don't get covered over. That is, active people, people who accomplish things (people who get somewhere) are always unencumbered, are people who don't stagnate.

What reply can be offered? Probably no reply will sway the person who interprets the proverb this way. Perhaps, then, we must conclude that (as the critic Northrop Frye said) reading is a picnic to which the writer brings the words and the reader brings the meanings. The remark is witty and is probably true. Certainly readers over the years have brought very different meanings to such works as the Bible and *Hamlet*.

Even if readers can never absolutely prove the truth of their interpretations, all readers have the obligation to make as convincing a case as possible. When you write about literature, you probably will begin (in your marginal jottings and in other notes) by setting down random expressions of feeling and even unsupported opinions, but later, when you are preparing to share your material with a reader, you will have to go further. You will have to try to show your reader *why* you hold the opinion you do. You must *argue* your case. In short,

- you have to offer plausible supporting evidence and
- you have to do so in a coherent and rhetorically effective essay.

That is, you'll have to make the reader in effect say, "Yes, I see exactly what you mean, and what you say makes a good deal of sense." You may not thoroughly convince your readers, but they will at least understand *why* you hold the views you do.

FORM AND MEANING

Let's turn now to a work not much longer than a proverb—a very short poem by Robert Frost (1874–1963):

THE SPAN OF LIFE

The old dog barks backward without getting up.
I can remember when he was a pup.

Read the poem aloud once or twice, physically experiencing Frost's "performance in words." Notice that the first line is harder to say than the second line, which more or less trips off the tongue. Why? Because in the first line we must pause between *old* and *dog*, between *backward* and *without*, and between *without* and *getting*—and perhaps between *back* and *ward*. Further, when we read the poem aloud, or with the mind's ear, in the first line we hear four consecutive stresses in *old dog barks back*, a noticeable contrast to the rather jingling "when he was a pup" in the second line. No two readers will read the lines in exactly the same way, but it is probably safe to say that most readers will agree that in the first line they may stress fairly heavily as many as eight syllables, whereas in the second line they may stress only three or four:

The OLD DOG BARKS BACKWARD withOUT GETTing UP,
I can reMEMber when HE was a PUP.

And so we can say that the *form* (a relatively effortful, hard-to-speak line, followed by a bouncy line) shapes and indeed is part of the *content* (a description of a dog that no longer has the energy or the strength to leap up, followed by a memory of the dog as a puppy).

Thinking further about Frost's poem, we notice something else about the form. The first line is about a dog, but the second line is about a dog *and* a human being ("*I* can remember"). The speaker must be getting on, too. And although nothing is said about the dog as a *symbol* of human life, surely the reader, prompted by the title of the poem, makes a connection between the life span of a dog and that of a human being. Part of what makes the poem effective is that this point is *not* stated explicitly, not belabored. Readers have the pleasure of making the connection for themselves—under Frost's careful guidance.

Everyone knows that puppies are frisky and that old dogs are not—though perhaps not until we encountered this poem did we think twice about the fact that "the old dog barks backward without getting up." Or let's put it this way: Other people may have noticed this behavior, but perhaps only Frost thought (to use Lady Murasaki's words), "There must never come a time . . . when people do not know about this." And, fortunately for all of us, Frost had the ability to put his perception into memorable words. Part of what makes this performance in words especially memorable is, of course, the *relationship* between the two lines. Neither line in itself is anything very special, but because of the counterpoint the whole is more than the sum of the parts. Skill in handling language, obviously, is indispensable if the writer is to produce literature. A person may know a great deal about dogs, and may be a great lover of dogs, but knowledge and love are not enough equipment with which to write even a two-line poem about a dog (or the span of life, or both). Poems, like other kinds of literature, are produced by people who know how to delight us with verbal performances.

Presumably Frost reported his observation about the dog not simply as a piece of dog lore, but because it concerns all of us. It is news that stays news. Once you have read or heard the poem, you can never again look at a puppy or an old dog in quite the way you used to—and probably the poem will keep coming to mind as you feel in your bones the effects of aging. If it at first seems odd to say that literature influences us, think of the debate concerning pornography. The chief reason for opposing pornography is that it exerts a bad influence on those who consume it. If indeed books and pictures can exert a bad influence, it seems reasonable to think that other books and pictures can exert a good influence. Fairness requires us to mention, however, that many thoughtful people disagree, and argue that literature and art entertain us but do not really influence us in any significant way. In trying to solve this debate, perhaps one can rely only on one's own experience.

We can easily see that Robert Frost's "The Span of Life" is a work of literature—a work that uses language in a special way—if we contrast it with another short work in rhyme:

Thirty days hath September,
April, June, and November;
All the rest have thirty-one
Excepting February alone,
Which has twenty-eight in fine,
Till leap year gives it twenty-nine.

This information is important, but it is only information. The lines rhyme, giving the work some form, but there is nothing very interesting about it. (This is a matter of opinion; perhaps you will want to take issue.) It is true and therefore useful, but it is not of compelling interest. It is not news that stays news, probably because it only *tells* us facts rather than *shows* or *presents* human experience. We all remember the lines, but they do not hold our interest. "Thirty Days" does not offer either the pleasure of an insight or the pleasure of an interesting tune. It has nothing of what the poet Thomas Gray said characterizes literature: "Thoughts that breathe, and words that burn."

As we will see, there are many ways of writing about literature, but one of the most interesting is to write not simply about the author's "thoughts" (or ideas) as abstractions but about the particular *ways* in which an author makes thoughts memorable, chiefly through the manipulation of words that at least glow if they don't "burn."

The poet W. H. Auden once defined literature as "a game of knowledge." His reference to a "game" reminds us of Frost's comment that literature is "a performance." Games have rules, forms, and conformity to the rules is part of the fun of playing a game. We don't want the basketball player to pick up the ball and run with it, or the tennis player to do away with the net. The fun in writing literature comes largely from performing effectively within the rules, or from introducing new rules and then working within them. For Auden, a work of art is "a verbal contraption," and in a work of art (as in a game) "Freedom and Law, System and Order are united in harmony" (*The Dyer's Hand* [1968], 50, 71).

We don't play (or watch) games because they teach us to be good citizens, or even because they will make us healthier; we play and watch them because they give us pleasure. But Auden's definition of literature is not simply "a game"; it is "a game of knowledge." When Auden speaks of knowledge he is speaking of the writer's understanding of human experience. We are back to Lady Murasaki's comment that "there must never come a time, the writer feels, when people do not know" about certain experiences. This knowledge that Lady Murasaki and Auden speak of is conveyed through words, arranged as in a performance or a game. The performance may be very brief, as in the highly structured proverb about a rolling stone or the equally structured pair of lines about the old dog, or it may be extended into a novel of a thousand pages. Many of the later pages in this book will be devoted to talking about structure in fiction, drama, and poetry.

THE LITERARY CANON

You may have heard people talk about the **canon** of literature, that is, talk about the recognized body of literature. *Canon* comes from a Greek word for a *reed* (it's the same as our word *cane*); a reed or cane was used as a yardstick, and certain works were said to measure up to the idea of literature. Many plays by Shakespeare fit the measure and were accepted into

the canon early (and they have stayed there), but many plays by his contemporaries never entered the canon—in their own day they were performed, maybe applauded, and some were published, but later generations
have not valued them. In fact, some plays by Shakespeare, too, are almost
never taught or performed, for instance *Cymbeline* and *Timon of Athens.*
And, conversely, some writers are known chiefly for a single work, although
they wrote a great deal. The canon, in actuality, has always been highly varied. True, it chiefly contained the work of white males, but that was because in the Euro-American world until fairly recently white males were
the people doing most of the publishing, and white males controlled the
publishing industry. (The reasons why women and persons of color were
not doing much publishing are scarcely to the credit of white males, who
controlled society, but that's not the subject we are talking about here.)
Even in the traditional male-dominated canon, however, the range was
great, including, for instance, ancient epic poems by Homer, tragedies and
comedies by Shakespeare, brief lyrics by Emily Dickinson, and short stories
and novels by James Joyce, Virginia Woolf, and Ralph Ellison.

Further, the canon—the group of works esteemed by a community of
readers—keeps changing, partly because in different periods somewhat
different measuring rods are used. For instance, Shakespeare's *Troilus and
Cressida*—a play about war, in which heroism and worthy ideals are in
short supply—for several hundred years was performed only rarely, but
during the Vietnam War it became popular, doubtless because the play was
seen as an image of that widely unpopular war. More important, however,
than the shifting fortunes of individual works is the recent inclusion of material representing newly valued kinds of experiences. In our day we have
increasingly become aware of the voices of women and of members of minority cultures, for instance Native Americans, African-Americans, Latinos,
lesbians and gays. As a consequence, works by these people—giving voice
to identities previously ignored by the larger society—are now taught in literature classes.

What is or is not literature, then, changes over the years; in the language of today's criticism, "literature" as a category of "verbal production
and reception" is itself an "historical construction" rather than an unchanging reality. Insofar as a new generation finds certain verbal works pleasing,
moving, powerful, memorable, compelling—beautiful and true, one might
say—they become literature. Today a course in nineteenth-century
American literature is likely to include works by Harriet Beecher Stowe
and Frederick Douglass—but it probably also includes works by long-es-
tablished favorites such as Emerson, Hawthorne, and Whitman.

Some works have measured up for so long that they probably will always be valued, that is, they will always be part of the literary canon. But of

course one cannot predict the staying power of new works. Doubtless some stories, novels, poems, and plays—as well, perhaps, as television scripts and popular songs—will endure. Most of the literature of *any* generation, however, measures up only briefly; later generations find it dated, uninteresting, unexciting. Lincoln's address at Gettysburg has endured as literature, but Kennedy's inaugural address—much praised in its day—now strikes many readers as thin, hollow, strained, even corny. (These adjectives of course imply value judgments; anyone who offers such judgments needs to support them, to argue them, not merely assert them. Elsewhere in this book there is talk about arguing a thesis.) Even if Kennedy's inaugural address fades as literature, it will retain its historical importance. In this view, it belongs in a course in politics, but not in a course in literature.

LITERATURE, TEXTS, DISCOURSES, AND CULTURAL STUDIES

These pages have routinely spoken of *literature* and of literary *works,* terms recently often supplanted by *text.* Some say that *literature* is a word with elitist connotations. They may say, too, that a *work* is a crafted, finished thing, whereas a *text,* in modern usage, is something that in large measure is created (i.e., given meaning) by a reader. Further, the word *text* helps to erase the line between, on the one hand, what traditionally has been called literature—for instance, canonized material—and, on the other hand, popular verbal forms such as science fiction, Westerns, sermons, political addresses, interviews, advertisements, comic strips, and bumper stickers—and, for that matter, nonverbal products such as sports events, architecture, fashion design, automobiles, and the offerings in a shopping mall. Texts or *discourses* of this sort (said to be parts of what is called a *discursive practice* or a *signifying practice*) in recent years have increasingly interested many people who used to teach literature ("great books") but who now teach *cultural studies.* In these courses the emphasis is not on objects inherently valuable and taught apart from the conditions of their production. Rather, the documents—whether plays by Shakespeare or comic books—are studied in their social and political contexts, especially in view of the conditions of their production, distribution, and consumption. Thus, *Hamlet* would be related to the economic and political system of England around 1600, and *also* to the context today—the educational system, the theater industry, and so on—that produces the work. To study a work otherwise—to study a literary work as an esthetic object, something to be enjoyed and admired apart from its context—is, it is claimed, to "sacralize" it, to treat it as a sacred thing, and in effect to mummify it. (One might ask if it is really a bad thing

to treat with respect—at least at the start—a work by, say, Shakespeare or
George Eliot.)

IN BRIEF: A CONTEMPORARY AUTHOR
SPEAKS ABOUT LITERATURE

Finally, in an effort to establish an idea of what literature is, let's listen to
the words of John Updike, an author of stories, novels, and poems. Updike,
as a highly successful writer, could of course be examined in the context of
cultural studies: How are his novels promoted? To what extent do reviews
of his books affect the sales? To what extent do Updike's reviews of other
people's books affect sales? What sorts of people (race, class, gender) read
Updike? But Updike's own abundant comments about writing are almost
entirely concerned with esthetic matters, as in the following passage. He is
talking about stories, but we can apply his words to all sorts of literature:

> I want stories to startle and engage me within the first few sentences, and in
> their middle to widen or deepen or sharpen my knowledge of human activity,
> and to end by giving me a sensation of completed statement.

Suggestions for Further Reading

Subsequent chapters will cite a fair number of recent titles relevant to this
chapter, but for a start a reader might first turn to an old but readable, hu-
mane, and still useful introduction, David Daiches, *A Study of Literature*
(1948). Another book of the same generation, and still a useful introduction, is a businesslike survey of theories of literature, by René Wellek and
Austin Warren, *Theory of Literature*, 2nd ed. (1956). For a fairly recent,
readable study, see Gerald Graff, *Professing Literature: An Institutional
History* (1987).

Some basic reference works should be mentioned: C. Hugh Holman
and William Harmon have written an introductory dictionary of movements, critical terms, literary periods, and genres: *A Handbook to
Literature*, 6th ed. (1992). For fuller discussions of critical terms, see
Wendell V. Harris, *Dictionary of Concepts in Literary Criticism and
Theory* (1992), which devotes several pages to each concept (for instance,
"author," "context," "evaluation," "feminist literary criticism," "narrative")
and gives a useful reading list for each entry. Fairly similar to Harris's book
are Irene Makaryk, ed., *Encyclopedia of Contemporary Literary Theory:
Approaches, Scholars, Terms* (1993), and Michael Groden and Martin

Kreiswirth, eds., *The Johns Hopkins Guide to Literary Theory and Criticism* (1994). *The Johns Hopkins Guide,* though it includes substantial entries on individual critics as well as on critical schools, is occasionally disappointing in the readability of some of its essays and especially in its coverage, since it does not include critical terms other than names of schools of criticism. Despite its title, then, it does not have entries for "theory" or for "criticism," nor does it have entries for such words as "canon" and "evaluation." In coverage (and also in the quality of many entries) it is inferior to an extremely valuable work with a misleadingly narrow title, *The New Princeton Encyclopedia of Poetry and Poetics,* eds. Alex Preminger and T. V. F. Brogan (1993). Although *The New Princeton Encyclopedia* of course does not include terms that are unique to, say, drama or fiction, it does include generous, lucid entries (with suggestions for further reading) on such terms as "allegory," "criticism," "canon," "irony," "sincerity," "theory," and "unity," and the long entries on "poetics," "poetry," and "poetry theories of" are in many respects entries on "literature."

For a collection of essays on the canon, see *Canons,* ed. Robert von Hallberg (1984); see also an essay by Robert Scholes, "Canonicity and Textuality," in *Introduction to Scholarship in Modern Languages and Literatures,* ed. Joseph Gibaldi, 2nd ed. (1992), 138–158. Gibaldi's collection includes essays on related topics, for instance literary theory (by Jonathan Culler) and on cultural studies (by David Bathrick).

6

What Is Interpretation?

INTERPRETATION AND MEANING

We can define **interpretation** as a setting forth of the meaning, or, better, a setting forth of one or more of the meanings of a work of literature. This question of *meaning* versus *meanings* deserves a brief explanation. Although some critics believe that a work of literature has a single meaning, the meaning it had for the author, most critics hold that a work has several meanings, for instance the meaning it had for the author, the meaning(s) it had for its first readers (or viewers, if the work is a drama), the meaning(s) it had for later readers, and the meaning(s) it has for us today. Take *Hamlet* (1600-01), for example. Perhaps this play about a man who has lost his father had a very special meaning for Shakespeare, who had recently lost his own father. Further, Shakespeare had earlier lost a son named Hamnet, a variant spelling of Hamlet. The play, then, may have had important psychological meanings for Shakespeare—but the audience could not have shared (or even known) these meanings.

What *did* the play mean to Shakespeare's audience? Perhaps the original audience of *Hamlet*—people living in a monarchy, presided over by Queen Elizabeth I—were especially concerned with the issue (specifically raised in *Hamlet*) of whether a monarch's subjects ever have the right to overthrow the monarch. But obviously for twentieth-century Americans the interest in the play lies elsewhere, and the play must mean something else. If we are familiar with Freud, we may see in the play a young man who subconsciously

90

lusts after his mother and seeks to kill his father (in the form of Claudius, Hamlet's uncle). Or we may see the play as largely about an alienated young man in a bourgeois society. Or—but the interpretations are countless.

IS THE AUTHOR'S INTENTION A GUIDE TO MEANING?

Shouldn't we be concerned, one might ask, with the *intentions* of the author? The question is reasonable, but there are difficulties, as the members of the Supreme Court find when they try to base their decisions on the original intent of the writers of the Constitution. First, for older works we almost never know what the intention is. Authors did not leave comments about their intentions. We have *Hamlet,* but we do not have any statement of Shakespeare's intention concerning this or any other play. One might argue that we can deduce Shakespeare's intention from the play itself, but to argue that we should study the play in the light of Shakespeare's intention, and that we can know his intention by studying the play, is to argue in a circle. We can say that Shakespeare must have intended to write a tragedy (if he intended to write a comedy he failed) but we can't go much further in talking about his intention.

Even if an author has gone on record, expressing an intention, we may think twice before accepting the statement as decisive. The author may be speaking facetiously, deceptively, mistakenly, or (to be brief) unconvincingly. For instance, Thomas Mann said, probably sincerely and accurately, that he wrote one of his novels merely in order to entertain his family—but we may nevertheless take the book seriously and find it profound.

IS THE WORK THE AUTHOR'S OR THE READER'S?

A good deal of recent critical theory argues that writers' views are by no means definitive, especially since writers—however independent they may think they are—largely reflect the ideas of their age. In current terminology, to accept the artist's statements about a work is "to privilege intentionalism." The idea that the person who seems to have created the work cannot comment definitively on it is especially associated with Roland Barthes (1915-80), author of a much-reprinted essay entitled "The Death of the Author," and Michel Foucault (1926-84), author of an equally famous essay entitled "What Is an Author?" (Barthes's essay appears in his *Image-Music-Text,* Foucault's in *Foucault Reader.*) Foucault, for example, assumes that the concept of the author is a repressive invention designed to impede the free circulation of ideas. In Foucault's view, the work belongs—or ought to belong—to the *perceiver*, not to the alleged maker.

Much can be said on behalf of this idea—and much can be said against it. On its behalf, one can again say that we can never entirely recapture the writer's intentions and sensations. Suppose, for instance, we are reading a work by Langston Hughes (1902-67), the African-American poet, essayist, and dramatist. None of us can exactly recover Hughes's attitudes; we cannot exactly re-create in our minds what it was like to be Langston Hughes in the 1930s and 1940s—an age that preceded the Civil Rights movement. We can read his texts, but we necessarily read them through our own eyes and in our own times, the 1990s.

Similarly, we can read or see a performance of an ancient Greek tragedy (let's say Sophocles's *King Oedipus*), but surely we cannot experience the play as did the Greeks, for whom it was part of an annual ritual. Further, a Greek spectator probably had seen earlier dramatic versions of the story. The Oedipus legend was, so to speak, part of the air that the Greeks breathed. Moreover we know (or think we know) things that the Greeks did not know. If we are familiar with Freud's view of the Oedipus complex—the idea that males wish to displace their fathers by sleeping with their mothers—we probably cannot experience Sophocles's *King Oedipus* without in some degree seeing it through Freud's eyes.

However, *against* the idea that works have no inherent core of meaning that all careful readers can perceive, one can argue that a competent writer shapes the work so that his or her meaning is largely evident to a competent reader—that is, to a reader familiar with the language and with the conventions of literature. (Writers of course do not mindlessly follow conventions; they can abide by, challenge, or even violate conventions, putting them to fresh purposes. But to deeply enjoy and understand a given work—say, an elegy—one needs some familiarity with other works of a similar kind.) Many people who write about literature assume a community of informed readers, and indeed it seems to be supported by common sense.

WHAT CHARACTERIZES
A GOOD INTERPRETATION?

Even the most vigorous advocates of the idea that meaning is indeterminate do not believe that all interpretations are equally significant. Rather, they believe that an interpretive essay is offered against a background of ideas, shared by essayist and reader, as to what constitutes a *persuasive argument*. Thus, an essay (even if it is characterized as "interpretive free play" or "creative engagement") will have to be coherent, plausible, and rhetorically effective. The *presentation* as well as the interpretation is significant. This means (to repeat a point made in Chapter 2) that the essayist cannot merely set down random expressions of feeling or unsupported opinions. The essayist must, on the contrary, convincingly *argue* a thesis—must point to evidence so that the reader will not only know what the essayist believes but will also understand why he or she believes it.

There are lots of ways of making sense (and even more ways of making nonsense), but one important way of helping readers to see things from your point of view is to do your best to face all of the complexities of the work. Put it this way: Some interpretations strike a reader as better than others because they are *more inclusive,* that is, because they *account for more of the details of the work.* The less-satisfactory interpretations leave a reader pointing to some aspects of the work—to some parts of the whole—and saying, "Yes, but your explanation doesn't take account of. . . ." This does not mean, of course, that a reader must feel that a persuasive interpretation says the last word about the work. We always realize that the work—if we value it highly—is richer than the discussion, but, again, for us to value an interpretation we must find the interpretation plausible and inclusive.

Interpretation often depends on making connections not only among various elements of the work (for instance among the characters in a story, or among the images in a poem), and between the work and other works by the author, but also on making connections between the particular work and a **cultural context.** The "cultural context" usually includes other writers and specific works of literature, since a given literary work participates in a tradition. That is, if a work looks toward life, it also looks toward other works. A sonnet, for example, is about human experience, but it is also part of a tradition of sonnet-writing. The more works of literature you are familiar with, the better equipped you are to interpret any particular work. Here is the way Robert Frost put it, in the preface to *Aforesaid:*

> A poem is best read in the light of all the other poems ever written. We read A the better to read B (we have to start somewhere; we may get very little out of A). We read B the better to read C, C the better to read D, D the better to go back and get something more out of A. Progress is not the aim, but circulation. The thing is to get among the poems where they hold each other apart in their places as the stars do.

Given the (debatable) views (1) that a work of literature may have several or even many meanings, that (2) some meanings may be unknowable to a modern spectator, and that (3) meaning is largely or even entirely determined by the viewer's particular circumstances, some students of literature prefer to say that they offer a "commentary" on the "significance" of a work rather than an "interpretation" of the "meaning."

AN EXAMPLE: INTERPRETING
PAT MORA'S "IMMIGRANTS"

Let's think about interpreting a short poem by a contemporary poet, Pat Mora.

IMMIGRANTS

wrap their babies in the American flag,
feed them mashed hot dogs and apple pie,
name them Bill and Daisy,
buy them blonde dolls that blink
blue eyes or a football and tiny cleats
before the baby can even walk,
speak to them in thick English,
      hallo, babee, hallo.
whisper in Spanish or Polish
when the babies sleep, whisper
in a dark parent bed, that dark
parent fear, "Will they like
our boy, our girl, our fine american
boy, our fine american girl?"

Perhaps most readers will agree that the poem expresses or dramatizes a desire, attributed to "immigrants," that their child grow up in an Anglo mode. (Mora is not saying that *all* immigrants have this desire; she has simply invented one speaker who says such-and-such. Of course *we* may say that Mora says all immigrants have this desire, but that is our interpretation.) For this reason the parents call their children Bill and Daisy (rather than, say, José and Juanita), and give them blonde dolls and a football (rather than dark-haired dolls and a soccer ball). Up to this point, the parents seem a bit silly in their mimicking of Anglo ways. But the second part of the poem gives the reader a more interior view of the parents, bringing out the fear and hope and worried concern that lie behind the behavior: some unspecified "they" may not "like / our boy, our girl." Who are "they"? Most readers probably will agree that "they" refers to native-born citizens, especially the blonde, blue-eyed all-American Anglo types that until recently constituted "the establishment" in the United States.

One can raise further questions about the interpretation of the poem. Exactly what does the poet mean when she says that immigrants "wrap their babies in the American flag"? Are we to take this literally? If not, how are we to take it? And why in the last two lines is the word "american" not capitalized? Is Mora imitating the non-native speaker's uncertain grasp of English punctuation? (But if so, why does Mora capitalize "American" in the first line, and "Spanish" and "Polish" later in the poem?) Or is she per-haps implying some mild reservation about becoming 100 percent American, some suggestion that in changing from Spanish or Polish to "american" there is some sort of loss?

A reader might seek Mora out, and ask her why she did not capitalize "american" in the last line, but Mora might not be willing to answer, or she might not give a straight answer, or she might say that she doesn't really know why, it just seemed right when she wrote the poem. Most authors do in fact take this last approach. When they are working as writers, they work by a kind of instinct, a kind of feel for the material. Later they can look crit-ically at their writing, but that's another sort of experience.

To return to our basic question: What characterizes a good interpreta-tion? The short answer is, *evidence*, and especially evidence that seems to cover all relevant issues. In an essay it is not enough merely to assert an in-terpretation. Your readers don't expect you to make an airtight case, but be-cause you are trying to help readers to understand a work—to see a work the way you do—you are obliged

- to offer reasonable supporting evidence,
- to take account of what might be set forth as counterevidence to your thesis.

Of course your essay may originate in an intuition or an emotional re-sponse, a sense that the work is about such-and-such, but this intuition or emotion must then be examined, and it must stand a test of reasonableness. (It's usually a good idea to jot down in a journal your first responses to a work, and in later entries to reflect on them.) It is not enough in an essay merely to set forth your response. Your readers will expect you to *demon-strate* that the response is something that they can to a large degree share. They may not be convinced that the interpretation is right or true, but they must at least feel that the interpretation is plausible and in accord with the details of the work, rather than, say, highly eccentric and irreconcilable with some details.

THINKING CRITICALLY ABOUT LITERATURE

Usually you will begin with a strong *response* to your reading—interest, boredom, bafflement, annoyance, shock, pleasure, or whatever. Fine. Then, if you are going to think critically about the work, you will go on to *examine* your response in order to understand it, or to deepen it, or to change it.

How can you change a response? Critical thinking involves seeing an is-sue from all sides, to as great a degree as possible. As you know, in ordinary language *to criticize* usually means to find fault, but in literary studies it does not have a negative connotation. Rather, it means *to examine carefully.* (The word *criticism* comes from a Greek verb meaning *to distinguish, to decide, to judge.*) Nevertheless, in one sense the term *critical thinking* does approach the usual meaning, since critical thinking requires you to take a skeptical view of your response. You will, so to speak, argue with yourself, seeing if your response can stand up to doubts.

Let's say that you have found a story implausible. Question yourself:

- Exactly what is implausible in it?
- Is implausibility always a fault?
- If so, exactly why?

Your answers may deepen your response. Usually, in fact, you will find supporting evidence for your response, but in your effort to distinguish and to decide and to judge, try also (if only as an exercise) to find **counterevidence.** See what can be said against your position. (The best lawyers, it is said, prepare two cases—their own, and the other side's.) As you consider the counterevidence you will sometimes find that it requires you to adjust your thesis. Fine. You may even find yourself developing an entirely different response. That's also fine, though of course the paper that you ultimately hand in should clearly argue a thesis.

Critical thinking, in short, means examining or exploring one's own responses, by questioning and testing them. Critical thinking is not so much a skill (though it does involve the ability to understand a text) as it is a *habit of mind,* or, rather, several habits, including

- openmindedness
- intellectual curiosity
- willingness to work.

It may involve, for instance, the willingness to discuss the issues with others, and to do research, a topic that will be treated separately in Chapter 15, on writing a research paper.

THREE STUDENT INTERPRETATIONS OF ROBERT FROST'S "STOPPING BY WOODS ON A SNOWY EVENING"

Read Frost's "Stopping by Woods on a Snowy Evening," and then read the first interpretation, written by a first-year student. This interpretation is followed by a discussion that is devoted chiefly to two questions:

- What is the essayist's thesis?
- Does the essayist offer convincing evidence to support the thesis?

Two additional essays by first-year students, offering different interpretations of the poem, provide further material for you to analyze critically.

Robert Frost
STOPPING BY WOODS ON A SNOWY EVENING

Whose woods these are I think I know.
His house is in the village though;
He will not see me stopping here
To watch his woods fill up with snow.

My little horse must think it queer
To stop without a farmhouse near
Between the woods and frozen lake
The darkest evening of the year.

He gives his harness bells a shake
To ask if there is some mistake.
The only other sound's the sweep
Of easy wind and downy flake.

The woods are lovely, dark and deep.
But I have promises to keep,
And miles to go before I sleep,
And miles to go before I sleep.

Darrel MacDonald
                    Stopping by Woods and Going On
        Robert Frost's "Stopping by Woods on a Snowy
Evening" is about what the title says it is. It is also
about something more than the title says.
        When I say it is about what the title says, I mean
that the poem really does give us the thoughts of a
person who pauses (that is, a person who is "stopping")
by woods on a snowy evening. (This person probably is a
man, since Robert Frost wrote the poem and nothing in
the poem clearly indicates that the speaker is not a
man. But, and this point will be important, the speaker
perhaps feels that he is not a very masculine man. As we
will see, the word "queer" appears in the poem, and,
also, the speaker uses the word "lovely," which sounds
more like the word a woman would use than a man.) In
line 3 the speaker says he is "stopping here," and it is
clear that "here" is by woods, since "woods" is

mentioned not only in the title but also in the first
line of the poem, and again in the second stanza, and
still again in the last stanza. It is equally clear
that, as the title says, there is snow, and that the
time is evening. The speaker mentions "snow" and "downy
flake," and he says this is "The darkest evening of the
year."

But in what sense is the poem about more than the
title? The title does not tell us anything about the man
who is "stopping by woods," but the poem--the man's
meditation--tells us a lot about him. In the first
stanza he reveals that he is uneasy at the thought that
the owner of the woods may see him stopping by the
woods. Maybe he is uneasy because he is trespassing, but
the poem does not actually say that he has illegally
entered someone else's property. More likely, he feels
uneasy, almost ashamed, of watching the "woods fill up
with snow." That is, he would not want anyone to see
that he actually is enjoying a beautiful aspect of
nature and is not hurrying about whatever his real
business is in thrifty Yankee style.

The second stanza gives more evidence that he feels
guilty about enjoying beauty. He feels so guilty that he
even thinks the horse thinks there is something odd
about him. In fact, he says that the horse thinks he is
"queer," which of course may just mean odd, but also (as
is shown by The American Heritage Dictionary) it can
mean "gay," "homosexual." A real man, he sort of
suggests, wouldn't spend time looking at snow in the
woods.

So far, then, the speaker in two ways has indicated
that he feels insecure, though perhaps he does not
realize that he has given himself away. First, he
expresses uneasiness that someone might see him watching
the woods fill up with snow. Second, he expresses
uneasiness when he suggests that even the horse thinks
he is strange, maybe even "queer" or unmanly, or at
least unbusinesslike. And so in the last stanza, even
though he finds the woods beautiful, he decides not to

stop and to see the woods fill up with snow. And his description of the woods as "lovely"--a woman's word--sounds as though he may be something less than a he-man. He seems to feel ashamed of himself for enjoying the sight of the snowy woods and for seeing them as "lovely," and so he tells himself that he has spent enough time looking at the woods and that he must go on about his business. In fact, he tells himself <u>twice</u> that he has business to attend to. Why? Perhaps he is insisting too much. Just as we saw that he was excessively nervous in the first stanza, afraid that someone might see him trespassing and enjoying the beautiful spectacle, now at the end he is again afraid that someone might see him loitering, and so he very firmly, using repetition as a form of emphasis, tries to reassure himself that he is not too much attracted by beauty and is a man of business who keeps his promises.

Frost gives us, then, a man who indeed is seen "stopping by woods on a snowy evening," but a man who, afraid of what society will think of him, is also afraid to "stop" long enough to fully enjoy the sight that attracts him, because he is driven by a sense that he may be seen to be trespassing and also may be thought to be unmanly. So after only a brief stop in the woods he forces himself to go on, a victim (though he probably doesn't know it) of the work ethic and of an over-simple idea of manliness.

Let's examine this essay briefly.

The **title** is interesting. It gives the reader a good idea of which literary work will be discussed ("Stopping by Woods") *and* it arouses interest, in this case by a sort of word-play ("Stopping . . . Going On"). A title of this sort is preferable to a title that merely announces the topic, such as "An Analysis of Frost's 'Stopping by Woods'" or "On a Poem by Robert Frost."

The opening paragraph helpfully names the exact topic (Robert Frost's poem) and arouses interest by asserting that the poem is about something more than its title. The writer's thesis presumably will be a fairly specific assertion concerning what else the poem is "about."

The body of the essay, beginning with the second paragraph, begins to develop the thesis. (The **thesis** perhaps can be summarized thus: "The speaker, insecure of his masculinity, feels ashamed that he responds with pleasure to the sight of the snowy woods.") The writer's evidence in the second paragraph is that the word "queer" (a word sometimes used to mean homosexuals) appears, and that the word "lovely" is "more like the word a woman would use than a man." Readers of MacDonald's essay may at this point be unconvinced by this evidence, but probably they suspend judgment. In any case, he has offered what he considers to be evidence in support of his thesis.

The next paragraph dwells on what is said to be the speaker's uneasiness, and the following paragraph returns to the word "queer," which, MacDonald correctly says, can mean "gay, homosexual." The question of course is whether *here,* in this poem, the word has this meaning. Do we agree with MacDonald's assertion, in the last sentence of this paragraph, that Frost is suggesting that "A real man . . . wouldn't spend time looking at snow in the woods"? Clearly this is the way MacDonald takes the poem—but is his response to these lines reasonable? After all, what Frost says is this: "The little horse must think it queer / To stop without a farmhouse near." Is it reasonable to see a reference to homosexuality (rather than merely to oddness) in *this* use of the word "queer"? Hasn't MacDonald offered a response that, so to speak, is private? It is *his* response—but are we likely to share it, to agree that we see it in Frost's poem?

The next paragraph, amplifying the point that the speaker is insecure, offers as evidence the argument that "lovely" is more often a woman's word than a man's. Probably most readers will agree on this point, though many or all might deny that only a gay man would use the word "lovely." And what do you think of MacDonald's assertions that the speaker of the poem "was excessively nervous in the first stanza" and is now "afraid that someone might see him loitering"? In your opinion does the text lend much support to MacDonald's view?

The concluding paragraph effectively reasserts and clarifies MacDonald's thesis, saying that the speaker hesitates to stop and enjoy the woods because "he is driven by a sense that he may be seen to be trespassing and also may be thought to be unmanly."

The big question, then, is whether the thesis is argued *convincingly.* It certainly *is* argued, not merely asserted, but how convincing is the evidence? Does MacDonald offer enough to make you think that his response is one that you can share? Has he helped you to enjoy the poem by seeing things that you may not have noticed—or has he said things that, however interesting, seem to you not to be in close contact with the poem as you see it?

Here are two other interpretations of the same poem.

Sara Fong

"Stopping by Woods on a Snowy Evening"
as a Short Story

Robert Frost's "Stopping by Woods on a Snowy Evening" can be read as a poem about a man who pauses to observe the beauty of nature, and it can also be read as a poem about a man with a death wish, a man who seems to long to give himself up completely to nature and thus escape his responsibilities as a citizen. Much depends, apparently, on what a reader wants to emphasize. For instance, a reader can emphasize especially appealing lines about the beauty of nature: "The only other sound's the sweep / Of easy wind and downy flake," and "The woods are lovely, dark and deep." On the other hand, a reader can emphasize lines that show the speaker is fully aware of the responsibilities that most of us agree we have. For instance, at the very start of the poem he recognizes that the woods are not his but are owned by someone else, and at the end of the poem he recognizes that he has "promises to keep" and that before he sleeps (dies?) he must accomplish many things (go for "miles").

Does a reader have to choose between these two interpretations? I don't think so; to the contrary, I think it makes sense to read the poem as a kind of very short story, with a character whose developing thoughts make up a plot with four stages. In the first stage, the central figure is an ordinary person with rather ordinary thoughts. His very first thought is of the owner of the woods. He knows who the owner is, and since the owner lives in the village, the poet feels safe in trespassing, or at least in watching the woods "fill up with snow." Then, very subtly, the poet begins to tell us that although this seems to be an ordinary person thinking ordinary thoughts, he is a somewhat special person in a special situation. First of all, the horse thinks something is strange. He shakes his bells, wondering why the driver doesn't keep moving, as presumably ordinary drivers would. Second, we are told

that this is "The darkest evening of the year." Frost
could simply have said that the evening is dark, but he
goes out of his way to make the evening a special
evening.

We are now through with the first ten lines, and
only six lines remain, yet in these six lines the story
goes through two additional phases. The first three of
these lines ("The only other sound's the sweep / Of easy
wind and downy flake" and "The woods are lovely, dark
and deep") are probably the most beautiful lines, in the
sense that they are the ones that make us say, "I wish I
were there," or "I'd love to experience this." We feel
that the poet has moved from the ordinary thoughts of
the first stanza, about such business-like things as who
owns the woods and where the owner's house is, to less
materialistic thoughts, thoughts about the beauty of the
non-human world of nature. And now, with the three final
lines, we get the fourth stage of the story, the return
to the ordinary world of people, the world of
"promises." But this world that we get at the end is not
exactly the same as the world we got at the beginning.
The world at the beginning of the poem is a world of
property (who owns the woods, and where the house is),
but the world at the end of the poem is a world of
unspecified and rather mysterious responsibilities
("promises to keep," "miles to go before I sleep"). It
is almost as though the poet's experience of the beauty
of nature--a beauty that for a moment made him forget
the world of property--has in fact served to sharpen his
sense that human beings have responsibilities. He
clearly sees that "The woods are lovely, dark and deep,"
and then he says (I add the underscore) "But I have
promises to keep." The "but" would be logical if after
saying that the woods are lovely, dark and deep, he had
said something like "But in the daylight they look
different," or "But one can freeze to death in them."
The logic of what Frost says, however, is not at all
clear: "The woods are lovely, dark and deep, / But I have
promises to keep." What is the logical connection? We

have to supply one, something like "but, because we are human beings we have responsibilities; we can refresh ourselves by perceiving the beauties of nature, and we can even for a moment get so caught up that we seem to enter an enchanted forest ('the woods are lovely, dark and deep'), but we cannot forget our responsibilities."

My point is not that Frost ends with an important moral, and it is also not that we have to choose between saying it is a poem about nature or a poem about a man with a death wish. Rather, my point is that the poem takes us through several stages and that, although the poem begins and ends with the speaker in the woods, the speaker has undergone mental experiences--has, we might say, gone through a plot with a conflict (the appeal of the snowy woods versus the call to return to the human world). It's not a matter of good versus evil and of one side winning. Frost in no way suggests that it is wrong to feel the beauty of nature--even to the momentary exclusion of all other thoughts. But the poem is certainly not simply a praise of the beauty of nature. Frost shows us, in this mini-story or mini-drama, one character who sees the woods as property, then sees them as a place of almost overwhelming beauty, and then (maybe refreshed by this experience) rejoins the world of chores and responsibilities.

EXERCISES

1. What is the thesis of the essay?
2. Does the essayist offer convincing evidence to support the thesis?
3. Do you consider the essay to be well written, poorly written, or something in between? On what evidence do you base your opinion?

Peter Franken

The Meaning of
"Stopping by Woods on a Snowy Evening"
Although on the surface there is nothing about religion in Robert Frost's "Stopping by Woods on a Snowy Evening," I think the poem is basically about a person's

realization that he or she has a religious duty to help other people.

   In Stanza One the poet tells us that he knows who owns the woods. The owner is God. Of course some individual may, during his lifetime, think that he owns the woods, but he is only the steward of the woods, a sort of caretaker. The true owner is God, whose "house is in the village," that is, who has a church in the village. At this stage in the poem, the poet is mistaken when he says that God will not see him, because God sees everything. So the poet's statement here is an example of unconscious irony.

   In Stanzas Two and Three the poet tells us that God sent a sort of message to him, through the horse. The horse shakes his harness bells, telling the speaker that he (the speaker) is making a "mistake." It may also be that in the picture of a snowy night and a domestic animal Robert Frost is trying to subtly suggest that we remember the scene of the birth of Jesus, in a manger, with domestic animals. In any case, although the scene is very peaceful and quiet (except for the harness bells and the sound of the "easy wind"), God is watching over the speaker of this poem.

   In Stanza Four, in the first line ("The woods are lovely, dark and deep") Robert Frost tells us of man's love of God's creation, and in the other lines of the stanza he says that proper love of the creation leads to an awareness of our responsibilities to other human beings. Robert Frost is very effective because he uses the device of understatement. He does not tell us exactly what these responsibilities are, so he leaves it to our imagination, but we can easily think of our many duties to our family and our fellow-citizens and our country.

EXERCISES

1. What is the thesis of the essay?
2. Does the essayist offer convincing evidence to support the thesis?

3. Do you consider the essay to be well written, poorly written, or something in between? On what evidence do you base your opinion?

Suggestions for Further Reading

The entries on "interpretation" in the reference works cited on pages 88–89 ("What Is Literature?") provide a good starting point, as does Steven Mailloux's entry on "interpretation" in *Critical Terms for Literary Study*, eds. Frank Lentricchia and Thomas McLaughlin (1990). You may next want to turn to a short, readable but highly thoughtful book by Monroe Beardsley, *The Possibility of Criticism* (1970). Also of interest are: E. D. Hirsch, *Validity in Interpretation* (1967); Paul B. Armstrong, *Conflicting Readings: Variety and Validity in Interpretation* (1990); and Umberto Eco, with Richard Rorty, Jonathan Culler, and Christine Brooke-Rose, *Interpretation and Overinterpretation* (1992). This last title includes three essays by Eco, with responses by Rorty, Culler, and Brooke-Rose, and a final "Reply" by Eco.

7

What Is Evaluation?

CRITICISM AND EVALUATION

Although, as noted previously, in ordinary usage "criticism" implies finding fault, and therefore implies evaluation—"this story is weak"—in fact most literary criticism is *not* concerned with evaluation. Rather, it is chiefly concerned with *interpretation* (the setting forth of meaning) and with *analysis* (examination of relationships among the parts, or of causes and effects). For instance, an interpretation may argue that in *Death of a Salesman* Willy Loman is the victim of a cruel capitalistic economy, and an analysis may show how the symbolic setting of the play (a stage direction tells us that "towering, angular shapes" surround the salesman's house) contributes to the meaning. In our discussion of "What Is Literature?" we saw that an analysis of Robert Frost's "The Span of Life" (p. 83) called attention to the contrast between the meter of the first line (relatively uneven or irregular, with an exceptional number of heavy stresses) and the meter of the second (relatively even and jingling). The analysis also called attention to the contrast between the content of the first line (the old dog) and the second (the speaker's memory of a young dog):

> The old dog barks backward without getting up.
> I can remember when he was a pup.

In our discussion we did not worry about whether this poem deserves an A, B, or C, nor about whether it was better or worse than some other poem by Frost, or by some other writer. And, to repeat, if one reads books and journals devoted to literary study, one finds chiefly discussions of meaning. For the most part, critics assume that the works they are writing about have value and are good enough to merit attention, and so critics largely concern themselves with other matters.

Evaluative Language and the Canon

Still, some critical writing is indeed concerned with evaluation—with saying that works are good or bad, dated or classic, major or minor. (The language need not be as explicit as these words are; evaluation can also be conveyed through words such as *moving, successful, effective, important,* or, on the other hand, *tedious, unsuccessful, weak,* and *trivial.*) In reviews of plays, books, movies, musical and dance performances, and films, professional critics usually devote much of their space to evaluating the work or the performance, or both. The reviewer seeks, finally, to tell readers whether to buy a book or a ticket—or to save their money and their time.

In short, although in our independent reading we read what we like, and we need not argue that one work is better than another, the issue of evaluation is evident all around us.

ARE THERE CRITICAL STANDARDS?

One approach to evaluating a work of literature, or, indeed, to evaluating anything at all, is to rely on personal taste. This approach is evident in a statement such as "I don't know anything about modern art, but I know what I like." The idea is old, at least as old as the Roman saying, *De gustibus nonestdisputandum* ("There is no disputing tastes").

If we say, "This is a good work," or "This book is greater than that book," are we saying anything beyond "I like this" and "I like this better than that"? Are all expressions of evaluation really nothing more than expressions of taste? Most people believe that if there are such things as works of art, or works of literature, there must be standards by which they can be evaluated, just as most other things are evaluated by standards. The standards for evaluating a scissors, for instance, are perfectly clear: It ought to cut cleanly, it ought not to need frequent sharpening, and it ought to feel comfortable in the hand. We may also want it to look nice (perhaps to be painted—or on the contrary to reveal its stainless steel), and to be inexpensive, rustproof, and so on, but in any case we can easily state our standards. Similarly, there are agreed-on standards for evaluating figure skating, gymnastics, fluency in language, and so on.

But what are the standards for evaluating literature? In earlier pages we have implied one standard: In a good work of literature, all of the parts contribute to the whole, making a unified work. Some people would add that mere unity is not enough; a work of high quality needs not only to be unified but needs also to be complex. The writer offers a "performance in words" (Frost's words, again), and when we read, we can see if the writer has successfully kept all of the Indian clubs in the air. If, for instance, the stated content of the poem is mournful, yet the meter jingles, we can probably say that the performance is unsuccessful; at least one Indian club is clattering on the floor.

Here are some of the standards commonly set forth:

- Personal taste
- Truth, realism
- Moral content
- Aesthetic qualities, for instance unity

Let's look at some of these in detail.

Morality and Truth as Standards

"It is always a writer's duty to make the world better." Thus writes Dr. Samuel Johnson, in 1765, in his "Preface to Shakespeare." In this view, *morality* plays a large role; a story that sympathetically treats lesbian or gay love from a traditional Judeo-Christian perspective probably is regarded as a bad story, or at least not as worthy as a story that celebrates heterosexual married love. On the other hand, a gay or lesbian critic, or anyone not committed to traditional Judeo-Christian values, might regard the story highly because, in such a reader's view, it helps to educate readers and thereby does something "to make the world better."

But there are obvious problems. For one thing, a gay or lesbian story might strike even a reader with traditional values as a work that is effectively told, with believable and with memorable characters, whereas a story of heterosexual married love might be unbelievable, awkwardly told, trite, sentimental, or whatever. (More about sentimentality in a moment.) How much value does one give to the ostensible content of the story, the obvious moral or morality, and how much value does one give to the artistry exhibited in telling the story?

People differ greatly about moral (and religious) issues. Edward FitzGerald's translation of *The Rubáiyát of Omar Khayyám* suggests that God doesn't exist, or—perhaps worse—if He does exist, He doesn't care about us. That God does not exist is a view held by many moral people; it is also a view opposed by many moral people. The issue then may become a matter of *truth*. Does the value of the poem depend on which view is right? In fact, does a reader have to subscribe to FitzGerald's view to enjoy (and to evaluate highly) the following stanza from the poem, in which FitzGerald suggests that the pleasures of this world are the only paradise that we can experience?

> A book of verses underneath the bough,
> A jug of wine, a loaf of bread—and thou
> Beside me singing in the wilderness—
> Oh, wilderness were paradise enow!

Some critics can give high value to a literary work only if they share its beliefs, if they think that the work corresponds to reality. They measure the work against their vision of the truth.

Other readers can highly value a work of literature that expresses ideas they do not believe, arguing that literature does not require us to believe in its views. Rather, this theory claims, literature gives a reader a strong sense of *what it feels like* to hold certain views—even though the reader does not share those views. Take, for instance, a lyric poem in which Christina Rossetti (1830–94), a devout Anglican, expresses both spiritual numbness and spiritual hope. Here is one stanza from "A Better Resurrection":

> My life is like a broken bowl,
> A broken bowl that cannot hold
> One drop of water for my soul
> Or cordial in the searching cold;
> Cast in the fire the perished thing;
> Melt and remould it, till it be
> A royal cup for Him, my King:
> O Jesus, drink of me.

One need not be an Anglican suffering a crisis to find this poem of considerable interest. It offers insight into a state of mind, and the truth or falsity of religious belief is not at issue. Similarly, one can argue that although *The Divine Comedy* by Dante Alighieri (1265-1321) is deeply a Roman Catholic work, the non-Catholic reader can read it with interest and pleasure because of (for example) its rich portrayal of a wide range of characters, the most famous of whom perhaps are the pathetic lovers Paolo and Francesca. In Dante's view, they are eternally damned because they were unrepentant adulterers, but a reader need not share this belief.

Other Ways to Think about Truth and Realism

Other solutions to the problem of whether a reader must share a writer's beliefs have been offered. One extreme view says that beliefs are irrelevant, since literature has nothing to do with truth. In this view, a work of art does not correspond to anything "outside" itself, that is, to anything in the real world. If a work of art has any "truth," it is only in the sense of being internally consistent. Thus Shakespeare's *Macbeth,* like, say, "Rock-a-bye Baby," isn't making assertions about reality. *Macbeth* has nothing to do with the history of Scotland, just as (in this view) Shakespeare's *Julius Caesar* has nothing to do with the history of Rome, although Shakespeare borrowed some of his material from history books. These tragedies, like lullabies, are worlds in themselves—not to be judged against historical accounts of Scotland or Rome—and we are interested in the characters in the plays only as they exist *in the plays.* We may require, for instance, that the characters be consistent, believable, and engaging, but we cannot require that they correspond to historical figures. Literary works are neither true nor false; they are only (when successful) coherent and interesting. The poet William Butler Yeats perhaps had in mind something along these lines when he said that you can refute a philosopher, but you cannot refute the song of sixpence. And indeed "Sing a song of sixpence, / Pocket full of rye," has endured for a couple of centuries, perhaps partly because it has nothing to do with truth or falsity; it has created its own engaging world.

The view that we should not judge literature by how much it corresponds to our view of the world around us is held by many literary critics, and there probably is something (maybe a great deal) to it. For instance, some argue that there is no fixed, unchanging, "real" world around us; there is only what we perceive, what we ourselves "construct," and each generation, indeed each individual, constructs things differently.

And yet one can object, offering a commonsense response: Surely when we see a play, or read an engaging work of literature, whether it is old or new, we feel that somehow the work says something about the life around us, the real world. True, some of what we read—let's say, detective fiction—is chiefly fanciful; we read it to test our wits, or to escape, or to kill time. But most literature seems to be connected to life. This commonsense view, that literature is related to life, has an ancient history, and in fact almost everyone in the Western world believed it from the time of the ancient Greeks until the nineteenth century, and of course many people—including authors and highly skilled readers—still believe it today.

For instance, a concern for accuracy characterizes much writing. Many novelists do a great deal of research, especially into the settings where they will place their characters. And they are equally concerned with style—with the exactness of each word that they use. Flaubert is said to have spent a day writing a sentence and another day correcting it. The German author Rainer Maria Rilke has a delightful passage in *The Notebooks of Malte Laurids Brigge* (1910), in which he mentions someone who was dying in a hospital. The dying man heard a nurse mispronounce a word, and so (in Rilke's words) "he postponed dying." First he corrected the nurse's pronunciation, Rilke tells us, and "then he died. He was a poet and hated the approximate."

Certainly a good deal of literature, most notably the realistic short story and the novel, is devoted to giving a detailed picture that at least *looks like* the real world. One reason we read the fiction of Kate Chopin is to find out what "the real world" of Creole New Orleans in the late nineteenth century was like—as seen through Chopin's eyes, of course. (One need not be a Marxist to believe, with Karl Marx, that one learns more about Industrial England from the novels of Dickens and Mrs. Gaskell than from economic treatises.) Writers of stories, novels, and plays are concerned about giving plausible, indeed precise and insightful, images of the relationships between people. Writers of lyric poems presumably are specialists in presenting human feelings, the experience of love, for instance, or of the loss of faith. And presumably we are invited to compare the writer's created world to the world that we live in, perhaps to be reminded that our own lives can be richer than they are.

Even when a writer describes an earlier time, the implication is that the description is accurate, and especially that people *did* behave the way the writer says they did—and the way our own daily experience shows us that people do behave. Here is George Eliot at the beginning of her novel *Adam Bede* (1859):

> With a single drop of ink for a mirror, the Egyptian sorcerer undertook to reveal to any chance comer far-reaching visions of the past. This is what I undertake to do for you, reader. With this drop of ink at the end of my pen, I will show you the roomy workshop of Jonathan Burge, carpenter and builder in the village of Hayslope, as it appeared on the 18th of June, in the year of Our Lord, 1799.

Why do novelists such as George Eliot give us detailed pictures, and cause us to become deeply involved in the lives of their characters? Another novelist, D. H. Lawrence, offers a relevant comment in the ninth chapter of *Lady Chatterley's Lover* (1928):

> It is the way our sympathy flows and recoils that really determines our lives. And here lies the vast importance of the novel, properly handled. It can inform and lead into new places the flow of our sympathetic consciousness, and it can lead our sympathy away in recoil from things gone dead. Therefore, the novel, properly handled, can reveal the most secret places of life. . . .

In Lawrence's view, we can evaluate a novel in terms of its moral effect on the reader; the good novel, Lawrence claims, leads us into worlds—human relationships—that deserve our attention, and leads us away from "things gone dead," presumably relationships and values—whether political, moral, and religious—that no longer deserve to survive. To be blunt, Lawrence claims that good books improve us. His comment is similar to a more violent comment, quoted earlier, by Franz Kafka: "A book must be an ice-axe to break the frozen sea inside us."

Realism, of course, is not the writer's only tool. In *Gulliver's Travels* Swift gives us a world of Lilliputians, people about six inches tall. Is his book pure fancy, unrelated to life? Not at all. We perceive that the Lilliputians are (except for their size) pretty much like ourselves, and we realize that their tiny stature is an image of human pettiness, an *un*realistic device that helps us to see the real world more clearly.

The view that we have been talking about—that writers do connect us to the world—does not require realism, but it does assume that writers see, understand, and, through the medium of their writings, give us knowledge, deepen our understanding, and even perhaps improve our character. If, the argument goes, a work distorts reality—let's say because the author sees women superficially—the work is inferior. Such an assumption is found, for instance, in a comment by Elaine Savory Fido, who says that the work of Derek Walcott, a Caribbean poet and dramatist, is successful when Walcott deals with racism and with colonialism but is unsuccessful when he deals with women. "His treatment of women," Fido says in an essay in the *Journal of Commonwealth Literature* (1986),

> is full of clichés, stereotypes and negativity. I shall seek to show how some of his worst writing is associated with these portraits of women, which sometimes lead him to the brink of losing verbal control, or give rise to a retreat into abstract, conventional terms which prevent any real treatment of the subject. (109)

We need not be concerned here with whether or not Fido's evaluations of Walcott's works about women and about colonialism are convincing; what concerns us is her assumption that works can be—should be—evaluated in terms of the keenness of the writer's perception of reality.

Although we *need* not be concerned with an evaluation, we may may wish to be concerned with it, and, if so, we will probably find, perhaps to our surprise, that in the very process of arguing our evaluation (perhaps only to ourselves) we are also interpreting and reinterpreting. That is, we find ourselves observing passages closely, from a new point of view, and we may therefore find ourselves seeing them differently, finding new meanings in them.

IS SENTIMENTALITY A WEAKNESS— AND IF SO, WHY?

The presence of *sentimentality* is often regarded as a sign that a writer has failed to perceive accurately. Sentimentality is usually defined as excessive emotion, especially an excess of pity or sorrow. But when one thinks about it, who is to say when an emotion is "excessive"? Surely (to take an example) parents can be grief-stricken by the death of a child; and just as surely they may continue to be grief-stricken for the rest of their lives. Well, how about a child's grief for a dead pet, or an adult's grief over the death of an elderly person, a person who has lived a full life, for whom death might serve as a relief? Again, can any of us say how someone else ought to feel?

What each reader can say, however, is that the *expression* of grief in a particular literary work is or is not successful, convincing, engaging, moving. Though readers may not be able to say that the emotion is proper or improper, they can say that the literary expression of that emotion is successful or not. Consider the following poem by Eugene Field (1850-95):

LITTLE BOY BLUE

The little toy dog is covered with dust,
    But sturdy and stanch he stands;
And the little toy soldier is red with rust,
    And his musket moulds in his hands.
Time was when the little toy dog was new,
    And the soldier was passing fair;
And that was the time when our Little Boy Blue
    Kissed them and put them there.

"Now, don't you go till I come," he said,
    "And don't you make any noise!"
So, toddling off to his trundle-bed,
    He dreamt of the pretty toys;
And, as he was dreaming, an angel song
    Awakened our Little Boy Blue—
Oh! the years are many, the years are long,
    But the little toy friends are true!

Ay, faithful to Little Boy Blue they stand,
    Each in the same old place—
Awaiting the touch of a little hand,
    The smile of a little face;
And they wonder, as waiting the long years through
    In the dust of that little chair,
What has become of our Little Boy Blue,
    Since he kissed them and put them there.

Why do many readers find this poem sentimental, and of low quality? Surely not because it deals with the death of a child. Many other poems deal with this subject sympathetically, movingly, interestingly. Perhaps one sign of weak writing in "Little Boy Blue" is the insistence on the word *little*. The boy is little (five times, counting the title), the dog is little (twice), the toy soldier is little (once), the toys collectively are little (once), and Little Boy Blue has a little face, a little hand, and a little chair. Repetition is not an inherently bad thing, but perhaps here we feel that the poet is too insistently tugging at our sympathy, endlessly asserting the boy's charm yet not telling us anything interesting about the child other than that he was little and that he loved his "pretty toys." Real writers don't simply accept and repeat the greeting card view of reality. Children are more interesting than "Little Boy Blue" reveals, and adults react to a child's death in a more complex way.

Further, the boy's death is in no way described or explained. A poet of course is not required to tell us that the child died of pneumonia, or in an automobile accident, but since Field did choose to give us information about the death we probably want something better than the assertion that when a child dies it is "awakened" by an "angel song." We might ask ourselves if this is an interesting, plausible, healthy way of thinking of the death of a child. In talking about literature we want to be cautious about using the word "true," for reasons already discussed, but can't we say that Field's picture of childhood and his explanation of death simply don't ring true? Don't we feel that he is talking nonsense? And finally, can't we be excused for simply not believing that the speaker of the poem, having left the arrangement of toys undisturbed for "many" years, thinks that therefore "the little toy friends are true," and that they "wonder" while "waiting the long years through?" More nonsense. If we recall D. H. Lawrence's comment, we may feel that in this poem the poet has *not* properly directed "the flow of our sympathetic consciousness."

Let us look now at another poem on the death of a child, this one by X. J. Kennedy (b. 1929).

LITTLE ELEGY
FOR A CHILD WHO SKIPPED ROPE

Here lies resting, out of breath,
Out of turns, Elizabeth
Whose quicksilver toes not quite
Cleared the whirring edge of night.

Earth whose circles round us skim
Till they catch the lightest limb,
Shelter now Elizabeth
And for her sake trip up Death.

This is a "little" elegy—literally, since it is only eight lines long—for another child. We can't know for sure how the poet really felt, but will you agree that the work itself (presumably the expression of feeling) is both tender-hearted and restrained? It is also—we can use the word—true; the passing days (alluded to here in the reference to the ever-turning earth) really do finally catch everyone, even someone with "the lightest limb." Further, the poem is also witty: In the first stanza Elizabeth is said to be "Out of turns," a child's expression appropriately describing a child at play, but here also meaning that Elizabeth is no longer turning about in this world, and also that she died too early, before her expected time or turn. Notice, too, the fresh use of "out of breath," here meaning not only "breathless from exertion" (as a girl skipping rope would sometimes be) but also "unbreathing, dead."

In the second stanza the poet addresses the "Earth." Its revolutions (which resemble the circular motion of the skipping rope) catch all of us, but the earth will also "shelter" the dead girl, in a grave. The poem ends with a small, bitter joke about tripping up Death, thus continuing the imagery of skipping rope. The last line conveys (with great restraint) the unreconciled attitude most of us feel when hearing of the death of a child. No such note of resentment occurs in Field's poem; one almost believes that Field thinks the death of Little Boy Blue is a very beautiful thing. His poem is all sweetness, uncomplicated by any perception of the pain that death causes.

Let us look at one more poem about death, although here the subject is not a child but several young men. The author is Gwendolyn Brooks (b. 1917).

WE REAL COOL

The Pool Players.
Seven at the Golden Shovel

We real cool. We
Left school. We

Lurk late. We
Strike straight. We

Sing sin. We
Drink gin. We

Jazz June. We
Die soon.

The subtitle pretty much tells us that the speakers are seven people who hang out at a pool hall called The Golden Shovel, and the last line tells us that they "Die soon," that is, while still young. The speaker uses Black English (one characteristic is the omission of the verb, as in "We real cool," instead of "We are real cool"), and he speaks for the group. The title and the first line of the poem each begin with the word "we," and the sense of group identity is emphasized by the fact that each line—except the last—ends with "we."

The death of these seven dropouts is communicated not only by what the poem explicitly says but also by what it does not say, or, rather, by what is missing. The "we" that occurs at the end of each of the first seven lines is missing from the eighth line; the group is no more.

Beside the fact that they die—that we see them disappear—what can we say about them? The young men have a strong sense of group identity but they have no connection with anyone else, except with June, a person who apparently exists only as a sexual object. There are no adults in the poem, and no whites. They live in an isolated world. We can say at least two other things about them: (1) They speak sentences of only three words, sentences of the utmost simplicity; and (2) the simplicity in fact is deceptive, because the language is vigorous, marked by strong rhythm and by interesting alliteration (repetition of initial sounds, as in "Lurk late," and "Jazz June"). The speaker has something urgent to say, and he says it memorably. (Of course it is really Gwendolyn Brooks who is doing the talking, but Brooks has chosen to create this effective spokesperson, this character who holds our interest.) The poem, in short, communicates not only the group's severe limitations (behavior that will lead to early deaths) but also communicates the group's strengths (a sense of fellow-feeling, a skill with language).

And can't we also say that the poem communicates the sadness of the waste of human lives, without tearfully tugging at our sleeve? Don't we feel that although the poet sympathizes with these seven young men (and all others who resemble them), she nevertheless does not try to sweeten the facts and take us into an unreal Little-Boy-Blue world where we can feel good about our response to death. She does not sentimentalize; she looks without flinching, and she tells it as it is. Perhaps we can even say that although The Golden Shovel and these seven young men may be inventions, the poem is a fiction that speaks the truth.

No one can tell you how you should feel about these three poems, but ask yourself if you agree with some or all of what has been said about them. Also ask yourself on what standards you base your own evaluation of them. Perhaps one way to begin is to ask yourself which of the first two poems ("Little Boy Blue" and "Little Elegy") you would prefer to read if you were so unfortunate as to have lost a child or a young sibling. Then explain *why* you answered as you did.

📖 Suggestions for Further Reading

Most of the reference works cited at the end of the discussion of "What Is Literature?" (page 88) include entries on "evaluation." But for additional short discussions see Chapter 18 ("Evaluation") in René Wellek and Austin Warren, *Theory of Literature,* 2nd ed. (1948); Chapter 5 ("On Value-Judgments") in Northrop Frye, *The Stubborn Structure* (1970); Chapter 4 ("Evaluation") in John M. Ellis, *The Theory of Literary Criticism* (1974). For a longer discussion see Chapters 10 and 11 ("Critical Evaluation" and "Aesthetic Value") in Monroe C. Beardsley, *Aesthetics* (1958). Also of interest is Joseph Strelka, ed., *Problems of Literary Evaluation* (1969). In Strelka's collection you may find it best to begin with the essays by George Boas, Northrop Frye, and David Daiches, and then to browse in the other essays.

8

Writing about Literature: An Overview

THE NATURE OF CRITICAL WRITING

In everyday talk the commonest meaning of **criticism** is something like "finding fault." And to be critical is to be censorious. But a critic can see excellences as well as faults. Because we turn to criticism with the hope that the critic has seen something we have missed, the most valuable criticism is not that which shakes its finger at faults but that which calls our attention to interesting things going on in the work of art. Here is a statement by W. H. Auden (1907–73), suggesting that criticism is most useful when it calls our attention to things worth attending to:

> What is the function of a critic? So far as I am concerned, he can do me one or more of the following services:
>
> 1. Introduce me to authors or works of which I was hitherto unaware.
> 2. Convince me that I have undervalued an author or a work because I had not read them carefully enough.
> 3. Show me relations between works of different ages and cultures which I could never have seen for myself because I do not know enough and never shall.
> 4. Give a "reading" of a work which increases my understanding of it.
> 5. Throw light upon the process of artistic "Making."
> 6. Throw light upon the relation of art to life, science, economics, ethics, religion, etc.
>
> —*The Dyer's Hand* (New York, 1963), pp. 8–9

Auden does not neglect the delight we get from literature, but he extends (especially in his sixth point) the range of criticism to include topics beyond the literary work itself. Notice too the emphasis on observing, showing, and illuminating, which suggests that the function of critical writing is not very different from the commonest view of the function of imaginative writing.

SOME CRITICAL APPROACHES
Formalist (or New) Criticism; Deconstruction; Reader-Response Criticism; Archetypal (or Myth) Criticism; Historical Scholarship, Marxist Criticism, The New Historicism, and Biographical Criticism; Psychological (or Psychoanalytic) Criticism; Gender (Feminist, and Lesbian and Gay) Criticism

Whenever we talk about a work of literature or of art, or, for that matter, even about a so-so movie or television show, what we say depends in large measure on certain conscious or unconscious assumptions that we make: "I liked it; the characters were very believable" (here the assumption is that characters ought to be believable); "I didn't like it; there was too much violence" (here the assumption is that violence ought not to be shown, or if it is shown it should be made abhorrent); "I didn't like it; it was awfully slow" (here the assumption probably is that there ought to be a fair amount of physical action, perhaps even changes of scene, rather than characters just talking); "I didn't like it; I don't think topics of this sort ought to be discussed publicly" (here the assumption is a moral one, that it is indecent to present certain topics); "I liked it partly because it was refreshing to hear such frankness" (here again the assumption is moral, and more or less the reverse of the previous one).

In short, whether we realize it or not, we judge the work from a particular viewpoint—its realism, its morality, or whatever.

Professional critics, too, work from assumptions, but their assumptions are usually highly conscious, and the critics may define their assumptions at length. They regard themselves as, for instance, Freudians or Marxists or gay critics. They read all texts through the lens of a particular theory, and their focus enables them to see things that otherwise might go unnoticed. It should be added, however, that if a lens or critical perspective or interpretive strategy helps us to see certain things, it also limits our vision. Many critics therefore regard their method not as an exclusive way of thinking but only as a useful tool.

What follows is a brief survey of the chief current approaches to literature. You may find, as you read these pages, that one or another approach sounds especially congenial, and you may therefore want to make use of it in your reading and writing. On the other hand, it's important to remember that works of literature are highly varied, and, second, we read them for various purposes—to kill time, to enjoy fanciful visions, to be amused, to explore alien ways of feeling, and to learn about ourselves. It may be best, therefore, to try to respond to each text in the way that the text seems to require rather than to read all texts according to a single formula. You'll find, of course, that some works will lead you to want to think about them from several angles. A play by Shakespeare may stimulate you to read a book about the Elizabethan playhouse, and another that offers a Marxist interpretation of the English Renaissance, and still another that offers a feminist analysis of Shakespeare's plays. All of these approaches, and others, may help you to deepen your understanding of the literary works that you read.

Formalist Criticism (New Criticism)

Formalist criticism emphasizes the work as an independent creation, a self-contained unit, something to be studied in itself, not as part of some larger context, such as the author's life or an historical period. This kind of study is called formalist criticism because the emphasis is on the *form* of the work, the relationships between the parts—the construction of the plot, the contrasts between characters, the functions of rhymes, the point of view, and so on.

Cleanth Brooks, perhaps America's the most distinguished formalist critic, in an essay in the *Kenyon Review* (Winter 1951), reprinted in *The Modern Critical Spectrum,* eds. Gerald Jay Goldberg and Nancy Marmer Goldberg (1962), set forth what he called his "articles of faith":

That literary criticism is a description and an evaluation of its object.

That the primary concern of criticism is with the problem of unity—the kind of whole which the literary work forms or fails to form, and the relation of the various parts to each other in building up this whole.

That the formal relations in a work of literature may include, but certainly exceed, those of logic.

That in a successful work, form and content cannot be separated.

That form is meaning.

If you have read the earlier pages of this book you are already familiar with most of these ideas, but in the next few pages we will look into some of them in detail.

Formalist criticism is, in essence, *intrinsic* criticism, rather than extrinsic, for (at least in theory) it concentrates on the work itself, independent of its writer and the writer's background—that is, independent of biography, psychology, sociology, and history. The discussions of a proverb ("A rolling stone") and of a short poem by Frost ("The Span of Life") on pages 79–83 are brief examples. The gist is that a work of literature is complex, unified, and free-standing. In fact, of course, we usually bring outside knowledge to the work. For instance, a reader who is familiar with, say, *Hamlet,* can hardly study some other tragedy by Shakespeare, let's say *Romeo and Juliet,* without bringing to the second play some conception of what Shakespearean tragedy is or can be. A reader of Alice Walker's *The Color Purple* inevitably brings unforgettable outside material (perhaps the experience of being an African-American, or at least some knowledge of the history of African-Americans) to the literary work. It is very hard to talk only about *Hamlet* or *The Color Purple* and not at the same time talk about, or at least have in mind, aspects of human experience.

Formalist criticism, of course, begins with a personal response to the literary work, but it goes on to try to account for the response by closely examining the work. It assumes that the author shaped the poem, play, or story so fully that the work guides the reader's responses. The assumption that "meaning" is fully and completely presented within the text is not much in favor today, when many literary critics argue that the active or subjective reader (or even what Judith Fetterley, a feminist critic, has called "the resisting reader") and not the author of the text makes the "meaning." Still, even if one grants that the reader is active, not passive or coolly objective, one can hold with the formalists that the author is active too, constructing a text that in some measure controls the reader's responses. Of course, during the process of writing about our responses we may find that our responses change. A formalist critic would say that we see with increasing clarity what the work is really like, and what it really means. (Similarly, when authors write and revise a text they may change their understanding of what they are doing. A story that began as a lighthearted joke may turn into something far more serious than the writer imagined at the start, but, at least for the formalist critic, the final work contains a stable meaning that all competent readers can perceive.)

In practice, formalist criticism usually takes one of two forms, **explication** (the unfolding of meaning, line by line or even word by word) or **analysis** (the examination of the relations of parts). The essay on Yeats's "The Balloon of the Mind" (p. 255) is an explication, a setting forth of the implicit meanings of the words. The essays on Kate Chopin's "The Story of an Hour" (pp. 29 and 175) and on Tennessee Williams's *The Glass Menagerie* (p. 205) are analyses. The three essays on Frost's "Stopping by Woods on a Snowy Evening" (pp. 97–104) are chiefly analyses but with some passages of explication.

To repeat: Formalist criticism assumes that a work of art is stable. An artist constructs a coherent, comprehensible work, thus conveying to a reader an emotion or an idea. T. S. Eliot said that the writer can't just pour out emotions onto the page. Rather, Eliot said in an essay entitled "Hamlet and His Problems" (1919), "The only way of expressing emotion in the form of art is by finding an 'objective correlative'; in other words, a set of objects, a situation, a chain of events which shall be the formula of the *particular* emotion." With this in mind, consider again Robert Frost's "The Span of Life," a poem already discussed on page 83:

> The old dog barks backward without getting up.
> I can remember when he was a pup.

The image of an old dog barking backward, and the speaker's memory—apparently triggered by the old dog's bark—of the dog as a pup, presumably is the "objective correlative" of Frost's emotion or idea; Frost is "expressing emotion" through this "formula." And all of us, as competent readers, can grasp pretty accurately what Frost expressed. Frost's emotion, idea, meaning, or whatever is "objectively" embodied in the text. Formalist critics try to explain how and why literary works—*these* words, in *this* order—constitute unique, complex structures that embody or set forth meanings.

Formalist criticism, also called the **New Criticism** (to distinguish it from the historical and biographical writing that in earlier decades had dominated literary study) began to achieve prominence in the late 1920s, and was the dominant form from the late 1930s until about 1970, and even today it is widely considered the best way for a student to begin to study a work of literature. For one thing, formalist criticism empowers the student; that is, the student confronts the work immediately, and is not told first to spend days or weeks or months, for instance, reading Freud and his followers in order to write a psychoanalytic essay or reading Marx and Marxists in order to write a Marxist essay, or doing research on "necessary historical background" in order to write an historical essay.

Deconstruction

Deconstruction, or deconstructive or poststructural criticism, can almost be characterized as the opposite of everything for which formalist criticism stands. Deconstruction begins with the assumptions that the world is unknowable and that language is unstable, elusive, unfaithful. (Language is all of these things because meaning is largely generated by opposition: "Hot" means something in opposition to "cold," but a hot day may be 90 degrees whereas a hot oven is at least 400 degrees; and a "hot item" may be of any temperature.) Deconstructionists seek to show that a literary work (usually called "a text" or "a discourse") inevitably is self-contradictory. Unlike formalist critics—who hold that a competent author constructs a coherent work with a stable meaning, and that competent readers can perceive this meaning—deconstructionists (e.g., Barbara Johnson, in *The Critical Difference* [1980]) hold that a work has no coherent meaning at the center. Jonathan Culler, in *On Deconstruction* (1982), says that "to deconstruct a discourse is to show how it undermines the philosophy it asserts" (86). (Johnson and Culler provide accessible introductions, but the major document is Jacques Derrida's seminal, difficult work, *Of Grammatology* [1967, trans. 1976].) The text is only marks on paper, and therefore so far as a reader goes the author of a text is not the writer but the reader; texts are "indeterminate," "open," and "unstable."

Despite the emphasis on indeterminacy, one sometimes detects in deconstructionist interpretations a view associated with Marxism. This is the idea that authors are "socially constructed" from the "discourses of power" or "signifying practices" that surround them. Thus, although authors may think they are individuals with independent minds, their works usually reveal—unknown to the authors—the society's economic base. Deconstructionists "interrogate" a text, and they reveal what the authors were unaware of or had thought they had kept safely out of sight. That is, deconstructionists often find a rather specific meaning—though this meaning is one that might surprise the author.

Deconstruction is valuable insofar as—like the New Criticism—it encourages close, rigorous attention to the text. Furthermore, in its rejection of the claim that a work has a single stable meaning, deconstruction has had a positive influence on the study of literature. The problem with deconstruction, however, is that too often it is reductive, telling the same story about every text—that here, yet again, and again, we see how a text is incoherent and heterogeneous. There is, too, an irritating arrogance in some deconstructive criticism: "The author could not see how his/her text is fundamentally unstable and self-contradictory, but *I* can and now will interrogate the text and will issue my report." Readers should, of course, not prostrate themselves before texts, but there is something askew about an approach that often leads readers to conclude that they know a good deal more than the benighted author.

Aware that their emphasis on the instability of language implies that their own texts are unstable or even incoherent, some deconstructionists seem to aim at entertaining rather than at edifying. They probably would claim that they do not deconstruct meaning in the sense of destroying it; rather, they might say, they exuberantly multiply meanings, and to this end they may use such devices as puns, irony, and allusions, somewhat as a poet might, and just as though (one often feels) they think they are as creative as the writers they are commenting on. Indeed, for many deconstructionists, the traditional conception of "literature" is merely an elitist "construct." All "texts" or "discourses" (novels, scientific papers, a Kewpie doll on the mantel, watching TV, suing in court, walking the dog, and all other signs that human beings make) are of a piece; all are unstable systems of signifying, all are fictions, all are "literature." If literature (in the usual sense) occupies a special place in deconstruction it is because literature delights in its playfulness, it fictiveness, whereas other discourses nominally reject playfulness and fictiveness.

Reader-Response Criticism

Probably all reading includes some sort of response—"This is terrific," "This is a bore," "I don't know what's going on here"—and probably almost all writing about literature begins with some such response, but specialists in literature disagree greatly about the role that response plays, or should play, in experiencing literature and in writing about it.

At one extreme are those who say that our response to a work of literature should be a purely aesthetic response—a response to a work of art—and not the response we would have to something comparable in real life. To take an obvious point: If in real life we heard someone plotting a murder, we would intervene, perhaps by calling the police or by attempting to warn the victim. But when we hear Macbeth and Lady Macbeth plot to kill King Duncan, we watch with deep *interest;* we hear their words with *pleasure,* and maybe we even look forward to seeing the murder and to seeing what the characters then will say and what will happen to the murderers.

When you think about it, the vast majority of the works of literature do not have a close, obvious resemblance to the reader's life. Most readers of *Macbeth* are not Scots, and no readers are Scottish kings or queens. (It's not just a matter of older literature; no readers of Toni Morrison's *Beloved* are nineteenth-century African-Americans.) The connections readers make between themselves and the lives in most of the books they read are not, on the whole, connections based on ethnic or professional identities, but, rather, connections with states of consciousness, for instance a young person's sense of isolation from the family, or a young person's sense of guilt for initial sexual experiences. Before we reject a work either because it seems too close to us ("I'm a man and I don't like the depiction of this man"), or on the other hand too far from our experience ("I'm not a woman, so how can I enjoy reading about these women?"), we probably should try to follow the advice of Virginia Woolf, who said, "Do not dictate to your author; try to become him." Nevertheless, some literary works of the past may today seem intolerable, at least in part. There are passages in Mark Twain's *Huckleberry Finn* that deeply upset us today. We should, however, try to reconstruct the cultural assumptions of the age in which the work was written. If we do so, we may find that if in some ways it reflected its age, in other ways it challenged that culture.

Still, some of our experiences, some of *what we are*, may make it virtually impossible for us to read a work sympathetically or "objectively," experiencing it only as a work of art and not as a part of life. Take so humble a form of literature as the joke. A few decades ago jokes about nagging wives and mothers-in-law were widely thought to be funny. Our fairly recent heightened awareness of sexism today makes those jokes unfunny. Twenty years ago the "meaning" of a joke about a nagging wife or about a mother-in-law was, in effect, "Here's a funny episode that shows what women typically are." Today the "meaning"—at least as the hearer conceives it—is "The unfunny story you have just told shows that you have stupid, stereotypical views of women." In short, the joke may "mean" one thing to the teller, and a very different thing to the hearer.

Reader-response criticism, then, says that the "meaning" of a work is not merely something put into the work by the writer; rather, the "meaning" is an interpretation created or constructed or produced by the reader as well as the writer. Stanley Fish, an exponent of reader-response theory, in *Is There a Text in This Class?* (1980), puts it this way: "Interpretation is not the art of construing but of constructing. Interpreters do not decode poems; they make them" (327).

Let's now try to relate these ideas more specifically to comments about literature. If "meaning" is the production or creation not simply of the writer but also of the perceiver, does it follow that there is no such thing as a "correct" interpretation of the meaning of a work of literature? Answers to this question differ. At one extreme, the reader is said to construct or reconstruct the text under the firm guidance of the author. That is, the author so powerfully shapes or constructs the text—encodes an idea—that the reader is virtually compelled to perceive or reconstruct or decode it the way the author wants it to be perceived. (We can call this view *the objective view*, since it essentially holds that readers look objectively at the work and see what the author put into it.) At the other extreme, the reader constructs the meaning according to his or her own personality—that is, according to the reader's psychological identity. (We can call this view *the subjective view*, since it essentially holds that readers inevitably project their feelings into what they perceive.) An extreme version of the subjective view holds that there is no such thing as literature; there are only texts, some of which some readers regard in a particularly elitist way.

Against the objective view one can argue thus: No author can fully control a reader's response to every detail of the text. No matter how carefully constructed the text is, it leaves something—indeed, a great deal—to the reader's imagination. For instance, when Macbeth says that life "is a tale /

Told by an idiot, full of sound and fury / Signifying nothing," are we getting a profound thought from Shakespeare or, on the contrary, are we getting a shallow thought from Macbeth, a man who does not see that his criminal deeds have been played out against a heaven that justly punishes his crimes? In short, the objective view neglects to take account of the fact that the author is not continually at our shoulder making sure that we interpret the work in a particular way.

It is probably true, as Flannery O'Connor says in *Mystery and Manners* (1957), that good writers select "every word, every detail, for a reason, every incident for a reason" (75), but there are always *gaps or indeterminacies,* to use the words of Wolfgang Iser, a reader-response critic. Readers always go beyond the text, drawing inferences, and evaluating the text in terms of their own experience. In the Old Testament, for instance, in Genesis, the author tells us (Chapter 22) that God commanded Abraham to sacrifice his son Isaac, and then says that "Abraham rose up early in the morning" and prepared to fulfill the command. We are not explicitly told *why* Abraham "rose up early in the morning," or how he spent the intervening night, but some readers take "early in the morning" to signify (reasonably?) that Abraham has had a sleepless night. Others take it to signify (reasonably?) that Abraham is prompt in obeying God's command. And of course some readers fill the gap with both explanations, or with neither. Doubtless much depends on the reader, but there is no doubt that readers "naturalize"—make natural, according to their own ideas—what they read.

In an extreme form the subjective view denies that authors can make us perceive the meanings that they try to put into their works. This position suggests that every reader has a different idea of what a work means, an idea that reflects the reader's own ideas. Every reader, then, is Narcissus, who looked into a pool of water and thought he saw a beautiful youth but really saw only a reflection of himself. But does every reader see his or her individual image in each literary work? Of course not. Even *Hamlet,* a play that has generated an enormous range of interpretation, is universally seen as a tragedy, a play that deals with painful realities. If someone were to tell us that *Hamlet* is a comedy, and that the end, with a pile of corpses, is especially funny, we would not say, "Oh, well, we all see things in our own way." Rather, we would make our exit as quickly as possible.

Many people who subscribe to one version or another of a reader-response theory would agree that they are concerned not with all readers but with what they call *informed readers* or *competent readers.* Thus, informed or competent readers are familiar with the conventions of literature. They understand, for instance, that in a play such as *Hamlet* the characters usually speak in verse. Such readers, then, do not express amazement that Hamlet often speaks metrically, and that he sometimes uses rhyme. These readers understand that verse is the normal language for most of the characters in the play, and therefore such readers do not characterize Hamlet as a poet. Informed, competent readers, in short, know the rules of the game. There will still, of course, be plenty of room for differences of interpretation. Some people will find Hamlet not at all blameworthy; others will find him somewhat blameworthy; and still others may find him highly blameworthy. In short, we can say that a writer works against a background that is *shared* by readers. As readers, we are familiar with various kinds of literature, and we read or see *Hamlet* as a particular kind of literary work, a tragedy, a play that evokes (in Shakespeare's words) "woe or wonder," sadness and astonishment. Knowing (to a large degree) how we ought to respond, our responses thus are not merely private.

Consider taking, as a guide to reading, a remark made by Mencius (372–289 BC), the Chinese Confucian philosopher. Speaking of reading *The Book of Odes*, the oldest Chinese anthology, Mencius said that "a reader must let his thought go to meet the intention as he would a guest." Of course we often cannot be sure about the author's intention (we do not know what Shakespeare intended to say in *Hamlet;* we have only the play itself), and even those relatively few authors who have explicitly stated their intentions may be untrustworthy for one reason or another. Still, there is something highly attractive in Mencius's suggestion that when we read we should—at least for a start—treat our author not with suspicion or hostility but with goodwill and with the expectation of pleasure.

What are the implications of reader-response theory for writing an essay on a work of literature? Even if we agree that we are talking only about competent readers, does this mean, then, that *almost* anything goes in setting forth one's responses in an essay? Almost all advocates of any form of reading-response criticism agree on one thing: There are agreed-upon rules of *writing* if not of reading. This one point of agreement can be amplified to contain at least two aspects: (1) we all agree (at least more or less) as to what constitutes evidence, and (2) we all agree that a written response should be coherent. If you say that you find Hamlet to be less noble than his adversary, Claudius, you will be expected to provide evidence by pointing to specific passages, to specific things that Hamlet and Claudius say and do. And you will be expected to order the material into an effective, coherent sequence, so that the reader can move easily through your essay and will understand what you are getting at.

Archetypal (or Myth) Criticism

Carl G. Jung, the Swiss psychiatrist, in *Contributions to Analytical Psychology* (1928), postulates the existence of a "collective unconscious," an inheritance in our brains consisting of "countless typical experiences [such as birth, escape from danger, selection of a mate] of our ancestors." Few people today believe in an inherited "collective unconscious," but many people agree that certain repeated experiences, such as going to sleep and hours later awakening, or the perception of the setting and of the rising sun, or of the annual death and rebirth of vegetation, manifest themselves in dreams, myths, and literature—in these instances, as stories of apparent death and rebirth. This archetypal plot of death and rebirth is said to be evident in Coleridge's *The Rime of the Ancient Mariner,* for example. The ship suffers a deathlike calm and then is miraculously restored to motion, and, in a sort of parallel rebirth, the mariner moves from spiritual death to renewed perception of the holiness of life. Another archetypal plot is the quest, which usually involves the testing and initiation of a hero, and thus essentially represents the movement from innocence to experience. In addition to archetypal plots there are archetypal characters, since an archetype is any recurring unit. Among archetypal characters are the Scapegoat (as in Shirley Jackson's "The Lottery," page 356), the Hero (savior, deliverer), the Terrible Mother (witch, stepmother—even the wolf "grandmother" in the tale of Little Red Riding Hood), and the Wise Old Man (father figure, magician).

Because, the theory holds, both writer and reader share unconscious memories, the tale an author tells (derived from the collective unconscious) may strangely move the reader, speaking to his or her collective unconscious. As Maud Bodkin puts it, in *Archetypal Patterns in Poetry* (1934), something within us "leaps in response to the effective presentation in poetry of an ancient theme" (4). But this emphasis on ancient (or repeated) themes has made archetypal criticism vulnerable to the charge that it is reductive. The critic looks for certain characters or patterns of action, and values the work if the motifs are there, meanwhile overlooking what is unique, subtle, distinctive, and truly interesting about the work. That is, to put the matter crudely, a work is regarded as good if it is pretty much like other works, with the usual motifs and characters. A second weakness in some archetypal criticism is that in the search for the deepest meaning of a work the critic may crudely impose a pattern, seeing (for instance) The Quest in every walk down the street. But perhaps to say this is to beg the question; it is the critic's job to write so persuasively that the reader at least tentatively accepts the critic's view. For a wide-ranging study of one particular motif, see Barbara Fass Leavy's *In Search of the Swan Maiden* (1994), a discussion of the legend of a swan maiden who is forced to marry a mortal because he possesses something of hers, usually a garment or an animal skin. Leavy analyzes several versions of the story, which she takes to be a representation not only of female rage against male repression but also a representation of male fear of female betrayal. Leavy ends her book by examining this motif in Ibsen's *A Doll's House*. Her claim is that when Nora finds a lost object, the dance costume, she can flee from the tyrannical domestic world and thus she regains her freedom.

If archetypal criticism sometimes seems farfetched, it is nevertheless true that one of its strengths is that it invites us to use comparisons, and comparing is often an excellent way to see not only what a work shares with other works but what is distinctive in the work. The most successful practitioner of archetypal criticism was the late Northrop Frye (1912-91), whose numerous books help readers to see fascinating connections between works. For Frye's explicit comments about archetypal criticism, as well as for examples of such criticism in action, see especially his *Anatomy of Criticism* (1957) and *The Educated Imagination* (1964). On archetypes see also Chapter 16, "Archetypal Patterns," in Norman Friedman, *Form and Meaning in Fiction* (1975).

Historical Scholarship

Historical criticism studies a work within its historical context. Thus, a student of *Julius Caesar, Hamlet,* or *Macbeth*—plays in which ghosts appear—may try to find out about Elizabethan attitudes toward ghosts. We may find, for instance, that the Elizabethans took ghosts more seriously than we do, or, on the other hand, we may find that ghosts were explained in various ways, for instance sometimes as figments of the imagination and sometimes as shapes taken by the devil in order to mislead the virtuous. Similarly, an historical essay concerned with *Othello* may be devoted to Elizabethan attitudes toward Moors, or to Elizabethan ideas of love, or, for that matter, to Elizabethan ideas of a daughter's obligations toward her father's wishes concerning her suitor. The historical critic assumes (and one can hardly dispute the assumption) that writers, however individualistic, are shaped by the particular social contexts in which they live. One can put it this way: The goal of historical criticism is to understand how people in the past thought and felt. It assumes that such understanding can enrich our understanding of a particular work. The assumption is, however, disputable, since one may argue that the artist—let's say Shakespeare—may *not* have shared the age's view on this or that. All of the half-dozen or so Moors in Elizabethan plays other than *Othello* are villainous or foolish, but this evidence, one can argue, does not prove that *therefore* Othello is villainous or foolish.

Marxist Criticism

One form of historical criticism is **Marxist criticism,** named for Karl Marx (1818-83). Actually, to say "one form" is misleading, since Marxist criticism today is varied, but essentially it sees history primarily as a struggle between socioeconomic classes, and it sees literature (and everything else) as the product of economic forces of the period.

For Marxists, economics is the "base" or "infrastructure"; on this base rests a "superstructure" of ideology (law, politics, philosophy, religion, and the arts, including literature), reflecting the interests of the dominant class. Thus, literature is a material product, produced—like bread or battleships—in order to be consumed in a given society. Like every other product, literature is the product of work, and it *does* work. A bourgeois society, for example, will produce literature that in one way or another celebrates bourgeois values, for instance individualism. These works serve to assure the society that produces them that its values are solid, even universal. The enlightened Marxist writer or critic, on the other hand, exposes the fallacy of traditional values and replaces them with the truths found in Marxism. In the heyday of Marxism in the United States, during the depression of the 1930s, it was common for such Marxist critics as Granville Hicks to assert that the novel must show the class struggle.

Few critics of any sort would disagree that works of art in some measure reflect the age that produced them, but most contemporary Marxist critics go further. First, they assert—in a repudiation of what has been called "'vulgar' Marxist theory"—that the deepest historical meaning of a literary work is to be found in what it does *not* say, what its ideology does not permit it to express. Second, Marxists take seriously Marx's famous comment that "the philosophers have only *interpreted* the world in various ways; the point is to *change* it." The critic's job is to change the world, by revealing the economic basis of the arts. Not surprisingly, most Marxists are skeptical of such concepts as "genius" and "masterpiece." These concepts, they say, are part of the bourgeois myth that idealizes the individual and detaches it from its economic context. For an introduction to Marxist criticism, see Terry Eagleton, *Marxism and Literary Criticism* (1976).

The New Historicism

A recent school of scholarship, called the **New Historicism,** insists that there is no "history" in the sense of a narrative of indisputable past events. Rather, the New Historicism holds that there is only our version—our narrative, our representation—of the past. In this view, each age projects its own preconceptions on the past; historians may think they are revealing the past but they are revealing only their own historical situation and their personal preferences. Thus, in the nineteenth century and in the twentieth almost up to 1992, Columbus was represented as the heroic benefactor of humankind who discovered the New World. But even while plans were being made to celebrate the five-hundredth anniversary of his first voyage across the Atlantic, voices were raised in protest: Columbus' did not "discover" a New World; after all, the indigenous people knew where they were, and it was Columbus who was lost, since he thought he was in India. In short, people who wrote history in, say, 1900, projected onto the past their current views (colonialism was a Good Thing), and people who in 1992 wrote history projected onto that same period a very different set of views (colonialism was a Bad Thing). Similarly, ancient Greece, once celebrated by historians as the source of democracy and rational thinking, is now more often regarded as a society that was built on slavery and on the oppression of women. And the Renaissance, once glorified as an age of enlightened thought, is now often seen as an age that tyrannized women, enslaved colonial people, and enslaved itself with its belief in witchcraft and astrology. Thinking about these changing views, one feels the truth of the witticism that the only thing more uncertain than the future is the past.

The New Historicism is especially associated with Stephen Greenblatt, who popularized the term in 1982 in the preface to a collection of essays published in the journal *Genre*. Greenblatt himself has said of the New Historicism that "it's no doctrine at all" (*Learning to Curse* [1990]) but the term is nevertheless much used, and, as the preceding remarks have suggested, it is especially associated with power, most especially with revealing the tyrannical practices of a society that others have glorified. The New Historicism was in large measure shaped by the 1960s; the students who in the 1960s protested against the war in Vietnam by holding demonstrations, in the 1980s—they were now full professors—protested against Ronald Reagan by writing articles exposing Renaissance colonialism. Works of literature were used as a basis for a criticism of society. Academic writing of this sort was not dry, impartial, unimpassioned scholarship; rather, it connected the past with the present, and it offered value judgments. In Greenblatt's words,

> Writing that was not engaged, that withheld judgments, that failed to connect the present with the past seemed worthless. Such connection could be made either by analogy or causality; that is, a particular set of historical circumstances could be represented in such a way as to bring out homologies with aspects of the present or, alternatively, those circumstances could be analyzed as the generative forces that led to the modern condition. (*Learning to Curse* 167)

For a collection of 15 essays exemplifying the New Historicism, see H. Aram Veeser, ed., *The New Historicism* (1989).

Biographical Criticism

One kind of historical research is the study of *biography*, which for our purposes includes not only biographies but also autobiographies, diaries, journals, letters, and so on. What experiences did (for example) Mark Twain undergo? Are some of the apparently sensational aspects of *Huckleberry Finn* in fact close to events that Twain experienced? If so, is he a "realist"? If not, is he writing in the tradition of the "tall tale"?

The really good biographies not only tell us about the life of the author but they enable us to return to the literary texts with a deeper understanding of how they came to be what they are. If, for example, you read Richard B. Sewall's biography of Emily Dickinson, you will find a wealth of material concerning her family and the world she moved in—for instance, the religious ideas that were part of her upbringing.

Biographical study may illuminate even the work of a living author. If you are writing about the poetry of Adrienne Rich, for example, you may want to consider what she has told us in many essays about her life, especially about her relations with her father and her husband.

Psychological (or Psychoanalytic) Criticism

One form that biographical study may take is **psychological** or **psychoanalytic criticism,** which usually examines the author and the author's writings in the framework of Freudian psychology. A central doctrine of Sigmund Freud (1856-1939) is the Oedipus complex, the view that all males (Freud seems not to have made his mind up about females) unconsciously wish to displace their fathers and to sleep with their mothers. According to Freud, hatred for the father and love of the mother, normally repressed, may appear disguised in dreams. Works of art, like dreams, are disguised versions of repressed wishes.

Consider, for instance, Edgar Allan Poe. An orphan before he was three years old, he was brought up in the family of John Allan, but he was never formally adopted. His relations with Allan were stormy, though he seems to have had better relations with Allan's wife and still better relations with an aunt, whose daughter he married. In the Freudian view, Poe's marriage to his cousin (the daughter of a mother figure) was a way of sleeping with his mother. According to psychoanalytic critics, if we move from Poe's life to his work, we see, it is alleged, this hatred for his father and love for his mother. Thus, the murderer in "The Cask of Amontillado" is said to voice Poe's hostility toward his father, and the wine vault in which much of the story is set (an encompassing structure associated with fluids) is interpreted as symbolizing Poe's desire to return to his mother's womb. In Poe's other works, the longing for death is similarly taken to embody his desire to return to the womb.

Of course other psychoanalytic interpretations of Poe have been offered. For instance, Kenneth Silverman, author of a biography entitled

Edgar Allan Poe (1991) and the editor of a collection entitled *New Essays on Poe's Major Tales* (1993), emphasizes the fact that Poe was orphaned before he was three, and was separated from his brother and his infant sister. In *New Essays* Silverman relates this circumstance to the "many instances of engulfment" that he finds in Poe's work. Images of engulfment, he points out, "are part of a still larger network of images having to do with biting, devouring, and similar oral mutilation." Why are they common in Poe? Here is Silverman's answer:

> Current psychoanalytic thinking about childhood bereavement explains the fantasy of being swallowed up as representing a desire, mixed with dread, to merge with the dead; the wish to devour represents a primitive attempt at preserving loved ones, incorporating them so as not to lose them. (20)

Notice that psychoanalytic interpretations usually take us away from what the author consciously intended; they purport to tell us what the work reveals, whether or not the author was aware of this meaning. The "meaning" of the work is found not in the surface content of the work but in the author's psyche.

One additional example—and it is the most famous—of a psychoanalytic study of a work of literature may be useful. In *Hamlet and Oedipus* (1949) Ernest Jones, amplifying some comments by Freud, argued that Hamlet delays killing Claudius because Claudius (who has killed Hamlet's father and married Hamlet's mother) has done exactly what Hamlet himself wanted to do. For Hamlet to kill Claudius, then, would be to kill himself.

If this approach interests you, take a look at Norman N. Holland's *Psychoanalysis and Shakespeare* (1966), or Frederick Crews's study of Hawthorne, *The Sins of the Fathers* (1966). Crews, for instance, finds in Hawthorne's work evidence of unresolved Oedipal conflicts, and he accounts for the appeal of the fictions thus: The stories "rest on fantasy, but on the shared fantasy of mankind, and this makes for a more penetrating fiction than would any illusionistic slice of life" (263). For applications to other authors, look at Simon O. Lesser's *Fiction and the Unconscious* (1957), or at an anthology of criticism, *Literature and Psychoanalysis*, edited by Edith Kurzweil and William Phillips (1983).

Psychological criticism can also turn from the author and the work to the reader, seeking to explain why we, as readers, respond in certain ways. Why, for example, is *Hamlet* so widely popular? A Freudian answer is that it is universal because it deals with a universal (Oedipal) impulse. One can, however, ask whether it appeals as strongly to women as to men (again, Freud was unsure about the Oedipus complex in women) and, if so, why it appeals to them. Or, more generally, one can ask if males and females read in the same way.

Gender (Feminist, and Lesbian and Gay) Criticism

This last question brings us to **gender criticism.** As we have seen, writing about literature usually seeks to answer questions. Historical scholarship, for instance, tries to answer such questions as, What did Shakespeare and his contemporaries believe about ghosts? or How did Victorian novelists and poets respond to Darwin's theory of evolution? Gender criticism, too, asks questions. It is especially concerned with two issues, one about reading and one about writing: Do men and women read in different ways, and Do they write in different ways?

Feminist criticism can be traced back to the work of Virginia Woolf (1882-1941), but chiefly it grew out of the Women's Movement of the 1960s. The Women's Movement at first tended to hold that women are pretty much the same as men and therefore should be treated equally, but much recent feminist criticism has emphasized and explored the differences between women and men. Because the experiences of the sexes are different, the argument goes, the values and sensibilities are different, and their responses to literature are different. Further, literature written by women is different from literature written by men. Works written by women are seen by some feminist critics as embodying the experiences of a minority culture—a group marginalized by the dominant male culture. (If you have read Charlotte Perkins Gilman's "The Yellow Wallpaper" or Susan Glaspell's "Trifles" you'll recall that these literary works themselves are largely concerned about the differing ways that males and females perceive the world.) Of course, not all women are feminist critics, and not all feminist critics are women. Further, there are varieties of feminist criticism, but for a good introduction see *The New Feminist Criticism: Essays on Women, Literature, and Theory* (1985), edited by Elaine Showalter. For the role of men in feminist criticism, see *Engendering Men* (1990), edited by Joseph A. Boone and Michael Cadden (1990). At this point it should also be said that some theorists, who hold that identity is socially constructed, strongly dispute the value of establishing "essentialist" categories such as *heterosexual, gay,* and *lesbian*—a point that we will consider in a moment.

Feminist critics rightly point out that men have established the conventions of literature and that men have established the canon—that is, the body of literature that is said to be worth reading. Speaking a bit broadly, in this patriarchal or male-dominated body of literature, men are valued for being strong and active, whereas women are expected to be weak and passive. Thus, in the world of fairy tales, the admirable male is the energetic hero (Jack, the Giant-Killer) but the admirable female is the passive Sleeping Beauty. Active women such as the wicked stepmother or—a disguised form of the same thing—the witch are generally villainous. (There are of course exceptions, such as Gretel, in "Hansel and Gretel.") A woman hearing or reading the story of Sleeping Beauty or of Little Red Riding Hood (rescued by the powerful woodcutter), or any other work in which women seem to be trivialized will respond differently from a man. For instance, a woman may be socially conditioned into admiring Sleeping Beauty but only at great cost to her mental well-being. A more resistant female reader may recognize in herself no kinship with the beautiful, passive Sleeping Beauty and may respond to the story indignantly. Another way to put it is this: The male reader perceives a romantic story, but the resistant female reader perceives a story of oppression.

For discussions of the ways in which, it is argued, women *ought* to read, you may want to look at *Gender and Reading* (1986), edited by Elizabeth A. Flynn and Patrocino Schweikart, and especially at Judith Fetterley's book, *The Resisting Reader* (1978). Fetterley's point, briefly, is that women should resist the meanings (that is, the visions of how women ought to behave) that male authors—or female authors who have inherited patriarchal values—bury in their books. "To read the canon of what is currently considered classic American literature is perforce to identify as male," Fetterley says. "It insists on its universality in specifically male terms." Fetterley argues that a woman must read as a woman, "exorcising the male mind that has been implanted in women." In resisting the obvious meanings—for instance, the false claim that male values are universal values—women may discover more significant meanings. Fetterley argues that Faulkner's "A Rose for Emily"

> is a story not of a conflict between the South and the North or between the old order and the new; it is a story of the patriarchy North and South, new and old, and of the sexual conflict within it. As Faulkner himself has implied, it is a story of a woman victimized and betrayed by the system of sexual politics, who nevertheless has discovered, within the structures that victimize her, sources of power for herself. . . . "A Rose for Emily" is the story of how to murder your gentleman caller and get away with it. (34-35)

Fetterley goes on to argue that the society made Emily a "lady"—society dehumanized her by elevating her. For instance, Emily's father, seeking to shape her life, stood in the doorway of their house and drove away her suitors. So far as he was concerned, Emily was a nonperson, a creature whose own wishes were not to be regarded; he alone would shape her future. Because society (beginning with her father) made her a "lady"—a creature so elevated that she is not taken seriously as a passionate human being—she is able to kill Homer Barron and not be suspected. Here is Fetterley speaking of the passage in which the townspeople crowd into her house when her death becomes known:

> When the would-be "suitors" finally get into her father's house, they discover the consequences of his oppression of her, for the violence contained in the

rotted corpse of Homer Barron is the mirror image of the violence represented in the tableau, the back-flung front door flung back with a vengeance. (42)

Feminist criticism has been concerned not only with the depiction of women and men in a male-determined literary canon and with female responses to these images but also with yet another topic: women's writing. Women have had fewer opportunities than men to become writers of fiction, poetry, and drama—for one thing, they have been less well educated in the things that the male patriarchy valued—but even when they *have* managed to write, men sometimes have neglected their work simply because it had been by a woman. Feminists have further argued that certain forms of writing have been especially the province of women—for instance journals, diaries, and letters; and predictably, these forms have not been given adequate space in the traditional, male-oriented canon.

In 1972, in an essay entitled "When We Dead Awaken: Writing as Re-Vision," the poet and essayist Adrienne Rich effectively summed up the matter:

> A radical critique of literature, feminist in its impulse, would take the work first of all as a clue to how we live, how we have been living, how we have been led to imagine ourselves, how our language has trapped as well as liberated us; and how we can begin to see—and therefore live—afresh. . . . We need to know the writing of the past and know it differently than we have ever known it; not to pass on a tradition but to break its hold over us.

Much feminist criticism concerned with women writers has emphasized connections between the writer's biography and her life. Suzanne Juhasz, in her introduction to *Feminist Critics Read Emily Dickinson* (1983), puts it this way:

> The central assumption of feminist criticism is that gender informs the nature of art, the nature of biography, and the relation between them. Dickinson is a woman poet, and this fact is integral to her identity. Feminist criticism's sensitivity to the components of female experience in general and to Dickinson's identity as a woman generates essential insights about her. . . . Attention to the relationship between biography and art is a requisite of feminist criticism. To disregard it further strengthens those divisions continually created by traditional criticism, so that nothing about the woman writer can be seen whole. (1-5)

Lesbian and gay criticism have their roots in feminist criticism; that is, feminist criticism introduced many of the questions that these other, newer developments are now exploring.

In 1979, in a book called *On Lies, Secrets, and Silence,* Adrienne Rich reprinted a 1975 essay on Emily Dickinson, "Vesuvius at Home." In her new preface to the reprinted essay she said that a lesbian-feminist reading of Dickinson would not have to prove that Dickinson slept with another woman. Rather, lesbian-feminist criticism "will ask questions hitherto passed over; it will not search obsessively for heterosexual romance as the key to a woman artist's life and work" (157-58). Obviously such a statement is also relevant to a male artist's life and work. It should be mentioned, too, that Rich's comments on lesbian reading and lesbianism as an image of creativity have been much discussed. For a brief survey, see Marilyn R. Farwell, "Toward a Definition of the Lesbian Literary Imagination," *Signs* 14 (1988): 100-18.

Before turning to some of the questions that lesbian and gay critics address it is necessary first to say that lesbian criticism and gay criticism are not—to use a word now current in much criticism—symmetrical, chiefly because lesbian and gay relationships themselves are not symmetrical. For instance, straight society has traditionally been more tolerant of—or blinder to—lesbianism than to male homosexuality. Further, lesbian literary theory has tended to see its affinities more with feminist theory than with gay theory; that is, the emphasis has been on gender (male/female) rather than on sexuality (homosexuality/bisexuality/heterosexuality). On the other hand, some gays and lesbians have been writing what is now being called *queer theory*.

Now for some of the questions that this criticism addresses: (1) Do lesbians and gays read in ways that differ from the ways straight people read? (2) Do they write in ways that differ from those of straight people? (For instance, Gregory Woods argues in *Lesbian and Gay Writing: An Anthology of Critical Essays* [1990], edited by Mark Lilly, that "modern gay poets . . . use . . . paradox, as weapon and shield, against a world in which heterosexuality is taken for granted as being exclusively natural and healthy" [176]. Another critic, Jeffrey Meyers, writing in *Journal of English and Germanic Philology* 88 [1989]:126-29, in an unsympathetic review of a book on gay writers contrasts gay writers of the past with those of the present. According to Meyers, closeted homosexuals in the past, writing out of guilt and pain, produced a distinctive literature that is more interesting than the productions of today's uncloseted writers.) (3) How have straight writers portrayed lesbians and gays, and how have lesbian and gay writers portrayed straight women and men? (4) What strategies did lesbian and gay writers use to make their work acceptable to a general public in an age when lesbian and gay behavior was unmentionable?

Questions such as these have stimulated critical writing especially about bisexual and lesbian and gay authors (for instance Virginia Woolf, Gertrude Stein, Elizabeth Bishop, Walt Whitman, Oscar Wilde, E. M. Forster, Hart Crane, Tennessee Williams), but they have also led to interesting writing on such a topic as Nathaniel Hawthorne's attitudes toward women. "An account of Hawthorne's misogyny that takes no account of his own and his culture's gender anxieties," Robert K. Martin says in Boone and Cadden's *Engendering Men,* "is necessarily inadequate" (122).

Shakespeare's work—and not only the sonnets, which praise a beautiful male friend—has stimulated a fair amount of gay criticism. Much of this criticism consists of "decoding" aspects of the plays. For instance, Seymour Kleinberg argues, in *Essays on Gay Literature* (1985), ed. Stuart Kellogg, that Antonio in *The Merchant of Venice,* whose melancholy is not made clear by Shakespeare, is melancholy because (again, this is according to Kleinberg) Antonio's lover, Bassanio, is deserting him, and because Antonio is ashamed of his own sexuality:

> Antonio is a virulently anti-Semitic homosexual and is melancholic to the point of despair because his lover, Bassanio, wishes to marry an immensely rich aristocratic beauty, to leave the diversions of the Rialto to return to his own class and to sexual conventionality. Antonio is also in despair because he despises himself for his homosexuality, which is romantic, obsessive, and exclusive, and fills him with sexual shame. (113)

Several earlier critics had suggested that Antonio is a homosexual, hopelessly pining for Bassanio, but Kleinberg goes further, and argues that Antonio and Bassanio are lovers, not just good friends, and that Antonio's hopeless and shameful (because socially unacceptable) passion for Bassanio becomes transformed into hatred for the Jew, Shylock. The play, according to Kleinberg, is partly about "a world where . . . sexual guilt is translated into ethnic hatred" (124).

Examination of matters of gender obviously can help to illuminate literary works, but it should be added, too, that some—perhaps most—critics write also as activists, reporting their findings not only to help us to understand and to enjoy the works of (say) Whitman, but also to change society's view of sexuality. Thus, in *Disseminating Whitman* (1991), Michael Moon is impatient with earlier critical rhapsodies about Whitman's universalism. It used to be said that Whitman's celebration of the male body was a sexless celebration of brotherly love in a democracy, but the gist of Moon's view is that we must neither whitewash Whitman's poems with such high-minded talk, nor reject them as indecent; rather, we must see exactly what Whitman is saying about a kind of experience that society had shut its eyes to, and we must take Whitman's view seriously. Somewhat similarly, Gregory Woods in *Articulate Flesh* (1987) points out that until a few years ago discussions of Hart Crane regularly condemned his homosexuality, as is evident, for instance, in L. S. Dembo's characterization of Crane (quoted by Woods) as "uneducated, alcoholic, homosexual, paranoic, suicidal" (140). Gay and lesbian writers do not adopt this sort of manner. But it should also be pointed out that today there are straight critics who study lesbian or gay authors and write about them insightfully and without hostility.

One assumption in much lesbian and gay critical writing is that although gender greatly influences the ways in which we read, reading is a skill that can be learned, and therefore straight people—aided by lesbian and gay critics—can learn to read, with pleasure and profit, lesbian and gay writers. This assumption of course also underlies much feminist criticism, which often assumes that men must stop ignoring books by women and must learn (with the help of feminist critics) how to read them, and, in fact, how to read—with newly opened eyes—the sexist writings of men of the past and present.

In addition to the titles mentioned earlier concerning gay and lesbian criticism, consult Eve Kosofsky Sedgwick, *Between Men: English Literature and Male Homosocial Desire* (1985) and an essay by Sedgwick, "Gender Criticism," in *Redrawing the Boundaries,* ed. Stephen Greenblatt and Giles Gunn (1992).

While many in the field of lesbian and gay criticism have turned their energies toward examining the effects that an author's—or a character's—sexual identity may have upon the text, others have begun to question, instead, the concept of sexual identity itself.[1] Drawing upon the work of the French social historian Michel Foucault, critics such as David Halperin (*One Hundred Years of Homosexuality and Other Essays on Greek Love* [1990]) and Judith Butler (*Gender Trouble* [1989]) explore how various categories of identity, such as "heterosexual" and "homosexual," represent ways of defining human beings that are distinct to particular cultures and historical periods. These critics, affiliated with what is known as the "social constructionist" school of thought, argue that however a given society (modern American, for instance, or ancient Greek) interprets sexuality will determine the particular categories within which individuals come to understand and to name their own desires. For such critics the goal of a lesbian or gay criticism is not to define the specificity of a lesbian or gay literature or mode of interpretations, but to show how the ideology (the normative understanding of a given culture) makes it seem natural to think about sexuality in terms of such identities as lesbian, gay, bisexual, or straight. By challenging the authority of those terms, or "denaturalizing" them, and by calling attention to moments in which literary (and nonliterary) representations make assumptions that reinforce the supposed inevitability of those distinctions, such critics attempt to redefine our understandings of the relations between sexuality and literature. They hope, in

[1]This paragraph and the next two are by Lee Edelman of Tufts University.

short, to make clear that sexuality is always, in a certain sense, "literary"; it is a representation of a fiction that society has constructed in order to make sense out of experience.

Because such critics have challenged the authority of the opposition between heterosexuality and homosexuality, and have read it as a historical construct rather than as a biological or psychological absolute, they have sometimes resisted the very terms "lesbian" and "gay." Many now embrace what is called queer theory as an attempt to mark their resistance to the categories of identity they see our culture as imposing upon us.

Works written within this mode of criticism are often influenced by deconstructionist or psychoanalytic thought. They examine works by straight authors as frequently as they do works by writers who might be defined as lesbian or gay. Eve Kosofsky Sedgwick's reading of *Billy Budd* in her book, *Epistemology of the Closet* (1990), provides a good example of this sort of criticism. Reading Claggart as "the homosexual" in the text of Melville's novella, Sedgwick is not interested in defining his difference from other characters. Instead, she shows how the novella sets up a large number of oppositions—such as public and private, sincerity and sentimentality, health and illness—all of which have a relationship to the way in which a distinct "gay" identity was being produced by American society at the end of the nineteenth century. Other critics whose work in this field may be useful for students of literature are D. A. Miller, *The Novel and the Police* (1988); Diana Fuss, *Essentially Speaking* (1989) and *Identification Papers* (1995); Judith Butler, *Bodies That Matter* (1993); and Lee Edelman, *Homographesis: Essays in Gay Literary and Cultural Theory* (1993).

This chapter began by making the obvious point that all readers, whether or not they consciously adopt a particular approach to literature, necessarily read through particular lenses. More precisely, a reader begins with a frame of interpretation—historical, psychological, sociological, or whatever—and from within the frame selects one of the several competing methodologies. Critics often make great—even grandiose—claims for their approaches. For example, Frederic Jameson, a Marxist, begins *The Political Unconscious: Narrative as a Socially Symbolic Act* (1981) thus:

> This book will argue the priority of the political interpretation of literary texts. It conceives of the political perspective not as some supplemental method, not as an optional auxiliary to other interpretive methods current today—the psychoanalytic or the myth-critical, the stylistic, the ethical, the structural—but rather as the absolute horizon of all reading and all interpretation. (7)

Readers who are chiefly interested in politics may be willing to assume "the priority of the political interpretation . . . as the absolute horizon of all reading and all interpretation," but other readers may respectfully decline to accept this assumption.

In talking about a critical approach, sometimes the point is made by saying that readers decode a text by applying a grid to it; the grid enables them to see certain things clearly. Good; but what is sometimes forgotten is that (since there is no such thing as a free lunch) a lens or a grid—an angle of vision or interpretive frame and a methodology—also prevents a reader from seeing certain other things. This is to be expected. What is important, then, is to remember this fact, and thus not to deceive ourselves by thinking that our keen tools enable us to see the whole. A psychoanalytic reading of, say, *Hamlet,* may be helpful, but it does not reveal all that is in *Hamlet,* and it does not refute the perceptions of another approach, let's say an historical study. Each approach may illuminate aspects neglected by others.

It is too much to expect a reader to apply all useful methods (or even several) at once—that would be rather like looking through a telescope with one eye and through a microscope with the other—but it is not too much to expect readers to be aware of the limitations of their methods. If one reads much criticism, one finds two kinds of critics. There are, on the one hand, critics who methodically and mechanically peer through a lens or grid, and they of course find what one can easily predict they will find. On the other hand, there are critics who (despite what may be inevitable class and gender biases) are at least relatively open-minded in their approach—critics who, one might say, do not at the outset of their reading believe that their method assures them that (so to speak) they have got the text's number and that by means of this method they will expose the text for what it is. The philosopher Richard Rorty engagingly makes a distinction somewhat along these lines, in an essay he contributed to Umberto Eco's *Interpretation and Overinterpretation* (1992). There is a great difference, Rorty suggests,

> between knowing what you want to get out of a person or thing or text in advance and [on the other hand] hoping that the person or thing or text will help you want something different—that he or she or it will help you to change your purposes, and thus to change your life. This distinction, I think, helps us highlight the difference between methodical and inspired readings of texts. (106)

Rorty goes on to say he has seen an anthology of readings on Conrad's *Heart of Darkness,* containing a psychoanalytic reading, a reader-response reading, and so on. "None of the readers had, as far as I could see," Rorty says,

> been enraptured or destabilized by *Heart of Darkness.* I got no sense that the book had made a big difference to them, that they cared much about Kurtz or Marlow or the woman "with helmeted head and tawny cheeks" whom Marlow

sees on the bank of the river. These people, and that book, had no more changed these readers' purposes than the specimen under the microscope changes the purpose of the histologist. (107)

The kind of criticism that Rorty prefers he calls "unmethodical" criticism and "inspired" criticism. It is, for Rorty, the result of an "encounter" with some aspect of a work of art "which has made a difference to the critic's conception of who she is, what she is good for, what she wants to do with herself. . . " (107). This is not a matter of "respect" for the text, Rorty insists. Rather, he says, "love" and "hate" are better words, "For a great love or a great loathing is the sort of thing that changes us by changing our purposes, changing the uses to which we shall put people and things and texts we encounter later" (107).

📖 Suggestions for Further Reading

Because a massive list of titles may prove discouraging rather than helpful, it seems advisable here to give a short list of basic titles. (Titles already mentioned in this chapter—which are good places to begin—are *not* repeated in the following list.)

A good sampling of contemporary criticism (60 or so essays or chapters from books), representing all of the types discussed in this commentary except lesbian and gay criticism, can be found in *The Critical Tradition: Classic Texts and Contemporary Trends*, ed. David H. Richter (1989).

For a readable introduction to various approaches, written for students who are beginning the study of literary theory, see Steven Lynn, *Texts and Contexts* (1994). For a more advanced survey, that is, a work that assumes some familiarity with the material, see a short book by K. M. Newton, *Interpreting the Text: A Critical Introduction to the Theory and Practice of Literary Interpretation* (1990). A third survey, though considerably longer than the books by Lynn and Newton, is narrower because it confines itself to a study of critical writings about Shakespeare: Brian Vickers, *Appropriating Shakespeare: Contemporary Critical Quarrels* (1993), offers an astringent appraisal of deconstruction, New Historicism, psychoanalytic criticism, feminist criticism, and Marxist criticism. For a collection of essays on Shakespeare written from some of the points of view that Vickers deplores, see John Drakakis, ed., *Shakespearean Tragedy* (1992).

Sympathetic discussions (usually two or three pages long) of each approach, with fairly extensive bibliographic suggestions, are given in the appropriate articles in the four encyclopedic works by Harris, Makaryk, Groden and Kreiswirth, and Preminger and Brogan, listed on pages 88–89, at the end of Chapter 5, though only Groden and Kreiswirth (*Johns Hopkins Guide*) discuss lesbian and gay criticism (under "Gay Theory and

Criticism"). For essays discussing feminist, gender, Marxist, psychoanalytic, deconstructive, New Historicist, and cultural criticism—as well as other topics not covered in this chapter—see Stephen Greenblatt and Giles Gunn, eds., *Redrawing the Boundaries: The Transformation of English and American Literary Studies* (1992).

Formalist Criticism (The New Criticism)

Cleanth Brooks, *The Well Wrought Urn: Studies in the Structure of Poetry* (1947), especially Chapters 1 and 11 ("The Language of Paradox" and "The Heresy of Paraphrase"); W. K. Wimsatt, *The Verbal Icon* (1954), especially "The Intentional Fallacy" and "The Affective Fallacy"; Murray Krieger, *The New Apologists for Poetry* (1956); and, for an accurate overview of a kind of criticism often misrepresented today, Chapters 9-12 in volume 6 of René Wellek, *A History of Modern Criticism: 1750-1950* (1986).

Deconstruction

Christopher Norris, *Deconstruction: Theory and Practice* (1982); Vincent B. Leitch, *Deconstructive Criticism: An Advanced Introduction and Survey* (1983); Christopher Norris, ed., *What Is Deconstruction?* (1988); Christopher Norris, *Deconstruction and the Interests of Theory* (1989).

Reader-Response Criticism

Wolfgang Iser, *The Act of Reading: A Theory of Aesthetic Response* (1978); Wolfgang Iser, *Prospecting: From Reader Response to Literary Anthropology* (1993); Susan Sulleiman and Inge Crossman, eds., *The Reader in the Text* (1980); Jane P. Tompkins, ed. *Reader-Response Criticism* (1980); Norman N. Holland, *The Dynamics of Literary Response* (1973, 1989); Steven Mailloux, *Interpretive Conventions: The Reader in the Study of American Fiction* (1982).

Archetypal Criticism

G. Wilson Knight, *The Starlit Dome* (1941); Richard Chase, *Quest for Myth* (1949); Murray Krieger, ed., *Northrop Frye in Modern Criticism* (1966); Frank Lentricchia, *After the New Criticism* (1980).

Historical Criticism

For a brief survey of some historical criticism of the first half of this century, see René Wellek, *A History of Modern Criticism: 1750-1950,* volume 6 (1986), Chapter 4 ("Academic Criticism"). E. M. W. Tillyard, *The Elizabethan World Picture* (1943) and Tillyard's *Shakespeare's History Plays* (1944), both of which related Elizabethan literature to the beliefs of the age, are good examples of the historical approach.

Marxist Criticism

Raymond Williams, *Marxism and Literature* (1977); Tony Bennett, *Formalism and Marxism* (1979); Lydia Sargent, ed., *Women and Revolution: A Discussion of the Unhappy Marriage of Marxism and Feminism* (1981); and for a brief survey of American Marxist writers of the 1930s and 1940s, see Chapter 5 of volume 6 of René Wellek, *A History of Modern Criticism* (1986).

New Historicism

Stephen Greenblatt, *Renaissance Self-Fashioning from More to Shakespeare* (1980), especially the first chapter; Brook Thomas, *The New Historicism and Other Old-Fashioned Topics* (1991).

Biographical Criticism

Leon Edel, *Literary Biography* (1957); Estelle C. Jellinek, ed., *Women's Autobiography: Essays in Criticism* (1980); James Olney, *Metaphors of Self: The Meaning of Autobiography* (1981). Among the most distinguished twentieth-century literary biographies is Richard Ellmann, *James Joyce* (1959, rev. ed. 1982).

Psychological (or Psychoanalytical) Criticism

Edith Kurzweil and William Phillips, eds., *Literature and Psychoanalysis* (1983); Maurice Charney and Joseph Reppen, eds., *Psychoanalytic Approaches to Literature and Film* (1987); Madelon Sprengnether, *The Spectral Mother: Freud, Feminism, and Psychoanalysis* (1990); Frederick Crews, *Out of My System* (1975).

Gender (Feminist, and Lesbian and Gay) Criticism

Gayle Greene and Coppèlia Kahn, eds., *Making a Difference: Feminist Literary Criticism* (1985), including an essay by Bonnie Zimmerman on lesbian criticism; Catherine Belsey and Jane Moore, eds., *The Feminist Reader: Essays in Gender and the Politics of Literary Criticism* (1989); Toril Moi, ed., *French Feminist Thought* (1987); Elizabeth A. Flynn and Patrocinio P. Schweikart, eds., *Gender and Reading: Essays on Readers, Texts, and Contexts* (1986); Barbara Christian, *Black Feminist Criticism: Perspectives on Black Women Writers* (1985); Shoshana Felman, *What Does a Woman Want? Reading and Sexual Difference* (1993); Robert Martin, *The Homosexual Tradition in American Poetry* (1979). Henry Abelove et al., eds., *The Lesbian and Gay Studies Reader* (1993) has only a few essays concerning literature, but it has an extensive bibliography on the topic.

A last word: If you want to read only a few pages about the nature and value of criticism, look at Helen Vendler's introduction and "The Function of Criticism" in a collection of her essays, *The Music of What Happens* (1988). Vendler is aware that most criticism today is ideological—Marxist, Freudian, or whatever, and it is therefore concerned with the interpretation of meaning—but she is less concerned with ideology and meaning than with the causes of "the aesthetic power of the art work":

> It is natural that people under new cultural imperatives should be impelled to fasten new interpretations (from the reasonable to the fantastic) onto aesthetic objects from the past. But criticism cannot stop there. The critic may well begin, "Look at it this way for a change," but the sentence must continue, "and now don't you see it as more intelligibly beautiful and moving?" That is, if the interpretation does not reveal some hitherto occluded aspect of the aesthetic power of the art work, it is useless as art criticism (though it may be useful as cultural history or sociology or psychology or religion). (2)

PART 3

*Up Close:
Thinking Critically
about Literary Forms*

9

Writing about Essays

The word **essay** entered the English language in 1597, when Francis Bacon called a small book of ten short prose pieces *Essays*. Bacon borrowed the word from Michel de Montaigne, a French writer who in 1580 had published some short prose pieces under the title *Essais*—that is, "testings" or "attempts," from the French verb *essayer*, "to try." Montaigne's title indicated that his graceful and personal jottings—the fruit of pleasant study and meditation—were not fully thought-out treatises but rather sketches that could be amplified and amended.

If you keep a journal, you are working in Montaigne's tradition. You jot down your tentative thoughts, perhaps your responses to a work of literature, partly to find out what you think and how you feel. Montaigne said, in the preface to his book, "I am myself the subject of my book," and in all probability you are the real subject of your journal. Your entries, recorded responses to other writers and your reflections on those responses, require you to examine yourself.

SOME KINDS OF ESSAYS

If you have already taken a course in composition (or even if you haven't) you are probably familiar with the chief kinds of essays. Essays are usually classified—roughly, of course—along the following lines: **meditation** (or **speculation** or **reflection**); **argument** (or **persuasion**); **exposition** (or **information**); **narration** and **description.**

Of these, the **meditative** (or **speculative** or **reflective**) essay is the closest to Montaigne. In a meditative essay, the writer seems chiefly concerned with exploring an idea or a feeling. The organization usually seems casual, not a careful and evident structure but a free flow of thought—what the Japanese (who wrote with brush and ink) called "following the brush."

149

The essayist is thinking, but he or she is not especially concerned with arguing a case, or even with being logical. We think along with the essayist, chiefly because we find the writer's tentative thoughts engaging. Of course the writer may in the long run be pressing a point, advancing an argument, but the emphasis is on the free play of mind, not on an orderly and logical analysis.

In the **argumentative** (or **persuasive**) essay, the organization probably is apparent, and is reasonable: For instance, the writer may announce a problem, define some terms, present and refute solutions that the writer considers to be inadequate, and then, by way of a knock-down ending, offer what he or she considers to be the correct solution.

The **expository** essay, in which the writer is chiefly concerned with giving information (for instance on how to annotate a text, or how to read a poem, or how to use a word processor), ordinarily has an equally clear organization. Clear organization is necessary in such an essay because the reader is reading not in order to come into contact with an interesting mind that may keep doubling back on its thinking (as in a meditative essay), and not in order to come to a decision about some controversial issue (as in an argumentative essay), but in order to gain information.

Narrative and **descriptive** essays usually really are largely meditative essays. For instance, a narrative essay may recount some happening—often a bit of autobiography—partly to allow the writer and the reader to meditate on it. Similarly, a description, let's say of a spider spinning a web, or of children playing in the street, usually turns out to be offered not so much as information—it thus is unlike the account of how to annotate a text—but rather is offered as something for the writer and reader to enjoy in itself, and perhaps to think further about.

Of course most essays are not pure specimens. For instance, an informative essay, let's say on how to use a word processing program, may begin with a paragraph that seeks to persuade you to use this particular software. Or it might begin with a very brief narrative, an anecdote of a student who switched from one program to another program, again in order to persuade the reader to use this software. Similarly, an argument—and probably most of the essays that you write in English courses will be arguments advancing a thesis concerning the meaning or structure of a literary work—may include some exposition, for instance a very brief summary, in order to remind the reader of the gist of the work you will be arguing about.

THE ESSAYIST'S PERSONA

Many of the essays that give readers the most pleasure are, like entries in a journal, chiefly reflective. An essay of this kind sets forth the writer's attitudes or states of mind, and the reader's interest in the essay is almost entirely in the way the writer sees things. It's not so much *what* the writers see and say as *how* they say what they see. Even in narrative essays—essays that recount events, for example, a bit of biography—our interest is more in the essayists' *responses* to the events than in the events themselves. When we read an essay, we almost say, "So that's how it feels to be you," and "Tell me more about the way you see things." The bit of history is less important than the memorable presence of the writer.

When you read an essay, try to imagine the kind of person who wrote it, the kind of person who seems to be speaking it. Then slowly reread the essay, noticing *how* the writer conveyed this personality or persona or "voice" (even while he or she was writing about a topic "out there"). The writer's persona may be revealed, for example, by common or uncommon words, by short or long sentences, by literal or figurative language, or by offering familiar or erudite examples.

Let's take a simple, familiar example of words that establish a persona. Lincoln begins the Gettysburg Address with "Four score and seven years ago." He might have said "Eighty-seven years ago"—but the language would have lacked the biblical echo, and the persona would have been that of an ordinary person rather than that of a man who has about him something of the tone of an Old Testament prophet. This religious tone is entirely fitting, since President Lincoln was speaking at the dedication of a cemetery for "these hallowed dead" and was urging the audience to give all of their energies to ensure that the dead men had not died in vain.

By such devices as the **choice of words,** the **length of sentences,** and the **sorts of evidence** offered, an author sounds to the reader solemn or agitated or witty or genial or severe. If you read Martin Luther King's "I Have a Dream," you will notice that he begins his essay (originally it was a speech, delivered at the Lincoln Memorial on the one-hundredth anniversary of Lincoln's Emancipation Proclamation) with these words: "Five score years ago. . . ." King is deliberately echoing Lincoln's words, partly in tribute to Lincoln but also to help establish himself as the spiritual descendent of Lincoln and, further back, of the founders of the Judaeo-Christian tradition.

Tone

Only by reading closely can we hear in the mind's ear the writer's tone—whether it is ironic or earnestly straightforward, indignant or genial. Perhaps you have heard the line from Owen Wister's novel *The Virginian:* "When you call me that, smile." Words spoken with a smile mean something different from the same words forced through clenched teeth. But while speakers can communicate or, we might say, can guide the responses of their audience by body language and gestures, by facial expressions, and by changes in tone of voice, writers have only words in ink on paper. As a writer, you are learning control of tone; that is, you take pains in your choice of words, in the way you arrange sentences, and even in the punctuation marks you may find yourself changing in your final draft. These skills will pay off doubly if you apply them to your reading by putting yourself in the place of the writer whose work you are reading.

As a reader, you must make some effort to "hear" the writer's tone as part of the meaning the words communicate. Skimming is not adequate to that task. Thinking carefully about the works means, first of all, reading them carefully, listening for the sound of the speaking voice so that you can respond to the persona—the personality or character the author presents in the essay.

WRITING ABOUT AN ESSAYIST'S STYLE

Since much of the pleasure we receive from an essay is derived from the essayist's style—the *how* with which an essayist conveys an attitude toward some aspect of reality that is revealed—your instructor may ask you to analyze the writer's style.

Read the following essay by Joan Didion. While reading it, annotate it wherever you are inclined (you may want to express responses in the margin and to underline puzzling words or passages that strike you as especially effective or as especially clumsy). Then reread the essay; since you will now be familiar with the essay as a whole, you may want to make further annotations, such as brief comments on Didion's use of repetition or of short and long sentences.

Joan Didion, a fifth-generation Californian, was born in Sacramento in 1934. In 1956 she was graduated from the University of California, Berkeley, and in the same year she published her first story and won a contest sponsored by *Vogue* magazine. Since then she has written essays, stories, screenplays, and novels. All of her writing, she says, is an "act of saying *I*, of imposing oneself upon other people, of saying *listen to me, see it my way, change your mind.*"

Joan Didion
LOS ANGELES NOTEBOOK

There is something uneasy in the Los Angeles air this afternoon, some unnatural stillness, some tension. What it means is that tonight a Santa Ana will begin to blow, a hot wind from the northeast whining down through the Cajon and San Gorgonio Passes, blowing up sandstorms out along Route 66, drying the hills and nerves to the flash point. For a few days now we will see smoke back in the canyons, and hear sirens in the night. I have neither heard nor read that a Santa Ana is due, but I know it, and almost everyone I have seen today

knows it too. We know it because we feel it. The baby frets. The maid sulks. I
rekindle a waning argument with the telephone company, then cut my losses
and lie down, given over to whatever it is in the air. To live with the Santa Ana
is to accept, consciously or unconsciously, a deeply mechanistic view of human
behavior.

I recall being told, when I first moved to Los Angeles and was living on an   2
isolated beach, that the Indians would throw themselves into the sea when the
bad wind blew. I could see why. The Pacific turned ominously glossy during a
Santa Ana period, and one woke in the night troubled not only by the peacocks
screaming in the olive trees but by the eerie absence of surf. The heat was sur-
real. The sky had a yellow cast, the kind of light sometimes called "earthquake
weather." My only neighbor would not come out of her house for days, and
there were no lights at night, and her husband roamed the place with a ma-
chete. One day he would tell me that he had heard a trespasser, the next a rat-
tlesnake.

"On nights like that," Raymond Chandler once wrote about the Santa Ana,   3
"every booze party ends in a fight, meek little wives feel the edge of the carving
knife and study their husband's necks. Anything can happen." That was the kind
of wind it was. I did not know then that there was any basis for the effect it had
on all of us, but it turns out to be another of these cases in which science bears
out folk wisdom. The Santa Ana, which is named for one of the canyons it
rushes through, is a *foehn* wind, like the *foehn* of Austria and Switzerland and
the *hamsin* of Israel. There are a number of persistent malevolent winds, perhaps the best known of which are the mistral of France and the Mediterranean
sirocco, but a *foehn* wind has distinct characteristics: it occurs on the leeward
slope of a mountain range and, although the air begins as a cold mass, it is
warmed as it comes down the mountain and appears finally as a hot dry wind.
Whenever and wherever a *foehn* blows, doctors hear about headaches and nau-
sea and allergies, about "nervousness," about "depression." In Los Angeles
some teachers do not attempt to conduct formal classes during a Santa Ana because the children become unmanageable. In Switzerland the suicide rate goes
up during the *foehn,* and in the courts of some Swiss cantons the wind is considered a mitigating circumstance for crime. Surgeons are said to watch the wind,
because blood does not clot normally during a *foehn.* A few years ago an Israeli
physicist discovered that not only during such winds, but for the ten or twelve
hours which precede them, the air carries an unusually high ratio of positive to
negative ions. No one seems to know exactly why that should be; some talk
about friction and others suggest solar disturbances. In any case the positive
ions are there, and what an excess of positive ions does, in the simplest terms, is
make people unhappy. One cannot get much more mechanistic than that.

Easterners commonly complain that there is no "weather" at all in   4
Southern California, that the days and the seasons slip by relentlessly, numb-
ingly bland. That is quite misleading. In fact the climate is characterized by in-
frequent but violent extremes: two periods of torrential subtropical rains which
continue for several weeks and wash out the hills and send subdivisions sliding
toward the sea; about twenty scattered days a year of the Santa Ana, which,

with its incendiary dryness, invariably means fire. At the first prediction of a Santa Ana, the Forest Service flies men and equipment from northern California into the southern forests, and the Los Angeles Fire Department cancels its ordinary non-firefighting routines. The Santa Ana caused Malibu to burn the way it did in 1956, and Bel Air in 1961, and Santa Barbara in 1964. In the winter of 1966–67 eleven men were killed fighting a Santa Ana fire that spread through the San Gabriel Mountains.

Just to watch the front-page news out of Los Angeles during a Santa Ana   5 is to get very close to what it is about the place. The longest single Santa Ana period in recent years was in 1957, and it lasted not the usual three or four days but fourteen days, from November 21 until December 4. On the first day 25,000 acres of the San Gabriel Mountains were burning, with gusts reaching 100 miles an hour. In town, the wind reached Force 12, or hurricane force, on the Beaufort Scale; oil derricks were toppled and people ordered off the downtown streets to avoid injury from flying objects. On November 22 the fire in the San Gabriels was out of control. On November 24 six people were killed in automobile accidents, and by the end of the week the Los Angeles *Times* was keeping a box score of traffic deaths. On November 26 a prominent Pasadena attorney, depressed about money, shot and killed his wife, their two sons, and himself. On November 27 a South Gate divorcée, twenty-two, was murdered and thrown from a moving car. On November 30 the San Gabriel Fire was still out of control, and the wind in town was blowing eighty miles an hour. On the first day of December four people died violently, and on the third the wind began to break.

It is hard for people who have not lived in Los Angeles to realize how rad-   6 ically the Santa Ana figures in the local imagination. The city burning is Los Angeles's deepest image of itself: Nathanael West perceived that, in *The Day of the Locust;* and at the time of the 1965 Watts riots what struck the imagination most indelibly were the fires. For days one could drive the Harbor free-way and see the city on fire, just as we had always known it would be in the end. Los Angeles weather is the weather of catastrophe, of apocalypse, and, just as the reliably long and bitter winters of New England determine the way life is lived there, so the violence and the unpredictability of the Santa Ana af-fect the entire quality of life in Los Angeles, accentuate its impermanence, its unreliability. The wind shows us how close to the edge we are.

[1968]

Annotations and Journal Entries

While reading the essay a second time, one student planning to write on Didion's style here marked the first paragraph thus:

long sentence

There is something uneasy in the Los Angeles air this afternoon, some unnatural stillness some tension. What it means is that tonight a Santa Ana will begin to blow, a hot wind from the northeast whining down through the Cajon and San Gorgonio Passes, blowing up sandstorms out along Route 66, drying the hills and the nerves to the flash point. For a few days now we will see smoke back in the canyons, and hear sirens in the night. I have neither heard nor read that a Santa Ana is due, but I

short sentences

know it, and almost everyone I have seen today knows it too. We know it because we feel it. The baby frets. The maid sulks. I rekindle a waning argument with the telephone company, then cut my losses and lie down, given over to whatever it is in the air. To live with the Santa Ana is to ac-

thesis?

cept, consciously or unconsciously, a deeply mechanistic view of human behavior.

He marked other paragraphs in more or less the same way, and later in the day wrote the following entry in his journal:

Tuesday. She really seems to get the effect of this terrible, oppressive wind. Didion repeats a lot ("something . . . some . . . some," all in the first sentence). I think she is trying to give us the feel of a wind that won't let up, that keeps hammering at us and driving us crazy. But what persona do I find in this essay? I'm not sure. Sometimes she seems school-teacherish, with that lecture on foehn winds. And in paragraph 4 when she says "That is quite misleading," that's a little sharp. Maybe the wind is getting her down!!

Tuesday night. I'm still not all that wild about the tone in "That is quite misleading," but I guess "school-teacherish" isn't quite the way to describe Didion on the whole. How many school teachers read Raymond? She does sound a bit teachery in the first sentence of the last paragraph ("It is hard for people who have not lived in Los Angeles to realize that. . . ."), but I guess that a writer sometimes has to give a little lecture. Maybe when she says "It is hard, etc." she is really trying to be helpful, reassuring us that if we don't realize whatever her point is, we aren't therefore idiots. She knows that lots of her readers don't know much about L.A. so she is being helpful.

Later, drawing largely on his annotations in the text and on his entries in his journal, this student jotted down the following notes in preparation for drafting an essay on Didion's style in "Los Angeles Notebook":

```
persona (as revealed by style?)
    rather personal ("I recall being told," in parag. 1)
    sometimes a bit of the school teacher
        (for instance on foehn wind, in 3
        "This is quite misleading" in 4)
    but: very interesting; very informative; a good
        teacher she seems to know what she is talking
        about; details about foehn wind in par. 4; facts
        about what the Santa Ana did to Malibu in 1956,
        Bel Air in 1961, Santa Barbara in 1964.  Also
        facts about longest Santa Ana (14 days, in 1957)
        in parag. 5.
style (chief characteristics that I see)
    some long sentences and some short sentences
        long sentences: Second: 45 words; prob. longest
            in essay; no, longest is next-to-last, 53
            words!!!  The point?  Long, blowing,
            continuing wind?  Certainly seems so in 3d
            sentence, with wind "whining, blowing,
            drying"; it just keeps going on and on.
        short sentences: "We know it because we feel it.
        The baby frets. The maid sulks."
            The point?  Impatience?  Inability to think,
            to accomplish anything that takes a little
            time? General nervousness?
    repetition of words: "something," "some," "some" in
        first par. In 3, "about" appears three times in one
        sentence--and also three "ands" here.  So, length plus
        repetition = suggestion of the driving, continuing
        wind.
```

A Sample Essay on Joan Didion's Style

Ultimately, the student wrote the following short essay. You'll notice that it draws heavily on the notes on style and hardly at all on the notes on persona. Notes written during pre-writing are a source to draw on. Resist the temptation to work in, at all costs, everything you've produced.

Joan Didion's Style: Not Hot Air

In "Los Angeles Notebook" Joan Didion has a point to make. A sentence at the end of her first paragraph states the point concisely: "To live with the Santa Ana is to accept, consciously or unconsciously, a deeply mechanistic view of human behavior." But she doesn't simply make the point; her essay tries to make the point effectively, to make us <u>feel</u> the truth of what she says. I think she succeeds, partly because she knows what she is talking about (she gives lots of details about the destructive effects of the wind) and partly because she uses certain stylistic devices, especially very short and very long sentences, and repetition.

Her first sentence is probably of average length, but it repeats "some" (once in the form of "something") three times:

There is something uneasy in the Los Angeles air this afternoon, some unnatural stillness, some tension.

The sentence is not monotonous, but the repetition perhaps makes it seem a bit longer than it really is, and the repetition suggests a lack of change, a lack of progress. As the reader soon finds, it helps to suggest the driving and unchanging wind. The second sentence, forty-five words long, makes the point clear:

What it means is that tonight a Santa Ana will begin to blow, a hot wind from the northeast whining down through the Cajon and San

Gorgonio Passes, blowing up sandstorms out
along Route 66, drying the hills and the
nerves to the flash point.

The length of the sentence, and the use of whining,
blowing, and drying--continuous actions--makes the
sentence go on and on, giving an effect of the constant
wind.

The length of even this unusually long sentence is
exceeded by the next-to-last sentence in the essay,
fifty-three words about the catastrophic weather of Los
Angeles. But this next-to-last sentence, which again
suggests the relentless wind, is followed by a sentence
of only eleven words, and in fact Didion earlier in the
essay writes a number of fairly short or even very short
sentences. These short sentences, like the long ones,
contribute to the reader's response. If the long
sentences suggest the wind, the short sentences suggest
the nervousness, crankiness, or fidgetiness of the
person who experiences the wind, or who even only senses
the coming of the wind: "We know it because we feel it.
The baby frets. The maid sulks." These choppy
sentences seem to fret and sulk.

In "Los Angeles Notebook" Didion gives us many facts
about the destructive effect of the Santa Ana, which, she
explains, is a foehn wind. Her essay is informative and
she is a good teacher, but her most effective method of
teaching is not the use of facts but the use of a style
that helps the reader to feel the impact of the foehn.

📖 Suggestions for Further Reading

For a collection of essays, with a useful introduction, see Philip Lopate, ed., *The Art of the Personal Essay: An Anthology from the Classical Era to the Present* (1994). On the essay see also: Graham Good, *The Observing Self: Rediscovering the Essay* (1988); Alexander J. Butrym, ed., *Essays on the Essay: Redefining the Genre* (1989).

✓ A Checklist: Getting Ideas for Writing about Essays

Persona and Tone

1. What sort of *persona* does the writer create?
2. How does the writer create this persona? (For example, does the writer use colloquial language or formal language or technical language? Short sentences or long ones? Personal anecdotes? Quotations from authorities?)
3. What is the tone of the essay? Is it, for example, solemn, or playful? Is the tone consistent? If not, how do the shifts affect your understanding of the writer's point or your identification of the writer's persona?

Kind of Essay

1. What kind of essay is it? Is it chiefly a presentation of facts (for example, an exposition, a report, a history)? Or is it chiefly an argument? Or a meditation? (Probably the essay draws on several kinds of writing, but which kind is it primarily? How are the other kinds related to the main kind?)
2. What does it seem to add up to? If the essay is chiefly meditative or speculative, how much emphasis is placed on the persona? That is, if the essay is a sort of thinking-out-loud, is your interest chiefly in the announced or ostensible topic, or in the writer's mood and personality? If the essay is chiefly a presentation of facts, does it also have a larger implication? For instance, if it narrates a happening (history), does the reader draw an inference—find a meaning—in the happening? If the essay is chiefly an argument, what is the thesis? How is the thesis supported? (Is it supported, for example, by induction, deduction, analogy, or emotional appeal?) Do you accept the assumptions (explicit and implicit)?

Structure

1. Is the title appropriate? Propose a better title, if possible.
2. Did the opening paragraph interest you? Why, or why not? Did the essay continue more or less as expected, or did it turn out to be rather different from what you anticipated?

3. Prepare an outline of the essay. What effect does the writer seem to be aiming at by using this structure?

Value

1. What is especially good (or bad) about the essay? Is it logically persuasive? Or entertaining? Or does it introduce an engaging persona? Or (if it is a narrative) does it tell a story effectively, using (where appropriate) description, dialogue, and commentary, and somehow make you feel that this story is worth reporting?

2. Does the writer seem to hold values that you share? Or cannot share? Explain.

3. Do you think that most readers will share your response, or do you think that for some reason—for example, your age, or your cultural background—your responses are unusual? Explain.

10

Writing about Fiction: The World of the Story

PLOT AND CHARACTER

Plot has two chief meanings: (1) what happens, the gist of the narrative, and (2) the writer's arrangement or structuring of the material into a story. Thus, in the first sense all tellings of the life of Lincoln have the same plot, but in the second sense a writer who begins with the assassination and then gives the earlier material is setting forth a plot that differs from one given by a writer who begins at the beginning.

It is usual to say that a plot has an **introduction,** a **complication,** and a **resolution;** that is, it gets under way, then some difficulty or problem or complexity arises (usually a **conflict** of opposed wills or forces), and finally there is some sort of settling down. A somewhat metaphoric way of putting it is to say that the plot can often be seen as the tying and then the untying of a knot; the end is the **dénouement** (French for "untying").

Still another way of looking at the organization of the happenings in many works of fiction is to see the plot as a pyramid or triangle. The German critic Gustav Freytag, in *Techniques of the Drama* (1863), introduced this conception in examining the five-act structure of plays, but it can be applied to some fiction, too. In this view, we begin either with an unstable situation or with an apparently stable situation that is soon disrupted; that is, some difficulty or problem or complexity arises (usually a **conflict** of opposed wills or forces). The early happenings, with their increasing tension, constitute a **rising action,** which culminates in a **climax** or **crisis** or **turning point.** (The word *climax* comes from a Greek word meaning "ladder." Originally, the climax was the entire rising action, but the word has come to mean the high point or end of the rising action.) What follows the decisive moment is the **falling action,** which ends in a stable situation—a situation that the reader takes to be final. Of course, the characters need not die; the reader feels, however, that nothing more is to be said about them. Here is a diagram showing Freytag's Pyramid. Remember, however, that a story *need* not have this structure.

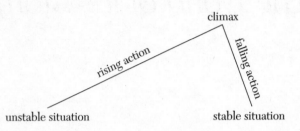

Early fiction tends to have a good deal of physical action—wanderings, strange encounters, births, and deaths. But in some fiction, little seems to happen. These apparently plotless stories, however, usually involve a *mental action*—a significant perception, a decision, a failure of the will—and the process of this mental action is the plot.

The sense of causality is in part rooted in **character.** Things happen, in most good fiction, at least partly because the people have certain personalities or characters (moral, intellectual, and emotional qualities) and, given their natures, because they respond plausibly to other personalities. What their names are and what they look like may help you understand them, but probably the best guide to characters is what they do. As we get to know more about their drives and goals—especially the choices they make—we enjoy seeing the writer complete the portraits, finally presenting us with a coherent and credible picture of people in action. In this view, plot and character are inseparable. Plot is not simply a series of happenings, but happenings that come out of character, that reveal character, and that influence character. Henry James puts it thus: "What is character but the determination of incident? What is incident but the illustration of character?" But, of course, characters are not defined only by what they do. The narrator often describes them, and the characters' words and dress reveal aspects of them.

You may want to set forth a character sketch, describing some person in the story or novel. You will probably plan to convey three things:

appearance,
personality, and

character—"character" here meaning not a figure in a literary work but the figure's moral or ethical values.

Of course, "character" in this sense may not be utterly distinct from "personality," but personality is more a matter of psychology than of ethics. For example, wit, irritability, and fastidiousness can be regarded as parts of personality, but generosity, cowardice, and temperance can be regarded as parts of character or of morality. The distinction is not always clear, but it is evident enough when we speak of someone as "a diamond in the rough." We probably mean that the person is morally solid (a matter of character) though given to odd or even rude expressions of personality.

In preparing a character sketch, take these points into consideration:

1. What the person says (but remember that what he or she says need not be taken at face value; the person may be hypocritical or self-deceived or biased)
2. What the person does
3. What others (including the narrator of the story) say about the person
4. What others do (their actions may help indicate what the person could do but does not do)
5. What the person looks like—face, body, clothes. These may help convey the personality, or they may in some measure help disguise it.

Writing about a Character

A character sketch (remember—we have made a distinction between character and personality, but when one speaks of a "character sketch" one means all aspects of a figure in a work of literature, *not* simply the moral sense), such as "Holden Caulfield: Adolescent Snob or Suffering Saint?" may be complex and demanding, especially if the character (the figure) is complex. Notice that in the example just referred to, the writer sees that Holden might (at least at first glance) be interpreted in two very different ways, a snob or a saint. In fact, the student who wrote the essay argued that Holden has touches of the adolescent snob but is chiefly a suffering saint.

An essay on a character, you will recall, is necessarily in some degree an interpretation, and, thus, even such an essay has a thesis or argument holding it together. Usually, however, you will want to do more than set forth your view of a character. Probably, you will discuss the character's function or contrast him or her with other characters or trace the development of personality. (One of the most difficult topics, the character of the narrator, will be discussed later in this chapter, under the heading "Point of View.") You probably will still want to keep in mind the five suggestions for getting

at a character (as well as others on page 163), but you will also want to go
further, relating your findings to additional matters of the sort we will examine now.

Organizing an Analysis of a Character

As you read and reread, you will highlight and annotate the text and will jot
down notes, recording (in whatever order they come to you) your thoughts
about the character you are studying. Reading with a view toward writing,
you'll want to

1. jot down traits as they come to mind ("kind," "forgetful," "enthusias-
   tic"); and
2. look back at the text, searching for supporting evidence (characteristic
   actions, brief supporting quotations), and of course you will also look
   for counterevidence so that you may modify your earlier impressions.

Brainstorming leads to an evaluation and a shaping of your ideas.
Evaluating and shaping lead to a tentative outline. A tentative outline leads
to the search for supporting evidence—the material that will constitute the
body of your essay.

When you set out to write a first draft, review your annotations and
notes, and see if you can summarize your view of the character in one or
two sentences:

X is. . . .

or

Although X is. . . , she is also. . . .

That is, *try to formulate a thesis sentence or a thesis paragraph*—a proposition that you will go on to support.

You want to let your reader know early, probably in your first sentence—and almost certainly by the end of your first paragraph—which
character you are writing about and what your overall thesis is.

The body of your essay will be devoted to supporting your thesis. If you
have asserted that although so-and-so is cruel and domineering he nevertheless is endowed with a conscience, you will go on in your essay to support those assertions with references to passages that demonstrate them.
This support does *not* mean that you tell the plot of the whole work; an essay on a character is by no means the same as a summary of the plot. Since
you must support your generalizations, you will have to make brief references to specific episodes that reveal his personality, and almost surely you
will quote an occasional word or passage.

An essay on a character may be organized in many possible ways. Much will depend on your purpose and thesis. For instance, you may want to show how the character develops—gains knowledge or matures or disintegrates. Or you may want to show what the character contributes to the story or play as a whole. Or, to give yet another example, you may want to show that the character is unbelievable. Still, although no single organization is always right, two methods are common and effective.

One effective way of organizing an essay on a character is to let the organization of your essay follow closely the sequence of the literary work; that is, you might devote a paragraph to the character as we first perceive him or her and then in subsequent paragraphs go on to show that this figure is later seen to be more complex than he or she at first appears. Such an essay may trace your changing responses.

A second effective way of organizing an essay on a character is to set forth, early in the essay, the character's chief traits—let's say the chief strengths and two or three weaknesses—and then go on to study each trait you have listed. The organization would (in order to maintain the reader's interest) probably begin with the most obvious points and then move on to the less obvious, subtler points. The body of your essay, in any case, is devoted to offering evidence that supports your generalizations about the character.

What about a concluding paragraph? The concluding paragraph ought *not* to begin with the obviousness of "Thus, we see," or "In conclusion," or "I recommend this story because. . . ." In fact, after you have given what you consider to be a sound sketch of the character, it may be appropriate simply to quit. Especially if your essay has moved from the obvious traits to the more subtle and more important traits, and if your essay is fairly short (say, fewer than 500 words), a reader may not need a conclusion. Further, why blunt what you have just said by adding an unnecessary and merely repetitive summary? If you do feel that a conclusion is necessary, you may find it effective to write a summary of the character, somewhat as you did in your opening. For the conclusion, relate the character's character to the entire literary work; that is, try to give the reader a sense of the role that the character plays.

A Sample Essay on a Character: "Holden's Kid Sister"

A student decided to write about Phoebe, Holden Caulfield's sister in J. D. Salinger's *The Catcher in the Rye*. Before writing, he reread the book, highlighting certain passages about Phoebe. He then reviewed the text and jotted down some key ideas, reproduced on the next page.

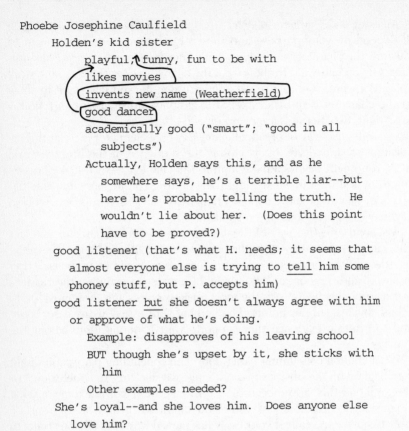

```
Phoebe Josephine Caulfield
    Holden's kid sister
            playful, funny, fun to be with
            likes movies
            invents new name (Weatherfield)
            good dancer
            academically good ("smart"; "good in all
                subjects")
            Actually, Holden says this, and as he
                somewhere says, he's a terrible liar--but
                here he's probably telling the truth.  He
                wouldn't lie about her.  (Does this point
                have to be proved?)
        good listener (that's what H. needs; it seems that
            almost everyone else is trying to tell him some
            phoney stuff, but P. accepts him)
        good listener but she doesn't always agree with him
            or approve of what he's doing.
            Example: disapproves of his leaving school
            BUT though she's upset by it, she sticks with
                him
            Other examples needed?
        She's loyal--and she loves him.  Does anyone else
            love him?
```

This material provided much of the first draft, which was submitted to peer review. The student then revised the draft, partly in accordance with the suggestions offered and partly in the light of his own further thinking. Here is the final version.

Holden's Kid Sister

Phoebe Josephine Caulfield, Holden's ten-year-old sister in J. D. Salinger's The Catcher in the Rye, is a child with a mind of her own. She doesn't care for her middle name, and so on the first page of one of her many notebooks she gives herself a new one: "Phoebe Weatherfield Caulfield." She is, we gather, playful and imaginative, but she is also in touch with reality, and able to get along well in the world. She has friends, and at school she is "good in all subjects." The quality that most impresses a reader, however, is not her academic success but her loyalty to Holden, and even when she criticizes Holden she does so out of deep love for him.

Since Holden is the narrator of the book, all that we know of Phoebe is seen through his eyes, but there is no reason to doubt his comments about her. Fairly early in the book, in Chapter 10, he gives us a long description, in the course of which he says that she is "pretty and smart," a redhead, "skinny," and (more important, of course) "affectionate." Later Holden tells us that she shares his taste in movies, and that she is a perfect partner when she dances with him. That is, Phoebe is on Holden's wave-length; the two can move in harmony, and not only when they dance. For instance, she is a good listener, and Holden desperately needs someone who can listen to him, since most of the people in his world are big talkers and are trying to impose their own values on him.

This is not to say, however, that Phoebe approves of all of Holden's actions. When she learns that he has left school, she is upset with him, but the reader always feels that any criticism she makes proceeds from her love for Holden. She is so loyal to him that she wants to leave school and go with him when he tells her

he plans to run away from New York and hitchhike to the
West. Her loyalty, her refusal to leave him, causes him
to abandon his desperate plan to flee.

Her sincerity and her love for Holden are not enough
to restore him to mental health (at the end of the book
we learn that he "got sick and all," and is now in some
sort of asylum), but the reader knows that if any
character in the book can provide the human warmth that
Holden requires, that character is his bright, strong-
willed, loving "kid sister."

A few comments on this essay:

1. The title is informative and at least moderately interesting—more interesting, for example, than "Phoebe Caulfield."

2. The writer does not cite pages because the instructor did not ask him to do so, but if your instructor asks you to give references, use the form prescribed. (On citations, see pages 324–30.)

3. The opening paragraph announces the topic, gives a brief description of Phoebe (her age, her imaginativeness), and ends by focusing on her most important trait, her love for Holden.

4. The body of the essay (paragraphs 2 and 3) offers a few additional minor details, but chiefly it supports (by means of the comment on dancing) the earlier generalization that Phoebe is uniquely in harmony with Holden. It does not summarize the plot, but it does refer to certain episodes, and it interprets them in order to show how they reveal Phoebe's character.

5. The final paragraph, the fourth, offers additional support (her plan to run away with Holden), and it concludes with a glance at the conclusion of the novel. Thus the essay more or less echoes the chronology of the book, but these last sentences are not mere plot-telling. Rather, they solidify the writer's view of Phoebe's character and her importance to Holden.

FORESHADOWING

The writer of fiction provides a coherent world in which the details work together. **Foreshadowing,** which eliminates surprise or at least greatly reduces it and thus destroys a story that has nothing except a surprise ending to offer, is a powerful tool in the hands of the writer of serious fiction. Even in such a story as Faulkner's "A Rose for Emily," in which we are surprised to learn near the end that Miss Emily has slept beside the decaying corpse of her dead lover, from the outset we expect something strange; that is, we are not surprised by the surprise, only by its precise nature. The first sentence of the story tells us that after Miss Emily's funeral (the narrator begins at the end) the townspeople cross her threshold "out of curiosity to see the inside of her house, which no one save an old manservant . . . had seen in at least ten years." As the story progresses, we see Miss Emily prohibiting people from entering the house, and we hear that after a certain point no one ever sees Homer Barron again, that "the front door remained closed," and (a few paragraphs before the end of the story) that the townspeople "knew that there was one room in that region above the stairs which no one had seen in forty years." The paragraph preceding the revelation that "the man himself lay in bed" is devoted to a description of Homer's dust-covered clothing and toilet articles. In short, however much we are unprepared for the precise revelation, we are prepared for some strange thing in the house; and, given Miss Emily's purchase of poison and Homer's disappearance, we have some idea of what will be revealed.

Joyce's "Araby" (it is printed on page 352) is another example of a story in which the beginning is a preparation for all that follows. Consider the first two paragraphs:

> North Richmond Street, being blind, was a quiet street except at the hour when the Christian Brothers' school set the boys free. An uninhabited house of two stories stood at the blind end, detached from its neighbours in a square ground. The other houses of the street, conscious of decent lives within them, gazed at one another with brown imperturbable faces.
>
> The former tenant of our house, a priest, had died in the back drawing-room. Air, musty from having been long enclosed, hung in all the rooms, and the waste room behind the kitchen was littered with old useless papers. Among these I found a few paper-covered books, the pages of which were curled and damp: *The Abbot,* by Walter Scott, *The Devout Communicant* and *The Memoirs of Vidocq.* I liked the last best because its leaves were yellow. The wild garden behind the house contained a central apple-tree and a few straggling bushes under one of which I found the late tenant's rusty bicycle pump. He had been a very charitable priest; in his will he had left all his money to institutions and the furniture of his house to his sister.

Of course the full meaning of the passage will not become apparent until you have read the entire story. In a sense, a story has at least three lives:

- when we read the story, sentence by sentence, trying to turn the sequence of sentences into a consistent whole;

- when we have finished reading the story and we think back on it as a whole, even if we think no more than "That was a waste of time"; and
- when we reread a story, knowing already even as we read the first line how it will turn out at the end.

Let's assume that you have not read the whole of "Araby." On the basis only of a reading of the first two paragraphs, what might you highlight or underline? Here are the words that one student marked:

blind	musty
quiet	kitchen was littered
set the boys free	leaves were yellow
brown imperturbable faces	wild garden . . . apple-tree
priest	charitable priest

No two readers will come up with exactly the same list (if you live on North Richmond Street, you will probably underline it and put an exclamation mark in the margin; if you attended a parochial school, you'll probably underline "Christian Brothers' school"), but perhaps most readers, despite their varied experience, would agree that Joyce is giving us a picture of what he elsewhere called the "paralysis" of Ireland. How the story will turn out is, of course, unknown to a first-time reader. Perhaps the paralysis will increase, or perhaps it will be broken. Joyce goes on adding sentence to sentence, trying to shape the reader's response, and the reader goes on reading, making meaning out of the sentences.

As we read further in the story, we are not surprised to learn that the boy for a while manufactured quasi-religious experiences, religion being dead—remember the dead priest and his rusty bicycle pump. In his ears, shop-boys sing "litanies," his girlfriend's name springs to his lips "in strange prayers," and his vision of her is a "chalice" that he carries "safely through a throng of foes." He plans to visit a bazaar, and he promises to bring her a gift; but after he has with some difficulty arrived at the bazaar, he is vastly disappointed by the trivial conversation of the attendants, by the counting of the day's receipts (money-changers in the temple), and by the darkness ("the upper part of the hall was now completely dark"). The last line of the story runs thus: "Gazing up into the darkness I saw myself as a creature driven and derided by vanity; and my eyes burned with anguish and anger." Everything in the story coheres; the dead-end street, the dead priest, the rusty pump—all are perfect preludes to this story about a boy's recognition of the nothingness that surrounds him. The "vanity" that drives and derides him is not only the egotism that moved him to think he could bring the girl a fitting gift but also the nothingness that is spoken of in the biblical "Vanity of vanities, all is vanity."

In preparing to write about foreshadowing,

- Reread the story; now that you know how it ends, you will be able to see how certain early details are relevant to the ending.
- Underline or highlight these details, and perhaps jot down brief notes in the margins, such as "images of emptiness" or "later turns out ironically."
- At a later stage in the process of writing, you probably will find it useful to jot down on a sheet of paper key phrases from the text and to annotate them with such comments as "The first of many religious images" and "same image appears later."

Organizing an Essay on Foreshadowing

What is the best way to organize an essay on foreshadowing? Probably you will work through the evidence chronologically, though your initial paragraph may discuss the end and indicate that the remainder of the essay will be concerned with tracing the way in which the author prepares the reader for this end and simultaneously maintains the right amount of suspense. If the suspense is too slight, we stop reading, not caring what comes next. If it is too great, we are perhaps reading a story in which the interest depends entirely on some strange happening rather than a story with sufficiently universal application to make it worthy of a second reading.

Your essay may study the ways in which details gain in meaning as the reader gets farther into the story. Or it may study the author's failure to keep details relevant and coherent, the tendency to introduce material for its momentary value at the expense of the larger design. An essay on an uneven story may do both: It may show that although there are unfortunate irrelevancies, considerable skill is used in arousing and interestingly fulfilling the reader's expectations. If you feel that the story is fundamentally successful, the organization of your thoughts may reflect your feelings. After an initial paragraph stating the overall position, you may discuss the failures and then go on at greater length to discuss the strengths, ending strongly on your main point. If you feel that the story is essentially a failure, perhaps first discuss its merits briefly and then go on to your main point—the unsatisfactory nature of the story. To reverse this procedure would be to leave the reader with an impression contrary to your thesis.

SETTING AND ATMOSPHERE

Foreshadowing normally makes use of **setting.** The setting or environment in the first two paragraphs of Joyce's "Araby" is not mere geography, not mere locale: It provides an **atmosphere,** an air that the characters breathe, a world in which they move. Narrowly speaking, the setting is the physical surroundings—the furniture, the architecture, the landscape, the climate— and these often are highly appropriate to the characters who are associated with them. Thus, in Emily Brontë's *Wuthering Heights* the passionate Earnshaw family is associated with Wuthering Heights, the storm-exposed moorland, whereas the mild Linton family is associated with Thrushcross Grange in the sheltered valley below. Hawthorne's "Young Goodman Brown" also has two settings, Salem in the daytime and a nearby forest at night. A reader of the story probably consciously or unconsciously comes to believe that Salem is associated with order, decency, the good, and the dark forest with chaos and evil.

Broadly speaking, setting includes not only the physical surroundings but a point or several points in time. The background against which we see the characters and the happenings may be specified as morning or evening, spring or fall, and this temporal setting in a good story will probably be highly relevant; it will probably be part of the story's meaning, perhaps providing an ironic contrast (think of the festive, carnival setting in Poe's "The Cask of Amontillado," a story of a murder) or perhaps exerting an influence on the characters.

Note: Although your instructor may ask you to write a paragraph describing the setting, more often he or she will want something more complicated, such as an essay on the *function* of the setting. For such an essay, you may find it useful to begin with a paragraph or two describing the setting or settings, but be sure to go on to analyze the significance of this material.

SYMBOLISM

Writers of fiction do not write only about things that have happened to them. They write about things they have seen or heard, and also about thoughts and emotions.

Inevitably, writers use symbols. Symbols are neither puzzles nor colorful details but are among the concrete embodiments that give the story whatever accuracy it has. For instance, in "Ripe Figs" (p. 3), Maman-Nainaine tells Babette that when the figs are ripe Babette can visit her cousins. Of course Maman may merely be setting an arbitrary date, but as we read the story we probably feel—because of the emphasis on the *ripening* of the figs, which occurs in the spring or early summer—that the ripening of the figs in some way suggests the maturing of Babette. If we do get such ideas, we will in effect be saying that the story is not simply an anecdote about an old woman whose behavior is odd. True, the narrator of the story, after telling us of Maman-Nainaine's promise, adds, "Not that the ripening of figs had the least thing to do with it, but that is the way Maman-Nainaine was." That is, the narrator sees nothing special—merely Maman-Nainaine's eccentricity—in the connection between the ripening of the figs and Babette's visit to her cousins. Readers, however, may see more than the narrator sees or says. They may see in Babette a young girl maturing; they may see in Maman-Nainaine an older woman who, almost collaborating with nature, helps Babette to mature.

Let's assume that if writers use symbols, they want readers to perceive—at least faintly—that certain characters or places or seasons or happenings have rich implications, stand for something more than what they are on the surface. How do writers help us to perceive these things? *By emphasizing them*—for instance, by describing them at some length, or *by introducing them at times when they might not seem strictly necessary*, or *by calling attention to them repeatedly*.

Consider, for example, Chopin's treatment of the season in which "The Story of an Hour" (p. 13) takes place. The story has to take place at *some* time, but Chopin does not simply say, "On a spring day," or an autumn day, or whatever, and let things go at that. Rather, she tells us about the sky, the trees, the rain, the twittering sparrows—and all of this in an extremely short story in which we might think there is no time for talk about the setting. After all, none of this material is strictly necessary to a story about a woman who has heard that her husband was killed in an accident, who grieves, then recovers, and then dies when he suddenly reappears.

Why, then, does Chopin give such emphasis to the season? Probably because she is using the season symbolically. In this story, the spring is not just a bit of detail added for realism. Chopin puts considerable emphasis on it, loading it with suggestions of renewal, of the new life that Louise achieves for a moment. But here, a caution. To say that the spring in this story is symbolic is not to say that whenever spring appears in a story it always stands for renewal—or that whenever winter appears it always stands for death. Nor does it mean that since spring recurs, Louise will be reborn. In short, in *this* story Chopin uses the season to convey certain specific implications.

Is the railroad also a symbol? Probably not—though readers may disagree. I think that the railroad accident in "The Story of an Hour" is just a railroad accident, essential to the plot but not to our sense of what the story is about. Chopin doesn't seem to be using this even to say something about (for instance) modern travel, or about industrialism. The steam-propelled railroad train could of course be used symbolically, to say something about industrialism displacing an agrarian economy, but does Chopin give her train any such association? If she had wished to do so, she would probably have talked about the enormous power of the train, she would have let us hear the shriek of its whistle, and let us see the smoke pouring out of the smokestack and the intense fire burning in the engine, or let us sense its indifference as it charged through the countryside, defacing the landscape and displacing farm workers. Had she done so, it would be a different story. Or she might have made the train a symbol of fate overriding human desires, but, again, she does not endow her train with such suggestions. She gives virtually no emphasis to the train, so it is reasonable to believe that it has virtually no significance for the reader. (Incidentally, Chopin's father had died in a train accident, and so it is conceivable that the episode in the story has some special significance for Chopin, but that is a matter for a psychoanalytic interpretation.)

A Sample Essay on Setting as Symbol: "Spring Comes to Mrs. Mallard"

The following essay is about Kate Chopin's "The Story of an Hour" (page 13). If you have not yet read the story, take a moment now to do so.

Amy Jones, a first-year student, has kindly provided her last notes, a scratch outline that guided her while she wrote her first draft. Not all of the notes ended up in the final version, of course, but they obviously were a great help in shaping the essay.

```
thesis: setting here not place but time--springtime
title?
        Chopin and Spring
        Chopin's Spring
        Mrs. M's Spring
        Mrs. M's Symbolic Spring
        Spring in "The Story of an Hour"
        Spring Comes to Mrs. M
        Setting as Symbol
        Setting as Symbol: Spring in . . .

setting in "Hour"
Define setting??? place and time
        Chopin doesn't give date (or city); but in a house
spring:
        "the tops of the trees . . . were all aquiver with
            the new spring" (parag. 5)
        "sparrows were twittering in the eaves" (parag. 5)
        "There were patches of blue sky showing here and
            there through the clouds" (parag. 6)
```

why clouds? brightness pushing through
darkness, like joyous new life pushing aside
grief???

~~"spring days and summer days" special significance
of summer?? Or just means "lots of days"?~~

~~old way of life~~

~~"Louise, open the door! I beg; open the door"~~

elixir (near end) medicine???

doctors say died of heart disease

End with a quotation? Or with something about life
turning to death?

*Title implies
thesis.
Opening
paragraph
identifies author
and story; topic
(setting) is
introduced.*

Spring Comes to Mrs. Mallard

In reading Kate Chopin's "The Story of an
Hour" a reader is hardly aware of where the
story is set. We are not told the country or
the city, or the period, and so (if we think
about it at all) we probably assume the story
is set during Chopin's own lifetime, perhaps
even during the year in which she wrote it, in
Chopin's own territory, although there really
is nothing very specific about Louisiana in
this story. Nor do we learn, at the very
beginning of the story, whether the action is
taking place indoors or outdoors. However,
since the story begins by telling us that Mrs.
Mallard's sister, Josephine, gently broke the
news of the death of Mr. Mallard, we probably
assume it is taking place at Mrs. Mallard's
house. This assumption is confirmed a little
later, when we hear that Mrs. Mallard, once

*Transition
("But") leads to
next point (that
the season is
emphasized).*

she had heard the terrible news, "went away to
her room alone" (13).

But if Kate Chopin doesn't tell us
anything about the society in which the
figures in the story live, she tells us quite

a bit about the time of the year during which the story takes place. The story is very short--only about two and a half pages--but Chopin finds space in which to tell us not only that the time was spring, but also that from a window in her room Mrs. Mallard

Quotation introduced as supporting evidence (set off because it is longer than four lines).

> could see the tops of trees that were all aquiver with the new spring life. The delicious breath of rain was in the air. In the street below a peddler was crying his wares. The notes of a distant song which some one was singing finally reached her faintly, and countless sparrows were twittering in the eaves.(13)

This is the fullest description of the time of year in the story, but there are other shorter references, so we can say that the springtime is given considerable emphasis, considering how short the story is. For

Brief quotations used as additional evidence.

instance, the quoted paragraph is followed by a shorter paragraph that mentions "patches of blue sky" (13), and in fact "blue sky is mentioned again, two paragraphs later. There is nothing especially remarkable about the sky being blue, and so one might wonder why Chopin bothers to tell us that the sky is blue when she doesn't even tell us where her story is set. And then, in the next paragraph, she tells us more about the sky: "There was something coming to her. . . . What was it? She did not know. . . . But she felt it creeping out of the sky, reaching toward her through the sounds, the scents, the color that filled the air" (13).

Thesis is further clarified.

Given this emphasis on the spring air, we can now see that Chopin is contrasting two aspects of setting, the season versus the place, springtime versus the closed room. The spring air is invading the room in which Mrs.Mallard has locked herself. At first Mrs. Mallard resists the mysterious invasion: "She was beginning to recognize this thing that was approaching to possess her, and she was striving to beat it back" (13), but, the reader comes to understand, "this thing" is the spirit of "the new spring life" which, we learned earlier in the story, set the tops of the trees aquiver. The trees, the swallows, and the blue sky are signs of the spring, and the spring symbolizes life. The locked room, where Mrs. Mallard goes to grieve, is a place of mourning, of death, but Mrs. Mallard is a living creature and though she sincerely grieves she cannot shut out life.

Thesis is hammered home.

Now it is clear why Chopin did not bother to tell us in what city, or even in what kind of house, the action takes place. It doesn't matter. What does matter is the feeling of new life that Mrs. Mallard feels, and this can best be shown by relating it to springtime, a time of new life.

Concluding paragraph furthers the argument (passage about "elixer") and also, in its final sentences, wraps up essay.

Even though she has confined herself to her room, through the window Mrs. Mallard drinks the spring air. In Chopin's words, "She was drinking in the very elixir of life through that open window" (14). An elixir, according to The American Heritage Dictionary, Third Edition, is "a substance believed to maintain life indefinitely." This word is an effective word to describe the way Mrs. Mallard feels, as the sights and sounds of spring press upon her and give her a new sense of life. But of course although spring renews life indefinitely, each year bringing new vegetation, people do not live indefinitely. In fact Mrs. Mallard will live for less than an hour. Chopin does not make it clear to a reader whether Mrs. Mallard dies because she really has "heart trouble," as we are told in the first paragraph, or because she has lived an intense spring moment as an individual and so she cannot stand the thought of a lifetime with her husband. But what is perfectly clear is that one aspect of the setting--springtime, a season full of new life--is essential to convey to the reader a sense of Mrs. Mallard's new (and tragically brief) feelings.

[New page]

Work Cited

Documentation Chopin, Kate. "The Story of an Hour." Rpt. in Sylvan Barnet, A Short Guide to Writing about Literature. 7th ed. New York: HarperCollins, 1996. 13-14.

POINT OF VIEW

The Dublin in "Araby" (p. 352) is the Dublin that James Joyce thought existed, but it must be remembered that although an author *writes* a story, someone else *tells* it. We hear the story from a particular **point of view,** and this point of view in large measure determines our response to the story. A wide variety of terms has been established to name differing points of view, but the following labels are among the commonest. We may begin with two categories: third-person points of view (in which the narrator is, in the crudest sense, not a participant in the story) and first-person points of view (in which the "I" who narrates the story plays a part in it).

Third-Person Narrators

The **third-person point of view** itself has several subdivisions. At one extreme is the **omniscient narrator,** who knows everything that is going on and can tell us the inner thoughts of all the characters. The omniscient narrator may editorialize, pass judgments, reassure the reader, and so forth, in which case he or she may sound like the author. Here is Thomas Hardy's editorially omniscient narrator in *Tess of the D'Urbervilles,* telling the reader that Tess was mistaken in imagining that the countryside proclaimed her guilt:

> But this encompassment of her own characterization, based upon shreds of convention, peopled by phantoms and voices antipathetic to her, was a sorry and mistaken creation of Tess's fancy—a cloud of moral hobgoblins by which she was terrified without reason.

Still, even this narrator is not quite Hardy; he does not allude to his other books, his private life, or his hope that the book will sell. If he is Hardy, he is only one aspect of Hardy, quite possibly a fictional Hardy, a disembodied voice with particular characteristics.

Another sort of third-person narrator, **selective omniscient,** takes up what Henry James called a "center of consciousness," revealing the thoughts of one of the characters but (for the most part) seeing the rest of the characters from the outside only. Wayne Booth, in a thoughtful study of Jane Austen's *Emma,* explains the effectiveness of selective omniscience in this novel. He points out that Emma is intelligent, witty, beautiful, and rich. But she is flawed by pride, and, until she discovers and corrects her fault, she almost destroys herself and her friends. How may such a character be made sympathetic, so that we will hope for the happy conclusion to the comedy? "The solution to the problem of maintaining sympathy despite almost crippling faults," Booth says,

> was primarily to use the heroine herself as a kind of narrator, though in third person, reporting on her own experience.... By showing most of the story through Emma's eyes, the author insures that we shall travel with Emma rather than stand against her. It is not simply that Emma provides, in the unimpeachable evidence of her own conscience, proof that she has many redeeming qualities that do not appear on the surface; such evidence could be given with authorial commentary, though perhaps not with such force and con-

viction. Much more important, the sustained inside view leads the reader to hope for good fortune for the character with whom he travels, quite independently of the qualities revealed.

—*The Rhetoric of Fiction,* 2nd ed. (Chicago, 1983), pp. 245-46

Booth goes on to point out in a long and careful analysis that "sympathy for Emma can be heightened by withholding inside views of others as well as by granting them of her."

In writing about point of view, one tries to suggest what the author's choice of a particular point of view contributes to the story. Wayne Booth shows how Jane Austen's third-person point of view helps keep sympathetic a character who otherwise might be less than sympathetic. Notice that Booth states the problem—how to draw an intelligent but proud woman so that the reader will wish for a happy ending—and he presents his answer convincingly, moving from "It is not simply . . . ." to "Much more important . . . ." (To reverse the order would cause a drop in interest.) He then moves from a discussion of the inside treatment of Emma to the outside treatment of the other characters, thus substantiating and enlarging his argument.

Possibly one could reverse this procedure, beginning with a discussion of the treatment of the characters other than Emma and then closing in on Emma, but such an essay may seem slow in getting under way. The early part may appear unfocused. The reader will for a while be left wondering why in an essay on point of view in *Emma* the essayist does not turn to the chief matter, the presentation of the central character.

The third-person narrator, then, although not in the ordinary sense a character in the story, is an important voice in the story, who helps give shape to it. Another type of third-person narrator is the so-called **effaced narrator.** (Some critics use the term **dramatic point of view** or **objective point of view.**) This narrator does not seem to exist, for (unlike the editorially omniscient narrator) he or she does not comment in his or her own voice and (unlike the omniscient and selective omniscient narrators) does not enter any minds. It is almost improper to speak of an effaced narrator as "he" or "he or she," for no evident figure is speaking. The reader hears dialogue and sees only what a camera or a fly on the wall would see. The following example is from Hemingway's "The Killers":

> The door of Henry's lunchroom opened and two men came in. They sat down at the counter.
> "What's yours?" George asked them.
> "I don't know," one of the men said. "What do you want to eat, Al?"
> "I don't know," said Al. "I don't know what I want to eat."

But even an effaced narrator has, if we think a moment, a kind of personality. The story the narrator records may seem "cold" or "scientific" or "reportorial" or "objective," and such a **tone** or voice (attitude of the narrator, as it is detected) may be an important part of the story. Rémy de Gourmont's remark, quoted in Ezra Pound's *Literary Essays,* is relevant: "To be impersonal is to be personal in a special kind of way. . . . The objective is one of the forms of the subjective."

In writing about a third-person narrator, speak of "the narrator" or "the speaker," not of "the author."

First-Person Narrators

To turn to **first-person,** or **participant, points of view:** The "I" who narrates the story (recall that at the end of "Araby" the narrator says, "I saw myself as a creature driven and derided by vanity") may be a major character in it (as he is in "Araby," in *The Catcher in the Rye,* and in Mark Twain's *Huckleberry Finn*), or may be a minor character, a mere witness (Dr. Watson narrates tales about Sherlock Holmes, Nick Carraway narrates the story of Gatsby in *The Great Gatsby*). Of course, the narrator, even when a relatively minor character, is still a character, and, therefore, in some degree the story is about him or her. Although *The Great Gatsby* is primarily about Gatsby, it is also about Nick's changing perception of Gatsby.

First-person narrators may not fully understand their own report. Take Huck Finn in *The Adventures of Huckleberry Finn.* In one passage Huck describes the "astonishing things" performed at a circus he witnessed, including a drunk who badgered the ringmaster until he was permitted to try to ride a horse. Of course, the drunk turns out to be an expert performer and is part of the circus act, but Huck thinks the ringmaster was genuinely deceived by a performer who "had got up that joke all out of his own head." In using Huck as the narrator, Mark Twain uses an **innocent eye,** a device in which a good part of the effect consists in the discrepancy between the narrator's imperfect awareness and the reader's superior awareness. Mark Twain makes much more important use of the device in another passage in *Huckleberry Finn,* when Huck is listening to Jim, an escaped slave:

> Jim talked out loud all the time while I was talking to myself. He was saying how the first thing he would do when he got to a free state he would go to saving up money and never spend a single cent, and when he got enough he would buy his wife, which was owned on a farm close to where Miss Watson lived; and then they would both work to buy the two children, and if their master wouldn't sell them, they'd get an Ab'litionist to go and steal them.
>
> It most froze me to hear such talk. He wouldn't ever dared to talk such talk in his life before. Just see what a difference it made in him the minute he

judged he was about free. It was according to the old saying, "Give a nigger an inch and he'll take an ell." Thinks I, this is what comes of my not thinking. Here was this nigger, which I had as good as helped to run away, coming right out flat-footed and saying he would steal his children—children that belonged to a man I didn't even know; a man that hadn't ever done me no harm.

I was sorry to hear Jim say that, it was such a lowering of him.

Of course, we hear *unconscious* irony in Huck's words, especially in his indignation that Jim "would steal his children—children that belonged to a man I didn't even know." In short, Huck is an **unreliable narrator.**

On the other hand, we sometimes feel that a first-person narrator (Conrad's Marlow in several novels is an example) is a very thinly veiled substitute for the author. Nevertheless, the words of a first-person narrator require the same kind of scrutiny that we give to the words of the other characters in a story or play. The reader must deduce the personality from what is said. For instance, the narrator of "Araby" never tells us that he was a good student, but, from such a passage as the following, we can deduce that he was a bookish boy until he fell in love: "I watched my master's face pass from amiability to sternness; he hoped I was not beginning to idle."

A first-person narrator is not likely to give us the help that an editorially omniscient narrator gives. We must deduce from this passage from "Araby" that the narrator's uncle drinks too much: "At nine o'clock I heard my uncle's latchkey in the hall-door. I heard him talking to himself and heard the hall-stand rocking when it had received the weight of his overcoat. I could interpret these signs." In a first-person narrative it is sometimes difficult for the reader to interpret the signs. In a sense the author has given the reader two stories: the story the narrator tells and the story of a narrator telling a story.

An essay on point of view in a first-person story will probably characterize the narrator at some length. For instance, it will point out that the narrator is a not-too-bright adult who is eagerly telling a new acquaintance something about life in this town. The essay will then go on to show how this narrator's character colors the story that he or she tells. The essay will, for instance, explain that because the narrator is rather simple, he does not understand that he is in fact recounting a story about murder and not—as he thinks—a curious accident; that is, the essay will discuss how the reader's response resembles or differs from the narrator's.

In writing about point of view in a first-person narrative, such as *Huckleberry Finn,* after an introductory remark to the effect that Huckleberry Finn narrates the story, use the character's name or a pronoun ("Huck fails to see. . . .") in speaking of the narrator.

Caution: Essays on narrative point of view have a way of slipping into essays on what the story is about. Of course, point of view *is* relevant to the theme of the story, but if you are writing about point of view, keep this focus in sight, explaining, for instance, how it shapes the theme.

NOTES AND A SAMPLE ESSAY ON NARRATIVE POINT OF VIEW IN JAMES JOYCE'S "ARABY"

Here are some of the notes—a journal entry and a rough outline—and the final version of an essay on the narrator in Joyce's "Araby." The story is printed in Appendix A, p. 352. Doubtless some of the notes were based on passages that the student had underlined or highlighted in the text.

1st person point of view, but <u>what sort of person?</u>

Several sorts

Opening it seems <u>objective</u> point of view

Boy is sensitive to beauty: likes a book because

pages are yellow (191); plays in stable where he

hears "music from the buckled harness" (192);

Boy is shy: hardly talks to girl: "I had never

spoken to her" (192); "At last she spoke to me"

(193) *Here narrator is <u>personal</u>, not objective omniscient*

But he plays with other boys; they don't seem

to regard him as different. Typical boy?

Prob. not. ~~"My eyes were often full of~~

~~tears" (193).~~ *But not from "the rough tribes from*

the cottages."

But narrator is no longer a kid; grownup,

looking back on childhood; sometimes he

<u>seems almost amused</u> by his childhood ("Her

name sprang to my lips at moments in strange

prayers and praise which I myself did not

understand, 192-93; <u>sometimes seems a bit</u>

<u>hard on his earlier self:</u> "all my foolish

blood"; "What innumerable follies laid waste

my waking and sleeping thoughts," 193); ~~My~~

~~soul luxuriated" (193)~~ *So, a <u>third</u> aspect to narrator*

The third aspect or maybe even a fourth

Ending: very hard on self: "I saw myself as a
creature driven and derided by vanity" (196)
But opening is very different, unemotional. In
fact, come to think of it, opening isn't
even clearly a firstperson narrator. *But there
is a special personality in semi-comic comment about
houses themselves were "conscious of decent lives
within them."*

The Three First-Person Narrators of Joyce's "Araby"

James Joyce's "Araby" is told by a first-person
narrator, but this point of view is not immediately
evident to a reader. The story at first seems to be told
by an objective third-person narrator:

> North Richmond Street, being blind, was a
> quiet street except at the hour when the
> Christian Brothers' School set the boys free.
> An uninhabited house of two stories stood at
> the blind end, detached from its neighbors in
> a square ground. The other houses of the
> street, conscious of decent lives within them,
> gazed at one another with brown imperturbable
> faces.[1]

These words seem objective and omniscient, but the very
next paragraph begins by saying, "The former tenant of
our house. . . ." The word "<u>Our</u>" indicates that the
narrative point of view is first-person. On rereading
the first paragraph of the story, a reader probably
still feels that the paragraph is chiefly objective, but
perhaps the reader now gets a little sense of an
individualized speaker in the passage about the houses
being "conscious of decent lives within them," and the

---

[1]Joyce's "Araby" appears in Sylvan Barnet, Morton Berman,
and William Burto, eds., *An Introduction to Literature*,
10th ed. (New York: HarperCollins, 1993), 191-96. All
quotations are from this text.

houses have "imperturbable faces." That is, the narrator personifies the houses, making them "conscious" and rather smug. Apparently he is detached, and somewhat amused, as he thinks back to the middle-class neighborhood of his childhood.

In many passages, however, the narrator describes his romantic childhood without any irony. For instance, he says that when he was in love with the girl, his "body was like a harp and her words and gestures were like fingers running upon the wires" (193). We can say, then, that so far the narrator has two aspects: (1) an adult, who looks back objectively, or maybe with a little sense of irony, and (2) an adult who looks back almost nostalgically at himself when he was a child in love.

But there is a third aspect to the narrator, revealed in several passages. For instance, he says that the girl's name was "like a summons to all [his] foolish blood" (192) and that he engaged in "innumerable follies" (193). What may seem to be the strongest passage of this sort is at the very end of the story, and it is the strongest partly because it is in such an emphatic place: "Gazing up into the darkness I saw myself as a creature driven and derided by vanity . . . " (196). But this passage is not exactly what it first seems to be. The narrator is <u>not</u> condemning himself, saying that as a child he was "driven and derided by vanity." He is saying, now, as an adult, that <u>at the time of the experience</u> he saw himself as driven and derided by vanity.

The fact that he says "I saw myself" is almost a way of saying "I saw myself, <u>falsely</u>, as . . . ." That is, the narrator makes it clear that he is giving the child's view, and the reader understands that the child was unusually sensitive. In several passages the narrator has distanced himself from the child (as in the "foolish blood" passage) but the reader does not see the child as foolish, just as highly romantic. The very fact that the narrator calls the child "foolish" is enough

for a reader mentally to come to the child's defense,
and in effect say, "Oh, no, don't be so hard on
yourself."

The earlier passages in which the narrator condemns
his childhood experience thus serve to help the reader
to take the child's part. And now, at the end of the
story, when the narrator reports the child's severe
judgment on himself, the reader leaps to the child's
defense. If the narrator had <u>not</u> occasionally commented
negatively on his childhood, readers might themselves
have thought that the child was acting absurdly, and
also thought that the narrator was too pleased with
himself, but since the narrator occasionally passes a
negative judgment on the child, and ends by telling us
that the child judged himself severely too, the reader
almost certainly wants to reassure the child that his
behavior was not nearly so bad as he thought it was--and
in fact it was really quite touching.

In some ways, then, this narrator is an unreliable
narrator. Such a narrator is usually a naive person, who
doesn't understand what is really going on in the story.
The narrator of "Araby" is not naive--he is obviously a
very sophisticated person--but sometimes is an
unreliable guide so far as his own childhood goes. But
because the narrator sometimes takes a very critical
view of his childhood, a reader mentally defends the
child. The third (critical) aspect of the narrator,
then, actually serves to make the reader value the
child's behavior rather than judge it negatively.

A few comments on this essay may be useful:

1. **The title** is engaging—the idea of *three* first-person narrators at first
sounds paradoxical. And it probably is enough if a title is engaging and
proves to be relevant. But keep in mind that the best title often is one that
gives the reader a hint of your thesis. Here, for instance, the title might have
been "How Reliable Is the Narrator in 'Araby'?" or perhaps "Reliable and
Unreliable Narrators in Joyce's 'Araby.'" This last version catches a reader's
attention for two reasons: It speaks of narrators (most readers will wonder
who narrates the story other than the narrator they have in mind), and it

raises the issue of reliability (most readers probably assume that the narrator is reliable). Again, none of this is to say that the student's title is weak. The point here is to indicate that the choice of a title is important.

2. **The organization** is reasonable. It begins with the beginning and it ends with the end. Such an organization is not a requirement, but it is not to be shunned. Do not, however, allow such an organization to turn what should be an analytic essay into a long summary of the story. You are arguing a thesis, not writing a summary.

3. **The proportions are appropriate.** The thesis is that the third, or critical, voice in the essay is important in (paradoxically) getting sympathy for the boy, and so the third voice is given the most space.

4. **Quotations** are used in order to let the reader know exactly what the writer is talking about. They are used as part of the argument, not as padding.

THEME: VISION OR ARGUMENT?

Because modern fiction makes subtle use of it, point of view can scarcely be neglected in a discussion of **theme**—what a story is about. Perhaps unfairly, modern criticism is usually unhappy with suggestions of the author's voice in older fiction. We would rather see than be lectured. We are less impressed by

> It was the stillness of an implacable force brooding over an inscrutable intention

(from Conrad's *Heart of Darkness*) than by this passage from the same book:

> Black shapes crouched, lay, sat between the trees, leaning against the trunks, clinging to the earth, half coming out, half effaced within the dim light, in all the attitudes of pain, abandonment, and despair. Another mine on the cliff went off, followed by a slight shudder of the soil under my feet. The work was going on. The work! And this was the place where some of the helpers had withdrawn to die.

The second quotation, but not the first, gives us the sense of reality that we have come to expect from fiction. (Still, this is a critical assumption that can be questioned.) Thomas Hardy's novels in particular have been censured on this account; the modern sensibility is uneasy when it hears Hardy's own voice commenting on the cosmic significance of the happenings, as when in *Tess of the D'Urbervilles* the narrator says: "In the ill-judged execution of the well-judged plan of things, the call seldom produces the comer, the man to love rarely coincides with the hour for loving." The passage goes on in this vein at some length. Even in passages of dialogue, we sometimes feel that we are getting not a vision of life but a discourse on it, as in this famous exchange between Tess and her brother:

> "Did you say the stars were worlds, Tess?"
> "Yes."
> "All like ours?"
> "I don't know; but I think so. They sometimes seem to be like the apples on our stubbard-tree. Most of them splendid and sound—a few blighted."
> "Which do we live on—a splendid one or a blighted one?"
> "A blighted one."

Partly, we feel that overt commentary (even when put into the mouths of the characters) leaves the world of fiction and invites us to judge it separately as philosophy. Partly the difficulty is that twentieth-century novelists and readers have come to expect the novel to do something different from what Hardy and his contemporaries expected it to do. As the novelist Flannery O'Connor puts it in *Mystery and Manners* (1957), we expect a storyteller to speak "*with* character and action, not *about* character and action" (76).

Determining and Discussing the Theme

First, we can distinguish between *story* and *theme* in fiction. Story is concerned with "How does it turn out? What happens?" Theme is concerned with "What does it add up to? What motif holds the happenings together? What does it make out of life, and, perhaps, what wisdom does it offer?[2]"

In a good work of fiction, the details add up, or, to use Flannery O'Connor's words, they are "controlled by some overall purpose." In F. Scott Fitzgerald's *Thats by*, for example, are many references to popular music, especially to jazz. These references contribute to our sense of the reality in Fitzgerald's depiction of America in the 1920s, but they do more: They help comment on the shallowness of the white middle-class characters, and they sometimes (very gently) remind us of an alternative culture. One might study Fitzgerald's references to music with an eye toward getting a deeper understanding of what the novel is about.

---

[2]A theme in a literary work is sometimes distinguished from a *thesis*, an arguable message such as "People ought not to struggle against Fate." The theme, it might be said, is something like "The 3struggle against Fate" or "The Process of Maturing" or "The Quest for Love." In any case, the formulation of a theme normally includes an abstract noun or a phrase, but it must be remembered that such formulations as those in the previous sentence are finally only shorthand expressions for highly complex statements. For further comments on theme, see pp. 216–18 and 280–82.

Preliminary Notes and Two Sample Essays
on the Theme of Shirley Jackson's "The Lottery"

Here are the notes and the final essays of two students who chose to write about the theme of Jackson's "The Lottery." (The story is printed on pages 356 to 363 in Appendix A of this book.)

The first student, after reading and rereading the story, jotted down the following notes as a sort of preliminary outline. Some of the notes were based on passages he had underlined. Notice that the jottings include some material specifically on the story and other material—references to the outside world—that is relevant to what the student takes to be the theme of the story. When he reviewed his notes before starting on a first draft, the student deleted some of them, having decided that they were not especially useful for his essay. Still, they were worth jotting down; only in retrospect can a writer clearly see which notes are useful.

```
Is Jackson saying that human nature is evil? Prob. no; here,
    people just follow a tradition, and don't examine it.  Mr.
    Warner defends lottery, saying "There's always been a
    lottery." No real argument in defense of it.
We are least conscious of the things we take for granted; I
    recall someone's saying "a fish is not aware of water
    until it is out of it."
examples of blindly following society's customs
    compulsory schooling (how many people ever even remotely
        think of schooling their children at home?)
    school is 5 days a week, why not 4 or 6? Bachelor's
        degree is 4 years, why not 3 or 5?
    segregation (until 1960s; later in S. Africa)
    women not permitted to drive in Saudi Arabia
    women must wear veil in Saudi Arabia
    eating of meat; might a vegetarian society not look with
        horror at our habit of eating meat?
    slavery (thought to be "natural" by almost all societies
        until nineteenth century)
thoughtless following of custom in "The Lottery"
    exact words of ritual lost, but still necessary to
        address "each person approaching"
    original box one, but present box said to be made of
        parts of previous box
```

```
    lottery an established ritual: "The lottery was
       conducted--as were the square dances, the teenage
       club, the Halloween program--by Mr. Summers, who had
       time and energy to devote to civic activities."
       Important: the lottery is a civic activity, a social
       action, a summer (pun?) ritual.
Evil?  Certainly yes, since killing an innocent, but no one
  in the story says it's evil.
       BUT Adams does say that in the north village "they're
          talking of giving up the lottery," and his wife says
          "Some places have already quit lotteries."
       Also: a girl whispers, "I hope it's not Nancy," so at
          least one person feels uneasy about the whole thing.
Are these people evil?  No, they seem pretty decent.  They
  just don't much question what they are doing, and they do
  something terrible
the box
     black = death?
     made out of pieces of old box
     "faded," "splintered badly": does this symbolize a need
        for a new tradition?
the papers
       earlier, wood chips. At end, wind blows away slips of
          paper? Symbolic of life fluttering away (Prob. not)
the three-legged stool
     symbolic? If so, of what?
possible title
     The Violent Lottery
     The Irrational Lottery
     We All Participate in "The Lottery"
     The Meaning of the Lottery
```

A lot of the material here is good, though some of it would be more suited for an essay on symbolism, and it is chiefly this material that the writer wisely deleted in preparing to draft an essay on the theme of Jackson's story. After writing a draft and then revising it, the author submitted the revision to a group for peer review. Ultimately, he turned in the following essay.

We All Participate in "The Lottery"

The townsfolk in Shirley Jackson's "The Lottery"
engage in a horrible ritual. They stone an innocent
person to death. It would be horrible enough if the
person they stoned were guilty of some crime, and
stoning was a form of capital punishment that the
society practiced, but in the case of "The Lottery" the
person is not guilty of any crime. Tessie Hutchinson
simply has the bad luck to pick the wrong slip of paper
from a box, a paper marked with a black spot.

The people in this unnamed town every year hold a
lottery, to find a victim. On the whole, they seem to
believe that the lottery is necessary, or is natural; at
least they hardly question it. True, Mr. Adams says that
in the north village "they're talking of giving up the
lottery," and his wife says that "Some places have
already quit lotteries," but that's about as much as one
hears of anybody questioning this institution of
society. Probably most of the people in the village
would agree with Old Man Warner, who says that people
who talk about giving up the lottery are a "pack of
crazy fools." He adds, "There's always been a lottery,"
and that seems to be about the best answer that anyone
can give. Of course the people don't take any special
pleasure in the lottery, and there is at least one
expression of sympathy, when a girl says, "I hope it's
not Nancy." On the whole, however, the people seem to
believe that the lottery must be held, and someone has
to die.

It's important to notice that the lottery is one of
the "civic activities," that is, it is part of the
regular life of these people, part (so to speak) of the
air they breathe. For the most part they don't question
the lottery any more than we question compulsory
education, the length of the school year, or the eating
of meat. When one thinks about it, one might ask why the
government should have the power to compel parents to
send children to school, or, for that matter, why a
child shouldn't have the right to leave school whenever

he or she feels like it. Why should children have almost
no rights? People simply don't bother to think about
this issue, or about many others. For instance, I can
imagine that a member of a vegetarian society--say a
Hindu Brahmin society--must be horrified by the way
almost all Americans think nothing of raising animals
(bringing life into the world) for the sole purpose of
eating them. We just accept these things, without
thinking, but from the view of another culture they may
be horrible customs.

What Jackson seems to be saying to her readers is
this: "Unthinkingly you follow certain conventions.
These conventions seem to you to be natural, and for the
most part they are harmless, but some of them are
barbaric and destructive." That is, Jackson is telling
us to examine our lives, and to stop assuming that all
of our customs are right. Some of the beliefs we share
today may, in time, come to be seen to be as evil as
slavery or murder.

Now for the notes and the essay by a second student. This writer came
to a very different conclusion about the theme of "The Lottery." After reading this student's notes and her essay, you may want to compare the two essays. Do you find one essay more interesting than the other? More persuasive? If so, why? You may feel that even though the essays come to different
conclusions, the two essays are equally interesting and equally valid.

surprise and shock
    shock
      violence (at end)
          esp. shocking because violence comes from
              people who seem normal and decent
          (only a few expressions of hesitation; Mr. and
              Mrs. Adams)
          Jackson claimed violence was normal (quote passage)
    (talk of giving up lotteries)
      surprise
          we don't know, until late, what's going on;
          on rereading, we see lots of clues about what
              will happen
          Example: references to stones

Meanings?
    lottery = the draft in wartime?
    lottery = community violence? Example: War (??)
    lottery = violent U.S. society??
       "   " <u>any</u> violent custom; bad tradition?
   human nature corrupt? sinful? (Note name of Adams,
      also Graves) (other significant names: Summers,
      Warner); human tendency to look for a scapegoat.
      Is it true?
Jackson quoted on her meaning: "violence and general
   inhumanity" but do we have to believe her?   *Example of*
    Maybe just a horror story, without "meaning" *such a story?*
    <u>Are</u> normal people willing to kill without great
      provocation?
Possible titles
    Shirley Jackson on Human Nature
    Do We All Participate in "The Lottery"?
    How Fair is Shirley Jackson's Lottery?
    Is "The Lottery" Fair?

When you read the essay, you'll notice that for a title the author settled on the last of her four tentative titles. The first title, "Shirley Jackson on Human Nature," is too broad since the essay is not on all of Jackson's work but on only one story. The second tentative title, "Do We All Participate in 'The Lottery'?", is acceptable, but it sounds a bit clumsy, so the choice apparently came down to the last two titles or to some entirely new title that the writer might discover during the process of revising her drafts.

Notice also that some points mentioned in the preliminary notes—for instance, the reference to Mr. Summers and to Mr. Warner—are omitted from the essay. And some points scarcely mentioned in the outline are emphasized in the essay. In drafting and revising the essay, the writer found that certain things weren't relevant to her point, and so she dropped them and found that others required considerable amplification.

Is "The Lottery" Fair?

Probably all readers are surprised by the ending of
Shirley Jackson's "The Lottery." But the story does more
than offer a surprise. It shocks, because it seems to
say that people who are perfectly ordinary, just like

ourselves, are capable of killing an innocent neighbor for apparently no reason at all. On rereading the story, we can see that Jackson has carefully prepared for the ending, and we can admire her skill. For instance, the second paragraph tells us that "Bobby Martin had already stuffed his pockets full of stones, and the other boys soon followed his example, selecting the smoothest and roundest stones" (863). We almost feel, when we reread the story, that we should not have been surprised. But even after we see that the ending has been foreshadowed, we remain shocked by the violence, and by what the story says about human beings. But exactly what does it say about them? And does it say anything that strikes us as true?

If we assume that the story does say something about life, and is not simply a meaningless shocker, we may come up with several possible interpretations. Is Jackson saying that Americans seem peaceful and neighborly but really are quite willing to engage in violence? (Although she does not clearly set the story in an identifiable region, she clearly sets it in a small town in the United States.) Certainly newspapers every day tell us of violent acts, but the violent acts are usually of an individual (a mad killer, or a rapist) or are of nature (an earthquake, a tornado).

Of course someone might conceivably argue that this story, which is about a community, is a sort of allegory about the United States as a whole. It was written in 1948, only three years after the end of World War II, and someone might claim that it is about American willingness to use violence, that is, to go to war. Or one might even say that it is about the wartime draft, which was a sort of lottery that chose certain people whose lives were risked.

But to see the story as a reference to World War II seems very strained. Nothing in the story suggests a conscious conflict between groups, as, for instance, Jackson could have suggested if members of this town were allied against another town. And though the story certainly is set in the United States, nothing in the story calls attention to a particularly <u>American violence</u>.

Another way of thinking about "The Lottery" is to see it as a story about all human beings--not just Americans--who unthinkingly submit to destructive traditions. This interpretation can be better supported than the first interpretation. For instance, at least two people in the story briefly question the tradition of the lottery. Steve Adams says, "Over in the north village they're talking of giving up the lottery," and a moment later his wife adds, "Some places have already quit lotteries" (866). But of course the story tells us that this community does not give up the lottery; in fact, we are particularly shocked to learn, near the end, that Steve Adams is "in the front of the crowd of villagers" (868) when they attack Tessie Hutchinson.

It's obvious that the story is about a terrible tradition that is accepted with relatively little objection, but we can still ask what connection the story has with our own lives. What traditions do we engage in that are so deadly? The wartime draft has already been mentioned, but even pacifists probably would grant that most of the people who engage in war are aware that war is terrible, and thus they are unlike Jackson's villagers. The story may be about the deadliness of certain traditions, but a reader is left wondering which of our traditions are represented in Jackson's lottery. Racism and sexism have had terrible effects, but it is hard to relate the lottery, which picks a victim at random, to discrimination against people of a certain color or a certain sex.

A third view, and one that I think is somewhat sounder than the first two views, is that the story is about human nature. Although most people are decent, they are also capable of terrible irrational violence. In Christian terms this is explained by Original Sin, a sinfulness that we have inherited from Adam. Jackson certainly allows for the possibility of some sort of Biblical interpretation, since, as we have seen, Mr. Adams is one of the leaders of the assault, and he is accompanied by Mr. Graves. The original sin of the first Adam led to death, and thus to the grave.

Shirley Jackson herself from time to time offered comments on the story. According to Judy Oppenheimer, in Private Demons: The Life of Shirley Jackson, when the fiction editor of The New Yorker asked her if "there was anything special she was trying to convey," she said, "Not really." When the editor pressed her, and asked if the story "made its point by an ironic juxtaposition of ancient superstition and modern setting," Jackson said "Sure, that would be fine," since she didn't like to discuss her work (128). Her fullest comment, according to Oppenheimer, was given to a columnist who was writing for the San Francisco Chronicle:

> I suppose I hoped, by setting a particularly
> brutal rite in the present and in my own
> village, to shock the readers with a graphic
> demonstration of the pointless violence and
> general inhumanity of their own lives. (qtd.
> in Oppenheimer 131)

There are obvious problems with accepting this comment. First of all, as has been mentioned, Jackson offered contradictory comments on the meaning of the story. She seems not to have worried about being consistent. Second, the words she used by way of introducing her intention--"I suppose I hoped"--indicate that she herself was not entirely clear about what she had intended. Third, even if she did correctly state her intention, she may not have fulfilled it adequately.

Certainly the story shows people who seem quite decent but who with only a little hesitation participate in a barbaric ritual. Perhaps Jackson did intend to say in her story that this is what we are also like. And since the story is related to ancient rituals in which societies purify themselves by finding a scapegoat, Jackson seems to be saying that all people, no matter how normal or decent they seem, engage in violence that they think purifies them or is at least in some way necessary for their own wellbeing. But just because Jackson <u>said</u> something like this, and said it in a gripping story, it isn't necessarily true. Despite all of the realistic detail--for instance Mrs. Hutchinson's desperate charge that "It isn't fair"--the final picture of life that "The Lottery" gives does not seem to me to be at all realistic, and therefore I don't think the story says anything about life. The story surprises and it shocks, for instance like Poe's "The Fall of the House of Usher." Maybe it even shows "The pointless violence and general inhumanity" in the lives of Jackson's neighbors, but does it reflect the lives of her readers? Do apparently normal, decent people routinely engage in barbaric behavior? I'm not like these people, and I doubt that Jackson and her neighbors were like them either. "The Lottery" is a cleverly plotted story, but the more you look at it, and the more you admire the skillful foreshadowing, the more it seems to be a clever trick, and the less it seems to be related to life.

[New page]

Works Cited

Jackson, Shirley. "The Lottery." <u>The Harper Anthology of Fiction</u>. Ed. Sylvan Barnet. New York: HarperCollins, 1991. 862-68.

Oppenheimer, Judy. <u>Private Demons: The Life of Shirley Jackson</u>. New York: Putnam's, 1988.

📖 Suggestions for Further Reading

E. M. Forster's *Aspects of the Novel* (1927) remains an engaging introduction to the art of prose fiction, by an accomplished practitioner. Other highly readable books by story writers and novelists include: Flannery O'Connor, *Mystery and Manners* (1969); William Gass, *Fiction and the Figures of Life* (1971); Eudora Welty, *The Eye of the Story* (1977).

For academic studies, see also Robert Scholes and Robert Kellogg, *The Nature of Narrative* (1966, on oral as well as written fiction); Robert Liddell, *Robert Liddell on the Novel* (1969, a volume combining two earlier books by Liddell, *A Treatise on the Novel* and *Some Principles of Fiction*); Norman Friedman, *Form and Meaning in Fiction* (1975); Seymour Chatman, *Story and Discourse* (1978); Wayne C. Booth, *The Rhetoric of Fiction*, 2nd ed. (1983); and, for a study using the latest terminology, Gerald Prince, *Narratology* (1982). For essays defining the short story and sketching its history see Susan Lohafer and Jo Ellyn Clarey, eds., *Short Story Theory at a Crossroads* (1989).

Among journals devoted to narrative are: *Journal of Narrative Technique, Modern Fiction Studies, Novel: A Forum*, and *Studies in Short Fiction*.

✓ A Checklist: Getting Ideas for Writing about Fiction

Here are some questions that may help to stimulate ideas about stories. Not every question is, of course, relevant to every story, but if after reading a story and thinking about it, you then run your eye over these pages, you will probably find some questions that will help you to think further about the story—in short, that will help you to get ideas.

It's best to do your thinking with a pen or pencil in hand. If some of the following questions seem to you to be especially relevant to the story you will be writing about, jot down—freely, without worrying about spelling—your initial responses, interrupting your writing only to glance again at the story when you feel the need to check the evidence.

Title

1. Is the title informative? What does it mean or suggest? Did the meaning seem to change after you read the story? Does the title help you to formulate a theme?
2. If you had written the story, what title would you use?

Plot

1. Does the plot grow out of the characters, or does it depend on chance or coincidence? Did something at first strike you as irrele-

vant that later you perceived as relevant? Do some parts continue to strike you as irrelevant?

2. Does surprise play an important role, or does foreshadowing? If surprise is very important, can the story be read a second time with any interest? If so, what gives it this further interest?

3. What conflicts does the story include? Conflicts of one character against another? Of one character against the setting, or against society? Conflicts within a single character?

4. Are the conflicts resolved? If so, how?

5. Are certain episodes narrated out of chronological order? If so, were you puzzled? Annoyed? On reflection, does the arrangement of episodes seem effective? Why or why not? Are certain situations repeated? If so, what do you make out of the repetitions?

6. List the major structural units of the story. In a sentence or two summarize each unit that you have listed.

7. In a sentence summarize the conclusion or resolution. Do you find it satisfactory? Why, or why not?

Character

1. List the traits of the main characters.

2. Which character chiefly engages your interest? Why?

3. What purposes do minor characters serve? Do you find some who by their similarities and differences help to define each other or help to define the major character? How else is a particular character defined—by his or her words, actions (including thoughts and emotions), dress, setting, narrative point of view? Do certain characters act differently in the same, or in a similar, situation?

4. How does the author reveal character? By explicit authorial (editorial) comment, for instance, or, on the other hand, by revelation through dialogue? Through depicted action? Through the actions of other characters? How are the author's methods especially suited to the whole of the story?

5. Is the behavior plausible—that is, are the characters well motivated?

6. If a character changes, why and how does he or she change? (You may want to jot down each event that influences a change.) Or did you change your attitude toward a character not because the character changes but because you came to know the character better?

7. Are the characters round or flat? Are they complex, or, on the other hand, highly typical (for instance, one-dimensional represen-

tatives of a social class or age)? Are you chiefly interested in a character's psychology, or does the character strike you as standing for something, such as honesty or the arrogance of power?

8. How has the author caused you to sympathize with certain characters? How does your response—your sympathy or lack of sympathy—contribute to your judgment of the conflict?

Point of View

1. Who tells the story? How much does the narrator know? Does the narrator strike you as reliable? What effect is gained by using this narrator?

2. How does the point of view help shape the theme? After all, the basic story of Little Red Riding Hood—what happens—remains unchanged whether told from the wolf's point of view or the girl's, but (to simplify grossly) if we hear the story from the wolf's point of view, we may feel that the story is about terrifying yet pathetic compulsive behavior; if from the girl's point of view, about terrified innocence and male violence.

3. Does the narrator's language help you to construct a picture of the narrator's character, class, attitude, strengths, and limitations? (Jot down some evidence, such as colloquial or—on the other hand—formal expressions, ironic comments, figures of speech.) How far can you trust the narrator? Why?

Setting

1. Do you have a strong sense of the time and place? Is the story very much about, say, New England Puritanism, or race relations in the South in the late nineteenth century, or midwestern urban versus small-town life? If time and place are important, how and at what points in the story has the author conveyed this sense? If you do not strongly feel the setting, do you think the author should have made it more evident?

2. What is the relation of the setting to the plot and the characters? (For instance, do houses or rooms or their furnishings say something about their residents? Is the landscape important?) Would anything be lost if the descriptions of the setting were deleted from the story or if the setting were changed?

Symbolism

1. Do certain characters seem to you to stand for something in addition to themselves? Does the setting—whether a house, a farm, a landscape, a town, a period—have an extra dimension?

2. Do certain actions in the story—for instance entering a forest at night, or shutting a door, or turning off a light—seem symbolic? If so, symbolic of what?

3. If you do believe that the story has symbolic elements, do you think they are adequately integrated within the story, or do they strike you as being too obviously stuck in?

Style

(Style may be defined as *how* the writer says what he or she says. It is the writer's manner of expression. The writer's choice of words, of sentence structure, and of sentence length are all aspects of style. Example: "Shut the door," and "Would you mind closing the door, please," differ substantially in style. Another example: Lincoln begins the Gettysburg Address by speaking of "Four score and seven years ago," i.e., by using language that has a Biblical overtone. If he had said "Eighty-seven years ago," his style would have been different.)

1. How would you characterize the style? Simple? Understated? Figurative? Or what, and why?

2. How has the point of view shaped or determined the style?

3. Do you think that the style is consistent? If it isn't—for instance, if there are shifts from simple sentences to highly complex ones— what do you make of the shifts?

Theme

1. Do certain passages—the title, some of the dialogue, or some of the description, the names of certain characters—seem to you to point especially toward the theme? Do you find certain repetitions of words or pairs of incidents highly suggestive and helpful in directing your thoughts toward stating a theme? Flannery O'Connor, in *Mystery and Manners*, says, "In good fiction, certain of the details will tend to accumulate meaning from the action of the story itself, and when that happens, they become symbolic in the way they work." Does this story work that way?

2. Is the meaning of the story embodied in the whole story, or does it seem stuck in, for example in certain passages of editorializing?

3. Suppose someone asked you to state the point—the theme—of the story. Could you? And if you could, would you say that the theme of a particular story reinforces values you hold, or does it to some degree challenge them? (It is sometimes said that the best writers are subversive, forcing readers to see something that they do not want to see.)

11

Writing about Drama

The college essays you write about plays will be similar in many respects to analytic essays about fiction. Unless you are writing a review of a performance, you probably won't try to write about all aspects of a play. Rather, you'll choose some significant topic. For instance, if you are writing about Tennessee William's *The Glass Menagerie,* you might compare the aspirations of Jim Connor and Tom Wingfield, or you might compare Tom's illusions with those of his sister, Laura, and his mother, Amanda. Or you might examine the symbolism, perhaps limiting your essay to the glass animals but perhaps extending it to include other symbols, such as the fire escape, the lighting, and the Victrola. Similarly, if you are writing an analysis, you might decide to study the construction of one scene of a play, or, if the play does not have a great many scenes, even the construction of the entire play.

A list of questions on pages 229–231 may help you find a topic for the particular play you choose.

A SAMPLE ESSAY

The following essay discusses the structure of *The Glass Menagerie.* It mentions various characters, but, since its concern is with the arrangement of scenes, it does not (for instance) examine any of the characters in detail. An essay might well be devoted to examining (for example) Williams's assertion that "There is much to admire in Amanda, and as much to love and pity as there is to laugh at," but an essay on the structure of the play is probably not the place to talk about Williams's characterization of Amanda.

Preliminary Notes

After deciding to write on the structure of the play, with an eye toward seeing the overall pattern, the student reread *The Glass Menagerie*, jotted down some notes briefly summarizing each of the seven scenes, with an occasional comment, and then typed them. On rereading the typed notes, he added a few observations in handwriting.

1. begins with Tom talking to audience;
   ~~says he is a magician~~
   America, in 1930s
       "shouting and confusion"
   Father deserted
   Amanda nagging; ~~is she a bit cracked?~~   *nagging*
   Tom: bored, angry
   Laura: embarrassed, depressed
2. Laura: quit business school; sad, but
       Jim's name is mentioned, so,
       lighter tone introduced
3. Tom and Amanda argue ———————— *out and out battle*
   Tom almost destroys glass menagerie
   Rage: Can things get any worse?
4. T and A reconciled ———————— *reconciliation, and false hopes — then final collapse*
   T to try to get a "gentleman caller"
5. T tells A that Jim will visit
   things are looking up
6. Jim arrives; L terrified
   still, Aman thinks things can work out
7. Lights go out (foreshadowing dark ending?)
   Jim a jerk, clumsy; breaks unicorn, but L
   doesn't seem to mind. Maybe he <u>is</u> the right
   guy to draw her into normal world. Jim reveals
   he is engaged:
       "Desolation."
   Tom escapes into merchant marine, but
       can't   escape memories. Speaks to
       audience.
       L. blows out candles (does this mean he

forgets her? No, because he is
remembering her right now. I don't get
it, if the candles are supposed to be
symbolic.)

These notes enabled the student to prepare a rough draft, which he
then submitted to some classmates for peer review. (On peer review, see
pp. 27–28.)

Notice that the final version of the essay, printed below, is *not*
merely a summary (a brief retelling of the plot). Although it does indeed
include summary, it chiefly is devoted to showing *how* the scenes are
related.

Title is focused; it announces topic and thesis.

The Solid Structure of

The Glass Menagerie

In the "Production Notes" Tennessee Williams
calls The Glass Menagerie a "memory play," a
term that the narrator in the play also uses.

Opening paragraph closes in on thesis.

Memories often consist of fragments of
episodes which are so loosely connected that
they seem chaotic, and therefore we might
think that The Glass Menagerie will consist of
very loosely related episodes. However, the
play covers only one episode and though it
gives the illusion of random talk, it really
has a firm structure and moves steadily toward
a foregone conclusion.

Reasonable organization; the paragraph touches on the beginning and the end.

Tennessee Williams divides the play into
seven scenes. The first scene begins with a
sort of prologue and the last scene concludes
with a sort of epilogue that is related to the
prologue. In the prologue Tom addresses the
audience and comments on the 1930s as a time
when America was "blind" and was a place of
"shouting and confusion." Tom also mentions

Brief but effective quotations.

that our lives consist of expectations, and though he does not say that our expectations are unfulfilled, near the end of the prologue he quotes a postcard that his father wrote to the family he deserted: "Hello--Goodbye." In the epilogue Tom tells us that he followed his "father's footsteps," deserting the family. And just before the epilogue, near the end of Scene VII, we see what can be considered to Tom's sister Laura that he is engaged and therefore cannot visit Laura again. Thus the end is closely related to the beginning, and the play is the steady development of the initial implications.

Useful generalization based on earlier details.

The first three scenes show things going from bad to worse. Amanda is a nagging mother who finds her only relief in talking about the past to her crippled daughter Laura and her frustrated son Tom. When she was young she was beautiful and was eagerly courted by rich young men, but now the family is poor and this harping on the past can only bore or infuriate Tom and embarrass or depress Laura, who have no happy past to look back to, who see no happy future, and who can only be upset by Amanda's insistence that they should behave as she behaved long ago. The second scene deepens the despair: Amanda learns that the timorous Laura has not been attending a business school but has retreated in terror from this confrontation with the contemporary world. Laura's helplessness is made clear to the audience, and so is Amanda's lack of understanding. Near the end of the second scene, however, Jim's name is introduced; he is a boy Laura had a crush on

Chronological organization is reasonable. Opening topic sentence lets readers know where they are going.

Brief plot summary supports thesis.

in high school, and so the audience gets a
glimpse of a happier Laura and a sense that
possibly Laura's world is wider than the
stifling tenement in which she and her mother
and brother live. But in the third scene
things get worse, when Tom and Amanda have so
violent an argument that they are no longer on
speaking terms. Tom is so angry with his
mother that he almost by accident destroys his
sister's treasured collection of glass
animals, the fragile lifeless world which is
her refuge. The apartment is literally full of
the "shouting and confusion" that Tom spoke of
in his prologue.

Useful summary
and transition.

The first three scenes have revealed a
progressive worsening of relations; the next
three scenes reveal a progressive improvement
in relations. In Scene IV Tom and his mother
are reconciled, and Tom reluctantly--
apparently in an effort to make up with his
mother--agrees to try to get a friend to come
to dinner so that Laura will have "a gentleman
caller." In Scene V Tom tells his mother that
Jim will come to dinner on the next night, and
Amanda brightens, because she sees a
possibility of security for Laura at last. In
Scene VI Jim arrives, and despite Laura's
initial terror, there seems, at least in
Amanda's mind, to be the possibility that
things will go well.

The seventh scene, by far the longest, at
first seems to be fulfilling Amanda's hopes.
Despite the ominous fact that the lights go
out because Tom has not paid the electric
bill, Jim is at ease. He is an insensitive

oaf, but that doesn't seem to bother Amanda, and almost miraculously he manages to draw Laura somewhat out of her sheltered world. Even when Jim in his clumsiness breaks the horn of Laura's treasured glass unicorn, she is not upset. In fact, she is almost relieved because the loss of the horn makes the animal less "freakish" and he "will feel more at home with the other horses." In a way, of course, the unicorn symbolizes the crippled Laura, who at least for the moment feels less freakish and isolated now that she is somewhat reunited with society through Jim. But this is a play about life in a blind and confused world, and though in a previous age the father escaped, there can be no escape now. Jim reveals that he is engaged, Laura relapses into "desolation," Amanda relapses into rage and bitterness, and Tom relapses into dreams of escape. In a limited sense Tom does escape. He leaves the family and joins the merchant marine, but his last speech or epilogue tells us that he cannot escape the memory of his sister: "Oh, Laura, Laura, I tried to leave you behind me, but I am more faithful than I intended to be!" And so the end of the last scene brings us back again to the beginning of the first scene: we are still in a world of "the blind" and of "confusion." But now at the end of the play the darkness is deeper, the characters are lost forever in their unhappiness as Laura "blows the candles out," the darkness being literal but also symbolic of their extinguished hopes.

The essayist is thinking and commenting, not merely summarizing the plot.

Numerous devices, such as repeated
references to the absent father, to Amanda's
youth, to Laura's Victrola and of course to
Laura's glass menagerie help to tie the scenes

Useful, thoughtful summary of thesis. together into a unified play. But beneath
these threads of imagery, and recurring
motifs, is a fundamental pattern that involves
the movement from nagging (Scenes I and II) to
open hostilities (Scene III) to temporary
reconciliation (Scene IV) to false hopes
(Scenes V and VI) to an impossible heightening
of false hopes and then, in a swift descent,
to an inevitable collapse (Scene VII).
Tennessee Williams has constructed his play
carefully. G. B. Tennyson says that a
"playwright must 'build' his speeches, as the
theatrical expression has it." (13). But a
playwright must do more, he must also build
his play out of scenes. Like Ibsen, if
Williams had been introduced to an architect
he might have said, "Architecture is my
business too."

[New Page]

Works Cited

Tennyson, G. B. An Introduction to Drama. New
        York: Holt, 1967.
Williams, Tennessee. The Glass Menagerie.
        Literature for Composition. Ed. Sylvan
        Barnet et al. 3rd ed. New York:
        HarperCollins, 1992. 722-67.

The danger in writing about structure, especially if one proceeds by beginning at the beginning and moving steadily to the end, is that one will
simply tell the plot. This essay on *The Glass Menagerie* manages to say
things about the organization of the plot even as it tells the plot. It has a

point, hinted at in the pleasantly paradoxical title, developed in the body of the essay, and wrapped up in the last line.

TYPES OF PLAYS

Most of the world's great plays written before the twentieth century may be regarded as one of two kinds: **tragedy** or **comedy.** Roughly speaking, tragedy dramatizes the conflict between the vitality of the single life and the laws or limits of life. The tragic hero reaches a height, going beyond the experience of others but at the cost of his or her life. Comedy dramatizes the vitality of the laws of social life. In comedy, the good life is seen to reside in the shedding of an individualism that isolates, in favor of a union with a genial and enlightened society. These points must be amplified a bit before we go on to the point that, of course, any important play does much more than can be put into such crude formulas.

Tragedy

Tragic heroes usually go beyond the standards to which reasonable people adhere; they do some fearful deed that ultimately destroys them. This deed is often said to be an act of hubris, a Greek word meaning something like "overweening pride." It may involve, for instance, violating a taboo, such as that against taking life. But if the hubristic act ultimately destroys the man or woman who performs it, it also shows that person (paradoxically) to be in some way more fully a living being—a person who has experienced life more fully, whether by heroic action or by capacity for enduring suffering—than the other characters in the play. Othello kills Desdemona, Lear gives away his crown and banishes his one loving daughter, Antony loses his share of the Roman Empire; but all of these men seem to live more fully than the other characters in the plays—for one thing, they experience a kind of anguish unknown to those who surround them and who outlive them. (If the hero does not die, he or she usually is left in some deathlike state, as is the blind Oedipus in *King Oedipus.*)

In tragedy, we see humanity pushed to an extreme; in agony and grief the hero enters a world unknown to most and reveals magnificence. After his or her departure from the stage, we are left in a world of littler people. The closing lines of almost any of Shakespeare's tragedies may be used to illustrate the point. *King Lear,* for example, ends thus:

The oldest hath borne most: we that are young
Shall never see so much, nor live so long.

What has just been said may (or may not) be true of most tragedies, but it certainly is not true of all. If you are writing about a tragedy, you might consider whether the points just made are illustrated in your play. Is the hero guilty of *hubris*? Does the hero seem a greater person than the others in the play? An essay examining such questions probably requires not only a character sketch but also some comparison with other characters.

Tragedy commonly involves **irony** of two sorts: unconsciously ironic deeds and unconsciously ironic speeches. **Ironic deeds** have some consequence more or less the reverse of what the doer intends. Macbeth thinks that by killing Duncan he will gain happiness, but he finds that his deed brings him sleepless nights. Brutus thinks that by killing Caesar he will bring liberty to Rome, but he brings tyranny. In an unconsciously **ironic speech,** the speaker's words mean one thing to him or her but something more significant to the audience, as when King Duncan, baffled by Cawdor's treason, says:

> There's no art
> To find the mind's construction in the face:
> He was a gentleman on whom I built
> An absolute trust.

At this moment Macbeth, whom we have already heard meditating the murder of Duncan, enters. Duncan's words are true, but he does not apply them to Macbeth, as the audience does. A few moments later Duncan praises Macbeth as "a peerless kinsman." Soon Macbeth will indeed become peerless, when he kills Duncan and ascends to the throne.[1] Sophocles's use of ironic deeds and speeches is so pervasive, especially in *King Oedipus,* that **Sophoclean irony** has become a critical term. Here is a critic summarizing the ironies of *King Oedipus:*

> As the images unfold, the enquirer turns into the object of enquiry, the hunter into the prey, the doctor into the patient, the investigator into the criminal, the revealer into the thing revealed, the finder into the thing found, the savior into the thing saved ("I was saved, for some dreadful destiny"), the liberator into the thing released ("I released your feet from the bonds which pierced your ankles" says the Corinthian messenger), the accuser becomes the defendant,

---

[1]*Dramatic irony* (ironic deeds or happenings, and unconsciously ironic speeches) must be distinguished from *verbal irony,* which is produced when the speaker is *conscious* that his or her words mean something different from what they say. In *Macbeth* Lennox says: "The gracious Duncan / Was pitied of Macbeth. Marry, he was dead! / And the right valiant Banquo walked too late. / . . . / Men must not walk too late." He *says* nothing about Macbeth having killed Duncan and Banquo, but he *means* that Macbeth has killed them.

the ruler the subject, the teacher not only the pupil but also the object lesson, the example.

> —BERNARD KNOX, "Sophocles' Oedipus," in *Tragic Themes in Western Literature,* ed. Cleanth Brooks (New Haven, 1955), pp. 10-11

Notice, by the way, the neatness of that sentence; it is unusually long but it does not ramble, it does not baffle, and it does not suggest a stuffy writer. The verb *turns* governs the first two-thirds; and after the second long parenthetical statement, when the messenger's speech may cause the reader to forget the verb, the writer provides another verb, *becomes.*

When the deed backfires or has a reverse effect, such as Macbeth's effort to gain happiness has, we have what Aristotle called a **peripeteia,** or a **reversal.** When a character comes to perceive what has happened (Macbeth's "I have lived long enough: my way of life / Is fall'n into the sere, the yellow leaf"), he experiences (in Aristotle's language) an **anagnorisis,** or **recognition.** Strictly speaking, for Aristotle the recognition was a matter of literal identification, for example, that Oedipus was the son of a man he killed. In *Macbeth,* the recognition in this sense is that Macduff, "from his mother's womb / Untimely ripped," is the man who fits the prophecy that Macbeth can be conquered only by someone not "of woman born."

In his analysis of drama Aristotle says that the tragic hero comes to grief through his **hamartia,** a term sometimes translated as **tragic flaw** but perhaps better translated as **tragic *error*.** Thus, it is a great error for Othello to trust Iago and to strangle Desdemona, for Lear to give away his kingdom, and for Macbeth to decide to help fulfill the prophecies. If we hold to the translation "flaw," we begin to hunt for a fault in their characters; and we say, for instance, that Othello is gullible, Lear self-indulgent, Macbeth ambitious, or some such thing. In doing this, we may overlook their grandeur. To take a single example: Iago boasts he can dupe Othello because

> The Moor is of a free and open nature
> That thinks men honest that but seem to be so.

We ought to hesitate before we say that a man who trusts men because they seem to be honest has a flaw.

Writing about Tragedy

When writing about tragedy, probably the commonest essay topic is on the tragic hero. Too often the hero is judged mechanically: He or she must be noble, must have a flaw, must do a fearful deed, must recognize the flaw, must die. The previous paragraph suggests that Shakespeare's practice makes doubtful one of these matters, the flaw. Be similarly cautious about accepting the rest of the package unexamined. (This book has several times urged you to trust your feelings; don't assume that what you have been taught about tragedy—in these pages or elsewhere—must be true and that you should, therefore, trust such assertions even if they go against your own responses to a given play.) On the other hand, if "tragedy" is to have any meaning—any use as a term—it must have some agreed-upon attributes.

An essay that seeks to determine whether a character is a tragic character ought at its outset to make clear its conception of tragedy and the degree of rigidity, or flexibility, with which it will interpret some or all of its categories. For example, it may indicate that although nobility is a *sine qua non,* nobility is not equivalent to high rank. A middle-class figure with certain mental or spiritual characteristics may, in such a view, be an acceptable tragic hero.

An essay closely related to the sort we have been talking about measures a character by some well-known theory of tragedy. For example, one can measure Willy Loman, in *Death of a Salesman,* against Miller's essays on tragedy or against Aristotle's remarks on tragedy. The organization of such an essay is usually not a problem: Isolate the relevant aspects of the theoretical statement, and then examine the character to see if, point by point, he illustrates them. But remember that even if Willy Loman fulfills Arthur Miller's idea of a tragic figure, you need not accept him as tragic; conversely, if he does not fulfill Aristotle's idea, you need not deny him tragic status. Aristotle may be wrong.

Comedy

Although a comedy ought to be amusing, the plays that are called comedies are not just collections of jokes. Rather, they are works that are entertaining throughout and that end happily.

In comedy, the fullest life is seen to reside within enlightened social norms: At the beginning of a comedy we find banished dukes, unhappy lovers, crabby parents, jealous husbands, and harsh laws; but at the end we usually have a unified and genial society, often symbolized by a marriage feast to which everyone, or almost everyone, is invited. Early in *A Midsummer Night's Dream,* for instance, we meet quarreling young lovers and a father who demands that his daughter either marry a man she does not love or enter a convent. Such is the Athenian law. At the end of the play the lovers are properly matched, to everyone's satisfaction.

Speaking broadly, most comedies fall into one of two classes: **satiric comedy** and **romantic comedy.** In satiric comedy the emphasis is on the obstructionists—the irate fathers, hardheaded businessmen, and other members of the Establishment who at the beginning of the play seem to hold all the cards, preventing joy from reigning. They are held up to ridicule because they are repressive monomaniacs enslaved to themselves, acting mechanistically (always irate, always hardheaded) instead of responding genially to the ups and downs of life. The outwitting of these obstructionists, usually by the younger generation, often provides the resolution of the plot. Jonson, Molière, and Shaw are in this tradition; their comedy, according to an ancient Roman formula, "chastens morals with ridicule"; that is, it reforms folly or vice by laughing at it. In romantic comedy (one thinks of Shakespeare's *Midsummer Night's Dream, As You Like It,* and *Twelfth Night*) the emphasis is on a pair or pairs of delightful people who engage our sympathies as they run their obstacle race to the altar. Obstructionists are found here too, but the emphasis is on festivity.

Writing about Comedy

Essays on comedy often examine the nature of the humor. Why is an irate father, in this context, funny? Or why is a young lover, again in this context, funny? Commonly, one will find that at least some of the humor is in the disproportionate nature of their activities (they get terribly excited) and in their inflexibility. In both of these qualities they are rather like the cat in animated cartoons who repeatedly chases the mouse to his hole and who repeatedly bangs his head against the wall. The following is a skeleton of a possible essay on why Jaques in *As You Like It* is amusing:

> Jaques is insistently melancholy. In the Eden-like Forest of Arden, he sees only the dark side of things.
>
> His monomania, however, is harmless to himself and to others; because it causes us no pain, it may entertain us.
>
> Indeed, we begin to look forward to his melancholy speeches. We delight in hearing him fulfill our expectations by wittily finding gloom where others find mirth.
>
> We are delighted, too, to learn that this chastiser of others has in fact been guilty of the sort of behavior he chastises.
>
> At the end of the play, when four couples are wed, the inflexible Jaques insists on standing apart from the general rejoicing.

Such might be the gist of an essay. It needs to be supported with details, and it can be enriched, for example, by a comparison between Jaques's sort of jesting and Touchstone's; but it is at least a promising draft of an outline.

In writing about comedy you may be concerned with the function of one scene or character, but whatever your topic, you may find it helpful to begin by trying to decide whether the play is primarily romantic or primarily satiric (or something else). One way of getting at this is to ask yourself to what degree you sympathize with the characters. Do you laugh *with* them, sympathetically, or do you laugh *at* them, regarding them as at least somewhat contemptible?

Tragicomedy

The word *tragicomedy* has been used to denote (1) plays that seem tragic until the happy ending, (2) plays that combine tragic and comic scenes, and (3) plays that combine the anguish of tragedy with the improbable situations and unheroic characters and funny dialogue of comedy. It is this last sort of tragicomedy (also called "black comedy") that will occupy us here because it has attracted most of the best dramatists of our time, for example, Beckett, Genet, and Ionesco. They are the dramatists of the Absurd in two senses: the irrational and the ridiculous. These writers differ from one another and from play to play, but they all are preoccupied with the loneliness of people in a world without the certainties afforded by God or by optimistic rationalism. This loneliness is heightened by a sense of impotence derived partly from an awareness of our inability to communicate in a society that has made language meaningless, and partly from an awareness of the precariousness of our existence in an atomic age.

Landmarks on the road to people's awareness of their littleness are Darwin's *The Origin of Species* (1859), which reduced human beings to the product of "accidental variations"; Marx's writings, which attributed people's sense of alienation to economic forces and thus implied that people had no identity they could properly call their own; and Freud's writings, which by charting people's unconscious drives and anarchic impulses induced a profound distrust of the self.

The result of such developments in thought seems to be that a "tragic sense" in the twentieth century commonly means a despairing or deeply uncertain view, something very different from what it meant in Greece and in Elizabethan England. This uncertainty is not merely about the cosmos or even about character or identity. In 1888, in the preface to *Miss Julie*, Strindberg called attention to the new sense of the instability of character:

> I have made the people in my play fairly "characterless." The middle-class conception of a fixed character was transferred to the stage, where the middle class has always ruled. A character there came to mean an actor who was always one and the same, always drunk, always comic or always melancholy, and who needed to be characterized only by some physical defect such as a club foot, a wooden leg, or a red nose, or by the repetition of some such phrase such as, "That's capital," or "Barkis is willin'." . . . Since the persons in my play are modern characters, living in a transitional era more hurried and hysterical than the previous one at least, I have depicted them as more unstable, as torn and divided, a mixture of the old and the new.

Along with the sense of characterlessness, or at least of the mystery of character, developed in the drama (and in the underground film and novel) was a sense of plotlessness or of the fundamental untruthfulness of the traditional plot that moved by cause and effect. Ionesco, for example, has said that a play should be able to stop at any point; it ends only because—as in life—the audience at last has to go home to bed. Moreover, Ionesco has allowed directors to make heavy cuts, and he has suggested that endings other than those he wrote are possibilities. After all, in a meaningless world one can hardly take a dramatic plot seriously.

Every play is different from every other play; each is a unique and detailed statement, and the foregoing paragraphs give only the broadest outlines—tragedies, comedies, and tragicomedies seen at a distance, as it were. The analyst's job is to try to study the differences, as well as the similarities, in an effort (in Henry James's words) "to appreciate, to appropriate, to take intellectual possession, to establish in fine a relation with the criticized thing and make it one's own."

ASPECTS OF DRAMA

Theme

If we have perceived the work properly, we ought to be able to formulate its **theme**, its underlying idea, and perhaps we can even go so far as to say its moral attitudes, its view of life, its wisdom. Some critics, it is true, have argued that the concept of theme is meaningless. They hold that *Macbeth*, for example, gives us only an extremely detailed history of one imaginary man. In this view, *Macbeth* says nothing to you or me; it only says what happened to some imaginary man. Even *Julius Caesar* says nothing about the historical Julius Caesar or about the nature of Roman politics. On this we can agree; no one would offer Shakespeare's play as evidence of what the historical Caesar said or did. But surely the view that the concept of theme is meaningless and that a work tells us only about imaginary creatures is a desperate one. We *can* say that we see in *Julius Caesar* the fall of power or (if we are thinking of Brutus) the vulnerability of idealism or some such thing.

To the reply that these are mere truisms, we can counter: Yes, but the truisms are presented in such a way that they take on life and become a part of us rather than remain things of which we say, "I've heard it said, and I guess it's so." Surely we are in no danger of equating the play with the theme that we sense underlies it. If, for example, we say (as Ionesco himself said of his play) that *Rhinoceros* is "an attack on collective hysteria and the epidemics that lurk beneath the surface of reason," we do not believe that our statement of the theme is the equivalent of the play itself. We recognize that the play presents the theme with such detail that our statement is only a wedge to help us enter into the play, so that we may more fully appropriate it.

A brief illustration may be helpful here. A critic examining Ibsen's achievements begins by trying to see what some of the plays are in fact about.

> We must not waste more than a paragraph on such fiddle-faddle as the notion that *Ghosts* is a play about venereal disease or that *A Doll's House* is a play about women's rights. On these terms, *King Lear* is a play about housing for the elderly and *Hamlet* is a stage-debate over the reality of spooks. Venereal disease and its consequences are represented onstage in *Ghosts;* so, to all intents and purposes, is incest; but the theme of the play is inherited guilt, and the sexual pathology of the Alving family is an engine in the hands of that theme. *A Doll's House* represents a woman imbued with the idea of becoming a person, but it proposes nothing categorical about women becoming people; in fact, its real theme has nothing to do with the sexes. It is the irrepressible conflict of two different personalities which have founded themselves on two radically different estimates of reality.
>
> —ROBERT M. ADAMS, "Ibsen on the Contrary," in *Modern Drama,* ed.
> Anthony Caputi (New York, 1966), p. 345

Such a formulation can be most useful; a grasp of the theme helps us see what the plot is really all about, what the plot suggests in its universal meaning or applicability.

A few words about the preceding quotation may be appropriate here. Notice that Adam's paragraph moves from a vigorous colloquial opening through some familiar examples, including a brief comparison with plays by another dramatist, to a fairly formal close. The disparity in tone between opening and closing is not distressing because even in the opening we sense the writer's mastery of his material, and we sympathize with his impatience. Adams's next paragraph, not given here, extends his suggestion that the plays are not about nineteenth-century problems: He argues that under the bourgeois décor, under the frock coat and the bustle, we detect two kinds of people—little people and great people. His third paragraph elaborates this point by suggesting that, allowing for variations, the dichotomy consists of satyrs and saints, and he provides the details necessary to make this dichotomy convincing. Among Ibsen's little people, or satyrs, are Parson Manders, Peter Stockmann, Hjalmar Ekdal, and Torvald Helmer; among the great people, or saints, are Mrs. Alving, Thomas Stockmann, Gregers Werle, and Nora Helmer. In short, Adams's argument about Ibsen's themes advances steadily and is convincingly illustrated with concrete references.

Some critics (influenced by Aristotle's statement that a drama is an imitation of an action) use **action** in a sense equivalent to theme. In this sense, the action is the underlying happening—the inner happening—for example, "the enlightenment of someone" or "the coming of unhappiness" or "the finding of the self by self-surrender." One might say that the theme of *Macbeth*, for example, is embodied in some words that Macbeth himself utters: "Blood will have blood." Of course, this is not to say that these words and no other words embody the theme or the action. Francis Fergusson suggests that another expression in *Macbeth*, to the effect that Macbeth "outran the pauser, reason," describes the action of the play:

> To "outrun" reason suggests an impossible stunt, like lifting oneself by one's own bootstraps. It also suggests a competition or race, like those of nightmare, which cannot be won. As for the word "reason," Shakespeare associates it with nature and nature's order, in the individual soul, in society, and in the cosmos. To outrun reason is thus to violate nature itself, to lose the bearings of common sense and of custom, and to move into a spiritual realm bounded by the irrational darkness of Hell one way, and the superrational grace of faith the other way. As the play develops before us, all the modes of this absurd, or evil, or supernatural, action are attempted, the last being Malcolm's and Macduff's acts of faith.
>
> —*The Human Image in Dramatic Literature* (New York, 1957), p. 118

Critics like Fergusson, who are influenced by Aristotle's *Poetics*, assume that the dramatist conceives of an action and then imitates it or sets it forth by means of first a plot and characters and then by means of language, gesture, and perhaps spectacle and music. When the Greek comic dramatist Menander told a friend he had finished his play and now had only to write it, he must have meant that he had the action or the theme firmly in mind and had worked out the plot and the requisite characters. All that remained was to set down the words.

Plot

Plot is variously defined sometimes as equivalent to "story" (in this sense a synopsis of *Julius Caesar* has the same plot as *Julius Caesar*) but more often, and more usefully, as the dramatist's particular arrangement of the story. Thus, because Shakespeare's *Julius Caesar* begins with a scene dramatizing an encounter between plebeians and tribunes, its plot is different from that of a play on Julius Caesar in which such a scene (not necessary to the story) is omitted. Richard G. Moulton, discussing the early part of Shakespeare's plot in *Julius Caesar*, examines the relationship between the first two scenes.

> . . . The opening scene strikes appropriately the key-note of the whole action. In it we see the tribunes of the people—officers whose whole *raison d'être* is

to be the mouthpiece of the commonalty—restraining their own clients from the noisy honors they are disposed to pay Caesar. To the justification in our eyes of a conspiracy against Caesar, there could not be a better starting-point than this hint that the popular worship of Caesar, which has made him what he is, is itself reaching its reaction-point. Such a suggestion moreover makes the whole play one complete *wave* of popular fickleness from crest to crest.

The second is the scene upon which the dramatist mainly relies for the *crescendo* in the justification of the conspirators. It is a long scene, elaborately contrived so as to keep the conspirators and their cause before us at their very best, and the victim at his very worst.

—*Shakespeare as a Dramatic Artist* (Oxford, 1893), pp. 188-189

Moulton's discussion of the plot continues at length. One may argue that he presents too favorable a view of the conspirators (when he says we see the conspirators at their best, he seems to overlook their fawning), but that is not our concern here; here we have been talking about the process of examining juxtaposed scenes, a process Moulton's words illustrate well.

Handbooks on the drama often suggest that a plot (arrangement of happenings) should have a **rising action,** a **climax,** and a **falling action.** This sort of plot may be diagrammed as a pyramid: The tension rises through complications or **crises** to a climax, at which point the climax is the apex, and the tension allegedly slackens as we witness the **dénouement** (unknotting). Shakespeare sometimes used a pyramidal structure, placing his climax neatly in the middle of what seems to us to be the third of five acts. Roughly the first half of *Romeo and Juliet,* for example, shows Romeo winning Juliet; but when in 3.1 he kills her cousin Tybalt, Romeo sets in motion (it is often said) the second half of the play, the losing of Juliet and of his own life. Similarly, in *Julius Caesar* Brutus rises in the first half of the play, reaching his height in 3.1 with the death of Caesar; but later in this scene he gives Marc Anthony permission to speak at Caesar's funeral, and thus he sets in motion his own fall, which occupies the second half of the play. In *Macbeth,* the protagonist attains his height in 3.1 ("Thou hast it now: King"), but he soon perceives that he is going downhill:

> I am in blood
> Stepped in so far, that, should I wade no more,
> Returning were as tedious as go o'er.

In *Hamlet,* the protagonist proves to his own satisfaction Claudius's guilt in 3.2, by the play within the play, but almost immediately he begins to worsen his position by failing to kill Claudius when he is an easy target (3.3) and by contaminating himself with the murder of Polonius (3.4).

No law demands such a structure, and a hunt for the pyramid usually causes the hunter to overlook all the crises but the middle one. William Butler Yeats once suggestively diagrammed a good plot not as a pyramid but as a line moving diagonally upward, punctuated by several crises. And it has been said that in Beckett's *Waiting for Godot,* "nothing happens, twice." Perhaps it is sufficient to say that a good plot has its moments of tension, but that the location of these will vary with the play. They are the product of **conflict,** but it should be noted that not all conflict produces tension; there is conflict but little tension in a ball game when the home team is ahead 10–0 and the visiting pitcher comes to bat in the ninth inning with two out and none on base.

Regardless of how a plot is diagramed, the exposition is the part that tells the audience what it has to know about the past, the **antecedent action.** Two gossiping servants who tell each other that after a year away in Paris the young master is coming home tomorrow with a new wife are giving the audience the exposition. The exposition in Shakespeare's *Tempest* is almost ruthlessly direct: Prospero tells his naive daughter, "I should inform thee farther," and for about 150 lines he proceeds to tell her why she is on an almost uninhabited island. Prospero's harangue is punctuated by his daughter's professions of attention; but the Elizabethans (and the Greeks) sometimes tossed out all pretense at dialogue and began with a **prologue,** like the one spoken by the Chorus at the opening of *Romeo and Juliet:*

> Two households, both alike in dignity
> > In fair Verona, where we lay our scene,
> From ancient grudge break to new mutiny,
> > Where civil blood makes civil hands unclean.
> From forth the fatal loins of these two foes
> > A pair of star-crossed lovers take their life. . . .

But the exposition may also extend far into the play, being given in small, explosive revelations.

Exposition has been discussed as though it consists simply of informing the audience about events, but exposition can do much more. It can give us an understanding of the characters who themselves are talking about other characters, it can evoke a mood, and it can generate tension. When we summarize the opening act and treat it as "mere exposition," we are probably losing what is in fact dramatic in it. Moulton, in his analysis of the first two scenes in *Julius Caesar,* does not make the mistake of thinking that the first scenes exist merely to tell the audience certain facts.

In fact, exposition usually includes **foreshadowing.** Details given in the exposition, which we may at first take as mere background, often turn out to be highly relevant to later developments. For instance, in the very short first scene of *Macbeth* the Witches introduce the name of Macbeth, but in such words as "fair is foul" and "when the battle's lost and won" they also give glimpses of what will happen: Macbeth will become foul, and though he will seem to win (he becomes king), he will lose the most important battle. Similarly, during the exposition in the second scene we learn that Macbeth has loyally defeated Cawdor, who betrayed King Duncan, and Macbeth has been given Cawdor's title. Later we will find that, like Cawdor, Macbeth betrays Duncan; that is, in giving us the background about Cawdor, the exposition is also telling us (though we don't know it when we first see or read the play) something about what will happen to Macbeth.

Writing about Plot

In writing about an aspect of plot, you may want to consider one of the following topics:

1. Is the plot improbable? If so, is the play, therefore, weak?
2. Does a scene that might at first glance seem unimportant or even irrelevant serve an important function?
3. If certain actions that could be shown onstage take place offstage, what is the reason? In *Macbeth*, for instance, why do you suppose the murder of Duncan takes place offstage, whereas Banquo and Macduff's family are murdered onstage? Why, then, might Shakespeare have preferred not to show us the murder of Duncan? What has he gained? (A good way to approach this sort of question is to think of what your own reaction would be if the action were shown onstage.) *King Lear*
4. If the play has several conflicts—for example, between pairs of lovers or between parents and their children and also between the parents themselves—how are these conflicts related? Are they parallel? Or contrasting?
5. Does the arrangement of scenes have a structure? For instance, do the scenes depict a rise and then a fall?
6. Does the plot seem satisfactorily concluded? Any loose threads? If so, is the apparent lack of a complete resolution a weakness in the play?

An analysis of plot, then, will consider the arrangement of the episodes and the effect of juxtapositions, as well as the overall story. A useful essay may be written on the function of one scene. Such an essay may point out, for example, that the long, comparatively slow scene (4.3) in *Macbeth*, in which Malcolm, Macduff, an English doctor, and Ross converse near the palace of the King of England, is not so much a leisurely digression as may at first be thought. After reading it closely, you may decide that it has several functions. For example, it serves to indicate the following:

1. The forces that will eventually overthrow Macbeth are gathering.
2. Even good men must tell lies during Macbeth's reign.

3. Macbeth has the vile qualities that the virtuous Malcolm pretends to have.

4. Macbeth has failed—as the King of England has not—to be a source of health to the realm.

It doubtless will take an effort to come to these or other conclusions, but once you have come to such ideas (probably by means of brainstorming and listing), the construction of an essay on the function of a scene is usually fairly simple: An introductory paragraph announces the general topic and thesis—an apparently unnecessary scene will be shown to be functional—and the rest of the essay demonstrates the functions, usually in climactic order if some of the functions are more important than others.

How might you organize such an essay? If you think all of the functions are equally important, perhaps you will organize the material from the most obvious to the least obvious, thereby keeping the reader's attention to the end. If on the other hand, you believe that although justifications for the scene can be imagined, the scene is nevertheless unsuccessful, say so; announce your view early, consider the alleged functions one by one, and explain your reasons for finding them unconvincing as you take up each point.

Sometimes an analysis of the plot will examine the relationships between the several stories in a play: *A Midsummer Night's Dream* has supernatural lovers, mature royal lovers, young Athenian lovers, a bumpkin who briefly becomes the lover of the fairy queen, and a play (put on by the bumpkins) about legendary lovers. How these are held together and how they help define each other and the total play are matters that concern anyone looking at the plot of *A Midsummer Night's Dream.* Richard Moulton suggests that Shakespeare's subplots "have the effect of assisting the main stories, smoothing away their difficulties and making their prominent points yet more prominent." Moulton demonstrates his thesis at some length, but a very brief extract from his discussion of the Jessica–Lorenzo story in *The Merchant of Venice* may be enough to suggest the method. The main story concerns Shylock and his rivals, Antonio, Bassanio, and Portia. Shylock's daughter, Jessica, is not needed for the narrative purpose of the main story. Why, then, did Shakespeare include her? (*Remember:* When something puzzles you, you have an essay topic at hand.) Part of Moulton's answer runs thus:

> A Shylock painted without a tender side at all would be repulsive . . . and yet it appears how this tenderness has grown hard and rotten with the general debasement of his soul by avarice, until, in his ravings over his loss, his ducats and his daughter are ranked as equally dear.
>
> I would my daughter were dead at my foot, and the jewels in her ear! Would she were hearsed at my foot, and the ducats in her coffin!

For all this we feel that he is hardly used in losing her. Paternal feeling may take a gross form, but it is paternal feeling none the less, and cannot be denied our sympathy; bereavement is a common ground upon which not only high and low, but even the pure and the outcast, are drawn together. Thus Jessica at home makes us hate Shylock; with Jessica lost we cannot help pitying him.

—*Shakespeare as a Dramatic Artist*

Characterization and Motivation

Characterization, or personality, is defined most obviously, as in fiction (see p. 163), by what the characters do (a stage direction tells us that "Hedda paces up and down, clenching her fists"), by what they say (she asks her husband to draw the curtains), by what others say about them, and by the setting in which they move.

The characters are also defined in part by other characters whom they in some degree resemble. Hamlet, Laertes, and Fortinbras have each lost their fathers, but Hamlet spares the praying King Claudius, whereas Laertes, seeking vengeance on Hamlet for murdering Laertes's father, says he would cut Hamlet's throat in church; Hamlet meditates about the nature of action, but Fortinbras leads the Norwegians in a military campaign and ultimately acquires Denmark. Here is Kenneth Muir commenting briefly on the way Laertes helps us see Hamlet more precisely. (Notice how Muir first offers a generalization, then supports it with details, and finally, drawing a conclusion from the details he has just presented, offers an even more important generalization that effectively closes his paragraph.)

In spite of Hamlet's description of him as "a very noble youth," there is a coarseness of fibre in Laertes which is revealed throughout the play. He has the stock responses of a man of his time and position. He gives his sister copybook advice; he goes to Paris (we are bound to suspect) to tread the primrose path; and after his father's death and again at his sister's grave he shows by the ostentation and "bravery of his grief" that he pretends more than he really feels. He has no difficulty in raising a successful rebellion against Claudius, which suggests that the more popular prince could have done the same. Laertes, indeed, acts more or less in the way that many critics profess to think Hamlet ought to act; and his function in the play is to show precisely the opposite. Although Hamlet himself may envy Laertes' capacity for ruthless action we ought surely to prefer Hamlet's craven scruples.

—*Shakespeare: The Great Tragedies* (London, 1961), pp. 12–13

Muir has not exhausted the topic in this paragraph. If you are familiar with *Hamlet* you may want to think about writing an entire essay comparing Hamlet with Laertes.

Other plays provide examples of such **foils,** or characters who set one another off. Macbeth and Banquo both hear prophecies, but they act and react differently; Brutus is one kind of assassin, Cassius another, and Casca still another. In *Waiting for Godot,* the two tramps Didi and Gogo are contrasted with Pozzo and his slave Lucky, the former two suggesting (roughly) the contemplative life, the latter two the practical or active (and, it turns out, mistaken) life.

Any analysis of a character, then, will probably have to take into account, in some degree, the other characters that help show what he or she is, that help set forth his or her motivation (grounds for action, inner drives, goals). In Ibsen's *Doll's House,* Dr. Rank plays a part in helping define Nora:

> This is not Rank's play, it is Nora's. Rank is a minor character—but he plays a vital dramatic role. His function is to act as the physical embodiment, visible on the stage, of Nora's moral situation as she sees it. Nora is almost hysterical with terror at the thought of her situation—almost, but it is part of her character that with great heroism she keeps her fears secret to herself; and it is because of her reticence that Rank is dramatically necessary, to symbolize the horror she will not talk about. Nora feels, and we feel, the full awfulness of Rank's illness, and she transfers to herself the same feeling about the moral corruption which she imagines herself to carry. Nora sees herself, and we see her seeing herself (with our judgment), as suffering from a moral disease as mortal, as irremediable as Rank's disease, a disease that creeps on to a fatal climax. This is the foe that Nora is fighting so courageously.
>
> —JOHN NORTHAM, "Ibsen's Search for the Hero," in *Ibsen*, ed. Rolf Fjelde (Englewood Cliffs, NJ, 1965), p. 103

Conventions

Artists and their audience have some tacit—even unconscious—agreements. When we watch a motion picture and see an image dissolve and then reappear, we understand that some time has passed. Such a device, unrealistic but widely accepted, is a **convention.** In the theater, we sometimes see on the stage a room, realistic in all details except that it lacks a fourth wall; were that wall in place, we would see it and not the interior of the room. We do not regret the missing wall, and, indeed, we are scarcely aware that we have entered into an agreement to pretend that this strange room is an ordinary room with the usual number of walls. Sometimes the characters in a play speak verse, although outside the theater no human beings speak verse for more than a few moments. Again we accept the device because it allows the author to make a play, and we want a play. In *Hamlet* the characters are understood to be speaking Danish, in *Julius Caesar* Latin, in *A Midsummer Night's Dream* Greek, yet they all speak English for our benefit.

Two other conventions are especially common in older drama: the **soliloquy** and the **aside.** In the former, although a solitary character speaks his or her thoughts aloud, we do not judge him or her to be a lunatic; in the latter, a character speaks in the presence of others but is understood not to be heard by them, or to be heard only by those to whom he or she directs those words.

The soliloquy and the aside strike us as artificial—and they are. But they so strike us only because they are no longer customary. Because we are accustomed to it, we are not bothered by the artificiality of music accompanying dialogue in a motion picture. The conventions of the modern theater are equally artificial but are so customary that we do not notice them. The Elizabethans, who saw a play acted without a break, would probably find strange our assumption that, when we return to the auditorium after a ten-minute intermission, the ensuing action may be supposed to follow immediately the action before the intermission.

Costumes, Gestures, and Settings

The language of a play, broadly conceived, includes the costumes that the characters wear, the gestures that the characters make, and the settings in which the characters move. As Ezra Pound says, "The medium of drama is not words, but persons moving about on a stage using words."

Let's begin with **costume,** specifically with Nora Helmer's changes of costume in Ibsen's *A Doll's House.* In the first act, Nora wears ordinary clothing, but in the middle of the second act she puts on "a long, many-colored shawl" when she frantically rehearses her tarantella. The shawl is supposed to be appropriate to the Italian dance, but surely its multitude of colors also helps express Nora's conflicting emotions, her near hysteria, expressed, too, in the fact that "her hair comes loose and falls down over her shoulders," but "She doesn't notice." The shawl and her disheveled hair, then, *speak* to us as clearly as the dialogue does.

In the middle of the third act, after the party and just before the showdown, Nora appears in her "Italian costume," and her husband, Torvald, wears "evening dress" under an open black cloak. She is dressed for a masquerade (her whole life has been a masquerade, it turns out), and Torvald's formal suit and black cloak help express the stiffness and the blight that have forced her to present a false front throughout their years of marriage. A little later, after Nora sees that she never really has known her husband for the selfish creature he is, she leaves the stage, and when she returns she is "in an everyday dress." The pretense is over. She is no longer Torvald's "doll." When she finally leaves the stage—leaving the house—she "Wraps her shawl around her." This is not the "many-colored shawl" she used in re-hearsing the dance, but the "big, black shawl" she wears when she returns from the dance. The blackness of this shawl helps express the death of her old way of life; Nora is now aware that life is not child's play.

Ibsen did not invent the use of costumes as dramatic language; it goes back to the beginnings of drama, and one has only to think of Hamlet's "inky cloak" or of Lear tearing off his clothing or of the fresh clothing in which Lear is garbed after his madness in order to see how eloquently cos-tumes can speak. To this may be added the matter of disguises—for exam-ple, Edgar's disguise in *King Lear*—which are removed near the end of plays, when the truth is finally revealed and the characters can be fully themselves. In short, the removal of disguises *says* something.

Gestures, too, are a part of the language of drama. Helmer "playfully pulls [Nora's] ear," showing his affection—and his domineering condescen-sion; Nora claps her hands, Mrs. Linde (an old friend of Nora) "tries to read but seems unable to concentrate," and so forth. All such gestures clearly and naturally convey states of mind. One of the most delightful and reveal-ing gestures in the play occurs when, in the third act, Helmer demonstrates to Mrs. Linde the ugliness of knitting ("Look here: arms pressed close to the sides") and the elegance of embroidering (". . . with your right [hand] you move the needle—like this—in an easy, elongated arc"). None of his absurd remarks throughout the play is quite so revealing of his absurdity as is this silly demonstration.

Some gestures or stage directions that imply gestures are a bit more complex. For example, when Nora "walks cautiously over to the door to the study and listens," this direction conveys Nora's fear that her husband may detect her foibles—or even her crime. We read this stage direction almost at the start of the play, when we do not yet know who is who or what is what, but we do know from this gesture alone that Nora is not at ease even in her own home. When Mrs. Linde sees her former lover, Krogstad, she "starts, looks, turns away toward the window," a natural enough reaction but one that indicates her desire to escape from this confining box-set. Similarly, when Nora "wildly" dances during her rehearsal in the second act, the action indicates the terrible agitation in her mind. One other, qui-eter example: In Act III, when the dying Dr. Rank for the last time visits Nora in order to gain comfort, she lights his cigar, and a moment later Rank replies—these are his last words—"And thanks for the light." Thus, we not only hear words about a cigar, but we *see* an act of friendship, a flash of light in this oppressive household.

Gesture may be interpreted even more broadly: The mere fact that a character enters, leaves, or does not enter may be highly significant. John Russell Brown comments on the actions and the absence of certain words that in *Hamlet* convey the growing separation between King Claudius and his wife, Gertrude:

> Their first appearance together with a public celebration of marriage is a large and simple visual effect, and Gertrude's close concern for her son suggests a simple, and perhaps unremarkable modification. . . . But Claudius enters without Gertrude for his "Prayer Scene" (III.iii) and, for the first time, Gertrude enters without him for the Closet Scene (III.iv) and is left alone, again for the first time, when Polonius hides behind the arras. Thereafter earlier accord is revalued by an increasing separation, often poignantly silent, and unexpected. When Claudius calls Gertrude to leave with him after Hamlet has dragged off Polonius' body, she makes no reply; twice more he urges her and she is still silent. But he does not remonstrate or question; rather he speaks of his own immediate concerns and, far from supporting her with assurances, becomes more aware of his own fears:
>
> > O, come away!
> > My soul is full of discord and dismay. (V.i.44–45)
>
> Emotion has been so heightened that it is remarkable that they leave together without further words. The audience has been aware of a new distance between Gertrude and Claudius, of her immobility and silence, and of his self-concern, haste and insistence.
>
> —*Shakespeare's Plays in Performance* (New York, 1967), p. 139

Sometimes the dramatist helps us interpret the gestures; Shaw and O'Neill give notably full stage directions, but detailed stage directions before the middle of the nineteenth century are rare.

Drama of the nineteenth and early twentieth centuries (for example, the plays of Ibsen, Chekhov, and Odets) is often thought to be "realistic," but even a realistic playwright or stage designer selects his or her materials. A realistic **setting** (indication of the locale), then, can say a great deal, can serve as a symbol. Here is Ibsen on nonverbal devices:

> I can do quite a lot by manipulating the prosaic details of my plays so that they become theatrical metaphors and come to mean more than what they are; I have used costume in this way, lighting, scenery, landscape, weather; I have used trivial every-day things like inky fingers and candles; and I have used living figures as symbols of spiritual forces that act upon the hero. Perhaps these things could be brought into the context of a modern realistic play to help me to portray the modern hero and the tragic conflict which I now understand so well.
>
> —Quoted by JOHN NORTHAM, "Ibsen's Search for the Hero," p. 99

In the setting of *Hedda Gabler*, for example, Ibsen uses two suggestive details as more than mere background: Early in the play Hedda is distressed by the sunlight that shines through the opened French doors, a detail that we later see helps reveal her fear of the processes of nature. More evident and more pervasive is her tendency, when she cannot cope with her present situation, to move to the inner room, at the rear of the stage, in which hangs a picture of her late father. And over and over again in Ibsen we find the realistic setting of a nineteenth-century drawing room, with its heavy draperies and its bulky furniture, helping convey his vision of a bourgeois world that oppresses the individual who struggles to affirm other values.

Twentieth-century dramatists are often explicit about the symbolic qualities of the setting. Here is an example from O'Neill's *Desire under the Elms*. Only a part of the initial stage direction is given.

> The house is in good condition but in need of paint. Its walls are a sickly grayish, the green of the shutters faded. Two enormous elms are on each side of the house. They bend their trailing branches down over the roof. They appear to protect and at the same time subdue. There is a sinister maternity in their aspect, a crushing, jealous absorption. . . . They are like exhausted women resting their sagging breasts and hands and hair on its roof. . . .

A second example is part of Miller's description of the set in *Death of a Salesman*:

> Before us is the Salesman's house. We are aware of towering, angular shapes behind it, surrounding it on all sides. Only the blue light of the sky falls upon the house and forestage; the surrounding area shows an angry glow of orange. As more light appears, we see a solid vault of apartment houses around the small, fragile-seeming home.

Material such as this cannot be skimmed. These directions and the settings they describe are symbols that help give the plays their meaning. Not surprisingly, O'Neill's play has Freudian overtones, Miller's (in a broad sense) Marxist overtones. O'Neill is concerned about passion, Miller (notice the "solid vault of apartment houses" that menaces the salesman's house) about social forces that warp the individual. An essay might examine in detail the degree to which the setting contributes to the theme of the play. Take, for example, O'Neill's setting. The maternal elms are the most important aspect, but an essayist might first point out that the "good condition" of the house suggests it was well built, presumably some years ago. The need of paint, however, suggests both present neglect and indifference to decoration, and, indeed, the play is partly concerned with a strong, miserly father who regards his sons as decadent. The house, "a sickly grayish," helps embody the suggestion of old strength but present decadence. One might continue through the stage directions, explaining the relevance of the details. Contrasts between successive settings can be especially important.

Because Shakespeare's plays were performed in broad daylight on a stage that (compared with Ibsen's, O'Neill's, and Miller's) made little use of scenery, he had to use language to manufacture his settings. But the attentive ear or the mind's eye responds to these settings, too. Early in *King Lear*, when Lear reigns, we hear that we are in a country "With plenteous rivers, and wide-skirted meads"; later, when Lear is stripped of his power, we are in a place where "For many miles about / There's scarce a bush."

In any case, a director must provide some sort of setting—even if only a bare stage—and this setting will be part of the play. A recent production of *Julius Caesar* used great cubes piled on top of each other as the background for the first half of the play, suggesting the pretensions and the littleness of the figures who strutted on the stage. In the second half of the play, when Rome is in the throes of a civil war, the cubes were gone; a shaggy black carpet, darkness at the rear of the stage, and a great net hanging above the actors suggested that they were wretched little creatures groping in blindness. In a review of a production, you will almost surely want to pay some attention to the function of the setting.

Suggestions for Further Reading

Among useful reference works are: Stanley Hochman, ed., *McGraw-Hill Encyclopedia of World Drama*, 5 vols., 2nd ed. (1984); Phyllis Hartnoll, ed., *The Oxford Companion to the Theatre*, 4th ed. (1983); Martin Banham, ed., *Cambridge Guide to World Theatre* (1988); Myron Matlaw, *Modern World Drama: An Encyclopedia* (1972).

Two useful introductions to the nature of drama are Eric Bentley, *The Life of the Drama* (1964), and J. L. Styan, *The Elements of Drama* (1969). More specialized studies are: Eric Bentley, *The Playwright as Thinker* (1946); C. W. E. Bigsby, *A Critical Introduction to Twentieth-Century American Drama*, 3 vols. (1982–85); Sue-Ellen Case, *Feminism and the Theatre* (1984); Susan Bennett, *Theatre Audiences: A Theory of Production and Reception* (1990).

A quarterly journal, *Modern Drama*, publishes articles on American and English drama from 1850 to the present. It also includes an annual bibliography of studies of this material.

A Checklist: Getting Ideas for Writing about Drama

The following questions may help you to formulate ideas for an essay on a play.

Plot and Conflict

1. Does the exposition introduce elements that will be ironically fulfilled? During the exposition do you perceive things differently from the way the characters perceive them?

2. Are certain happenings or situations recurrent? If so, what significance do you attach to them?

3. If there is more than one plot, do the plots seem to you to be related? Is one plot clearly the main plot and another plot a sort of subplot, a minor variation on the theme?

4. Take one scene of special interest and indicate the structure, for example from stability at the beginning to the introduction of an instability, and then to a new sort of stability or resolution.

5. Do any scenes strike you as irrelevant?

6. Are certain scenes so strongly foreshadowed that you anticipated them? If so, did the happenings in these scenes merely fulfill your expectations, or did they also in some way surprise you?

7. What kinds of conflict are there? One character against another, one group against another, one part of a personality against another part in the same person?

8. How is the conflict resolved? By an unambiguous triumph of one side or by a triumph that is also in some degree a loss for the triumphant side? Do you find the resolution satisfying, or unsettling, or what? Why?

Character

1. What are the traits of the chosen character?

2. A dramatic character is not likely to be thoroughly realistic, a copy of someone we might know. Still, we can ask if the character is consistent and coherent. We can also ask if the character is complex or is, on the other hand, a rather simple representative of some human type.

3. How is the character defined? Consider what the character says and does and what others say about him or her and do to him or her. Also consider other characters who more or less resemble the character in question, because the similarities—and the differences—may be significant.

4. How trustworthy are the characters when they characterize themselves? When they characterize others?

5. Do characters change as the play goes on, or do we simply know them better at the end? If characters change, *why* do they change?

6. What do you make of the minor characters? Are they merely necessary to the plot, or are they foils to other characters? Or do they serve some other functions?

7. If a character is tragic, does the tragedy seem to proceed from a moral flaw, from an intellectual error, from the malice of others, from sheer chance, or from some combination of these?

8. What are the character's goals? To what degree do you sympathize with them? If a character is comic, do you laugh *with* or *at* the character?

9. Do you think the characters are adequately motivated?

10. Is a given character so meditative that you feel he or she is engaged less in a dialogue with others than in a dialogue with the self? If so, do you feel that this character is in large degree a spokesperson for the author, commenting not only on the world of the play but also on the outside world?

Nonverbal Language

1. If the playwright does not provide full stage directions, try to imagine for a least one scene what gestures and tones might accompany each speech. (The first scene is usually a good one to try your hand at.)

2. What do you make of the setting? Does it help reveal character? Do changes of scene strike you as symbolic? If so, symbolic of what?

The Play on Film

1. If the play has been turned into a film, what has been added? What has been omitted? Why?

2. Has the film medium been used to advantage—for example, in focusing attention through close-ups or reaction shots (shots showing not the speaker but a person reacting to the speaker)? Or do some of the inventions—for example, outdoor scenes that were not possible in the play—seem mere busywork, distracting from the urgency or the conflict or the unity of the play?

12

Writing about Poetry

THE SPEAKER AND THE POET

The **speaker** or **voice** or **mask** or **persona** (Latin for "mask") that speaks a poem is not usually identical with the poet who writes it. The author assumes a role, or counterfeits the speech of a person in a particular situation. Robert Browning, for instance, in "My Last Duchess" (1842) invented a Renaissance duke who, in his palace, talks about his first wife and his art collection with an emissary from a count who is negotiating to offer his daughter in marriage to the duke.

In reading a poem, then, the first and most important question to ask yourself is this: Who is speaking? If an audience and a setting are suggested, keep them in mind, too, although these are not always indicated in a poem. For instance, Emily Dickinson's "Wild Nights" (1861) is the utterance of an impassioned lover, but we need not assume that the beloved is actually in the presence of the lover. In fact, since the second line says, "Were I with thee," the reader must assume that the person addressed is *not* present. The poem apparently represents a state of mind—a sort of talking to oneself—rather than an address to another person.

Emily Dickinson (1830–86)
WILD NIGHTS—WILD NIGHTS

Wild Nights—Wild Nights,
Were I with Thee
Wild Nights should be
Our luxury!   4

Futile—the Winds
To a Heart in port—
Done with the Compass—
Done with the Chart!   8

Rowing in Eden
—Ah, the Sea!
Might I but moor—Tonight—
In Thee.   12

Clearly, the speaker is someone passionately in love. The following questions invite you to look more closely at how the speaker of "Wild Nights" is characterized.

Questions to Stimulate Ideas about "Wild Nights—Wild Nights"

This chapter will end with a list of many questions that you may ask yourself in order to get ideas for writing about any poem. Here, however, are a few questions about this particular poem, to help you to think about it.

1. How does this poem communicate the speaker's state of mind? For example, in the first stanza (lines 1–4), what—beyond the meaning of the words—is communicated by the repetition of "Wild Nights"? In the last stanza (lines 9–12), what is the tone of "Ah, the Sea!"? ("Tone" means something like emotional coloring, as for instance when one speaks of a "businesslike tone," a "bitter tone," or an "eager tone.")

2. Paraphrase (put into your own words) the second stanza. What does this stanza communicate about the speaker's love for the beloved? Compare your paraphrase and the original. What does the form of the original sentences (the *omission*, for instance, of the verbs of lines 5 and 6 and of the subject in lines 7 and 8) communicate?

3. Paraphrase the last stanza. How does "Ah, the Sea!" fit into your paraphrase? If you had trouble fitting it in, do you think the poem would be better off without it? If not, why not?

Although the voice speaking a poem often clearly is *not* the author's, in many other poems the voice does have the ring of the author's own voice, and to make a distinction between speaker and author may at times seem perverse. In fact, some poetry (especially contemporary American poetry) is highly autobiographical. Still, even in autobiographical poems it may be convenient to distinguish between author and speaker. The speaker of a given poem is, let's say, Sylvia Plath in her role as parent, or Sylvia Plath in her role as daughter, not simply Sylvia Plath the poet.

The Language of Poetry: Diction and Tone

How is a voice or mask or persona created? From the whole of language, the author consciously or unconsciously selects certain words and grammatical constructions; this selection constitutes the persona's diction. It is, then, partly by the diction that we come to know the speaker of a poem. Just as in life there is a difference between people who speak of a *belly-button*, a *navel*, and an *umbilicus*, so in poetry there is a difference between speakers who use one word rather than another. Of course, it is also possible that all three of these words are part of a given speaker's vocabulary, but the speaker's choice among the three would depend on the situation; that is, in addressing a child, the speaker would probably use the word *belly-button;* in addressing an adult other than a family member or close friend, the speaker might be more likely to use *navel,* and if the speaker is a physician addressing an audience of physicians, he or she might be most likely to use *umbilicus.* This is only to say that the dramatic situation in which one finds oneself helps define oneself, helps establish the particular role that one is playing.

Some words are used in virtually all poems: *I, see, and,* and the like. Still, the grammatical constructions in which they appear may help define the speaker. In Dickinson's "Wild Nights," for instance, such expressions as "Were I with Thee" and "Might I" indicate an educated speaker.

Speakers have attitudes toward themselves, their subjects, and their audiences, and, consciously or unconsciously, they choose their words, pitch, and modulation accordingly; all these add up to their tone. In written literature, tone must be detected without the aid of the ear, although it's a good idea to read poetry aloud, trying to find the appropriate tone of voice; that is, the reader must understand by the selection and sequence of words the way the words are meant to be heard—playfully, angrily, confidentially, ironically, or whatever. The reader must catch what Frost calls "the speaking tone of voice somehow entangled in the words and fastened to the page for the ear of the imagination."

Writing about the Speaker:
Robert Frost's "The Telephone"

Robert Frost once said that

> everything written is as good as it is dramatic. . . . [A poem is] heard as sung or
> spoken by a person in a scene—in character, in a setting. By whom, where and
> when is the question. By the dreamer of a better world out in a storm in au-
> tumn; by a lover under a window at night.

Suppose, in reading a poem Frost published in 1916, we try to establish "by
whom, where and when" it is spoken. We may not be able to answer all
three questions in great detail, but let's see what the poem suggests. As you
read it, you'll notice—alerted by the quotation marks—that the poem has
two speakers; the poem is a tiny drama. Thus, the closing quotation marks
at the end of line 9 signal to us that the first speech is finished.

Robert Frost (1874–1963)
THE TELEPHONE

"When I was just as far as I could walk
From here today
There was an hour
All still
When leaning with my head against a flower   5
I heard you talk.
Don't say I didn't, for I heard you say—
You spoke from that flower on the window sill—
Do you remember what it was you said?"

"First tell me what it was you thought you heard."   10

"Having found the flower and driven a bee away,
I leaned my head,
And holding by the stalk,
I listened and I thought I caught the word—
What was it? Did you call me by my name?   15
Or did you say—
Someone said 'Come'—I heard it as I bowed."

"I may have thought as much, but not aloud."

"Well, so I came."

Suppose we ask: Who are these two speakers? What is their relationship? What's going on between them? Where are they? Probably these
questions cannot be answered with absolute certainty, but some answers

are more probable than others. For instance, line 8 ("You spoke from that flower on the window sill") tells us that the speakers are in a room, probably of their home—rather than, say, in a railroad station—but we can't say whether they live in a farmhouse or in a house in a village, town, or city, or in an apartment.

Let's put the questions (even if they may turn out to be unanswerable) into a more specific form.

Questions

1. One speaker speaks lines 1–9, 11–17, and 19. The other speaks lines 10 and 18. Can you tell the gender of each speaker? For sure, probably, or not at all? On what do you base your answer?
2. Try to visualize this miniature drama. In line 7 the first speaker says, "Don't say I didn't...." What happens—what do you see in your mind's eye—after line 6 that causes the speaker to say this?
3. Why do you suppose the speaker of lines 10 and 18 says so little? How would you characterize the tone of these two lines? What sort of relationship do you think exists between the two speakers?
4. How would you characterize the tone of lines 11-17? Of the last line of the poem?

If you haven't jotted down your responses, consider doing so before reading what follows.

Journal Entries

Given questions somewhat like these, students were asked whether they could identify the speakers by sex, to speculate on their relationship, and then to add whatever they wished to say. One student recorded the following thoughts:

```
These two people care about each other--maybe husband
and wife, or lovers--and a man is doing most of the
talking, though I can't prove it.  He has walked as far
as possible--that is, as far as possible and still get
back on the same day--and he seemed to hear the other
person call him.  He claims that she spoke to him "from
that flower on the window sill," and that's why I think
the second person is a woman.  She's at home, near the
window.  Somehow I even imagine she was at the window
near the kitchen sink, maybe working while he was out on
this long walk.
```

Then she speaks one line; she won't say if she did
or didn't speak. She is very cautious or suspicious:
"First tell me what it was you thought you heard."
Maybe she doesn't want to say something and then have
her husband embarrass her by saying, "No, that's not
what I thought." Or maybe she just doesn't feel like
talking. Then he claims that he heard her speaking
through a flower, as though the flower was a telephone,
just as though it was hooked up to the flower on the
window sill. But at first he won't say what he
supposedly heard, or "thought" he heard. Instead, he
says that maybe it was someone else: "Someone said
'Come.'" Is he teasing her? Pretending that she may
have a rival?

Then she speaks--again just one line, saying, "I may
have thought as much, but not aloud." She won't admit
that she did think this thought. And then the man says,
"Well, so I came." Just like that; short and sweet. No
more fancy talk about flowers as telephones. He somehow
(through telepathy?) got the message, and so here he is.
He seems like a sensitive guy, playful (the stuff about
the flowers as telephones) but also he knows when to
stop kidding around.

Another student also identified the couple as a man and woman and
thought that this dialogue occurs after a quarrel:

As the poem goes on, we learn that the man wants to be
with the woman, but it starts by telling us that he
walked as far away from her as he could. He doesn't say
why, but I think from the way the woman speaks later in
the poem, they had a fight and he walked out. Then,
when he stopped to rest, he thought he heard her voice.
He really means that he was thinking of her and he was
hoping she was thinking of him. So he returns, and he
tells her he heard her calling him, but he pretends he
heard her call him through a flower on their window
sill. He can't admit that he was thinking about her.
This seems very realistic to me; when someone feels a
bit ashamed, it's sometimes hard to admit that you were

wrong, and you want the other person to tell you that
things are OK anyhow. And judging from line 7, when he
says "Don't say I didn't;" it seems that she is going to
interrupt him by denying it. She is still angry, or
maybe she doesn't want to make up too quickly. But he
wants to pretend that she called him back. So when he
says, "Do you remember what it was you said?" she won't
admit that she was thinking of him, and she says, "First
tell me what it was you thought you heard." She's
testing him a little. So he goes on, with the business
about flowers as telephones, and he says "someone"
called him. He understands that she doesn't want to be
pushed into forgiving him, so he backs off. Then she is
willing to admit that she did think about him, but still
she doesn't quite admit it. She is too proud to say
openly that she wants him back but she does say, "I may
have thought as much . . . . " And then, since they both
have preserved their dignity and also have admitted that
they care about the other, he can say, "Well, so I
came."

Further Thoughts about "The Telephone"

1. In a paragraph or two or three, *evaluate* one of these two entries recorded by students. Do you think the comments are weak, plausible, or convincing, and *why* do you think so? Can you offer additional supporting evidence, or counterevidence?

2. Two small questions: In a sentence or two, offer a suggestion why in line 11 Frost wrote, "and driven a bee away." After all, the bee plays no role in the poem. Second, in line 17 Frost has the speaker say, "I heard it as I bowed." Of course, "bowed" rhymes with "aloud," but let's assume that the need for a rhyme did not dictate the choice of this word. Do you think "I heard it as I bowed" is better than, say, "heard it as I waited" or "I heard it as I listened"? Why?

FIGURATIVE LANGUAGE

Robert Frost has said, "Poetry provides the one permissible way of saying one thing and meaning another." This, of course, is an exaggeration, but it shrewdly suggests the importance of figurative language—saying one thing in terms of something else. Words have their literal meanings, but they can also be used so that something other than the literal meaning is implied. "My love is a rose" is, literally, nonsense, for a person is not a five-petaled, many-stamened plant with a spiny stem. But the suggestions of rose (at least for Robert Burns, the Scottish poet who compared his beloved to a rose in the line, "My Love is like a red, red rose") include "delicate beauty," "soft," and "perfumed," and, thus, the word *rose* can be meaningfully applied—figuratively rather than literally—to "my love." The girl is fragrant; her skin is perhaps like a rose in texture and (in some measure) color; she will not keep her beauty long. The poet has communicated his perception very precisely.

People who write about poetry have found it convenient to name the various kinds of figurative language. Just as the student of geology employs such special terms as *kames* and *eskers*, the student of literature employs special terms to name things as accurately as possible. The following paragraphs discuss the most common terms.

In a **simile,** items from different classes are explicitly compared by a connective such as *like, as,* or *than,* or by a verb such as *appears* or *seems.* (If the objects compared are from the same class, for example, "Tokyo is like Los Angeles," no simile is present.)

Float like a butterfly, sting like a bee.

—MUHAMMAD ALI

It is a beauteous evening, calm and free.
The holy time is quiet as a Nun,
Breathless with adoration.

—WILLIAM WORDSWORTH

All of our thoughts will be fairer than doves.

—ELIZABETH BISHOP

Seems he a dove? His feathers are but borrowed.

—SHAKESPEARE

A **metaphor** asserts the identity, without a connective such as *like* or a verb such as *appears*, of terms that are literally incompatible.

Umbrellas clothe the beach in every hue.

—ELIZABETH BISHOP

The
whirlwind fife-and-drum of the storm bends the salt
marsh grass

—MARIANNE MOORE

In the following poem, Keats's excitement on reading George Chapman's sixteenth-century translation of the Greek poet Homer is communicated first through a metaphor and then through a simile.

John Keats (1795–1821)
ON FIRST LOOKING INTO CHAPMAN'S HOMER

Much have I traveled in the realms of gold,	
And many goodly states and kingdoms seen;	
Round many western islands have I been	
Which bards in fealty° to Apollo hold.	*loyalty* 4
Oft of one wide expanse had I been told,	
That deep-browed Homer ruled as his demesne:°	*property*
Yet did I never breathe its pure serene°	*vast expanse*
Till I heard Chapman speak out loud and bold:	8
Then felt I like some watcher of the skies	
When a new planet swims into his ken;	
Or like stout Cortez when with eagle eyes	
He stared at the Pacific—and all his men	12
Looked at each other with a wild surmise—	
Silent, upon a peak in Darien.°	*in Central America*

We might pause for a moment to take a closer look at Keats's poem. If you write an essay on the figurative language in this sonnet, you will probably discuss the figure involved in asserting that reading is a sort of traveling (it brings us to unfamiliar worlds) and especially that reading brings us to realms of gold. Presumably, the experience of reading is valuable. "Realms of gold" not only continues and modifies the idea of reading as travel, but in its evocation of El Dorado (an imaginary country in South America, thought to be rich in gold and, therefore, the object of search by Spanish explorers of the Renaissance) it introduces a suggestion of the Renaissance appropriate to a poem about a Renaissance translation of Homer. The figure of traveling is amplified in the next few lines, which assert that the "goodly states and kingdoms" and "western islands" are ruled by poets who owe allegiance to a higher authority, Apollo.

 The beginning of the second sentence (line 5) enlarges this already spacious area with its reference to "one wide expanse," and the ruler of this area (unlike the other rulers) is given the dignity of being named. He is Homer, "deep-browed," "deep" suggesting not only his high or perhaps furrowed forehead but the profundity of the thoughts behind the forehead. The speaker continues the idea of books as remote places, but now he also seems to think of this place as more than a rich area; instead of merely saying that until he read Chapman's translation he had not "seen" it (as in line

2) or "been" there (line 3), he says he never breathed its air; that is, the preciousness is not material but ethereal, not gold but something far more exhilarating and essential.

This reference to air leads easily to the next dominant image, that of the explorer of the illimitable skies (so vast is Homer's world) rather than of the land and sea. But the explorer of the skies is conceived as watching an *oceanic* sky. In hindsight we can see that the link was perhaps forged earlier in line 7, with "serene" (a vast expanse of air *or* water); in any case, there is an unforgettable rightness in the description of the suddenly discovered planet as something that seems to "swim" into one's ken.

After this climactic discovery we return to the Renaissance Spanish explorers (though Balboa, not Cortez, was the first white man to see the Pacific) by means of a simile that compares the speaker's rapture with Cortez's as he gazed at the expanse before him. The writer of an essay on the figurative language in a poem should, in short, try to call attention to the aptness (or ineptness) of the figures and to the connecting threads that make a meaningful pattern.

Two types of metaphor deserve special mention. In **synecdoche** the whole is replaced by the part, or the part by the whole. For example, "bread," in "Give us this day our daily bread," replaces all sorts of food. In **metonymy** something is named that replaces something closely related to it. For example, James Shirley names certain objects ("Scepter and crown," and "Scythe and spade"), using them to replace social classes (powerful people, and poor people) to which the objects are related:

Scepter and crown must tumble down
And in the dust be equal made
With the poor crooked scythe and spade.

The attribution of human feelings or characteristics to abstractions or to inanimate objects is called **personification.**

Memory,
that exquisite blunderer.

—AMY CLAMPITT

There's Wrath who has learnt every trick of guerilla warfare,
The shamming dead, the night-raid, the feinted retreat.

—W. H. AUDEN

Hope, thou bold taster of delight.

—RICHARD CRASHAW

Crashaw's personification, "Hope, thou bold taster of delight," is also an example of the figure called **apostrophe,** an address to a person or thing not literally listening. Wordsworth begins a sonnet by apostrophizing Milton:

Milton, thou shouldst be living at this hour,

and Ginsberg apostrophizes "gusts of wet air":

Fall on the ground, O great Wetness.

What conclusions can we draw about figurative language?

First, figurative language, with its literally incompatible terms, forces the reader to attend to the connotations (suggestions, associations) rather than to the denotations (dictionary definitions) of one of the terms.

Second, although figurative language is said to differ from ordinary discourse, it is found in ordinary discourse, as well as in literature. "It rained cats and dogs," "War is hell," "Don't be a pig," "Mr. Know-all," and other tired figures are part of our daily utterances. But through repeated use, these, and most of the figures we use, have lost whatever impact they once had and are only a shade removed from expressions that, though once figurative, have become literal: the *eye* of a needle, a *branch* office, the *face* of a clock.

Third, good figurative language is usually concrete, condensed, and interesting. The concreteness lends precision and vividness; when Keats writes that he felt "like some watcher of the skies / When a new planet swims into his ken," he more sharply characterizes his feelings than if he had said, "I felt excited." His simile isolates for us a precise kind of excitement, and the metaphoric "swims" vividly brings up the oceanic aspect of the sky. The effect of the second of these three qualities, condensation, can be seen by attempting to paraphrase some of the figures. A paraphrase will commonly use more words than the original, and it will have less impact—as the gradual coming of night usually has less impact on us than a sudden darkening of the sky, or as a prolonged push has less impact than a sudden blow. The third quality, interest, is largely dependent on the previous two; the successful figure often makes us open our eyes wider and take notice. Keats's "deep-browed Homer" arouses our interest in Homer as "thoughtful Homer" or "meditative Homer" does not. Similarly, when W. B. Yeats says:

An aged man is but a paltry thing,
A tattered coat upon a stick, unless

> Soul clap its hands and sing, and louder sing
> For every tatter in its mortal dress,

the metaphoric identification of an old man with a scarecrow jolts us out of all our usual unthinking attitudes about old men as kind, happy folk who are content to have passed from youth into age.

Preparing to Write about Figurative Language

As you prepare to write about figurative language, consider

1. the areas from which the images are drawn (for instance, religion, exploration, science, commerce, nature);
2. the kinds of images (for instance, similes, metaphors, overstatements, understatements);
3. any shifts from one type of imagery to another (for instance, from similes to metaphors, or from abundant figures of speech to literal speech) and the effects that the shifts arouse in you; and
4. the location of the images (perhaps they are concentrated at the beginning of the poem or in the middle or at the end) and if parts of the poem are richer in images than other parts, consider their effect on you.

If you underline or highlight images in your text or in a copy of the poem that you have written or typed, you'll probably be able to see patterns, and you can indicate the connections by drawing arrows or perhaps by making lists of related images. Thinking about these patterns, you will find ideas arising about some of the ways in which the poem makes its effect. With a little luck you will be able to formulate a tentative thesis for your essay, though as you continue to work—say, as you write a first draft—you will probably find yourself modifying the thesis in the light of additional thoughts that come to you while you are putting words onto paper.

Imagery and Symbolism

When we read *rose*, we may more or less call to mind a picture of a rose, or perhaps we are reminded of the odor or texture of a rose. Whatever in a poem appeals to any of our senses (including sensations of heat as well as of sight, smell, taste, touch, sound) is an image. In short, images are the sensory content of a work, whether literal or figurative. When a poet says "My rose" and is speaking about a rose, we have no figure of speech—though we still have an image. If, however, "My rose" is a shortened form of "My love is a rose," some would say that he or she is using a metaphor; but others would say that because the first term is omitted ("My love is"), the rose is a **symbol.** A poem about the transience of a rose might compel the reader to feel that the transience of female beauty is the larger theme even though it is never explicitly stated.

Some symbols are **conventional symbols**—people have agreed to accept them as standing for something other than their literal meanings: A poem about the cross is probably about Christianity; similarly, the rose has long been a symbol for love. In Virginia Woolf's novel *Mrs. Dalloway,* the husband communicates his love by proffering this conventional symbol: "He was holding out flowers—roses, red and white roses. (But he could not bring himself to say he loved her; not in so many words.)" Objects that are not conventional symbols, however, may also give rise to rich, multiple, indefinable associations. The following poem uses the traditional symbol of the rose, but in a nontraditional way.

> *William Blake (1757–1827)*
> THE SICK ROSE
>
> O rose, thou art sick!
> The invisible worm
> That flies in the night,
> In the howling storm,
>
> Has found out thy bed
> Of crimson joy,
> And his dark secret love
> Does thy life destroy.

A reader might perhaps argue that the worm is invisible (line 2) merely because it is hidden within the rose, but an "invisible worm / That flies in the night" is more than a long, slender, soft-bodied, creeping animal; and a rose that has, or is, a "bed / Of crimson joy" is more than a gardener's rose. Blake's worm and rose suggest things beyond themselves—a stranger, more vibrant world than the world we are usually aware of. They are, in short, symbolic, though readers will doubtless differ in their interpretations. Perhaps we find ourselves half thinking, for example, that the worm is male, the rose female, and that the poem is about the violation of virginity. Or that the poem is about the destruction of beauty: Woman's beauty, rooted in joy, is destroyed by a power that feeds on her. But these interpretations are not fully satisfying: The poem presents a worm and a rose, and yet it is not merely about a worm and a rose. These objects resonate, stimulating our thoughts toward something else, but the something else is elusive. This is not to say, however, that symbols mean whatever any reader says they mean. A reader could scarcely support an interpretation arguing that the poem is about the need to love all aspects of nature. All interpretations are not equally valid; it's the writer's job to offer a reasonably persuasive interpretation.

A symbol, then, is an image so loaded with significance that it is not simply literal, and it does not simply stand for something else; it is both itself *and* something else that it richly suggests, a kind of manifestation of something too complex or too elusive to be otherwise revealed. Blake's poem is about a blighted rose and at the same time about much more. In a symbol, as Thomas Carlyle wrote, "the Infinite is made to blend with the Finite, to stand visible, and as it were, attainable there."

STRUCTURE

The arrangement of the parts, the organization of the entire poem, is its **structure.** Sometimes a poem is divided into blocks of, say, four lines each, but even if the poem is printed as a solid block, it probably has some principle of organization—for example, from sorrow in the first two lines to joy in the next two, or from a question in the first three lines to an answer in the last line.

Consider this short poem by an English poet of the seventeenth century.

> *Robert Herrick (1591–1674)*
> UPON JULIA'S CLOTHES
>
> Whenas in silk my Julia goes,
> Then, then (methinks) how sweetly flows
> That liquefaction of her clothes.
>
> Next, when I cast mine eyes, and see
> That brave° vibration, each way free,   *splendid*
> O, how that glittering taketh me.

Annotating and Thinking about a Poem

David Thurston, a student, began thinking about this poem by copying it, double-spaced, and by making the following notes on his copy.

Upon Julia's Clothes

Whenas in silk my Julia goes, ——— *cool tone?*

"Then, then"—
more excited?
almost at a
loss for words?

Then, then (methinks) how sweetly flows
That liquefaction of her clothes.

Next, when I cast mine eyes, and see
That brave vibration, each way free, *free to do what?*
                                      free from what?
O, how that glittering taketh me.

emotional?

Thurston got further ideas by thinking about several of the questions
that, at the end of this chapter, we suggest you ask yourself while rereading
a poem. Among the questions are these:

> Does the poem proceed in a straightforward way, or at some point or
> points does the speaker reverse course, altering his or her tone or
> perception?
> What is the effect on you of the form?

With such questions in mind, Thurston was stimulated to see if
Herrick's poem has some sort of reversal or change and, if so, how it is related to the structure. After rereading the poem several times, thinking
about it in the light of these questions and perhaps others that came to
mind, he produced the following notes:

> Two stanzas, each of three lines, with the same
>   structure
> Basic structure of 1st stanza: When X (one line), then Y
>   (two lines)
> Basic structure of second stanza: Next (one line), then
>   Z (two lines)

When he marked the text after reading the poem a few times, he noticed
that the last line—an exclamation of delight ("O, how that glittering taketh
me")—is much more personal than the rest of the poem. A little further
thought enabled him to refine this last perception:

> Although the pattern of stanzas is repeated, the
> somewhat analytic, detached tone of the beginning
> ("Whenas," "Then," "Next") changes to an open,
> enthusiastic confession of delight in what the poet
> sees.

Further thinking led to this:

> Although the title is "Upon Julia's Clothes," and the
> first five lines describe Julia's silken dress, the poem
> finally is not only about Julia's clothing but about the
> effect of Julia (moving in silk that liquefies or seems
> to become a liquid) on the poet.

This is a nice observation, but when Thurston looked again at the poem the next day and started to write about it, he found that he was able to refine his observation.

> Even at the beginning, the speaker is not entirely
> detached, for he speaks of "my Julia."

In writing about Herrick's "Upon Julia's Clothes," Thurston reported, the thoughts did not come quickly or neatly. After two or three thoughts, he started to write. Only after drafting a paragraph and rereading the poem did he notice that the personal element appears not only in the last line ("taketh *me*") but even in the first line ("*my* Julia"). In short, for almost all of us, the only way to get to a good final essay is to read, to think, to jot down ideas, to write a draft, and revise and revise again. Having gone through such processes, the student came up with the following excellent essay.

The Student's Finished Essay: "Herrick's Julia, Julia's Herrick"

By the way, Thurston did not hit on the final version of his title ("Herrick's Julia, Julia's Herrick") until shortly before he typed his final version. His preliminary title was

> Structure and Personality in
> Herrick's "Upon Julia's Clothing"

That's a bit heavy-handed but at least it is focused, as opposed to such an uninformative title as "On a Poem." He soon revised his tentative title to

> Julia, Julia's Clothing, and Julia's Poet

That's quite a good title: It is neat, and it is appropriate, since it moves (as the poem and the essay do) from Julia and her clothing to the poet. Of course, it doesn't tell the reader exactly what the essay will be about, but it does stimulate the reader's interest. The essayist's final title, however, is even better:

Herrick's Julia, Julia's Herrick

Again, it is neat (the balanced structure, and structure is part of the student's topic), and it moves (as the poem itself moves) from Julia to the poet.

Herrick's Julia, Julia's Herrick

Robert Herrick's "Upon Julia's Clothes" begins as a description of Julia's clothing and ends as an expression of the poet's response not just to Julia's clothing but to Julia herself. Despite the apparently objective or detached tone of the first stanza and the first two lines of the second stanza, the poem finally conveys a strong sense of the speaker's excitement.

The first stanza seems to say, "Whenas" X (one line), "Then" Y (two lines). The second stanza repeats this basic structure of one line of assertion and two lines describing the consequence: "Next" (one line), "then" (two lines). But the logic or coolness of "Whenas," "Then," and "Next," and of such rather scientific language as "liquefaction" (a more technical-sounding word than "melting") and "vibration" is undercut by the breathlessness or excitement of "Then, then" (that is very different from a simple "Then"). It is also worth mentioning that although there is a personal rather than a fully detached note even in the first line, in "my Julia," this expression scarcely reveals much feeling. In fact, it reveals a touch of male chauvinism, a suggestion that the woman is a possession of the speaker's. Not until the last line does the speaker reveal that, far from Julia being his possession, he is possessed by Julia: "O, how that glittering taketh me." If he begins coolly, objectively, and somewhat complacently, and uses a structure that suggests a somewhat detached mind, in the exclamatory "O" he nevertheless at last confesses (to our delight) that he is enraptured by Julia.

Other things, of course, might be said about this poem. For instance, the writer says nothing about the changes in the meter and their possible value in the poem. Nor does he say anything about the sounds of any of the words (he might have commented on the long vowels in "sweetly flows" and shown how the effect would have been different if instead of "sweetly flows" Herrick had written "swiftly flits"), but such topics might be material for another essay. Furthermore, another reader might have found the poem less charming—even offensive in its exclusive concern with Julia's appearance and its utter neglect of her mind. Still, this essay is, in itself, an interesting and perceptive discussion of the way the poet used a repeated structure to set forth a miniature drama in which observation is, at the end, replaced by emotion.

Some Kinds of Structure

Repetitive

Although every poem has its own structure, if we stand back from a given poem we may see that the structure is one of three common sorts: repetitive, narrative, or logical. **Repetitive structure** is especially common in lyrics that are sung, where a single state of mind is repeated from stanza to stanza so that the stanzas are pretty much interchangeable. As we read through "Auld Lang Syne," for instance, we get reaffirmation rather than progression. Here is a passage from Whitman's "By Blue Ontario's Shore" that similarly has a repetitive structure:

> I will confront these shows of the day and night,
> I will know if I am to be less than they,
> I will see if I am not as majestic as they,
> I will see if I am not as subtle and real as they,
> I will see if I am to be less generous than they.

Narrative

In a poem with a **narrative structure** (we are not talking about "narrative poems," poems that tell a story, such as *The Odyssey* or *The Rime of the Ancient Mariner*, but about a kind of lyric poem) there is a sense of advance. Blake's "The Sick Rose" (p. 244) is an example. What comes later in the poem could not come earlier. The poem seems to get somewhere, to settle down to an end. A lyric in which the speaker at first grieves and then derives some comfort from the thought that at least he was once in love similarly has a narrative structure. Here is a short poem with a narrative structure.

William Wordsworth (1770–1850)
A SLUMBER DID MY SPIRIT SEAL

A slumber did my spirit seal;
I had no human fears:
She seemed a thing that could not feel
The touch of earthly years.

No motion has she now, no force;
She neither hears nor sees;
Rolled round in earth's diurnal° course,   *daily*
With rocks, and stones, and trees.

In the first stanza "did" and "seemed" establish the time as the past; in the
second stanza "now" establishes the time as the present. In the blank space
between the stanzas the woman has died. If we were required to summarize the stanzas very briefly, we might for the first stanza come up with, "I
thought she could not die," and for the second, "She is dead." But the poem
is not so much about the woman's life and death as about the speaker's response to her life and death.

If this poem is a sort of narrative of the speaker's change in perceptions, exactly what are the perceptions? Is the idea, as some readers have
argued, "I thought she seemed immortal, but now I am appalled that she is
reduced to mere earthly matter"? Or is it, as other readers have argued, "I
knew a woman who seemed more than earthly; now I see, pantheistically,
that in her death she is part of the grandness of nature"? According to the
first of these views, there is a chilling irony in the fact that the woman who
in the first stanza seemed exempt from "The touch of earthly years" is, in
the second stanza, laid in earth, with no motion of her own. She is as inert
as the "rocks, and stones, and trees." In this view, the poem moves from a
romantic state of mind to a report of facts, and the facts imply an abrupt
understanding of the brutality of death. But according to the second view,
the woman participates (with natural objects) in the grand motion of
"earth's diurnal course." In further support of this second view it can be argued that Wordsworth is known to have held pantheistic beliefs and that
the Latinism, *diurnal*—the longest word and the only unusual word in the
poem—adds dignity, especially in a line noted for melodiousness: "Rolled
round in earth's diurnal course." Perhaps one can even push this view further and say that the second stanza does not offer a sharp contrast to the
first but deepens it by revealing a mature and satisfying view of the
woman's true immortality, an immortality perceived only naively in the first
stanza.

Possibly the poem is of indeterminate meaning, and the disagreement cannot be settled, but you might spend a moment thinking about which of these views you prefer, and why. Or do you accept all of them? Or do you hold an entirely different view?

Logical

The third kind of structure commonly found is **logical structure.** The speaker argues a case and comes to some sort of conclusion. Probably the most famous example of a poem that moves to a resolution through an argument is Andrew Marvell's "To His Coy Mistress." The speaker begins, "Had we but world enough, and time" (that is, "if"), and for twenty lines he sets forth what he might do. At the twenty-first line he says, "But," and he indicates that the preceding twenty lines, in the subjunctive, are not a description of a real condition. The real condition (as he sees it) is that Time oppresses us, and he sets this idea forth in lines 21–32. In line 33 he begins his conclusion, "Now therefore," clinching it in line 45 with "Thus." Here is another example of a poem with a logical structure.

John Donne (1573–1631)
THE FLEA

Mark but this flea, and mark in this
How little that which thou deniest me is:
It sucked me first, and now sucks thee,
And in this flea our two bloods mingled be.
Thou knowest that this cannot be said   5
A sin, nor shame, nor loss of maidenhead;
 Yet this enjoys before it woo,
 And pampered swells with one blood made of two,
 And this, alas, is more than we would do.

O stay! Three lives in one flea spare,   10
Where we almost, yea, more than married are;
This flea is you and I, and this
Our marriage bed and marriage temple is.
Though parents grudge, and you, we're met
And cloistered in these living walls of jet.   15
 Though use° make you apt to kill me,   *custom*
 Let not to that, self-murder added be,
 And sacrilege, three sins in killing three.

Cruel and sudden! Hast thou since
Purpled thy nail in blood of innocence?   20
Wherein could this flea guilty be,

Except in that drop which it sucked from thee?
Yet thou triumph'st and saist that thou
Find'st not thyself, nor me, the weaker now.
   'Tis true. Then learn how false fears be;   25
   Just so much honor, when thou yield'st to me,
   Will waste, as this flea's death took life from thee.

The speaker is a lover who begins by assuring his mistress that sexual inter-course is of no more serious consequence than a flea bite. Between the first and second stanzas the woman has apparently threatened to kill the flea, moving the lover to exclaim in line 10, "O stay! Three lives in one flea spare." In this second stanza he reverses his argument, now insisting on the importance of the flea, arguing that since it has bitten both man and woman it holds some of their lives, as well as its own. Unpersuaded of its importance, the woman kills the flea between the second and third stanzas; and the speaker uses her action to reinforce his initial position when he says, beginning in line 25, that the death of the flea has no serious conse-quences and her yielding to him will have no worse consequences.

Verbal Irony

Among the commonest devices in poems with logical structure (although this device is employed elsewhere, too) is **verbal irony.** The speaker's words mean more or less the opposite of what they seem to say. Sometimes it takes the form of **understatement,** as when Andrew Marvell's speaker remarks with cautious wryness, "The grave's a fine and private place, / But none, I think, do there embrace," or when Sylvia Plath sees an intended suicide as "the big strip tease"; sometimes it takes the form of **overstatement,** or **hyperbole,** as when Donne's speaker says that in the flea he and the lady are "more than married." Speaking broadly, intensely emotional contemporary poems, such as those of Plath, often use irony to undercut—and thus make acceptable—the emotion.

Paradox

Another common device in poems with a logical structure is **paradox:** the assertion of an apparent contradiction, as in "This flea is you and I." But again it must be emphasized that irony and paradox are not limited to po-ems with a logical structure. In "Auld Lang Syne," for instance, there is the paradox that the remembrance of joy evokes a kind of sadness, and there is understatement in "we've wandered mony a weary fitt," which stands (roughly) for something much bigger, such as "we have had many painful experiences."

EXPLICATION

In Chapter 3, which included a discussion of Langston Hughes's "Harlem," we saw that an explication is a line-by-line commentary on what is going on in a text. (*Explication* literally means "unfolding," or "spreading out.") Although your explication will for the most part move steadily from the beginning to the end of the selection, try to avoid writing along these lines (or, one might say, along this one line): "In line one. . . , In the second line. . . , In the third line. . . ,"; that is, don't hesitate to write such things as

> The poem begins . . . In the next line . . . The speaker immediately adds . . .
> She then introduces . . . The next stanza begins by saying . . .

And of course you may discuss the second line before the first if that seems the best way of handling the passage.

An explication is not concerned with the writer's life or times, and it is not a paraphrase (a rewording)—though it may include paraphrase if a passage in the original seems unclear perhaps because of an unusual word or an unfamiliar expression. On the whole, however, an explication goes beyond paraphrase, seeking to make explicit what the reader perceives as implicit in the work. To this end it calls attention, as it proceeds, to the implications of

- words, especially of their tone (repetitions, shifts in levels of diction, for instance from colloquial to formal language, or from ordinary language to technical language);
- figures of speech;
- length of sentences (since an exceptionally short or exceptionally long sentence conveys a particular effect);
- sound effects, such as alliteration and rhyme; and
- structure (for instance, a question in one stanza, and the answer in the next, or a generalization and then a particularization, or a contrast of some sort).

To repeat, in short, an explication makes *explicit* what is implicit, especially in the words. It sets forth the reader's sense of the precise meaning of the work, word by word, or phrase by phrase, or line by line.

To begin with an almost absurdly simple example, if one were explicating a line that consisted of the words "Shut up," one would probably say something like this:

> The speaker rudely tells the hearer to be silent by
> using the imperative form--without even a "Please"--and

by using a highly colloquial expression (rather than,
say, "Be quiet"). The speaker thus reveals either his
or her anger or lack of concern for good manners, or both.

A Sample Explication of Yeats's "The Balloon of the Mind"

Take this short poem (published in 1917) by the Irish poet William Butler
Yeats (1865–1939). The "balloon" in the poem is a dirigible, a blimp.

> *William Butler Yeats*
> THE BALLOON OF THE MIND
>
> Hands, do what you're bid:
> Bring the balloon of the mind
> That bellies and drags in the wind
> Into its narrow shed.

Annotations and Journal Entries

A student began thinking about the poem by copying it, double-spaced.
Then she jotted down her first thoughts.

sounds abrupt

Hands, do what you're bid:

Bring the balloon of the mind   *balloon imagined by the mind? Or a mind like a balloon?*

That bellies and drags in the wind

Into its narrow shed.   *no real rhymes? line seems to drag— it's so long!*

Later she wrote some notes in a journal.

I'm still puzzled about the meaning of the words, "The
balloon of the mind." Does "balloon of the mind" mean a
balloon that belongs to the mind, sort of like "a
disease of the heart"? If so, it means a balloon that
the mind has, a balloon that the mind possesses, I guess
by imagining it. Or does it mean that the mind is like
a balloon, as when you say "he's a pig of a man,"
meaning he is like a pig, he is a pig? Can it mean
both? What's a balloon that the mind imagines? Something
like dreams of fame, wealth? Castles in Spain?
    Is Yeats saying that the "hands" have to work hard
to make dreams a reality? Maybe. But maybe the idea

really is that the mind is <u>like</u> a balloon--hard to keep
under control, floating around. Very hard to keep the
mind on the job. If the mind is like a balloon, it's
hard to get it into the hangar (shed).

   "Bellies." Is there such a verb? In this poem it
seems to mean something like "puffs out" or "flops
around in the wind." Just checked <u>The American Heritage
Dictionary</u>, and it says "belly" can be a verb, "to swell
out," "to bulge." Well, you learn something every day.

A later entry:

OK; I think the poem is about a writer trying to keep
his balloon-like mind under control, trying to keep it
working at the job of writing something, maybe writing
something with the "clarity, unity, and coherence" I
keep hearing about in this course.

Here is the student's final version of the explication.

Yeats's "Balloon of the Mind" is about writing poetry,
specifically about the difficulty of getting one's
floating thoughts down in lines on the page. The first
line, a short, stern, heavily stressed command to the
speaker's hands, perhaps implies by its severe or
impatient tone that these hands will be disobedient or
inept or careless if not watched closely: the poor
bumbling body so often fails to achieve the goals of the
mind. The bluntness of the command in the first line is
emphasized by the fact that all the subsequent lines
have more syllables. Furthermore, the first line is a
grammatically complete sentence, whereas the thought of
line 2 spills over into the next lines, implying the
difficulty of fitting ideas into confining spaces, that
is, of getting one's thoughts into order, especially
into a coherent poem.

   Lines 2 and 3 amplify the metaphor already stated in
the title (the product of the mind is an airy but
unwieldy balloon) and they also contain a second
command, "Bring." Alliteration ties this command
"Bring" to the earlier "<u>b</u>id"; it also ties both of these

verbs to their object, "balloon" and to the verb that
most effectively describes the balloon, "bellies." In
comparison with the abrupt first line of the poem, lines
2 and 3 themselves seem almost swollen, bellying and
dragging, an effect aided by using adjacent unstressed
syllables ("of the," "[bell]ies and," "in the") and by
using an eye rhyme ("mind" and "wind") rather than an
exact rhyme. And then comes the short last line: almost
before we could expect it, the cumbersome balloon--here
the idea that is to be packed into the stanza--is
successfully lodged in its "narrow shed." Aside from
the relatively colorless "into," the only words of more
than one syllable in the poem are "balloon," "bellies,"
and "narrow," and all three emphasize the difficulty of
the task. But after "narrow"--the word itself almost
looks long and narrow, in this context like a hangar--we
get the simplicity of the monosyllable "shed." The
difficult job is done, the thought is safely packed
away, the poem is completed--but again with an off rhyme
("bid" and "shed"), for neatness can go only so far when
hands and mind and a balloon are involved.

Note: The reader of an explication needs to see the text, and because the
explicated text is usually short, it is advisable to quote it all. (Remember,
your imagined audience probably consists of your classmates; even if they
have already read the work you are explicating, they have not memorized it,
and so you helpfully remind them of the work by quoting it.) You may
quote the entire text at the outset, or you may quote the first unit (for example a stanza), then explicate that unit, and then quote the next unit, and
so on. And if the poem or passage of prose is longer than, say, six lines, it is
advisable to number each line at the right for easy reference.

RHYTHM AND VERSIFICATION:
A GLOSSARY FOR REFERENCE

Rhythm

Rhythm (most simply, in English poetry, stresses at regular intervals) has a
power of its own. A highly pronounced rhythm is common in such forms of
poetry as charms, college yells, and lullabies; all of them are aimed at in-
ducing a special effect magically. It is not surprising that *carmen,* the Latin

word for poem or song, is also the Latin word for charm and the word from which our word *charm* is derived.

In much poetry, rhythm is only half heard, but its presence is suggested by the way poetry is printed. Prose (from Latin *prorsus*, "forward," "straight on") keeps running across the paper until the right-hand margin is reached; then, merely because the paper has given out, the writer or printer starts again at the left, with a small letter. But verse (Latin *versus*, "a turning") often ends well short of the right-hand margin. The next line begins at the left—usually with a capital—not because paper has run out but because the rhythmic pattern begins again. Lines of poetry are continually reminding us that they have a pattern.

Note that a mechanical, unvarying rhythm may be good to put the baby to sleep, but it can be deadly to readers who want to stay awake. Poets vary their rhythm according to their purposes; they ought not to be so regular that they are (in W. H. Auden's words) "accentual pests." In competent hands, rhythm contributes to meaning; it says something. Ezra Pound has a relevant comment: "Rhythm *must* have meaning. It can't be merely a careless dash off, with no grip and no real hold to the words and sense, a tumty tum tumty tum tum ta."

Consider this description of Hell from John Milton's *Paradise Lost* (stressed syllables are marked by / ; unstressed syllables by ⌣):

> Rocks, caves, lakes, fens, bogs, dens, and shades of death.

The normal line in *Paradise Lost* is written in iambic feet—alternate unstressed and stressed syllables—but in this line Milton immediately follows one heavy stress with another, helping communicate the "meaning"—the oppressive monotony of Hell. As a second example, consider the function of the rhythm in two lines by Alexander Pope:

> When Ajax strives some rock's vast weight to throw.
> The line too labors. and the words move slow.

The stressed syllables do not merely alternate with the unstressed ones; rather, the great weight of the rock is suggested by three consecutive stressed words, "rock's vast weight," and the great effort involved in moving it is suggested by another three consecutive stresses, "line too labors," and by yet another three, "words move slow." Note, also, the abundant pauses within the lines. In the first line, for example, unless one's speech is slovenly, one must pause at least slightly after "Ajax," "strives," "rock's," "vast," "weight," and "throw." The grating sounds in "Ajax" and "rock's" do their work, too, and so do the explosive *t*'s. When Pope wishes to suggest lightness, he reverses his procedure, and he groups *un*stressed syllables:

Not so, when swift Camilla scours the plain,
Flies o'er th' unbending corn, and skims along the main.

This last line has 12 syllables and is, thus, longer than the line about Ajax, but the addition of *along* helps communicate lightness and swiftness because in this line (it can be argued) neither syllable of *along* is strongly stressed. If *along* is omitted, the line still makes grammatical sense and becomes more regular, but it also becomes less imitative of lightness.

The very regularity of a line may be meaningful, too. Shakespeare begins a sonnet thus:

When I do count the clock that tells the time.

This line about a mechanism runs with appropriate regularity. (It is worth noting, too, that "*count the clock*" and "*tells the time*" emphasize the regularity by the repetition of sounds and syntax.) But notice what Shakespeare does in the middle of the next line:

And see the brave day sunk in hideous night.

The technical vocabulary of **prosody** (the study of the principles of verse structure, including meter, rhyme and other sound effects, and stanzaic patterns) is large. An understanding of these terms will not turn anyone into a poet, but it will enable you to write about some aspects of poetry more efficiently. The following are the chief terms of prosody.

Meter

Most poetry written in English has a pattern of stressed (accented) sounds, and this pattern is the **meter** (from the Greek word for "measure"). Strictly speaking, we really should not talk of "unstressed" or "unaccented" syllables, since to utter a syllable—however lightly—is to give it some stress. It is really a matter of *relative* stress, but the fact is that "unstressed" or "unaccented" are parts of the established terminology of versification.

In a line of poetry, the **foot** is the basic unit of measurement. It is on rare occasions a single stressed syllable; generally a foot consists of two or three syllables, one of which is stressed. The repetition of feet, then, produces a pattern of stresses throughout the poem.

Two cautions:

1. A poem will seldom contain only one kind of foot throughout; significant variations usually occur, but one kind of foot is dominant.

2. In reading a poem, one chiefly pays attention to the sense, not to a presupposed metrical pattern. By paying attention to the sense, one often finds (reading aloud is a great help) that the stress falls on a word that according to the metrical pattern would be unstressed. Or a word that according to the pattern would be stressed may be seen to be unstressed. Furthermore by reading for sense one finds that not all stresses are equally heavy; some are almost as light as unstressed syllables, and some have a **hovering stress;** that is, the stress is equally distributed over two adjacent syllables. To repeat: One reads for sense, allowing the syntax to help indicate the stresses.

Metrical Feet.   The most common feet in English poetry are the six listed below.

Iamb (adjective: **iambic**): one unstressed syllable followed by one stressed syllable. The iamb, said to be the most common pattern in English speech, is surely the most common in English poetry. The following example has four iambic feet:

My heart is like a sing -ing bird.

–CHRISTINA ROSSETTI

Trochee (trochaic): one stressed syllable followed by one unstressed.

We were very tired, we were very merry

–EDNA ST. VINCENT MILLAY

Anapest (anapestic): two unstressed syllables followed by one stressed.

There are man -y who say that a dog has his day.

–DYLAN THOMAS

Dactyl (dactylic): one stressed syllable followed by two unstressed. This trisyllabic foot, like the anapest, is common in light verse or verse suggesting joy, but its use is not limited to such material, as Longfellow's *Evangeline* shows. Thomas Hood's sentimental "The Bridge of Sighs" begins:

Take her up tenderly.

Spondee (spondaic): two stressed syllables; most often used as a substitute for an iamb or trochee.

Smart lad, to slip betimes away.

–A. E. HOUSMAN

Pyrrhic: two unstressed syllables; it is often not considered a legitimate foot in English.

Metrical Lines.   A metrical line consists of one or more feet and is named for the number of feet in it. The following names are used:

monometer: one foot   **pentameter:** five feet
dimeter: two feet   **hexameter:** six feet
trimeter: three feet   **heptameter:** seven feet
tetrameter: four feet

A line is scanned for the kind and number of feet in it, and the **scansion** tells you if it is, say, anapestic trimeter (three anapests):

As I came to the edge of the woods.

–ROBERT FROST

Or, in another example, iambic pentameter:

The summer thunder, like a wooden bell

–LOUISE BOGAN

A line ending with a stress has a **masculine ending;** a line ending with an extra unstressed syllable has a **feminine ending.** The **caesura** (usually indicated by the symbol / /) is a slight pause within the line. It need not be indicated by punctuation (notice the fourth and fifth lines in the following quotation), and it does not affect the metrical count:

> Awake, my St. John! / / leave all meaner things
> To low ambition, / / and the pride of kings.
> Let us / / (since Life can little more supply
> Than just to look about us / / and to die)   4
> Expatiate free / / o'er all this scene of Man;
> A mighty maze! / / but not without a plan;
> A wild, / / where weeds and flowers promiscuous shoot;
> Or garden, / / tempting with forbidden fruit.   8

—ALEXANDER POPE

The varying position of the caesura helps give Pope's lines an informality that plays against the formality of the pairs of rhyming lines.

An **end-stopped line** concludes with a distinct syntactical pause, but a **run-on line** has its sense carried over into the next line without syntactical pause. (The running-on of a line is called **enjambment.**) In the following passage, only the first is a run-on line:

Yet if we look more closely we shall find
Most have the seeds of judgment in their mind:
Nature affords at least a glimmering light;
The lines, though touched but faintly, are drawn right.

—ALEXANDER POPE

Meter produces **rhythm,** recurrences at equal intervals, but rhythm (from a Greek word meaning "flow") is usually applied to larger units than feet. Often it depends most obviously on pauses. Thus, a poem with run-on lines will have a different rhythm from a poem with end-stopped lines even though both are in the same meter. And prose, though it is unmetrical, may have rhythm, too.

In addition to being affected by syntactical pause, rhythm is affected by pauses attributable to consonant clusters and to the length of words. Polysyllabic words establish a different rhythm from monosyllabic words, even in metrically identical lines. One may say, then, that rhythm is altered by shifts in meter, syntax, and the length and ease of pronunciation. Even with no such shift, even if a line is repeated word for word, a reader may sense a change in rhythm. The rhythm of the final line of a poem, for example, may well differ from that of the line before even though in other respects the lines are identical, as in Frost's "Stopping by Woods on a Snowy Evening," which concludes by repeating "And miles to go before I sleep." One may simply sense that this final line ought to be spoken, say, more slowly and with more stress on "miles."

Patterns of Sound

Though rhythm is basic to poetry, **rhyme**—the repetition of the identical or similar stressed sound or sounds—is not. Rhyme is, presumably, pleasant in itself; it suggests order; and it also may be related to meaning, for it brings two words sharply together, often implying a relationship, as in the now trite *dove* and *love* or in the more imaginative *throne* and *alone.*

Perfect or **exact rhyme:** Differing consonant sounds are followed by identical stressed vowel sounds, and the following sounds, if any, are identical (*foe—toe; meet—fleet; buffer—rougher*). Notice that perfect rhyme involves identity of sound, not of spelling. *Fix* and *sticks,* like *buffer* and *rougher,* are perfect rhymes.

Half-rhyme (or off-rhyme): Only the final consonant sounds of the words are identical; the stressed vowel sounds, as well as the initial consonant sounds, if any, differ (*soul—oil; mirth—forth; trolley—bully*).

Eye-rhyme: The sounds do not in fact rhyme, but the words look as though they would rhyme (*cough—bough*).

Masculine rhyme: The final syllables are stressed and, after their differing initial consonant sounds, are identical in sound (*stark—mark; support—retort*).

Feminine rhyme (or double rhyme): Stressed rhyming syllables are followed by identical unstressed syllables (*revival—arrival; flatter—batter*). **Triple rhyme** is a kind of feminine rhyme in which identical stressed vowel sounds are followed by two identical unstressed syllables (*machinery—scenery; tenderly—slenderly*).

End rhyme (or terminal rhyme): The rhyming words occur at the ends of the lines.

Internal rhyme: At least one of the rhyming words occurs within the line (Oscar Wilde's "Each narrow *cell* in which we *dwell*").

Alliteration: Sometimes defined as the repetition of initial sounds ("All the *a*wful *a*uguries" or "*B*ring me my *b*ow of *b*urning gold"), and sometimes as the prominent repetition of a consonant ("a*f*ter life's *f*itful *f*ever").

Assonance: The repetition, in words of proximity, of identical vowel sounds preceded and followed by differing consonant sounds. Whereas *tide* and *hide* are rhymes, *tide* and *mine* are assonantal.

Consonance: The repetition of identical consonant sounds and differing vowel sounds in words in proximity (*fail—feel; rough—roof; pitter—patter*). Sometimes, consonance is more loosely defined merely as the repetition of a consonant (*fail—peel*).

Onomatopoeia: The use of words that imitate sounds, such as *hiss* and *buzz*. A common mistaken tendency is to see onomatopoeia everywhere—for example, in *thunder* and *horror*. Many words sometimes thought to be onomatopoeic are not clearly imitative of the thing they refer to; they merely contain some sounds that, when we know what the word means, seem to have some resemblance to the thing they denote. Tennyson's lines from "Come down, O maid" are usually cited as an example of onomatopoeia:

> The moan of doves in immemorial elms
> And murmuring of innumerable bees.

Stanzaic Patterns

Lines of poetry are commonly arranged into a rhythmical unit called a **stanza** (from an Italian word meaning "room" or "stopping-place").

Usually, all the stanzas in a poem have the same rhyme pattern. A stanza is sometimes called a **verse,** though *verse* may also mean a single line of poetry. (In discussing stanzas, rhymes are indicated by identical letters. Thus, *abab* indicates that the first and third lines rhyme with each other, while the second and fourth lines are linked by a different rhyme. An unrhymed line is denoted by *x.*) Common stanzaic forms in English poetry are the following:

Couplet: a stanza of two lines, usually, but not necessarily, with endrhymes. *Couplet* is also used for a pair of rhyming lines. The **octosyllabic couplet** is iambic or trochaic tetrameter:

Had we but world enough, and time,
This coyness, lady, were no crime.

—ANDREW MARVELL

Heroic couplet: a rhyming couplet of iambic pentameter, often "closed," that is, containing a complete thought, with a fairly heavy pause at the end of the first line and a still heavier one at the end of the second. Commonly, a parallel or an *antithesis* (contrast) is found within a line or between the two lines. It is called heroic because in England, especially in the eighteenth century, it was much used for heroic (epic) poems.

Some foreign writers, some our own despise;
The ancients only, or the moderns, prize.

—ALEXANDER POPE

Triplet (or **tercet**): a three-line stanza, usually with one rhyme.

Whenas in silks my Julia goes
Then, then (methinks) how sweetly flows
That liquefaction of her clothes.

—ROBERT HERRICK

Quatrain: a four-line stanza, rhymed or unrhymed. The **heroic** (or **elegiac) quatrain** is iambic pentameter, rhyming *abab;* that is, the first and third lines rhyme (so they are designated *a*), and the second and fourth lines rhyme (so they are designated *b*).

Sonnet: a 14-line poem, predominantly in iambic pentameter. The rhyme is usually according to one of the two following schemes. **The Italian** (or **Petrarchan**) **sonnet** has two divisions: the first 8 lines (rhyming *a b b a a b b a*) are the **octave;** the last 6 (rhyming *c d c d c d,* or a variant) are the **sestet.** Keats's "On First Looking into Chapman's Homer" (p. 240) is an Italian sonnet. The second kind of sonnet, the **English** (or **Shakespearean**) **sonnet,** is arranged usually into three quatrains and a couplet, rhyming *a b a b c d c d e f e f g g.* Many sonnets have a marked correspondence between the rhyme scheme and the development of the thought. Thus, an Italian sonnet may state a generalization in the octave and a specific example in the sestet. Or an English sonnet may give three examples—one in each quatrain—and draw a conclusion in the couplet.

Blank Verse and Free Verse

A good deal of English poetry is unrhymed, much of it in **blank verse,** that is, unrhymed iambic pentameter. Introduced into English poetry by Surrey in the middle of the sixteenth century, late in the century it became the standard medium (especially in the hands of Marlowe and Shakespeare) of English drama. A passage of blank verse that has a rhetorical unity is sometimes called a **verse paragraph.**

The second kind of unrhymed poetry fairly common in English, especially in the twentieth century, is **free verse** (or *vers libre*): rhythmical lines varying in length, adhering to no fixed metrical pattern, and usually unrhymed. The pattern is often largely based on repetition and parallel grammatical structure. Here is a sample of free verse.

> *Walt Whitman (1819–92)*
> WHEN I HEARD THE LEARN'D ASTRONOMER
>
> When I heard the learn'd astronomer,
> When the proofs, the figures, were ranged in columns before me,
> When I was shown the charts and diagrams, to add, divide, and
>   measure them.
> When I sitting heard the astronomer where he lectured with much
>   applause in the lecture-room.
> How soon unaccountable I became tired and sick,   5
> Till rising and gliding out I wander'd off by myself,
> In the mystical moist night-air, and from time to time,
> Look'd up in perfect silence at the stars.

What can be said about the rhythmic structure of this poem? Rhymes are absent, and the lines vary greatly in the number of syllables, ranging from 9 (the first line) to 23 (the fourth line), but when we read the poem we sense a rhythmic structure. The first four lines obviously hang together, each beginning with "When"; indeed, three of these four lines begin "When I." We may notice, too, that each of these four lines has more syllables than its predecessor (the numbers are 9, 14, 18, and 23); this increase in length, like the initial repetition, is a kind of pattern.

In the fifth line, however, which speaks of fatigue and surfeit, there is a shrinkage to 14 syllables, offering an enormous relief from the previous swollen line with its 23 syllables. The second half of the poem—the pattern established by "When" in the first four lines is dropped, and in effect we get a new stanza, also of four lines—does not relentlessly diminish the number of syllables in each succeeding line, but it *almost* does so: 14, 14, 13, 10.

The second half of Whitman's poem, thus, has a pattern, too, and this pattern is more or less the reverse of the first half of the poem. We may notice, too, that the last line (in which the poet, now released from the oppressive lecture hall, is in communion with nature) is very close to an iambic pentameter line; that is, the poem concludes with a metrical form said to be the most natural in English.

The effect of naturalness or ease in this final line, moreover, is increased by the absence of repetitions (e.g., not only of "When I," but even of such syntactic repetitions as "charts and diagrams," "tired and sick," "rising and gliding") that characterize most of the previous lines. Of course, this final effect of naturalness is part of a carefully constructed pattern in which rhythmic structure is part of meaning. Though at first glance free verse may appear unrestrained, as T. S. Eliot (a practitioner) said, "No *vers* is *libre* for the man who wants to do a good job"—or for the woman who wants to do a good job.

In recent years poets who write what earlier would have been called "free verse" have characterized their writing as **open form.** Such poets as Charles Olson, Robert Duncan, and Denise Levertov reject the "closed form" of the traditional, highly patterned poem, preferring instead a form that seems spontaneous or exploratory. To some readers the unit seems to be the phrase or the line rather than the group of lines, but Denise Levertov insists that the true writer of open-form poetry must have a "form sense"; she compares such a writer to "a sort of helicopter scout flying over the field of the poem, taking aerial photos and reporting on the state of the forest and its creatures—or over the sea to watch for the schools of herring and direct the fishing fleet toward them."[1] And, Levertov again, "Form is never more than a *revelation* of content."

SAMPLE ESSAY ON METRICS: "SOUND AND SENSE IN HOUSMAN'S 'EIGHT O'CLOCK'"

Once you have decided to write about some aspect of versification, write your own copy of the poem, double-spaced or even triple-spaced, providing plenty of space to mark the stresses, indicate pauses, and annotate in any other way that strikes you. At this stage, it's probably best to use pencil for

---

[1]"Some Notes on Organic Form," reprinted in *The Poetics of the New American Poetry*, ed. Donald M. Allen and Warren Tallman (New York, 1973), pp. 316–17.

your scansion, since on rereading the poem you may revise some of your views, and you can simply erase and revise.

Here is an excellent analysis by a student. Notice that she quotes the poem and indicates the metrical pattern and that she proceeds chiefly by explaining the effect of the variations or departures from the norm in the order in which they occur.

Notice, too, that although it is usually a good idea to announce your thesis early—that is, in the first paragraph—this writer does *not* say, "This paper will show that Housman effectively uses rhythm to support his ideas" or some such thing. It's sufficient that the writer announces her topic in the title and again, in slightly different words, in the first sentence (the paper will "analyze the effects of sounds and rhythms in Housman's 'Eight O'Clock'"). We know where we will be going, and we read with perhaps even a bit of suspense, looking to see what the analysis will produce.

Sound and Sense in Housman's "Eight O'Clock"

Before trying to analyze the effects of sounds and rhythms in Housman's "Eight O'Clock," it will be useful to quote the poem and to indicate which syllables are stressed and which are unstressed. It must be understood, however, that the following scansion is relatively crude, because it falsely suggests that all stressed syllables (marked ╱) are equally stressed, but of course they are not: in reading the poem aloud, one would stress some of them relatively heavily, and one would stress others only a trifle more than the unstressed syllables. It should be understood, too, that in the discussion that follows the poem some other possible scansions will be proposed.

He stood, | and heard | the steeple
   Sprinkle | the quar | ters on | the mor | ning town.
One, two, | three, four, | to mar | ket-place | and people
   It tossed | them down.

Strapped, noosed, | nighing | his hour.
   He stood | and coun | ted them | and cursed | his luck;
And then | the clock | collec | ted in | the tower
   Its strength, | and struck.

As the first line of the second stanza makes especially clear, the poem is about a hanging at eight o'clock, according to the title. Housman could have written about the man's thoughts on the justice or injustice of his fate, or about the reasons for the execution, but he did not. Except for the second line of the second stanza--"He stood and counted them and cursed his luck"--he seems to tell us little about the man's thoughts. But the poem is not merely a narrative of an event; the sound effects in the poem help to convey an idea as well as a story.

The first line establishes an iambic pattern. The second line begins with a trochee ("Sprinkle"), not an iamb, and later in the line possibly "on" should not be stressed even though I marked it with a stress and made it part of an iambic foot, but still the line is mainly iambic. The poem so far is a fairly jingling description of someone hearing the church clock chiming at each quarter of the hour. Certainly, even though the second line begins with a stress, there is nothing threatening in "Sprinkle," a word in which we almost hear a tinkle.

But the second half of the first stanza surprises us, and maybe even jolts us. In "One, two, three, four" we get four consecutive heavy stresses. These stresses are especially emphatic because there is a pause, indicated by a comma, after each of them. Time is not just passing to the chimes of a clock: this is a countdown, and we sense that it may lead to something significant. Moreover, the third line, which is longer than the two previous lines, does not end with a pause. This long line (eleven syllables) runs on into the next line, almost as though once the countdown has begun there is no stopping it. But then we do stop suddenly, because the last line of the stanza has only four syllables-- far fewer than we would have expected. In other words, this line stops unexpectedly because it has only two feet. The first line had three feet, and the second and third lines had

five feet. Furthermore, this short, final line of the stanza
ends with a heavy stress in contrast to the previous line,
which ends with an unstressed syllable, "people." As we will
see, the sudden stopping at the end is a sort of preview of a
life cut short. Perhaps it is also a preview of a man
dropping through a trapdoor and then suddenly stopping when
the slack in the hangman's rope has been taken up.

In the first line of the second stanza the situation is
made clear, and it is also made emphatic by three consecutive
stresses: "Strapped, noosed, nighing his hour." The pauses
before each of these stresses make the words especially
emphatic. And though I have marked the first two words of the
next line "He stood," possibly "He" should be stressed too.
In any case even if "He" is not heavily stressed, it is
certainly stressed more than the other unstressed syllables,
"and," "-ed" (in "counted"), and "his." Similarly in the
third line of the stanza an effective reading might even
stress the first word as well as the second, thus: "And
then." And although normal speech would stress only the
second syllable in "collected," in this poem the word appears
after "clock," and so one must pause after the k sound in
"clock" (one simply can't say "clock collected" without
pausing briefly between the two words), and the effect is to
put more than usual stress on the first syllable, almost
turning it into "collected." And so this line really can
reasonably be scanned like this:

And then the clock collected in the tower.

And again the third line of the stanza runs over into the
fourth, propelling us onward. The final line surely begins
with a stress, even though "Its" is not a word usually
stressed, and so in the final line we begin with two strong
stresses, "Its strength." This line, like the last line of
the first stanza, is unusually short, and it too ends with a
heavy stress. The total effect, then, of the last two lines

of this stanza is of a clock striking, not just sprinkling music but forcefully and emphatically and decisively striking. The pause after "strength" is almost like the suspenseful pause of a man collecting his strength before he strikes a blow, and that is what the clock does:

> And then the clock collected in the tower.
> Its strength and struck.

If "clock collected" has in its k sounds a sort of ticktock effect, the clock at the end shows its force, for when it strikes the hour, the man dies.

I said near the beginning of this essay that Housman did not write about the man's thought about the justice or injustice of the sentence, and I think this is more or less true, but if we take into account the sound effects in the poem we can see that in part the poem is about the man's thoughts: he sees himself as the victim not only of his "luck" but of this machine, this ticking, unstoppable contraption that strikes not only the hours but a man's life.

📖 Suggestions for Further Reading

Alex Preminger and T. V. F. Brogan, eds. *The New Princeton Encyclopedia of Poetry and Poetics* (1993), is an indispensable reference work, with entries ranging from a few sentences to half a dozen or so pages on prosody, genres, critical approaches, schools, and so on.

Some specialized studies: On prosody see Paul Fussell, *Poetic Meter and Poetic Form,* rev. ed. (1979) and (especially engaging) John Hollander, *Rhyme's Reason,* enlarged ed. (1989). Barbara Herrnstein Smith, *Poetic Closure: A Study of the Way Poems End* (1968) is an interesting study of a central topic. For poets talking about their art, see *The Poet's Work: 29 Masters of 20th Century Poetry on the Origins and Practice of their Art,* ed. Reginald Gibbons (1979). For good discussions (with interesting pictorial material) of 13 American poets from Whitman to Sylvia Plath, see *Voices and Visions: The Poet in America,* ed. Helen Vendler (1987). Helen Vendler is also the author of two important books on contemporary poetry, *Part of Nature, Part of Us: Modern American Poets* (1980), and *The Music of What Happens: Poems, Poets, Critics* (1988).

✓ A Checklist: Getting Ideas for Writing about Poetry

If you are going to write about a fairly short poem (say, under 30 lines), it's a good idea to copy out the poem, writing or typing it double-spaced. By writing it out you will be forced to notice details, down to the punctuation. After you have copied the poem, proofread it carefully against the original. Catching an error—even the addition or omission of a comma—may help you to notice a detail in the original that you might otherwise have overlooked. And of course, now that you have the poem with ample space between the lines, you have a worksheet with room for jottings.

A good essay is based on a genuine response to a poem; a response may be stimulated in part by first reading the poem aloud and then considering the following questions.

First Response
What was your response to the poem on first reading? Did some parts especially please or displease you, or puzzle you? After some study—perhaps checking the meanings of some of the words in a dictionary and reading the poem several times—did you modify your initial response to the parts and to the whole?

Speaker and Tone
1. Who is the speaker? (Consider age, sex, personality, frame of mind, and tone of voice.) Is the speaker defined fairly precisely (for instance, an older woman speaking to a child), or is the speaker simply a voice meditating? (Jot down your first impressions, then reread the poem and make further jottings, if necessary.)
2. Do you think the speaker is fully aware of what he or she is saying, or does the speaker unconsciously reveal his or her personality and values? What is your attitude toward this speaker?
3. Is the speaker narrating or reflecting on an earlier experience or attitude? If so, does he or she convey a sense of new awareness, such as of regret for innocence lost?

Audience
To whom is the speaker speaking? What is the situation (including time and place)? (In some poems, a listener is strongly implied, but in others, especially those in which the speaker is meditating, there may be no audience other than the reader, who "overhears" the speaker.)

Structure and Form
1. Does the poem proceed in a straightforward way, or at some point or points does the speaker reverse course, altering his or her tone or perception? If there is a shift, what do you make of it?

2. Is the poem organized into sections? If so, what are these sections—stanzas, for instance—and how does each section (characterized, perhaps, by a certain tone of voice, or a group of rhymes) grow out of what precedes it?

3. What is the effect on you of the form—say, quatrains (stanzas of four lines) or blank verse (unrhymed lines of ten syllables)? If the sense overflows the form, running without pause from (for example) one quatrain into the next, what effect is created?

Center of Interest and Theme

1. What is the poem about? Is the interest chiefly in a distinctive character, or in meditation? That is, is the poem chiefly psychological or chiefly philosophical?

2. Is the theme stated explicitly (directly) or implicitly? How might you state the theme in a sentence? What is lost by reducing the poem to a statement of a theme?

Diction

1. How would you characterize the language? Colloquial, or elevated, or what?

2. Do certain words have rich and relevant associations that relate to other words and help to define the speaker or the theme or both?

3. What is the role of figurative language, if any? Does it help to define the speaker or the theme?

4. What do you think is to be taken figuratively or symbolically, and what literally?

Sound Effects

1. What is the role of sound effects, including repetitions of sound (for instance, alliteration) and of entire words, and shifts in versification?

2. If there are off-rhymes (for instance "dizzy" and "easy," or "home" and "come"), what effect do they have on you? Do they, for instance, add a note of tentativeness or uncertainty?

3. If there are unexpected stresses or pauses, what do they communicate about the speaker's experience? How do they affect you?

13

Writing about Film

This chapter offers some comments about the nature of film, some definitions of indispensable technical terms, a few suggestions about topics, a sample essay by a student, and a list of questions that you may want to ask yourself as you begin to think about writing on a film.

FILM AS A MEDIUM

Perhaps one's first thought is that a film (excluding cartoons, documentaries, newsreels, and so on) is rather like a play: A story is presented by means of actors. The film, of course, regularly uses some techniques not possible in the playhouse, such as close-ups and rapid changes of scene, but even these techniques can usually be approximated in the playhouse—for example, by means of lighting. It may seem, then, that one can experience a film as though it were a photographic record of a play. And, indeed, some films are nothing more than film records of plays.

There are, however, crucial distinctions between film and drama. First, though drama uses such visual matters as gestures, tableaux effects, and scenery, the plays that we value most highly are *literature:* the word dominates, the visual component is subordinate. One need not be a film fanatic who believes that the invention of the sound track was an impediment to film in order to realize that a film is more a matter of pictures than of words. The camera usually roves, giving us crowded streets, empty skies, rainy nights, or close-ups of filled ashtrays and chipped coffee cups. A critic has aptly said that in Ingmar Bergman's *Smiles of a Summer Night* "the almost unbearably ornate crystal goblets, by their aspect and their positioning in the image, convey the oppressive luxuriousness of the diners' lives in purely and uniquely filmic terms." In the words of the Swiss director Eric Rohmer, "the cinema is the description of man and his surroundings."[1]

Some of the greatest sequences in cinema, such as the battle scene in Orson Welles's *Falstaff* (also titled *Chimes at Midnight*) or parts of the search for Anna in Michelangelo Antonioni's *L'Avventura,* have no dialogue but concentrate on purely visual matters. In *L'Avventura* a group of rich and bored Italians goes on a yachting excursion and visits a volcanic island off the coast of Sicily, where one member of the party—Anna—disappears. Anna's fiancé, Sandro, and Anna's best friend, Claudia, search for her, but during the search they find that they are attracted to each other and they become lovers; Claudia later discovers that Sandro is unfaithful to her—but she and Sandro both were unfaithful to Anna, and the implication is that Claudia and Sandro will (in their way) remain weary partners. During the film's two hours, long sequences occur when, in a conventional sense, little "happens"—for example, there are shots of the sea, or of a character far from the camera, walking on the island during bad weather. Of course, in this film the setting itself is an important part of the story, the barren and crumbling island being symbolic of the decadent people who walk on it and symbolic also of the vast inhospitable universe in which these figures—rendered small by their distance from the camera—aimlessly move. The long silences (episodes without dialogue or background music) are as important as what is said, and what is seen is more important than what is said.

In short, the speaker in a film does not usually dominate. In a play the speaker normally holds the spectator's attention, but in a film when a character speaks, the camera often gives us a **reaction shot,** focusing not on the speaker but on the face or gestures of a character who is affected by the speech, thus giving the spectator a visual interpretation of the words. In Truffaut's *400 Blows,* for example, we hear a reform school official verbally assault a boy, but we see the uncomfortable boy, not the official. Even when the camera does focus on the speaker, it is likely to offer an interpretation.

---

[1]Films made for television, however, in contrast to the films under discussion, are, for the most part, fairly close to drama. Outdoor scenes, except for car chases and crashes, are relatively few. These television films show people talking and moving on a stage, but the films convey relatively little sense of a large world. This is not surprising; television technology is still primitive, and (unlike film) television cannot clearly portray a distant object (for example a horseman on the skyline), nor can it sharply portray fine detail even of an object close to the camera. Perhaps one should add here, however, that in the middle 1960s some directors, especially Jean-Luc Godard, rejected the idea that cinema is primarily a visual medium. Godard's characters sit around (they scarcely seem to *act*) talking about politics and their emotions.

An extreme example is a scene from *Brief Encounter:* A gossip is talking, and the camera gives us a close-up of her jabbering mouth which monstrously fills the screen.

This distance between film and drama can be put in another way: A film is more like a novel than a play, the action being presented not directly by actors but by a camera, which, like a novelist's point of view, comments on the story while telling it. A novelist may, like a dramatist, convey information about a character through dialogue and gesture but may also simply tell us about the character's state of mind. Similarly, a film maker may use the camera to inform us about unspoken thought. In Murnau's *Last Laugh,* when the hotel doorman reads a note firing him, the camera blurs; when he gets drunk, the camera spins so that the room seems to revolve. Somewhat similarly, Antonioni's *Red Desert* occasionally uses out-of-focus shots to convey Giuliana's view of the world; when she is more at ease—for example, with her husband—the shots are in proper focus. In Bertolucci's *Conformist* a shot of a chase through the woods is filmed with a hand-held camera whose shaky images convey to us the agitated emotions of the chase. At the end of *Bonnie and Clyde,* when Clyde is riddled with bullets, because his collapse is shot in slow motion he seems endowed not only with unusual grace but also with almost superhuman powers of endurance.

Even the choice of film stock is part of the comment. A highly sensitive or "fast" film needs less light to catch an image than a "slow" film does, but it is usually grainier. Perhaps because black-and-white newsreels often use fast film, a grainy quality may suggest authenticity or realism. Moreover, fast film can be processed to show less subtle gradations from black to white than slow film does, and this high contrast makes it especially suitable for the harsh, unromantic *Battle of Algiers.* Different film stocks may be used within a single motion picture. In *Wild Strawberries,* for instance, Bergman uses high-contrast stock for the nightmare sequence, though elsewhere in the film the contrasts are subtle. Color film has its own methods of tone and texture control.

The medium, as everyone knows, is part of the message; Sir Laurence Olivier made Shakespeare's *Henry V* in color but *Hamlet* in black and white because these media say different things. Peter Brook's film of *King Lear* is also in black and white, with an emphasis on an icy whiteness that catches the play's spirit of old age and desolation; a *Lear* in color probably would have an opulence that would work against the lovelessness and desolation of much of the play. John Houseman said that he produced *Julius Caesar* in black and white because he wanted "intensity" rather than "grandeur" and because black and white evoked newsreels of Hitler and thus helped establish the connection between Shakespeare's play and relatively recent politics. Peter Ustinov said that he made *Billy Budd* in black and white because he wanted it to seem real; and Richard Brooks's *In Cold Blood,* also in black and white, tried to look like a documentary. Similarly, although by 1971 most fiction films were being made in color, Peter Bogdanovich made *The Last Picture Show* in black and white, partly to convey a sense of the unexciting life of a small town in America in the 1950s and partly to evoke the films of the fifties. When a film is made in color, however, the colors may be symbolic (or at least suggestive) as well as realistic. In *A Clockwork Orange,* for example, hot colors (oranges and reds) conveying vitality and aggressiveness in the first half of the film are displaced in the second half by cool colors (blues and greens) when the emphasis turns to "clockwork"—to mechanization.

The kind of lens used also helps determine what the viewer sees. In *The Graduate* Benjamin runs toward the camera (he is trying to reach a church before his girl marries another man), but he seems to make no progress because a telephoto lens was used and thus his size does not increase as it normally would. The lens, that is, helps communicate his desperate sense of frustration. Conversely, a wide-angle lens makes a character approach the camera with menacing rapidity; he quickly looms into the foreground. Of course, a film maker, though resembling a novelist in offering pervasive indirect comment, is not a novelist any more than he or she is a playwright or director of a play; the medium has its own techniques, and the film maker works with them, not with the novel's or the drama's. The wife who came out of the movie theater saying to her husband "What a disappointment; it was exactly like the book" knew what a film ought to be.

FILM TECHNIQUES

At this point it may be well to suspend generalizations temporarily and to look more methodically at some techniques of film making. What follows is a brief grammar and dictionary of film, naming and explaining the cinematic devices that help film makers embody their vision in a work of art. An essay on film will probably discuss some of these devices, but there is no merit in mechanically trotting them all out.

Shots

A shot is what is recorded between the time a camera starts and the time it stops, that is, between the director's call for "action" and the call to "cut." Perhaps the average shot is about 10 seconds (very rarely a fraction of a second, and usually not more than 15 or so seconds). The average film is about an hour and a half, with about 600 shots, but Hitchcock's *Birds* uses 1360 shots. Three common shots are (1) a **long shot** or **establishing shot,** showing the main object at a considerable distance from the camera and thus presenting it in relation to its general surroundings (for example, captured soldiers, seen across a prison yard, entering the yard); (2) a **medium shot,** showing the object in relation to its immediate surroundings (a couple of soldiers, from the knees up, with the yard's wall behind them); (3) a **close-up,** showing only the main object, or, more often, only a part of it (a soldier's face or his bleeding feet).

In the outside world we can narrow our vision to the detail that interests us by moving our head and by focusing our eyes, ignoring what is not of immediate interest. The close-up is the movie director's chief way of directing our vision and of emphasizing a detail. (Another way is to focus sharply on the significant image, leaving the rest of the image in soft focus.) The close-up, a way of getting emphasis, has been heavily used in recent years, not always successfully. As Dwight Macdonald said of *Midnight Cowboy* and *Getting Straight,* "a movie told in close-ups is like a comic book, or like a novel composed in punchy one-sentence paragraphs and set throughout in large caps. How refreshing is a long or middle shot, a glimpse of the real world, so lovely and so *far away,* in the midst of those interminable processions of [a] hairy ogre face."

Two excellent film versions of Shakespeare's *Henry V* nicely show the different effects that long shots and close-ups can produce. Sir Laurence Olivier's version (1944) used abundant long shots and, on the whole, conveyed a highly pictorial sweeping epic version of the war in which Henry was engaged. Made during World War II, the film was a patriotic effort to inspire the English by showing the heroism of combat. On the other hand, Kenneth Branagh's version, made in 1989, used lots of close-ups of soldiers with mudsplattered faces, emphasizing the grittiness of war. Olivier brought out the splendor and romance, Branagh the labor and pain of war.

While taking a shot, the camera can move: It can swing to the right or left while its base remains fixed (a **pan shot**), up or down while fixed on its axis (a **tilt shot**), forward or backward (a **traveling shot**), or in and out and up and down fastened to a crane (a **crane shot**). The **zoom lens,** introduced in the 1950s and widespread by the middle 1960s, enables the camera to change its focus fluidly so that it can approach a detail—as a traveling shot does—while remaining fixed in place. Much will depend on the angle (high or low) from which the shots are made. If the camera is high (a **high-angle shot**), looking down on figures, it usually will dwarf them, perhaps even reduce them to crawling insects, making them vulnerable, pitiful, or contemptible. The higher the angle, the more likely it is to suggest a God's-eye view of entrapped people. If the camera is low (a **low-angle shot**), close to the ground and looking up, thereby showing figures against the sky, it probably will give them added dignity. In Murnau's *Last Laugh,* we first get low-angle shots of the self-confident doorman, communicating his grand view of himself; later, when he loses his strength and is reduced to working as a lavatory attendant, we see him from above, and he seems dwarfed. But these are not invariable principles. A shot in *Citizen Kane,* for example, shows Kane from above, but it does not dwarf him; rather, it shows him dominating his wife and then in effect obliterating her by casting a shadow over her. Similarly, a low-angle shot does not always add dignity: Films in which children play important parts often have lots of low-angle shots showing adults as menacing giants; and in *Dr. Strangelove* Stanley Kubrick regularly photographed Colonel Jack D. Ripper from low angles, thus emphasizing the colonel's power. In *Citizen Kane,* Kane is often photographed from floor level, similarly emphasizing his power, but some low-angle shots late in the film, showing him in his cavernous mansion, help convey his loneliness. In short, by its distance from the subject, its height from the ground, and its angle of elevation, the camera comments on or interprets what happens. It seems to record reality, but it offers its own version. It is only a slight exaggeration to say that the camera always lies, that is, gives a personal vision of reality.

Slow motion and **fast motion** also offer comments. In Branagh's *Henry V,* for example, as in Orson Welles's *Falstaff,* part of a battle is filmed in slow motion, thus emphasizing the weariness of the soldiers. On the other hand, a fast motion shot of factory workers or of vacationers betting in Las Vegas will—probably comically—emphasize their frantic activity.

Sequences

A group of related scenes—such as the three scenes of soldiers mentioned earlier—is a **sequence,** though a sequence is more likely to have 30 scenes than 3. A sequence corresponds roughly to a chapter in a novel, the shots being sentences and the scenes being paragraphs. Within a sequence may be an **intercut,** a switch to another action that, for example, provides an ironic comment on the main action of the sequence. If intercuts are so abundant in a sequence that, in effect, two or more sequences are going at once (for example, shots of the villain about to ravish the heroine, alternating with shots of the hero riding to her rescue), we have **parallel editing** (also called a **cross-cut**). In the example just given, probably the tempo would increase, the shots being progressively shorter as we get to the rescue. Though often a sequence will have an early establishing shot, it need not. Sometimes an establishing shot is especially effective if delayed, as in Dreyer's *Day of Wrath,* in which scenes of a witch tied to the top rungs of a ladder lead to a long shot of the context: The witch has been tied to the top of a tall ladder near a great heap of burning faggots. Still at a distance, the next shot shows the soldiers tilting the ladder up into the air and onto the pyre.

Transitions

Within a sequence, the transitions normally are made by **straight cuts**—a strip of film is spliced to another, resulting in an instantaneous transfer from one shot to the next. Usually, an audience is scarcely (if at all) conscious of transitions from, say, a long shot of a character to a medium shot of him, or from a close-up of a speaker to a close-up of his auditor. But sometimes the director wants the audience to be fully aware of the change, as an author may emphasize a change by beginning a new paragraph or, even more sharply, by beginning a new chapter. Two older, and now rather unfashionable, relatively conspicuous transitions are sometimes still used, usually between sequences rather than within a sequence. These are the **dissolve** (the shot dissolves while a new shot appears to emerge from beneath it, there being a moment when we get a superimposition of both scenes), and the **fade** (in the **fade-out** the screen grows darker until black; in the **fade-in** the screen grows lighter until the new scene is fully visible). In effect the camera is saying "Let us now leave X and turn to Y," or "Two weeks later." In *2001* a prehistoric apelike creature discovers that it can use a bone as a tool, and it destroys a skeleton with it. Then it throws the bone triumphantly into the air, where the bone dissolves into a spaceship of the year 2001. The point is that the spaceship is the latest of our weapons and that progress is linked with destructiveness. Two older methods, even less in favor today than the dissolve and the fade but used in many excellent old films and in some modern films that seek an archaic effect, are the **wipe** (a sort of windshield wiper crosses the screen, wiping off the first scene and revealing the next), and the **iris** (in an **iris-in,** the new scene first appears in the center of the previous scene and then this circle expands until it fills the screen; an **iris-out** shows the new scene first appearing along the perimeter and then the circle closes in on the previous scene). Chaplin more than once ended a scene with an iris-out of the tramp walking jauntily toward the horizon. François Truffaut used iris shots in *The Wild Child,* suggesting by the encircling darkness the boy's isolation from most of the world surrounding him as he concentrated on a single object before him. In Kurosawa's *High and Low* a wipe is used with no archaic effect: An industrialist, trying to decide whether to pay an enormous ransom to free a child, has been told to toss the money from a train; the scene showing him arriving at his decision in his luxurious home is wiped off by a train that rushes across the screen. He has decided to pay.

Editing

All of the transitions discussed a moment ago are examples of editing techniques. A film, no less than a poem or a play or a picture or a palace, is something made, and it is not made by simply exposing some footage. Shots—often taken at widely separated times and places—must be appropriately joined. For example, we see a man look off to the right, and then we get a shot of what he is looking at and then a shot of his reaction. Until the shots are assembled, we don't have a film—we merely have the footage. V. I. Pudovkin put it this way: "The film is not *shot*, but built, built up from the separate strips of celluloid that are its raw material." This building-up is the process of **editing.** In *Film Technique* Pudovkin gives some examples of editing:

1. In the simplest kind of editing, the film tells a story from the best viewpoints, that is, sometimes from long shots, sometimes from medium shots, sometimes from close-ups.

2. Simultaneous actions, occurring in different places, can be narrated by cutting back and forth from one to the other.

3. Relationships can be conveyed by contrast (shots of starvation cut in with shots of gluttony), by symbolism (in Pudovkin's *Mother*, shots of an ice floe melting are cut into shots of a procession of workers, thereby suggesting that the workers' movement is a natural force coming to new life), and by *leitmotif* (that is, repetition of the same shot to emphasize a recurring theme).

More than a story can be told, of course; something of the appropriate emotion can be communicated by juxtaposing, say, a medium-long shot of a group of impassively advancing soldiers against a close-up of a single terrified victim. Similarly, emotion can be communicated by the duration of the shots (quick shots suggest haste; prolonged shots suggest slowness) and by the lighting (progressively darker shots can suggest melancholy; progressively lighter shots can suggest hope or joy). An extremely obvious but effective example occurs in Charlie Chaplin's *Modern Times* (1936), a satire on industrialism. We see a mass of workers hurrying to their jobs, and a moment later we see a herd of sheep on the move, this shot providing a bitter comic comment on the previous shot.

The Russian theorists of film called this process of building by quick cuts **montage.** The theory held that shots, when placed together, add up to more than the sum of the parts. Montage, for them, was what made a film a work of art and not a mere replica of reality. American writers commonly use the term merely to denote quick cutting, and French writers use it merely in the sense of cutting.[2]

---

[2]You don't have to be in Hollywood or in Russia or France to write a script. You may find it challenging and entertaining to recall either some incident you were involved in or a scene from a novel and then to recast it as a script, indicating shots, camera angles, lighting, and sound track.

All this talk about ingenious shots and their arrangement, then, assumes that the camera is a sort of pen, carefully setting forth images and thus at every point guiding the perceiver. The director (through the actors, camera technicians, cutters, and a host of others) makes an artifact, rather as a novelist makes a book or a sculptor makes a statue, and this artifact is a sort of elaborate contraption that manipulates the spectators by telling them at every second exactly how they ought to feel. But since, say, the 1950s, a reaction has occurred against such artistry, a feeling that although the elaborate editing of, say, Eisenstein and the other Russians is an esthetic triumph, it is also a moral failure because by its insistent tricky commentary it seems to deny the inherent worth of the event in itself as it happens. Moreover, just as the nineteenth-century narrator in the novel, who continually guided the reader ("Do not fear, gentle reader, for even at this moment plans were being laid. . . ") was in the twentieth-century novel sloughed off, forcing the readers in large measure to deduce the story for themselves, so too some contemporary film makers emphasize improvisation, fully aware that the film thus made will not at every point guide or dominate the viewer. Rather, the viewers of such a film become something of creators themselves, making the work of art by sorting out the relevant from the irrelevant images. Norman Mailer, in an essay on his film *Maidstone*, calls attention to the fact that in making this sort of film the camera, expecting an interesting bit of acting, may zoom in on what later turns out to be dull, but the scene is not deleted or shot again. The dull parts, the mistakes, are kept, and what was missed is not reenacted. In *Maidstone*, Mailer says, "When significant movement was captured, it was now doubly significant because one could not take it for granted. Watching film became an act of interpretation and restoration for what was missed."

THEME

It is time now to point out an obvious fact: Mastery of technique, though necessary to good film making, will not in itself make a good film. A good film is not a bag of cinematic devices but the embodiment, through cinematic devices, of a vision, an underlying theme. What is this theme or vision? It is a film maker's perception of some aspect of existence that he or she thinks is worthy of our interest. Normally, this perception involves characters and a plot. Though recent American films, relying heavily on color, rock music in stereophonic sound, quick cutting, and the wide screen, have tended to emphasize the emotional experience and deemphasize narrative, still most of the best cinema is concerned with what people do, that is, with character and plot. Character is what people are; plot is what happens; but the line between character and plot fades, for what people are is in large measure what they do, and what is done is in large measure the result of what people are.

Character and plot, then, finally are inseparable; in a good film, everything hangs together. Harold Lloyd said that he had idea men who suggested numerous bits of comic business, and then he chose "the ones that [he] thought would be most appropriate to the particular film we were doing." The operative words are "most appropriate." A very funny bit of business might not be appropriate—might somehow not seem to fit—in a particular film because it was not in harmony with the underlying theme or vision or idea, the "clothes rack" (Lloyd's term) on which the funny bits (the clothes) were hung. In *The Freshman*, Lloyd said, the underlying idea or theme was the student's enormous desire for popularity, and everything in the film had to further this theme. Consider the comments of the late Truffaut on the themes of *The 400 Blows* and *Jules and Jim*, and on the disastrous lack of a theme in *Shoot the Piano Player*:

> In *400 Blows*, I was guided by the desire to portray a child as honestly as possible, and to invest his actions with a moral significance. Similarly with *Jules and Jim*, my desire to keep the film from seeming either pornographic, indelicate, or conventional guided me. The trouble with *Shoot the Piano Player* was that I was able to do anything—that the subject itself didn't impose its own form. . . . As it stands, there are some nice bits in the film, but it can't be said: this is the best work on this particular theme. There isn't any theme.

(It does not follow, of course, that the artist is fully aware of the theme from the start. Antonioni mentions that "it often happens that I experience fragmentary feelings before the experiences themselves take hold." But if they do not finally take hold, the film will probably arouse the sort of response that Truffaut mentions in his comments on *Shoot the Piano Player*.)

And so we come back to the idea of a vision or, in a less exalted word, a theme. Some critics, we recall, have argued that the concept of theme is meaningless: A film is only a detailed presentation of certain imaginary people in imaginary situations, not a statement about an aspect of life. Susan Sontag, in a challenging essay in *Against Interpretation*, argues that our tendency to seek a meaning in what we perceive is a manifestation of a desire to control the work of art by reducing its rich particulars to manageable categories. But Sontag's view itself is reductive. If we read in a newspaper about a marriage or a business failure or a baseball game, we take it only as a particular happening of some interest, and we do not assume that it implies much if anything beyond itself. It tells of something that has happened, but it does not tell what ought to happen or what usually happens; that is, it does not imply anything about the ways of people in general. When, however, we read a novel, or see on the stage or screen a happening, we inevitably feel—if only because we are asked to give the event an hour or more of our attention—that it is offered to us as noteworthy, an example not of what *happened* (it didn't happen; it's fictional) but an example of what *happens*. The characters in the fictional work are (like the characters in newspaper items) individuals, not mere abstractions, but (unlike those in newspaper items) they are significant individuals, in some measure revealing to us a whole class of people or a way of life. An artist gives us a representation that can be thought about.

Sometimes we sense that a film has an arguable thesis. Stanley Kubrick, for example, has said that *A Clockwork Orange* "warns against the new psychedelic fascism—the eye-popping, multimedia, quadrasonic, drug-oriented conditioning of human beings by other human beings—which many believe will usher in the forfeiture of human citizenship and the beginning of zombiedom." A film maker, however, need not argue a thesis that is subject to verification (for example, that the older generation seeks to repress the younger generation); it is enough if he or she sees in the human experience something worth our contemplation (for example, the conflict between generations) and embodies it on film. A theme can usually be named by an abstract noun or phrase (the quest for happiness, the difficulty of achieving self-knowledge, the fragility of love) and though we recognize that any such formula is not the whole life, it is nonetheless important. Adequately embodied in a film (or in any other kind of art) this exploration of experience alters our experience of life, including our experience of ourselves. Let Truffaut have the last word on this topic:

> I also believe that every film must contain some degree of "planned violence" upon its audience. In a good film, people must be made to see something that they don't want to see: they must be made to approve of someone of whom they had disapproved, they must be forced to look where they had refused to look.

GETTING READY TO WRITE

Mastery of terminology does not make anyone a perceptive film critic, but it helps writers communicate their perceptions to their readers. Probably an essay on a film will not be primarily about the use of establishing shots or of wipes or of any such matters, but rather it will be about some of the reasons why a particular film pleases or displeases, succeeds or fails, seems significant or insignificant, and in discussing these large matters it is sometimes necessary (or at least economical) to use the commonest technical terms. Large matters are often determined in part by such seemingly small matters as the distance of the camera from its subject or the way in which transitions are made, and one may as well use the conventional terms. But it is also true that a film maker's technique and technology alone cannot make a first-rate film. An idea, a personal vision, a theme (see pp. 280–82) must be embodied in all that is flashed on the screen.

Writing an essay about a new film—one not yet available for study on the VCR—presents difficulties not encountered in writing about stories, plays, and poems. Because we experience film in a darkened room, we cannot easily take notes, and because the film may be shown only once, we cannot always take another look at passages that puzzle us. But some brief notes can be taken even in the dark; it is best to amplify them as soon as light is available, while one still knows what the scrawls mean. If you can see the film more than once, do so; and, of course, if the script has been published, study it. Draft your paper as soon as possible after your first viewing, and then see the film again. You can sometimes check hazy memories of certain scenes and techniques with fellow viewers. But even with multiple viewings and the aid of friends, it is almost impossible to get the details right; it is best for the writer to be humble and for the reader to be tolerant.

A SAMPLE ESSAY ON VISUAL SYMBOLS: "A JAPANESE MACBETH"

Printed here is a student's essay on a film. Because it is on a version of *Macbeth*, it is in some degree a comparison between a film and a play, but it does not keep shifting back and forth and does not make the obvious point that many differences are found. Rather, it fairly quickly announces that it will be concerned with one kind of difference—the use of visual symbols that the camera can render effectively—and it then examines four such symbols.

Here is the skeleton of the essay, "A Japanese *Macbeth*," paragraph by paragraph:

> The Japanese film of *Macbeth* is not a film of a stage performance; it is a cinematic version.
>
> The film sometimes changes Shakespeare's plot, but this essay will be concerned only with the changes that are visual symbols: the fog, the castle, the forest, the horses.
>
> The fog, the castle, and the forest can be treated briefly. The fog shows nature blinding man; the castle shows man's brief attempt to impose his will on the natural landscape; the forest shows nature entrapping man.

The nervous, active horses—which could not be actually shown on the
Elizabethan stage—suggest man's fierce, destructive passions.
The film, though literally false to the play, is artistically true.

This is a solid organization: The title, though not especially imaginative, at
least catches our interest and gives a good idea of the general topic; the first
paragraph introduces a significant point; and the second narrows it and announces precisely what the essay will cover. The third paragraph studies
three of the four symbols announced in the second paragraph, and the
fourth paragraph studies the fourth, more complicated symbol. The concluding paragraph in a way reaffirms the opening paragraph, but it does so
now in the light of concrete evidence that has been offered. Organizing the
essay is only part of the job. The writer of this essay has done more than
work out an acceptable organization; she has some perceptions to offer, and
she has found the right details and provided neat transitions so that the
reader can move through the essay with pleasure.

A Japanese <u>Macbeth</u>

*Essayist's general
position, and
implicit thesis, is
clear from the
start.*

A Japanese movie-version of <u>Macbeth</u> sounds
like a bad idea--until one sees Kurosawa's
film, <u>Throne of Blood</u>, in which Toshiro Mifune
plays Washizu, the equivalent of Macbeth. It
is a much more satisfying film than, say,
Oliver's <u>Othello</u>, largely because it is not
merely a filmed version of a play as it might
be performed on a stage, but rather it is a
freely re-created version that is designed for
the camera. The very fact that it is in
Japanese is probably a great help to
Westerners. If it were in English, we would
be upset at the way some speeches are cut, but
because it is in Japanese, we do not compare
the words to Shakespeare's, and we concentrate
on the visual aspects of the film.

*As the paragraph
proceeds, it zooms
in on the topic.*

There are several differences in the plots
of the two works. Among the alterations are
such things as these: Shakespeare's three
witches are reduced to one; Lady Washizu has a

miscarriage; Washizu is killed by his own troops and not by Macduff. But this paper will discuss another sort of change, the introduction of visual symbols, which the camera is adept at rendering, and which play an important part in the film. The four chief visual symbols are the fog, the castle, the forest, and the horses.

Essayist tells us exactly what will be covered in the rest of the essay.

   The fog, the castle, and the forest, though highly effective, can be dealt with rather briefly. When the film begins we get a slow panoramic view of the ruined castle seen through the fog. The film ends with a similar panoramic view. These two scenes end with a dissolve, though almost all of the other scenes end abruptly with sharp cuts, and so the effect is that of lingering sorrow at the transience of human creations, and awe at the permanence of the mysterious natural world, whose mist slowly drifts across what once was a mighty castle built by a great chief. The castle itself, when we come to see it in its original condition, is not a particularly graceful Japanese building. Rather, it is a low, strong building, appropriate for an energetic warrior. The interior scenes show low, oppressive ceilings, with great exposed beams that almost seem to crush the people within the rooms. It represents man's achievement in the center of the misty tangled forest of the mysterious world, but it also suggests, despite its strength, how stifling that achievement is, in comparison with the floating mists and endless woods. The woods,

Transition (through repetition of part of previous sentence) and helpful forecast.

Analysis, not mere plot telling.

Thoughtful interpretation.

rainy and misty, consist of curiously gnarled trees and vines, and suggest a labyrinth that has entrapped man, even though for a while man thinks he is secure in his castle. Early in the film we see Washizu riding through the woods, in and out of mists, and behind a maze of twisted trees that periodically hide him from our sight. Maybe it is not too fanciful to suggest that the branches through which we glimpse him blindly riding in the fog are a sort of net that entangles him. The trees and the mist are the vast unfathomable universe; man can build his castle, can make his plans, but he cannot subdue nature for long. He cannot have his way forever; death will ultimately catch him, despite his strength. One later scene of the forest must be mentioned. Near the end of the film, when the forest moves (the soldiers are holding up leafy boughs to camouflage themselves), we get a spectacular shot; Shakespeare talks of the forest moving, but in the film we see it. Suddenly the forest seems to give a shudder and to be alive, crawling as though it is a vast horde of ants. Nature is seen to rise up against Washizu's crimes.

Shakespeare's stage could do very little about such an effect as the fog, though his poetry can call it to mind, and it could do even less about the forest. Kurosawa did not feel bound to the text of the play: he made a movie, and he took advantage of the camera's ability to present impressive and significant scenic effects. Similarly, he made much use

Further interpretation.

Essayist moves chronologically.

Summary leads, at the end of the paragraph, to interpretation.

The first half of this paragraph is a well-handled comparison.

of horses, which, though mentioned in Shakespeare's play, could not be shown on the Elizabethan stage. In fact, in <u>Macbeth</u> Shakespeare more or less apologizes forShakespeare more or less apologizes for the absence of horses when one murderer explains to the other that when horsemen approach the palace it is customary for them to leave their horses and to walk the rest of the way. But the film gives us plenty of horses, not only at the start, when Washizu is galloping in the terrifying forest, but throughout the film, and they are used to suggest the terror of existence, and the evil passions in Washizu's heart. Shakespeare provided a hint. After King Duncan is murdered, Shakespeare tells us that Duncan's horses "Turned wild in nature, broke their stalls," and even that they ate each other (II.iv.16-18). In the film, when Washizu and his wife plot the murder of their lord, we see the panic-struck horses running around the courtyard of the castle--a sort of parallel to the scene of Washizu chaotically riding in and out of the fog near the beginning of the movie. The horses in the courtyard apparently have sensed man's villainous plots, or perhaps they are visual equivalents of the fierce emotions in the minds of Washizu and his wife. Later, when Washizu is planning to murder Miki (the equivalent of Banquo), we see Miki's white horse kicking at his attendants. Miki saddles the horse, preparing to ride into the hands of his assassins. Then Kurosawa cuts to a long

A reminder of a point made earlier, but now developed at length.

shot of the courtyard at night, where Miki's
attendants are nervously waiting for him to
return. Then we hear the sound of a galloping
horse, and suddenly the white horse comes
running in, riderless. Yet another use of this
motif is when we cut to a wild horse, after
Washizu's wife has said that she is pregnant.
In the film the wife has a miscarriage, and
here again the horse is a visual symbol of the
disorder engendered within her (the child
would be the heir to the usurped throne), as

Thoughtful
generalization.

the other horses were symbols for the disorder
in her mind and in Macbeth's. All of these
cuts to the horses are abrupt, contributing to
the sense of violence that the unrestrained
horses themselves embody. Moreover, almost
the only close-ups in the film are some shots
of horses, seen from a low angle, emphasizing
their powerful, oppressive brutality.

Conclusion is
chiefly a
restatement but
the last sentence
gives it an
interesting twist.

   Throne of Blood is not Shakespeare's
Macbeth--but even a filmed version of a staged
version of the play would not be Shakespeare's
Macbeth either, for the effect of a film is
simply not identical with the effect of a play
with live actors on the stage. But Throne of
Blood is a fine translation of Macbeth into an
approximate equivalent. Despite its lack of
faithfulness to the literal text, it is in a
higher way faithful. It is a work of art,
like its original.

THE BIG PICTURE

All works of art are contrivances, of course, but (as a Roman saying puts it) the art is to conceal art. Does the film seem arty, a mere *tour de force,* or does it have the effect of inevitability, the effect of rightness, conveying a sense that a vision has been honestly expressed? Are characters or scenes clumsily dragged in? Are unusual effects significant? Does the whole add up to something? Do we get scenes or characters or techniques that at first hold us by their novelty but then have nothing further to offer?

Some final advice: Early in the essay it is usually desirable to sketch enough of the plot to give the readers an idea of what happens. (In the previous essay the student does not sketch the plot, but she says it is a version of *Macbeth* and thus gives the necessary information.) Do not try to recount everything that happens; it can't be done, and the attempt will frustrate you and bore your readers. Once you introduce the main characters and devote a few sentences to the plot, thus giving the readers a comfortable seat, get down to the job of convincing them that you have something interesting to say about the film—that the plot is trivial, or that the hero is not really cool but cruel, or that the plot and the characters are fine achievements but the camera work is sometimes needlessly tricksy, or that all is well.

Incidentally, a convenient way to give an actor's name in your essay is to put it in parentheses after the character's name or role, thus: "The detective (Humphrey Bogart) finds a clue. . . ." Then, as you go on to talk about the film, use the names of the characters or the roles, not the names of the actors, except of course when you are talking about the actors themselves, as in "Bogart is exactly right for the part."

📖 Suggestions for Further Reading

For quick reference, see Ephraim Katz, *The Film Encyclopedia* (1980) and Leslie Halliwell, *The Filmgoer's Companion,* 9th ed. (1988). For somewhat fuller discussions of directors, ranging from two or three pages to eight or ten pages, see Richard Roud, ed., *Cinema: A Critical Dictionary: The Major Film-Makers,* 2 vols. (1980).

Good introductory books include Gerald Mast, *A Short History of the Movies,* 5th ed., rev. Bruce F. Kawin (1992); Leo Braudy, *The World in a Frame* (1984); Bruce F. Kawin, *How Movies Work* (1992); Thomas Sobchack and Vivian C. Sobchack, *An Introduction to Film,* 2nd ed. (1987); David Bordwell, *Making Meaning: Inference and Rhetoric in the Interpretation of Cinema* (1989); Edward R. Branigan, *Point of View in Cinema* (1984); Timothy Corrigan, *A Short Guide to Writing about Film*

(1989). For theory, see *Film Theory and Criticism,* 4th ed., eds. Gerald Mast, Marshall Cohen, and Leo Braudy (1992). For a highly influential feminist study, see Laura Mulvey, *Visual and Other Pleasures* (1989).

Articles on film can be located through *International Index to Film Periodicals.*

✓ A Checklist: Getting Ideas for Writing about Film

These questions may help bring impressions out into the open and may with some reworking provide topics for essays.

Preliminaries
Is the title significant? Are the newspaper or television advertisements appropriate?

Literary Adaptations
1. If the film is adapted from fiction or drama, does it slavishly follow its original and neglect the potentialities of the camera? Or does it so revel in cinematic devices that it distorts the original work? (Of course, an adaptation need not go to either extreme. *An Occurrence at Owl Creek Bridge* is a close adaptation of Ambrose Bierce's story, and yet it is visually interesting.)
2. If the film is adapted from fiction or drama, does it do violence to the theme of the original? Is the film better than its source? Are the additions or omissions due to the medium or to a crude or faulty interpretation of the original? Is the film *The Color Purple* more sensational or less than the book? In what ways can it be said that the film is different from the book?

Plot and Character
1. Can film deal as effectively with inner action—mental processes— as with external, physical action? In a given film, how is the inner action conveyed?
2. Are shots and sequences adequately developed, or do they seem jerky? (A shot may be jerky by being extremely brief or at an odd angle; a sequence may be jerky by using discontinuous images or fast cuts. Sometimes, of course, jerkiness may be desirable.) If such cinematic techniques as wipes, dissolves, and slow motion are used, are they meaningful and effective?
3. Are the characters believable?
4. Are the actors appropriately cast? (Wasn't it a mistake to cast Robert Redford as Gatsby? Tom Hanks as the lead in *Bonfire of the Vanities?*)

Sound Track

1. Does the sound track offer more than realistic dialogue? Is the music appropriate and functional? (Music may, among other things, imitate natural sounds, give a sense of locale or of ethnic group, suggest states of mind, provide ironic commentary, or—by repeated melodies—help establish connections.) Are volume, tempo, and pitch—whether of music or of such sounds as the wind blowing or cars moving—used to stimulate emotions?

PART 4

Inside: Style, Format, and Special Assignments

14

Style and Format

PRINCIPLES OF STYLE

Writing is hard work (Lewis Carroll's school in *Alice's Adventures in Wonderland* taught reeling and writhing), and there is no point fooling ourselves into believing that it is all a matter of inspiration. Evidence abounds that many of the poems, stories, plays, and essays that seem to flow so effortlessly as we read them were in fact the product of innumerable revisions. "Hard labor for life" was Conrad's view of his career as a writer. This labor for the most part is directed not to prettifying language but to improving one's thoughts and then getting the words that communicate these thoughts exactly.

The efforts are not guaranteed to pay off, but failure to expend effort is sure to result in writing that will strike the reader as confused. It won't do to comfort yourself with the thought that you have been misunderstood. You may know what you *meant to say*, but your reader is the judge of what indeed you *have said*.

Big books have been written on the elements of good writing, but the best way to learn to write is to generate ideas by such methods as annotating the text, listing, brainstorming, free writing, and making entries in a journal. Then, with some ideas at hand, you can write a first draft, which you will revise—perhaps in light of comments by your peers—and later will revise yet again, and again. After you hand your essay in, your instructor will annotate it. Study the annotations an experienced reader puts on your essay. In revising the annotated passages, you will learn what your weaknesses are. After drafting your next essay, put it aside for a day or so; when you reread it, preferably aloud, you may find much that bothers you. If the argument does not flow, check to see whether your organization is reasonable and whether you have made adequate transitions. Do not hesitate to delete interesting but irrelevant material that obscures the argument. Make the necessary revisions again and again if time permits. Revision is indispensable if you wish to avoid (in Maugham's words) "the impression of writing with the stub of a blunt pencil."

Still, a few principles can be briefly set forth here. On Dr. Johnson's belief that we do not so much need to be taught as to be reminded, these principles are brief imperatives rather than detailed instructions. They will not suppress your particular voice. Rather, they will get rid of static, enabling your voice to come through effectively. You have something to say, but you can say it only after your throat is cleared of "Well, what I meant was," and "It's sort of, well, you know." Your readers do *not* know; they are reading in order *to* know. The paragraphs that follow are attempts to help you let your individuality speak clearly.

Get the Right Word

Denotation

Be sure the word you choose has the right explicit meaning, or **denotation.** Don't say "tragic" when you mean "pathetic," "sarcastic" when you mean "ironic," "free verse" when you mean "blank verse," "disinterested" when you mean "uninterested."

Connotation

Be sure the word you choose has the right association or implication—that is, the right **connotation.** Here are three examples of words with the wrong connotations for their contexts: "The heroic spirit is not dead. It still *lurks* in the hearts of men." ("Lurks" suggests a furtiveness inappropriate to the heroic spirit. Something like "lives" or "dwells" is needed.) "Close study will *expose* the strength of Woolf's style." ("Reveal" would be better than "expose" here; "expose" suggests that some weakness will be brought to light, as in "Close study will expose the flimsiness of the motivation.") "Although Creon suffers, his suffering is not great enough to *relegate* him

Calvin and Hobbes   by Bill Watterson

to the role of tragic hero." (In place of "relegate," we need something like "elevate" or "exalt.")

Concreteness

Catch the richness, complexity, and uniqueness of things. Do not write "Here one sees his lack of emotion" if you really mean "Here one sees his indifference" or "his iciness" or "his impartiality" or whatever the exact condition is. Instead of "The clown's part in *Othello* is very small," write "The clown appears in only two scenes in *Othello*" or "The clown in *Othello* speaks only 30 lines." ("Very," as in "very small" or "very big," is almost never the right word. A role is rarely "very big"; it "dominates" or "overshadows" or "is second only to. . . .")

In addition to using the concrete word and the appropriate detail, use illustrative **examples.** Northrop Frye, writing about the perception of rhythm, illustrates his point:

> Ideally, our literary education should begin, not with prose, but with such things as "this little pig went to market"—with verse rhythm reinforced by physical assault. The infant who gets bounced on somebody's knee to the rhythm of "Ride a cock horse" does not need a footnote telling him that Banbury Cross is twenty miles northeast of Oxford. He does not need the information that "cross" and "horse" make (at least in the pronunciation he is most likely to hear) not a rhyme but an assonance. . . . All he needs is to get bounced.
>
> —*The Well-tempered Critic* (Bloomington, Ind., 1963), p. 25

Frye does not say our literary education should begin with "simple rhymes" or with "verse popular with children." He says "with such things as 'this little pig went to market,'" and then he goes on to add "Ride a cock horse." We know exactly what he means. Notice, too, that we do not need a third example. Be detailed, but know when to stop.

Repetition and Variation

Although some repetitions—say, of words like *surely* or *it is noteworthy*—reveal a tic that ought to be cured by revision, don't be afraid to repeat a word if it is the best word. The following paragraph repeats "interesting," "paradox," "Salinger," "what makes," and "book"; notice also "feel" and "feeling":

> The reception given to *Franny and Zooey* in America has illustrated again the interesting paradox of Salinger's reputation there; great public enthusiasm, of the *Time* magazine and Best Seller List kind, accompanied by a repressive coolness in the critical journals. What makes this a paradox is that the book's

themes are among the most ambitiously highbrow, and its craftsmanship most uncompromisingly virtuoso. What makes it an interesting one is that those who are most patronising about the book are those who most resemble its characters; people whose ideas and language in their best moments resemble Zooey's. But they feel they ought not to enjoy the book. There is a very strong feeling in American literary circles that Salinger and love of Salinger must be discouraged.

—MARTIN GREEN, *Re-appraisals* (New York, 1965), p. 197

Repetition, a device necessary for continuity and clarity, holds the paragraph together. Variations occur: "*Franny and Zooey*" becomes "the book," and then instead of "the book's" we get "its." Similarly, "those who" becomes "people," which in turn becomes "they." Such substitutions, which neither confuse nor distract, keep the paragraph from sounding like a broken phonograph record.

Pronouns are handy substitutes, and they ought to be used, but other substitutes need not always be sought. An ungrounded fear of repetition often produces a vice known as *elegant variation:* Having mentioned *Franny and Zooey* an essayist next speaks of "the previously mentioned work," then of "the tale," and finally of "this work of our author." This vice is far worse than repetition; it strikes the reader as silly.

Pointless variation of this sort, however, is not to be confused with a variation that communicates additional useful information, such as "these two stories about the Glass family"; this variation is entirely legitimate, indeed necessary, for it furthers the discussion. But elegant variation can be worse than silly; it can be confusing, as in "My first *theme* dealt with plot, but this *essay* deals with character." The reader wonders if the writer means to suggest that an essay is different from a theme.

Notice in these lucid sentences by Helen Gardner the effective repetition of "end" and "beginning":

Othello has this in common with the tragedy of fortune, that the end in no way blots out from the imagination the glory of the beginning. But the end here does not merely by its darkness throw up into relief the brightness that was. On the contrary, beginning and end chime against each other. In both the value of life and love is affirmed.

—*The Noble Moor* (Oxford, 1956), p. 203

The substitution of "conclusion" or "last scene" for the second "end" would be worse than pointless; it would destroy Gardner's point that there is *identity* or correspondence between beginning and end.

Do not repeat a word if it is being used in a different sense. Get a different word. Here are two examples of the fault: "This *theme* deals with the *theme* of the novel." (The first "theme" means "essay"; the second means "underlying idea," "motif.") "Caesar's *character* is complex. The comic *characters* too have some complexity." (The first "character" means "personality"; the second means "persons," "figures in the play.")

The Sound of Sense

Avoid awkward repetitions of sound, as in "The story is marked by a remarkable mystery," "The reason the season is Spring. . . ," "Circe certainly. . . ," "This is seen in the scene in which. . . ." These irrelevant echoes call undue attention to the words and thus get in the way of the points you are making. But wordplay can be effective when it contributes to meaning. Gardner's statement that in the beginning and the end of *Othello* "the value of life and love is affirmed" makes effective use of the similarity in sound between "life" and "love." Her implication is that these two things that sound alike are indeed closely related, an idea that reinforces her contention that the beginning and the end of the play are in a way identical.

Write Effective Sentences

Economy

Say everything relevant, but say it in the fewest words possible. The wordy sentence

> There are a few vague parts in the story that give it a mysterious quality.

may be written more economically as

> A few vague parts in the story give it a mysterious quality.

Nothing has been lost by deleting "There are" and "that." Even more economical is

> A few vague parts add mystery to the story.

The original version says nothing that the second version does not say, and says nothing that the third version—9 words against 15—does not say. If you find the right nouns and verbs, you can often delete adjectives and adverbs. (Compare "a mysterious quality" with "mystery.") Another example of wordiness is: "Sophocles's tragic play *Antigone* is mistitled because Creon is the tragic hero, and the play should be named for him." These 20 words can be reduced, with no loss of meaning, to 9 words: "Sophocles's *Antigone* is mistitled; Creon is the tragic hero."

Something is wrong with a sentence if you can delete words and not sense the loss. A chapter in a recent book on contemporary theater begins:

One of the principal and most persistent sources of error that tends to bedevil a considerable proportion of contemporary literary analysis is the assumption that the writer's creative process is a wholly conscious and purposive type of activity.

Well, there is something of interest here, but it comes along with a lot of hot air. Why that weaseling ("*tends* to bedevil," "a *considerable* proportion"), and why "type of activity" instead of "activity"? Those spluttering *p*'s ("principal and most persistent," "proportion," "process," "purposive") are a giveaway; the writer is letting off steam, not thinking. Pruned of the verbiage, what he says adds up to this:

One of the chief errors bedeviling much contemporary criticism is the assumption that the writer's creative process is wholly conscious and purposive.

If he were to complain that this revision deprives him of his style, might we not fairly reply that what he calls his style is the display of insufficient thinking, a tangle of deadwood?

Cut out all the deadwood, but in cutting it out, do not cut out supporting detail. Supporting detail is wordiness only when the details are so numerous and obvious that they offend the reader's intelligence.

The **passive voice** (wherein the subject is the object of the action) is a common source of wordiness. Do not say "This story was written by Melville"; instead, say "Melville wrote this story." The revision is one-third shorter, and it says everything that the longer version says. Sometimes, of course, the passive voice, although less vigorous, may be preferable to the active voice. Changing "The novel was received in silence" to "Readers neglected the novel" makes the readers' response more active than it was. The passive catches the passivity of the response. Furthermore, the revision makes "readers" the subject, but the true subject is (as in the original) the novel.

Parallels

Use parallels to clarify relationships. Few of us are likely to compose such deathless parallels as "I came, I saw, I conquered" or "of the people, by the people, for the people," but we can see to it that coordinate expressions correspond in their grammatical form. A parallel such as "He liked to read and to write" (instead of "He liked reading and to write") makes its point neatly. No such neatness appears in "Virginia Woolf wrote novels, delightful letters, and penetrating stories." The reader is left wondering what value the novels have. If one of the items has a modifier, usually all should have modifiers. Notice how the omission of "the noble" in the following sentence would leave a distracting gap: "If the wicked Shylock cannot enter the fairy story world of Belmont, neither can the noble Antony."

Other examples of parallels are: "Mendoza longs to be an Englishman and to marry the girl he loves" (*not* "Mendoza longs to be an Englishman and for the girl he loves"); "He talked about metaphors, similes, and symbols" (*not* "He talked about metaphors, similes, and about symbols"). If one wishes to emphasize the leisureliness of the talk, one might put it thus: "He talked about metaphors, about similes, and about symbols." The repetition of "about" in this version is not wordiness; because it emphasizes the leisureliness, it does some work in the sentence. Notice in the next example how Helen Gardner's parallels ("in the," "in his," "in his," "in the") lend conviction:

> The significance of *Othello* is not to be found in the hero's nobility alone, in his capacity to know ecstasy, in his vision of the world, and in the terrible act to which he is driven by his anguish at the loss of that vision. It lies also in the fact that the vision was true.
>
> —*The Noble Moor*, p. 205

Subordination

Make sure that the less important element is subordinate to the more important. In the following example the first clause, summarizing the writer's previous sentences, is a subordinate or dependent clause; the new material is made emphatic by being put into two independent clauses:

> As soon as the Irish Literary Theatre was assured of a nationalist backing, it started to dissociate itself from any political aim, and the long struggle with the public began.

The second and third clauses in this sentence, linked by "and," are coordinate—that is, of equal importance.

We have already discussed parallels ("I came, I saw, I conquered") and pointed out that parallel or coordinate elements should appear so in the sentence. The following line gives time and eternity equal treatment: "Time was against him; eternity was for him." The quotation about the Irish Literary Theatre is a **compound sentence**—composed of two or more clauses that can stand as independent sentences but that are connected with a coordinating conjunction such as *and, but, for, nor, yet,* and *if;* or with a correlative conjunction such as *not only . . . but also;* or with a conjunctive adverb such as *also* or *however;* or with a colon, a semicolon, or (rarely) a comma. But a **complex sentence** (an independent clause and one or more subordinate clauses) does not give equal treatment to each clause; whatever is outside the independent clause is subordinate, less important. Consider this sentence:

> Aided by Miss Horniman's money, Yeats dreamed of a poetic drama.

The writer puts Yeats's dream in the independent clause, subordinating the relatively unimportant Miss Horniman. (Notice, by the way, that emphasis by subordination often works along with emphasis by position. Here the independent clause comes *after* the subordinate clause; the writer appropriately put the more important material in the more emphatic position.)

Had the writer wished to give Miss Horniman more prominence, the passage might have run:

> Yeats dreamed of a poetic drama, and Miss Horniman subsidized that dream.

Here Miss Horniman at least stands in an independent clause, linked to the previous independent clause by "and." The two clauses, and the two people, are now of approximately equal importance.

If the writer had wanted to emphasize Miss Horniman and to deemphasize Yeats, he might have written:

> While Yeats dreamed of a poetic drama, Miss Horniman provided the money.

Here Yeats is reduced to the subordinate clause, and Miss Horniman is given the dignity of the only independent clause. (Again notice that the important point is also in the emphatic position, near the end of the sentence. A sentence is likely to sprawl if an independent clause comes first, followed by a long subordinate clause of lesser importance, such as the sentence you are now reading.)

In short, though simple sentences and compound sentences have their place, they make everything of equal importance. Since everything is not of equal importance, you must often write complex and compound-complex sentences, subordinating some things to other things.

Write Unified and Coherent Paragraphs

Unity

A unified paragraph is a group of sentences (rarely a single sentence) on a single idea. The idea may have several twists or subdivisions, but all the parts—the sentences—should form a whole that can be summarized in one sentence. A paragraph is, to put the matter a little differently, one of the major points supporting your thesis. If your essay is some 500 words long—about two double-spaced typewritten pages—you probably will not break it down into more than four or five parts or paragraphs. (But you *should* break your essay down into paragraphs, that is, coherent blocks that give the reader a rest between them. One page of typing is about as long as you can go before the reader needs a slight break.) A paper of 500 words with a dozen paragraphs is probably faulty not because it has too many ideas but because it has too few *developed* ideas. A short paragraph—especially one consisting of a single sentence—is usually anemic; such a paragraph may be acceptable when it summarizes a highly detailed previous paragraph or group of paragraphs, or when it serves as a transition between two complicated paragraphs, but usually summaries and transitions can begin the next paragraph.

Each paragraph has a unifying idea, which may appear as a **topic sentence.** Most commonly, the topic sentence is the first sentence, forecasting what is to come in the rest of the paragraph; or it may be the second sentence, following a transitional sentence. Less commonly, it is the last sentence, summarizing the points that the paragraph's earlier sentences have made. Least commonly—but thoroughly acceptable—the topic sentence may appear nowhere in the paragraph, in which case the paragraph has a **topic idea**—an idea that holds the sentences together although it has not been explicitly stated. Whether explicit or implicit, an idea must unite the sentences of the paragraph. If your paragraph has only one or two sentences, the chances are that you have not adequately developed its idea. You probably have not provided sufficient details—perhaps including brief quotations—to support your topic sentence or your topic idea.

A paragraph can make several points, but the points must be related, and the nature of the relationship must be indicated so that the paragraph has a single unifying point. Here is a paragraph, unusually brief, that may seem to make two points but that, in fact, holds them together with a topic idea. The author is Edmund Wilson:

> James Joyce's *Ulysses* was an attempt to present directly the thoughts and feelings of a group of Dubliners through the whole course of a summer day. *Finnegans Wake* is a complementary attempt to render the dream fantasies and the half-unconscious sensations experienced by a single person in the course of a night's sleep.
>
> —*The Wound and the Bow* (New York, 1947), p. 243

Wilson's topic idea is that *Finnegans Wake* complements *Ulysses*. Notice that the sentence about *Finnegans Wake* concludes the paragraph. Not surprisingly, Wilson's essay is about this book, and the structure of the paragraph allows him to get into his subject.

The next example may seem to have more than one subject (Richardson and Fielding were contemporaries; they were alike in some ways; they were different in others), but again the paragraph is unified by a topic idea (although Richardson and Fielding were contemporaries and were alike in some ways, they differed in important ways):

> The names of Richardson and Fielding are always coupled in any discussion of the novel, and with good reason. They were contemporaries, writing in the same cultural climate (*Tom Jones* was published in 1719, a year after *Clarissa*). Both had genius and both were widely recognized immediately. Yet they are utterly different in their tastes and temperaments, and therefore in their visions of city and country, of men and women, and even of good and evil.
> —ELIZABETH DREW, *The Novel* (New York, 1963), p. 59

This paragraph, like Edmund Wilson's, closes in on its subject.

The beginning and especially the end of a paragraph are usually the most emphatic parts. A beginning may offer a generalization that the rest of the paragraph supports. Or the early part may offer details, preparing for the generalization in the later part. Or the paragraph may move from cause to effect. Although no rule can cover all paragraphs (except that all must make a point in an orderly way), one can hardly go wrong in making the first sentence either a transition from the previous paragraph or a statement of the paragraph's topic. Here is a sentence that makes a transition and also states the topic: "Not only narrative poems but also meditative poems may have a kind of plot." This sentence gets the reader from plot in narrative poetry (which the writer has been talking about) to plot in meditative poetry (which the writer goes on to talk about).

Coherence

If a paragraph has not only unity but also a structure, then it has coherence, its parts fit together. Make sure that each sentence is properly related to the preceding and the following sentences. One way of gaining coherence is by means of transitions—words such as *furthermore, on the other hand,* and *but*. These words let the reader know how a sentence is related to the previous sentence.

Nothing is wrong with such obvious transitions as *moreover, however, but, for example, this tendency, in the next chapter,* and so on; but, of course, (1) these transitions should not start every sentence (they can be buried thus: "Zora Neale Hurston, moreover,. . . "), and (2) they need not appear anywhere in the sentence. The point is not that transitions must be explicit, but that the argument must proceed clearly. The gist of a paragraph might run thus: "Speaking broadly, there were in the Renaissance two comic traditions. . . . The first . . . The second . . . The chief difference . . . But both traditions. . . "

Here is a paragraph by Elizabeth Drew, discussing one aspect of Dickens's *Great Expectations*. The structure is basically chronological, but notice, too, the effective use of a parallel as a linking device within the last sentence. (The links are italicized.)

> Some of the most poignant scenes in the book are the *opening ones*, which describe the atmosphere in which Pip grows up. *He is introduced* as "a small bundle of shivers" alone in the graveyard, *which is followed* by the terrifying intrusion of the world of active violence and fear as the convict seizes him. *Then we see* the household at the forge, where he is made to feel guilty and ashamed of his very existence; the Christmas party at which he is baited and bullied by his elders; his treatment at the hands of the hypocritical Pumblechook; his introduction to Estella, who reveals to him that he is coarse and common. *Dickens knows* that in children "there is nothing so finely perceived and so finely felt, as injustice," and looking back on his childhood, *Pip too knows* that truth: "Within myself, I had sustained, from my babyhood, a perpetual conflict with injustice."
>
> —*The Novel*, p. 197

Introductory Paragraphs

Beginning a long part of one of his long poems, Byron aptly wrote, "Nothing so difficult as a beginning." Almost all writers—professionals as well as amateurs—find that the beginning paragraphs in their drafts are false starts. Don't worry too much about the opening paragraphs of your draft; you'll almost surely want to revise your opening later anyway, and when writing a first draft you merely need something—almost anything may do—to get you going. Though on rereading you will probably find that the first paragraph or two should be replaced, those opening words at least helped you break the ice.

In your finished paper the opening cannot be mere throat clearing. It should be interesting and informative. Don't paraphrase your title ("Sex in *1984*") in your first sentence: "This theme will study the topic of sex in *1984*." The sentence contains no information about the topic here, at least none beyond what the title already gave, and no information about you, either—that is, no sense of your response to the topic, such as might be present in, say, "In George Orwell's *1984* the rulers put a lot of energy into producing antisexual propaganda, but Orwell never convinces us of the plausibility of all of this activity."

Often you can make use of a quotation, either from the work or from a critic. After all, if a short passage from the work caught your attention and set you thinking and stimulated you to develop a thesis, it may well provide a good beginning for your essay.

Here is a nice opening from a chapter on Norman Mailer, by Richard Poirier: "Mailer is an unusually repetitious writer. Nearly all writers of any lasting interest are repetitious." The first sentence, simple though it is, catches our attention; the second gives the first a richer meaning than we had attributed to it. Poirier then goes on to give examples of major writers who are obsessed with certain topics, and he concludes the paragraph with a list of Mailer's obsessions.

Such an opening paragraph is a slight variant on a surefire method: *You cannot go wrong in stating your thesis* in your opening paragraph, moving from a rather broad view to a narrower one. If you look at the sample essays in this book, you will see that most good opening paragraphs clearly indicate the writer's thesis. Here is an introductory paragraph, written by a student, on the ways in which Shakespeare manages in some degree to present Macbeth sympathetically:

> Near the end of <u>Macbeth</u>, Malcolm speaks of Macbeth as a "dead butcher" (5.8.69), and there is some--perhaps much--truth in this characterization. Macbeth is the hero of the play, but he is also the villain. And yet to call him a villain is too simple. Despite the fact that he murders his king, his friend Banquo, and even the utterly innocent Lady Macduff and her children, he engages our sympathy, largely because Shakespeare continually reminds us that Macbeth never (despite appearances) becomes a cold-blooded murderer. Macbeth's violence is felt not only by his victims but by Macbeth himself; his deeds torture him, plaguing his mind. Despite all his villainy, he is a man with a conscience.

Concluding Paragraphs

With conclusions, as with introductions, try to say something interesting. It is not of the slightest interest to say "Thus we see . . . [here the writer echoes the title and the first paragraph]." Some justification may be made for a summary at the end of a long paper because the reader may have half-forgotten some of the ideas presented 30 pages earlier, but a paper that can be held easily in the mind needs something different. In fact, if your paper is short—say 2 or 3 pages—you may not need to summarize or to draw a conclusion. Just make sure that your last sentence is a good one and that the reader does not expect anything further.

If you do feel that a concluding paragraph (as opposed to a final paragraph) is appropriate or necessary, make sure that you do not merely echo what you have already said. A good concluding paragraph may round out the previous discussion, normally with a few sentences that summarize (without the obviousness of "We may now summarize"), but it may also draw an inference that has not previously been expressed. To draw such an inference is not to introduce a new idea—a concluding paragraph is hardly the place for a new idea—but is to see the previous material from a fresh perspective. A good concluding paragraph closes the issue while enriching it. Notice how the two examples that follow wrap things up and at the same time, open out by suggesting a larger frame of reference.

The first example is the conclusion to Norman Friedman's "Point of View in Fiction." In this fairly long discussion of the development of a critical concept, Friedman catalogs various points of view and then spends several pages arguing that the choice of a point of view is crucial if certain effects are to be attained. The omniscient narrator of a novel who comments on all that happens, Friedman suggests, is a sort of free verse of fiction, and an author may willingly sacrifice this freedom for a narrower point of view if he or she wishes to make certain effects. Friedman concludes:

> All this is merely to say, in effect, that when an author surrenders in fiction, he does so in order to conquer; he gives up certain privileges and imposes certain limits in order the more effectively to render his story-illusion, which constitutes artistic truth in fiction. And it is in the service of this truth that he spends his creative life.
>
> —*PMLA*, 70 (1955), 1160–84

Notice that Friedman devotes the early part of his paragraph to a summary of what has preceded, and then in the latter part he puts his argument in a new perspective.

A second example of a concluding paragraph that restates the old and looks toward the new comes from Richard B. Sewall's discussion of *The Scarlet Letter.*

> Henry James said that Hawthorne had "a cat-like faculty of seeing in the dark"; but he never saw through the dark to radiant light. What light his vision reveals is like the fitful sunshine of Hester's and Dimmesdale's meeting in the forest—the tragic opposite of Emerson's triumphant gleaming sun that "shines also today."
>
> —*The Vision of Tragedy* (New Haven, 1959), p. 91

Again, don't feel that you must always offer a conclusion in your last paragraph. Especially if your paper is fairly short—let's say fewer than five pages—when you have finished your analysis or explication it may be enough to stop. If, for example, you have been demonstrating throughout your paper that in *Julius Caesar* Shakespeare condensed the time (compared to his historical source) and thus gave the happenings in the play an added sense of urgency, you scarcely need to reaffirm this point in your last paragraph. Probably it will be conclusion enough if you just offer your final evidence in a well-written sentence and then stop.

✓ A Checklist: Revising Paragraphs

1. Does the paragraph say anything? Does it have substance?
2. Does the paragraph have a topic sentence? If so, is it in the best place? If the paragraph doesn't have a topic sentence, might one improve the paragraph? Or does it have a clear topic idea?
3. If the paragraph is an opening paragraph, is it interesting enough to attract and to hold a reader's attention? If it is a later paragraph, does it easily evolve out of the previous paragraph, and lead into the next paragraph?
4. Does the paragraph contain some principle of development, for instance from cause to effect, or from general to particular?
5. Does each sentence clearly follow from the preceding sentence? Have you provided transitional words or cues to guide your reader? Would it be useful to repeat certain key words, for clarity?
6. What is the purpose of the paragraph? Do you want to summarize, or give an illustration, or concede a point, or what? Is your purpose clear to you, and does the paragraph fulfill your purpose?
7. Is the closing paragraph effective, and not an unnecessary restatement of the obvious?

Write Emphatically

All that has been said about getting the right word, about effective sentences, and about paragraphs is related to the matter of **emphasis.** But we can add a few points here. The first rule (it will be modified in a moment) is: Be emphatic. But do not attempt to achieve emphasis, as Queen Victoria did, by a *style* consisting *chiefly* of *italics* and *exclamation* marks!!! Do not rely on such expressions as "very important," "definitely significant," and "really beautiful." The proper way to be emphatic is to find the right word, to use appropriate detail, to subordinate the lesser points, and to develop your ideas reasonably. The beginning and the end of a sentence (and of a paragraph) are emphatic positions; of these two positions, the end is usually the more emphatic. Here is a sentence that properly moves to an emphatic end:

> Having been ill-treated by Hamlet and having lost her father, Ophelia goes mad.

If the halves are reversed, the sentence peters out:

> Ophelia goes mad because she has been ill-treated by Hamlet and she has lost her father.

Still, even this version is better than the shapeless:

> Having been ill-treated by Hamlet, Ophelia goes mad, partly too because she has lost her father.

The important point, that she goes mad, is dissipated by the lame addition of words about her father. In short, avoid anticlimaxes such as "Macbeth's deed is reprehensible and serious."

The usual advice, build to emphatic ends, needs modification. Don't write something that sounds like an advertisement for *The Blood of Dracula:* "In her eyes DESIRE! In her veins—the blood of a MONSTER!!!" Be emphatic but courteous and sensible; do not shout.

Notes on the Dash and the Hyphen

1. **A pair of dashes**—here is an example—is used to insert and set off additional information. A pair of dashes is, in effect, like a pair of commas or like a pair of parentheses (see the preceding commas, and the parentheses here), but the dashes are more emphatic—some people would say more breathless—and therefore they should be used sparingly.

2. **To indicate a dash,** type two hyphens without hitting the spacebar before, between, or after them.

3. **Hyphenate "century" when it is used as an adjective.** "Nineteenth-century authors often held that. . . " But: "Eliot, born in the nineteenth century, often held that. . . " The principle is: Use a hyphen to join words that are used as a single adjective, for example, a "six-volume work," "an out-of-date theory," and so "a nineteenth-century author." Notice that the hyphen is neither preceded nor followed by a space.

REMARKS ABOUT MANUSCRIPT FORM

Basic Manuscript Form

Much of what follows is nothing more than common sense.

- Use good quality $8\frac{1}{2}'' \times 11''$ paper. Make a photocopy, or, if you have written on a word processor print out a second copy, in case the instructor's copy goes astray.
- If you write on a typewriter or a word processor, **double-space,** and type on one side of the page only; use a reasonably fresh ribbon. If you submit handwritten copy, use lined paper and write on one side of the page only in black or dark blue ink, on every other line.

- Use **one-inch margins** on all sides.
- Within the top margin, put your last name and then (after hitting the space bar twice) the **page number** (in arabic numerals), so that the number is flush with the right-hand margin.
- On the first page, below the top margin and flush with the left-hand margin, put **your full name,** your **instructor's name,** the **course number** (including the section), and the **date,** one item per line, double-spaced.
- **Center the title** of your essay. Remember that the title is important—it gives the readers their first glimpse of your essay. **Create your own title**—one that reflects your topic or thesis. For example, a paper on Shirley Jackson's "The Lottery" should not be called "The Lottery" but might be called

```
          Suspense in Shirley Jackson's "The Lottery"
```

or

```
                    Is "The Lottery" Rigged?
```

or

```
          Jackson's "The Lottery" and Scapegoat Rituals
```

These titles do at least a little in the way of rousing a reader's interest.
- **Capitalize the title thus:** Begin the first word of the title with a capital letter, and capitalize each subsequent word except articles (*a, an, the*), conjunctions (*and, but, if, when,* etc.), and prepositions (*in, on, with,* etc.):

```
             A Word on Behalf of Mrs. Mitty
```

Notice that you do *not* enclose your title within quotation marks, and you do not underline it—though if it includes the title of a story, *that* is enclosed within quotation marks, or if it includes the title of a novel or play, *that* is underlined (to indicate italics), thus:

```
   Jackson's "The Lottery" and the Scapegoat Tradition
```

and

```
             Gender Stereotypes in Macbeth
```

- **After writing your title, double-space,** indent five spaces, and begin your first sentence.

- Unless your instructor tells you otherwise, **use a paper clip** to hold the pages together. (Do not use a stiff binder; it will only add to the bulk of the instructor's stack of papers.)
- Extensive revisions should have been made in your drafts, but minor **last-minute revisions** may be made—neatly—on the finished copy. Proofreading may catch some typographical errors, and you may notice some small weaknesses. You can make corrections using the following proofreader's symbols in the next section.

Corrections in the Final Copy

Changes in wording may be made by crossing through words and rewriting them:

> The influence of Poe and Hawthorne ~~have~~ *has* greatly diminished.

Additions should be made above the line, with a caret below the line at the appropriate place:

> The influence of Poe and Hawthorne has *greatly* diminished.

Transpositions of letters may be made thus:

> The influence of Poe and Hawthorne has greatly diminished.

Deletions are indicated by a horizontal line through the word or words to be deleted. Delete a single letter by drawing a vertical or diagonal line through it; then indicate whether the letters on either side are to be closed up by drawing a connecting arc:

> The influence of Poe and Hawthorne has greatly diminished.

Separation of words accidentally run together is indicated by a vertical line, **closure by** a curved line connecting the letters to be closed up:

> The influence of Poe and Hauthorne has g reatly diminished.

Paragraphing may be indicated by the symbol ¶ before the word that is to begin the new paragraph:

> The influence of Poe and Hawthorne has greatly diminished. ¶The influence of Borges has very largely replaced that of earlier writers of fantasy.

Quotations and Quotation Marks

First, a word about the *point* of using quotations. Don't use quotations to pad the length of a paper. Rather, give quotations from the work you are discussing so that your readers will see the material you are discussing and (especially in a research paper) so that your readers will know what some of the chief interpretations are and what your responses to them are.

Note: The next few paragraphs do *not* discuss how to include citations of pages, a topic discussed in the next chapter under the heading "How to Document: Footnotes and Internal Parenthetical Citations."

The Golden Rule: If you quote, *comment on* the quotation. Let the reader know what you make of it and why you quote it.

Additional principles:

1. **Identify the speaker or writer of the quotation** so that the reader is not left with a sense of uncertainty. Usually, in accordance with the principle of letting readers know where they are going, this identification precedes the quoted material, but occasionally it may follow the quotation, especially if it will provide something of a pleasant surprise. For instance, in a discussion of Flannery O'Connor's stories, you might quote a disparaging comment on one of the stories and then reveal that O'Connor herself was the speaker.

2. If the quotation is part of your own sentence, **be sure to fit the quotation grammatically and logically into your sentence.**

> *Incorrect:* Holden Caulfield tells us very little about "what my lousy childhood was like."
> *Correct:* Holden Caulfield tells us very little about what his "lousy childhood was like."

3. **Indicate any omissions or additions.** The quotation must be exact. Any material that you add—even one or two words—must be enclosed within square brackets, thus:

```
Hawthorne tells us that "owing doubtless to the depth of
the gloom at that particular spot [in the forest], neither
the travellers nor their steeds were visible."
```

If you wish to omit material from within a quotation, indicate the ellipsis by three spaced periods. If your sentence ends in an omission, add a closed-up period and then three spaced periods to indicate the omission. The following example is based on a quotation from the sentences immediately preceding this one:

```
The instructions say that "If you . . . omit material from
within a quotation, [you must] indicate the ellipsis. .  .
. If your sentence ends in an omission, add a closed-up
period and then three spaced periods. . . .
```

Notice that although material preceded "If you," periods are not needed to indicate the omission because "If you" began a sentence in the original. Customarily, initial and terminal omissions are indicated only when they are part of the sentence you are quoting. Even such omissions need not be indicated when the quoted material is obviously incomplete—when, for instance, it is a word or phrase.

4. **Distinguish between short and long quotations,** and treat each appropriately. *Short quotations* (usually defined as fewer than five lines of typed prose or three lines of poetry) are enclosed within quotation marks and run into the text (rather than being set off, without quotation marks), as in the following example:

```
Hawthorne begins the story by telling us that "Young
Goodman Brown came forth at sunset into the street at
Salem village," thus at the outset connecting the village
with daylight.  A few paragraphs later, when Hawthorne
tells us that the road Brown takes was "darkened by all of
the gloomiest trees of the forest," he begins to associate
the forest with darkness--and a very little later with
evil.
```

If your short quotation is from a poem, be sure to follow the capitalization of the original, and use a slash mark (with a space before and after it) to indicate separate lines. Give the line numbers, if your source gives them, in parentheses, immediately after the closing quotation marks and before the closing punctuation, thus:

```
In Adrienne Rich's "Aunt Jennifer's Tigers," Rich says
that "Uncle's wedding band / Sits heavily upon Aunt
Jennifer's hand" (7-8).  The band evidently is a sign of
her oppression.
```

To set off a *long quotation* (more than four typed lines of prose or more than two lines of poetry), indent the entire quotation ten spaces from the left margin. Usually, a long quotation is introduced by a clause ending with a colon—for instance, "The following passage will make this point clear:" or "The closest we come to hearing an editorial voice is a long passage in the middle of the story:" or some such lead-in. After typing your lead-in, double-space, and then type the quotation, indented and double-spaced.

5. **Commas and periods go inside the quotation marks.**

> Chopin tells us in the first sentence that "Mrs. Mallard was afflicted with heart trouble," and in the last sentence the doctors say that Mrs. Mallard "died of heart disease."

Exception: If the quotation is immediately followed by material in parentheses or in square brackets, close the quotation, then give the parenthetic or bracketed material, and then—after closing the parenthesis or bracket—put the comma or period.

> Chopin tells us in the first sentence that "Mrs. Mallard was afflicted with heart trouble" (17), and in the last sentence the doctors say that Mrs. Mallard "died of heart disease" (18).

Semicolons, colons, and dashes go outside the closing quotation marks.

Question marks and exclamation points go inside if they are part of the quotation, outside if they are your own.

In the following passage from a student's essay, notice the difference in the position of the question marks. The first is part of the quotation, so it is enclosed within the quotation marks. The second question mark, however, is the student's, so it comes after the closing quotation mark.

> The older man says to Goodman Brown, "Sayest thou so?" Doesn't a reader become uneasy when the man immediately adds, "We are but a little way in the forest yet"?

Quotation Marks or Underlining?

Use quotation marks around titles of short stories and other short works—that is, titles of chapters in books, essays, and poems that might not be published by themselves. Underline (to indicate italics) titles of books, periodicals, collections of essays, plays, and long poems such as *The Rime of the Ancient Mariner*. Word processing software probably will let you use italic type (instead of underlining) if you wish.

15

Writing a Research Paper

WHAT RESEARCH IS NOT, AND WHAT RESEARCH IS

Jeff, in a Mutt and Jeff cartoon, sells jars of honey. He includes in each jar a dead bee as proof that the product is genuine. Some writers—even some professionals—seem to think that a hiveful of dead quotations or footnotes is proof of research. But research requires much more than the citation of authorities. What it requires, briefly, is informed, *thoughtful* analysis.

Because a research paper requires its writer to collect and interpret evidence—usually including the opinions of earlier investigators—one sometimes hears that a research paper, unlike a critical essay, is not the expression of personal opinion. Such a view is unjust both to criticism and to research. A critical essay is not a mere expression of personal opinions; if it is any good, it offers evidence that supports the opinions and thus persuades the reader of their objective rightness. A research paper is in the final analysis largely personal because the author continuously uses his or her own judgment to evaluate the evidence, deciding what is relevant and convincing. A research paper is not the mere presentation of what a dozen scholars have already said about a topic; it is a thoughtful evaluation of the available evidence, and so it is, finally, an expression of what the author thinks the evidence adds up to.

Research can be a tedious and frustrating business; hours are spent reading books and articles that prove to be irrelevant, pieces of evidence contradict themselves, and time is always short.

Still, even though research is time-consuming, those who engage in it feel (at least sometimes) an exhilaration, a sense of triumph at having studied a problem thoroughly and arrived at conclusions that—for the moment, anyway—seem objective and irrefutable. Later, new evidence may turn up and require a new conclusion, but until that time one has built something that will endure wind and weather.

PRIMARY AND SECONDARY MATERIALS

The materials of literary research may be conveniently divided into two sorts, primary and secondary. The *primary materials* or sources are the real subject of study; the *secondary materials* are critical and historical accounts already written about these primary materials. For example, if you want to know whether Shakespeare's attitude toward Julius Caesar was highly traditional or highly original (or a little of each), you read the primary materials (*Julius Caesar* and other Elizabethan writings about Caesar); and, since research requires that you be informed about the present state of thought on your topic, you also read the secondary materials (post-Elizabethan essays, books on Shakespeare, and books on Elizabethan attitudes toward Caesar, or, more generally, on Elizabethan attitudes toward Rome and toward monarchs).

A second example: If you are concerned with Charlotte Perkins Gilman's representation of medical treatment for women in her story "The Yellow Wallpaper," Gilman's story and her autobiographical writings are primary material, and one might also consider primary material the medical discussions of the period, especially the writings of S. Weir Mitchell, a physician who treated Gilman. Articles and books about Gilman and about medicine in the late nineteenth century are secondary sources.

FROM TOPIC TO THESIS

Almost every literary work lends itself to research. As has already been mentioned, a study of Shakespeare's attitude toward Julius Caesar would lead to a study of other Elizabethan works and of modern critical works. Similarly, a study of the ghost of Caesar—does it have a real, objective existence, or is it merely a figment of Brutus's imagination?—could lead to a study of Shakespeare's other ghosts (for instance, those in *Hamlet* and *Macbeth*), and a study of Elizabethan attitudes toward ghosts. Or, to take an example from our own century, a reader of Edward Albee's *The Sandbox* might want to study the early, critical reception of the play. Did the reviewers like it? More precisely, did the reviewers in relatively highbrow journals evaluate it differently from those in popular magazines and newspapers? Or, what has Albee himself said about the play in the decades that have passed since he wrote it? Do his comments in essays and interviews indicate that he now sees the play as something different from what he saw when he wrote it? Or, to take yet another example of a work from the middle of our century, a reader might similarly study George Orwell's *1984,* looking at its critical reception, or Orwell's own view of it, or, say, at the sources of Orwell's inspiration. Let's look, for a few minutes, at this last topic.

Assume that you have read George Orwell's *1984* and that, in preparing to do some research on it, browsing through *The Collected Essays, Journalism, and Letters,* you come across a letter (17 February 1944) in which Orwell says that he has been reading Evgenii Zamyatin's *We* and that he himself has been keeping notes for "that kind of book." And in *The Collected Essays, Journalism, and Letters* you also come across a review (4 January 1946) Orwell wrote of *We,* from which it is apparent that *We* resembles *1984.* Or perhaps you learned in a preface to an edition of *1984* that Orwell was influenced by *We,* and you have decided to look into the matter. You want to know exactly how great the influence is.

You borrow *We* from the library, read it, and perceive resemblances in plot, character, and theme. But it's not simply a question of listing resemblances between the two books. Your topic is: What do the resemblances add up to? After all, Orwell in the letter said he had already been working in Zamyatin's direction without even knowing Zamyatin's book, so your investigation may find, for example, that the closest resemblances are in relatively trivial details and that everything really important in *1984* was already implicit in Orwell's earlier books; or your investigation may find that Zamyatin gave a new depth to Orwell's thought; or it may find that though Orwell borrowed heavily from Zamyatin, he missed the depth of *We.*

In the earliest stage of your research, then, you don't know what you will find, so you cannot yet formulate a thesis (or, at best, you can formulate only a tentative thesis). But you know that there is a topic, that it interests you, and that you are ready to begin the necessary legwork.

LOCATING MATERIAL
First Steps

First, prepare a working bibliography, that is, a list of books and articles that must be looked at. The **library catalog** is an excellent place to begin. If your topic is Orwell and Zamyatin, you'll want at least to glance at whatever books by and about these two authors are available. When you have looked over the most promising portions of this material (in secondary sources, chapter headings and indexes will often guide you), you will have found some interesting things. But you want to get a good idea of the state of current scholarship on your topic, and you realize that you must go beyond the catalog's listings under *Orwell, Zamyatin,* and such obviously related topics as *utopian literature.* Doubtless there are pertinent articles in journals, but you cannot start thumbing through them at random.

The easiest way to locate articles and books on literature written in a modern language—that is, on a topic other than literature of the ancient world—is to consult the

MLA International Bibliography (1922-),

which until 1969 was published as part of *PMLA* (*Publications of the Modern Language Association*) and since 1969 has been published separately. It is also available on CD-ROM through WILSONDISC, and in fact the disc is preferable since it is updated quarterly, whereas the print version is more than a year behind the times.

MLA International Bibliography lists scholarly studies—books as well as articles in academic journals—published in a given year. Because of the great number of items listed, the print version of the bibliography runs to more than one volume, but material on writing in English (including, for instance, South African authors who write in English) is in one volume. To see what has been published on Orwell in a given year, then, in this volume you turn to the section on English literature (as opposed to American, Canadian, Irish, and so forth), and then to the subsection labeled 1900–99, to see if anything that sounds relevant is listed. But to find material on Zamyatin you will have to turn to the volume that lists publications on Russian writing.

Because your time is severely limited, you probably cannot read everything published on your topic. At least for the moment, therefore, you will use only the last five or ten years of this bibliography. Presumably, any important earlier material will have been incorporated into some of the recent studies listed, and if, when you come to read these recent studies, you find references to an article of, say, 1975 that sounds essential, of course you will read that article too.

Although *MLA International Bibliography* includes works on American literature, if you are doing research on an aspect of American literature you may want to begin with

American Literary Scholarship (1965-),

an annual publication noted for its broad coverage of articles and books on major and minor American writers, and perhaps especially valuable for its frank comments on the material that it lists.

On some recent topics—for instance the arguments for and against dropping *Huckleberry Finn* from high school curricula—there may be few or no books, and there may not even be material in the scholarly journals indexed in *MLA International Bibliography*. Popular magazines, however, such as *Atlantic, Ebony,* and *Newsweek*—unlisted in *MLA*—may include some useful material. These magazines, and about 200 others, are indexed in

Readers' Guide to Periodical Literature (1900-).

If, for example, you want to write a research paper on the controversy over *Huckleberry Finn*, or, say, on the popular reception given to Kenneth Branagh's recent films of Shakespeare's *Henry V* and *Much Ado about Nothing*, you can locate material (for instance, reviews of Branagh's films) through *Readers' Guide*. For that matter, you can also locate reviews of older films, let's say Olivier's films of Shakespeare's plays, by consulting the volumes for the years in which the films were released.

On many campuses *Readers' Guide* has been supplanted by

InfoTrac (1985-),

on CD-ROM. The disc is preinstalled in a microcomputer that can be accessed from a computer terminal. This index to authors and subjects in popular and scholarly magazines and in newspapers provides access to several database indexes, including:

- The *General Periodical Index,* available in the Academic Library Edition (about 1100 general and scholarly periodicals) and in the Public Library Edition (about 1100 popular magazines).
- The *Academic Index* (400 general-interest publications, all of which are also available in the Academic Library Edition of the General Periodicals Index).
- The *Magazine Index Plus* (the four most recent years of *The New York Times,* the two most recent months of the *Wall Street Journal,* and 400 popular magazines, all of which are included in the Public Library Edition of the General Periodicals Index).
- The *National Newspaper Index* (the four most recent years of the New York Times, the Christian Science Monitor, the Washington Post, and the Los Angeles Times).

Other Bibliographic Aids

There are hundreds of guides to publications and to reference works. For instance, *American Women Writers: Bibliographical Essays* (1983), edited by Maurice Duke, Jackson R. Bryer, and M. Thomas Inge includes scholarship through 1981 on 24 authors, including Bradstreet, Jewett, Chopin, Stein, O'Connor, Hurston, and Plath. *Black American Writers:*

Bibliographical Essays (1978), edited by M. Thomas Inge, Maurice Duke, and Jackson R. Bryer, covers slave narratives, as well as such later African-American writers as Hughes, Ellison, and Baldwin.

How do you find such books? Two invaluable guides to reference works (that is, to bibliographies and to such helpful compilations as handbooks of mythology, place names, and critical terms) are

James L. Harner, *Literary Research Guide: A Guide to Reference Sources for the Study of Literatures in English and Related Topics,* 2nd ed. (1993)

and

Michael J. Marcuse, *A Reference Guide for English Studies* (1990).

And there are guides to these guides: reference librarians. If you don't know where to turn to find something, turn to the librarian.

TAKING NOTES

Let's assume now that you have checked some bibliographies and that you have a fair number of references you must read to have a substantial knowledge of the evidence and the common interpretations of the evidence. Most researchers find it convenient, when examining bibliographies and the library catalog, to write down each reference on a 3″ × 5″ index card—one title per card. On the card put the author's full name (last name first), the exact title of the book or of the article, and the name of the journal (with dates and pages). Titles of books and periodicals (publications issued periodically—for example, monthly or four times a year) are underlined; titles of articles and of essays in books are put within quotation marks. It's also a good idea to put the library catalog number on the card to save time if you need to get the item for a second look.

Next, start reading or scanning the materials whose titles you have collected. Some of these items will prove irrelevant or silly; others will prove valuable in themselves and also in the leads they give you to further references, which you should duly record on 3″ × 5″ cards. Notes—aside from these bibliographic notes—are best taken on 4″ × 6″ cards. Smaller cards do not provide enough space for summaries of useful materials, but 4″ × 6″ cards—rather than larger cards—will serve to remind you that you should not take notes on everything. Be selective in taking notes.

Two Mechanical Aids: The Photocopier and the Word Processor

The ***photocopier*** of course enables you to take home from the library, with very little effort, lots of material (including material that does not circulate) that you might otherwise have to copy laboriously by hand. If, for instance, you are writing a paper on feminist responses to Faulkner's "A Rose for Emily," you can simply scan the material to locate the relevant pages, and then can photocopy the essays in journals, or the appropriate passages in books. Later, at your convenience, without making another trip to the library you can read or reread the photocopied material, highlighting or underlining the chief points. But (and this point is so important that it will be made again, in a moment) because it is easy to highlight or underline, you may mark almost everything. That is, you may not *think* about the material, as you would if you were taking notes by hand, where you would have a powerful incentive to think about whether the material really is noteworthy.

The great advantages of using a **word processor** have already been discussed in Chapter 2, but it is worth repeating here that a word processor is useful not only in the final stage, to produce a neat copy, but also in the early stages of research, when you are getting ideas and are taking notes.

If you take notes on the word processor, print them out and then scissor them apart. Although the slips will not be identical in size, you can still arrange them into appropriate packets, and (as with index cards) you can then arrange the packets into an appropriate sequence. At this point you can begin to draft your paper, working from your organized notes, or—and this is probably a better method—you can rearrange the sequence of notes in your word processor. That is, guided by the sequence of slips, you can move blocks of notes on the word processor into the sequence that you have tentatively settled on. After you have done this, you can start drafting your paper, writing a lead-in to the first quotation, printing the quotation (or part of it, or a summary of it), and commenting on it. *Caution:* Do not feel that you must use all of your notes. Your reader does not want to read a series of notes that are linked by thin connectives.

A Guide to Note Taking

1. **In the upper-left corner of the card specify the source in an abbreviated form.** The author's last name, or the name and the first word of the title are usually enough (unless the first word is "A," "An," or "The").

2. **Write summaries, not paraphrases** (that is, write abridgments rather than restatements which in fact may be as long as or longer than the original). There is rarely any point to paraphrasing. Generally speaking, either quote exactly (and put the passage in quotation marks, with a notation of the source, including the page number or numbers) or summarize, reducing a page or even an entire article or chapter of a book to a single $4'' \times 6''$ card. Even when you summarize, indicate your source (including the page numbers) on the card, so that you can give appropriate credit in your paper.

3. **Quote sparingly.** Of course in your summary you will sometimes quote a phrase or a sentence—putting it in quotation marks—but quote sparingly. You are not doing stenography; rather you are assimilating knowledge and you are thinking, and so for the most part your source should be digested rather than engorged whole. Thinking now, while taking notes, will also help you later to avoid plagiarism. If, on the other hand, when you take notes you mindlessly copy material at length, later when you are writing the paper you may be tempted to copy it yet again, perhaps without giving credit. Similarly, if you photocopy pages from articles or books, and then merely underline some passages, you probably will not be thinking; you will just be underlining. But if you make a terse summary on a note card you will be forced to think and to find your own words for the idea. Quote directly only those passages that are particularly effective, or crucial, or memorable. In your finished paper these quotations will provide authority and emphasis.

4. **Quote accurately.** After copying a quotation, check your card against the original, correct any misquotation, and then put a checkmark after your quotation to indicate that it is accurate. Verify the page number also, and then put a check on your card, after the page number. If a quotation runs from the bottom of, say, page 306 to the top of 307, on your card put a distinguishing mark (for instance two parallel vertical lines after the last word of the first page), so that if you later use only part of the quotation, you will know the page on which it appeared.

Use ellipses (three spaced periods) to indicate the omission of any words within a sentence. If the omitted words are at the end of the quoted sentence, put a period immediately at the point where you end the sentence, and then add three spaced periods to indicate the omission. Example:

> If the . . . words were at the end of the quoted sentence, put a period immediately at the end. . . .

Use square brackets to indicate your additions to the quotation. Here is an example.

> Here is an [uninteresting] example.

5. **Never copy a passage by changing an occasional word,** under the impression that you are thereby putting it into your own words. Notes of this sort may find their way into your paper, your reader will sense a style other than yours, and suspicions of plagiarism may follow. (For a detailed discussion of plagiarism, see pp. 324–26.)

6. **Write on one side of the card only.** Because when you set out to draft your paper you will probably want to spread out your notes so that you

can see all of the material simultaneously, notes on the back of a card are of little use and they will probably get overlooked. If a note won't fit on one side of a card, continue the note on a second card (and a third, if necessary), and put the appropriate number on each card.

7. **Comment on your notes.** Feel free to jot down your responses to the note. Indeed, consider it your obligation to *think* about the material, evaluating it and using it as a stimulus to further thought. For example, you may want to say "Gold seems to be generalizing from insufficient evidence," or "Corsa made the same point five years earlier"; but make certain that later you will be able to distinguish between these comments and the notes summarizing or quoting your source. A suggestion: surround all comments recording your responses with double parentheses, thus: ((. . .)).

8. **In the upper corner of each note card write a brief key**—for example, "Orwell's first reading of *We*" or "Characterization" or "Thought control"—so that later you can tell at a glance what is on the card.

As you work, you'll find yourself returning again and again to your primary materials—and you'll probably find to your surprise that a good deal of the secondary material is unconvincing or even wrong, despite the fact that it is printed in a handsome book or a scholarly journal. At times, under the weight of evidence, you will have to abandon some of your earlier views, but at times you will have your own opinions reinforced, and at times you will feel that your ideas have more validity than those you are reading. One of the things we learn from research is that not everything in print is true; this discovery is one of the pleasures we get from research.

DRAFTING THE PAPER

The difficult job of writing up your findings remains, but if you have taken good notes and have put useful headings on each card, you are well on your way. Read through the cards and sort them into packets of related material. Discard all notes, however interesting, that you now see are irrelevant to your paper. Go through the cards again and again, sorting and resorting, putting together what belongs together. Probably you will find that you have to do a little additional research—somehow you aren't quite clear about this or that—but after you have done this additional research, you should be able to arrange the packets into a reasonable and consistent sequence. You now have a kind of first draft, or at least a tentative organization for your paper. Two further pieces of advice:

1. Beware of the compulsion to include every note card in your essay; that is, beware of telling the reader, "A says . . . ; B says . . . ; C says. . . "
2. You must have a point, a thesis.

Remember: As you studied the evidence, you increasingly developed or documented or corrected a thesis. You may, for example, have become convinced that the influence of Zamyatin was limited to a few details of plot and character and that Orwell had already developed the framework and the chief attitudes that are implicit in *1984.* Similarly, now, as you write and revise your paper, you will probably still be modifying your thesis to some extent, discovering what in fact the evidence implies.

The final version of the paper, however, should be a finished piece of work, without the inconsistencies, detours, and occasional dead ends of an early draft. Your readers should feel that they are moving toward a conclusion (by means of your thoughtful evaluation of the evidence) rather than merely reading an anthology of commentary on the topic. And so we should get some such structure as: "There are three common views on . . . The first two are represented by *A* and *B;* the third, and by far the most reasonable, is *C*'s view that . . . *A* argues . . . but . . . The second view, *B*'s, is based on . . . but . . . Although the third view, *C*'s, is not conclusive, still . . . Moreover, *C*'s point can be strengthened when we consider a piece of evidence that he does not make use of. . . ."

Be sure, when you quote, to *write a lead-in,* such as "*X* concisely states the common view" or "*Z,* without offering any proof, asserts that. . . ." Let the reader know where you are going, or, to put it a little differently, let the reader know how the quotation fits into your argument.

Quotations and summaries, in short, are accompanied by judicious analyses of your own so that by the end of the paper your readers not only have read a neatly typed paper (see pages 309–11) and have gained an idea of what previous writers have said, but also are persuaded that under your guidance they have seen the evidence, heard the arguments justly summarized, and reached a sound conclusion.

A bibliography or list of works consulted (see pages 332–38) is usually appended to a research paper so that readers may easily look further into the primary and secondary material if they wish; but if you have done your job well, readers will be content to leave the subject where you left it, grateful that you have set matters straight.

DOCUMENTATION
What to Document: Avoiding Plagiarism

Honesty requires that you acknowledge your indebtedness for material, not only when you quote directly from a work, but also when you appropriate an idea that is not common knowledge. Not to acknowledge such borrowing is plagiarism. If in doubt whether to give credit, give credit.

You ought, however, to develop a sense of what is considered **common knowledge.** Definitions in a dictionary can be considered common knowledge, so there is no need to say, "According to Webster, a novel is . . . " (This is weak in three ways: It's unnecessary, it's uninteresting, and it's unclear, since "Webster" appears in the titles of several dictionaries, some good and some bad.) Similarly, the date of first publication of *The Scarlet Letter* can be considered common knowledge. Few can give it when asked, but it can be found out from innumerable sources, and no one need get the credit for providing you with the date. The idea that Hamlet delays is also a matter of common knowledge. But if you are impressed by So-and-so's argument that Claudius has been much maligned, you should give credit to So-and-so.

Suppose you happen to come across Frederick R. Karl's statement in the revised edition of *A Reader's Guide to the Contemporary English Novel* (New York: Farrar, Straus & Giroux, 1972) that George Orwell was "better as a man than as a novelist." This is an interesting and an effectively worded idea. You cannot use these words without giving credit to Karl. And you cannot retain the idea but alter the words, for example, to "Orwell was a better human being than he was a writer of fiction," presenting the idea as your own, for here you are simply lifting Karl's idea—and putting it less effectively. If you want to use Karl's point, give him credit and—since you can hardly summarize so brief a statement—use his exact words and put them within quotation marks.

What about a longer passage that strikes you favorably? Let's assume that in reading Alex Zwerdling's *Orwell and the Left* (New Haven: Yale, 1974) you find the following passage from page 105 interesting:

> *1984* might be said to have a predominantly negative goal, since it is much more concerned to fight *against* a possible future society than *for* one. Its tactics are primarily defensive. Winston Smith is much less concerned with the future than with the past—which is of course the reader's present.

You certainly *cannot* say:

```
The goal of 1984, can be said to be chiefly negative
because it is devoted more to opposing some future
society than it is to fighting for a future society.
Smith is more concerned with the past (our present) than
he is with the future.
```

This passage is simply a theft of Zwerdling's property: The writer has stolen Zwerdling's automobile and put a different color paint on it. How, then, can a writer use Zwerdling's idea? (1) Give Zwerdling credit and quote directly, or (2) give Zwerdling credit and summarize his point in perhaps a third of the length, or (3) give Zwerdling credit and summarize the point but include—within quotation marks—some phrase you think is especially quotable. Thus:

1. *Direct quotation.* In a study of Orwell's politics, Alex Zwerdling says, "*1984* might be said to have a predominantly negative goal, since it is much more concerned to fight *against* a possible future society than *for* one" (105).
2. *Summary.* The goal of *1984*, Zwerdling points out, is chiefly opposition to, rather than advocacy of, a certain kind of future society (105).
3. *Summary with selected quotation.* Zwerdling points out that the goal of *1984* is "predominantly negative," opposition to, rather than advocacy of, a certain kind of future society (105).

If for some reason you do not wish to name Zwerdling in your lead-in, you will have to give his name with the parenthetical citation so that a reader can identify the source:

```
The goal of 1984, one critic points out, is
"predominantly negative" (Zwerdling 105), opposition to,
rather than advocacy of, a certain kind of future
society.
```

But it is hard to imagine why the writer preferred to say "one critic," rather than to name Zwerdling immediately, since Zwerdling sooner or later must be identified.

How to Document:
Footnotes and Internal Parenthetical Citations

Documentation tells your reader exactly what your sources are. Until recently, the standard form was the footnote, which, for example, told the reader that the source of such-and-such a quotation was a book by so-and-so. But in 1984 the Modern Language Association, which had established the footnote form used in hundreds of journals, university presses, and classrooms, substituted a new form. It is this new form—parenthetical citations within the text (rather than at the foot of the page or the end of the essay)—that we will discuss at length. Keep in mind, though, that footnotes still have their uses.

Footnotes
If you are using only one source, your instructor may advise you to give the source in a footnote. (Check with your instructors to find out their preferred forms of documentation.)

Let's say that your only source is a textbook. Let's say, too, that all of your quotations will be from a single story—Kate Chopin's "The Story of an Hour"—printed in this book on pages 13–14. The simplest way to cite your source is (if you are using a typewriter rather than a word processing program) to type the digit 1 (elevated, and *without* a period after it) after your first reference to (or quotation from) the story and then to put a footnote at the bottom of the page, explaining where the story can be found. After the last line of type on the page, triple-space, indent five spaces from the left-hand margin, raise the typewriter carriage half a line, and type the arabic numeral 1. Do *not* put a period after it. Then lower the carriage half a line, hit the spacebar once, and type a statement (double-spaced) to the effect that all references are to this book. Notice that although the footnote begins by being indented five spaces, if the note runs to more than one line the subsequent lines are typed flush left.

[1] Chopin's story appears in Sylvan Barnet, ed., The Harper Anthology of Fiction (New York: HarperCollins, 1991), 25-27.

Your word processing software may do the job for you. It probably will automatically indent, elevate the footnote number, and print the note on the appropriate page.

If a book has two or three editors, give all the names but with the abbreviation "eds." instead of "ed." (*not* within quotation marks). If it has more than three editors, give the name of only the first editor, followed by "et al." (the Latin abbreviation for "and others") and "eds." See the next example.

Even if you are writing a comparison of, say, two stories in a book, you may use a note of this sort. It might run thus:

[1] All page references, given parenthetically within the essay, refer to stories in Sylvan Barnet et al., eds., Literature for Composition. 3rd ed. (New York: HarperCollins, 1992).

If you use such a note, do not put a footnote after each quotation that follows. Give the citations right in the body of the paper, by putting the page references in parentheses after the quotations.

Internal Parenthetical Citations
Information on pages 313–14 distinguishes between embedded quotations (which are short, are run right into your own sentence, and are enclosed

within quotation marks) and quotations that are set off on the page (for example, three or more lines of poetry, five or more lines of typed prose that are not enclosed within quotation marks).

For an embedded quotation, put the page reference in parentheses immediately after the closing quotation mark, *without* any intervening punctuation. Then, after the parenthesis that follows the number, put the necessary punctuation (for instance, a comma or a period).

```
Woolf says that there was "something marvelous as well
as pathetic" about the struggling moth (90). She goes on
to explain . . .
```

Notice that the period comes *after* the parenthetical citation. Notice, similarly, that in the next example *no* punctuation comes after the first citation—because none is needed—and a comma comes *after* (not before or within) the second citation, because a comma is needed in the sentence.

```
This is ironic because almost at the start of the story,
in the second paragraph, Richards with the best of
motives "hastened" (63) to bring his sad message; if he
had at the start been "too late" (64), Mallard would
have arrived at home first.
```

For a quotation that is not embedded within the text but is set off (indented ten spaces), put the parenthetical citation on the last line of the quotation, two spaces *after* the period that ends the quoted sentence.

```
Long sentences are not necessarily hard to follow. For
instance, a reader has no trouble with this sentence,
from Juanita Miranda's essay:
        The Philistine's scorn when he sees David,
        David's reply (a mixture of scorn and pity,
        for David announces that he comes "in the name
        of the Lord"), the observation that David was
        eager to do battle (he "ran toward the army to
        meet the Philistine"), the explanation that
        David cut off Goliath's head with Goliath's
        own sword--all of these details help us to see
        the scene, to believe in the characters, and
        yet of course the whole story is, on the
        literal level, remote from our experience.
        (249)
```

> Why is the sentence easy to follow? Partly because
> it uses parallel constructions ("The Philistine's scorn
> . . . , David's reply"; "the observation that . . . ,
> the explanation that"; "to see, . . . to believe"), and
> partly because Miranda does not hesitate to repeat the
> names of David and Goliath.

Notice that the indented quotation ends with a period. After the period there are two spaces and then the citation in parentheses.

For a drama in which the acts, scenes, and lines are numbered, give this information, in arabic numerals, in parentheses. A reference to act one, scene two, line 10 would appear thus: (1.2.10)

Four additional points:

1. "p." "pg.," and "pp." are *not* used in citing pages.
2. If a story is very short—perhaps running for only a page or two—your instructor may tell you not to cite the page for each quotation. Simply mention in the footnote that the story appears on, say, pages 200-02.
3. If you are referring to a poem, your instructor may tell you to use parenthetical citations of line numbers rather than of page numbers. But, again, your footnote will tell the reader that the poem can be found in this book, and on what page.
4. If you are referring to a play with numbered lines, your instructor may prefer that in your parenthetical citations you give act, scene, and line, rather than page numbers. Use arabic (not roman) numerals, separating the act from the scene, and the scene from the line, by periods. Here, then, is how a reference to act three, scene two, line 118 would be given: (3.2.118).

Parenthetical Citations and List of Works Cited

Footnotes have fallen into disfavor. Parenthetical citations are now usually clarified not by means of a footnote but by means of a list, headed Works Cited, given at the end of the essay. In this list you give alphabetically (last name first) the authors and titles that you have quoted or referred to in the essay.

Briefly, the idea is that the reader of your paper encounters an author's name and a parenthetical citation of pages. By checking the author's name in Works Cited, the reader can find the passage in the book. Suppose you are writing about Kate Chopin's "The Story of an Hour." Let's assume that you have already mentioned the author and the title of the story—that is, you have let the reader know the subject of the essay—and now you introduce a quotation from the story. (Notice the parenthetical citation of page numbers immediately after the quotation.)

```
True, Mrs. Mallard at first expresses grief when she
hears the news, but soon (unknown to her friends) she
finds joy in it. So, Richards's "sad message" (64),
though sad in Richards's eyes, is in fact a happy
message.
```

Turning to Works Cited, the reader, knowing the quoted words are by Chopin, looks for Chopin and finds the following:

```
Chopin, Kate. "The Story of an Hour." Literature for
     Composition, 3rd ed. Eds. Sylvan Barnet et al. New
     York: HarperCollins, 1992.
```

Thus the essayist is informing the reader that the quoted words ("sad message") are to be found on page 64 of this anthology.

If you have not mentioned Chopin's name in some sort of lead-in, you will have to give her name within the parentheses so that the reader will know the author of the quoted words:

```
What are we to make out of a story that ends by telling
us that the leading character has died "of joy that
kills" (Chopin 14)?
```

(Notice, by the way, that the closing quotation marks come immediately after the last word of the quotation; the citation and the final punctuation—in this case, the essayist's question mark—come *after* the closing quotation marks.)

If you are comparing Chopin's story with Gilman's "The Yellow Wallpaper," in Works Cited you will give a similar entry for Gilman—her name, the title of the story, the book in which it is reprinted, and the page numbers that the story occupies.

If you are referring to several works reprinted within one volume, instead of listing each item fully, it is acceptable in Works Cited to list each item simply by giving the author's name, the title of the work, then a period, two spaces, and the name of the anthologist, followed by the page numbers that the selection spans. Thus a reference to Chopin's "The Story of an Hour" would be followed only by: Barnet, 14–16. This form requires that the anthology itself be cited under the name of the first-listed editor, thus:

```
Barnet, Sylvan, et al., eds. Literature for Composition.
     4th ed. New York: HarperCollins, 1995.
```

If you are writing a research paper, you will use many sources. Within the essay itself you will mention an author's name, quote or summarize from this author, and follow the quotation or summary with a parenthetical citation of the pages. In Works Cited you will give the full title, place of publication, and other bibliographic material.

Here are a few examples, all referring to an article by Joan Templeton, "The *Doll House* Backlash: Criticism, Feminism, and Ibsen." The article appeared in *PMLA* 104 (1989): 28–40, but this information is given only in Works Cited, not within the text of the student's essay.

If in the text of your essay you mention the author's name, the citation following a quotation (or a summary of a passage) is merely a page number in parentheses, followed by a period, thus:

```
In 1989 Joan Templeton argued that many critics, unhappy
with recognizing Ibsen as a feminist, sought "to render
Nora inconsequential" (29).
```

Or:

```
In 1989 Joan Templeton noted that many critics, unhappy
with recognizing Ibsen as a feminist, have sought to
make Nora trivial (29).
```

If you don't mention the name of the author in a lead-in, you will have to give the name within the parenthetic citation:

```
Many critics, attempting to argue that Ibsen was not a
feminist, have tried to make Nora trivial (Templeton
29).
```

Notice in all of these examples that the final period comes after the parenthetic citation. *Exception:* If the quotation is longer than four lines and, therefore, is set off by being indented ten spaces from the left margin, end the quotation with the appropriate punctuation (period, question mark, or exclamation mark), hit the space bar twice, and type (in parentheses) the page number. In this case, do not put a period after the citation.

Another point: If your list of Works Cited includes more than one work by an author, in your essay when you quote or refer to one or the other you'll have to identify *which* work you are drawing on. You can provide the title in a lead-in, thus:

```
In "The Doll House Backlash: Criticism, Feminism, and
Ibsen," Templeton says, "Nora's detractors have often
been, from the first, her husband's defenders" (30).
```

Or you can provide the information in the parenthetic citation, giving a shortened version of the title—usually the first word, unless it is *A, An,* or *The,* in which case the second word usually will do, though certain titles may require still another word or two, as in this example:

```
According to Templeton, "Nora's detractors have often
been, from the first, her husband's defenders" ("Doll
House Backlash" 30).
```

Forms of Citation in Works Cited
In looking over the following samples of entries in Works Cited, remember:

1. The list of Works Cited appears at the end of the paper. It begins on a new page, and the page continues the numbering of the text.
2. The list of Works Cited is arranged alphabetically by author (last name first).
3. If a work is anonymous, list it under the first word of the title unless the first word is *A, An,* or *The,* in which case list it under the second word.
4. If a work is by two authors, although the book is listed alphabetically under the first author's last name, the second author's name is given in the normal order, first name first.
5. If you list two or more works by the same author, the author's name is not repeated but is represented by three hyphens followed by a period and two spaces.
6. Each item begins flush left, but if an entry is longer than one line, subsequent lines in the entry are indented five spaces.

For details about almost every imaginable kind of citation, consult Joseph Gibaldi, *MLA Handbook for Writers of Research Papers,* 4th ed. (New York: Modern Language Association, 1995). We give here, however, information concerning the most common kinds of citations.

Here are samples of the kinds of citations you are most likely to include in your list of Works Cited.

Entries (arranged alphabetically) begin flush with the left margin. If an entry runs more than one line, indent the subsequent line or lines five spaces from the left margin.

A Book by One Author:
```
Douglas, Ann. The Feminization of American Culture. New
    York: Knopf, 1977.
```
Notice that the author's last name is given first, but otherwise the name is given as on the title page. Do not substitute initials for names written out

on the title page, but you may shorten the publisher's name—for example, from Little, Brown and Company to Little.

Take the title from the title page, not from the cover or the spine, but disregard unusual typography—for instance, the use of only capital letters or the use of & for *and*. Underline the title and subtitle with one continuous underline, but do not underline the period. The place of publication is indicated by the name of the city. If the city is not well known or if several cities have the same name (for instance, Cambridge, Massachusetts, and Cambridge, England) the name of the state is added. If the title page lists several cities, give only the first.

A Book by More than One Author:

Gilbert, Sandra, and Susan Gubar, <u>The Madwoman in the</u>
    <u>Attic: The Woman Writer and the Nineteenth-Century</u>
    <u>Literary Imagination</u>. New Haven: Yale UP, 1979.

Notice that the book is listed under the last name of the first author (Gilbert) and that the second author's name is then given with first name (Susan) first. *If the book has more than three authors,* give the name of the first author only (last name first) and follow it with "et al." (Latin for "and others.")

A Book in Several Volumes:

McQuade, Donald, et al., eds. <u>The Harper American</u>
    <u>Literature</u>. 2nd ed. 2 vols. New York: HarperCollins,
    1994.

Pope, Alexander. <u>The Correspondence of Alexander Pope</u>. 5
    vols. Ed. George Sherburn. Oxford: Clarendon, 1955.

Notice that the total number of volumes is given after the title, regardless of the number that you have used.

If you have used more than one volume, within your essay you will parenthetically indicate a reference to, for instance, page 30 of volume 3 thus: (3:30). If you have used only one volume of a multivolume work—let's say you used only volume 2 of McQuade's anthology—in your entry in Works Cited write, after the period following the date, Vol. 2. In your parenthetical citation within the essay you will therefore cite only the page reference (without the volume number), since the reader will (on consulting Works Cited) understand that in this example the reference is in volume 2.

If, instead of using the volumes as whole, you used only an independent work within one volume—say an essay in volume 2—in Works Cited omit the abbreviation "vol." Instead, give an arabic 2 (indicating volume 2) followed by a colon, a space, and the page numbers that encompass the selection you used:

```
McPherson, James Alan. "Why I Like Country Music."
     The Harper American Literature. 2nd ed. 2 vols.
     New York: HarperCollins, 1994. 2:2304-15.
```

Notice that this entry for McPherson specifies not only that the book consists of two volumes, but also that only one selection ("Why I Like Country Music," occupying pages 2304–15 in volume 2) was used. If you use this sort of citation in Works Cited, in the body of your essay a documentary reference to this work will be only to the page; the volume number will *not* be added.

A Book with a Separate Title in a Set of Volumes:

```
Churchill, Winston. The Age of Revolution. Vol. 3 of A
     History of the English-Speaking Peoples. New York:
     Dodd, 1957.
Jonson, Ben. The Complete Masques. Ed. Stephen Orgel.
     Vol. 4 of The Yale Ben Jonson. New Haven: Yale UP,
     1969.
```

A Revised Edition of a Book:

```
Ellmann, Richard. James Joyce. Rev. ed. New York: Oxford
     UP, 1982.
Chaucer, Geoffrey. The Works of Geoffrey Chaucer. Ed. F.
     N. Robinson. 2nd ed. Boston: Houghton, 1957.
```

A Reprint, Such as a Paperback Version of an Older Hardcover Book:

```
Rourke, Constance. American Humor. 1931. Garden City,
     New York: Doubleday, 1953.
```

Notice that the entry cites the original date (1931) but indicates that the writer is using the Doubleday reprint of 1953.

An Edited Book Other than an Anthology:

```
Keats, John. The Letters of John Keats. Ed. Hyder Edward
     Rollins. 2 vols. Cambridge, Mass.: Harvard UP, 1958.
```

An Anthology:

You can list an anthology either under the editor's name or under the title.

A Work in a Volume of Works by One Author:

```
Sontag, Susan. "The Aesthetics of Silence." In Styles of
     Radical Will. New York: Farrar, 1969. 3-34.
```

This entry indicates that Sontag's essay, called "The Aesthetics of Silence" appears in a book of hers entitled *Styles of Radical Will*. Notice that the page numbers of the short work are cited (not page numbers that you may happen to refer to, but the page numbers of the entire piece).

A Work in an Anthology, That Is, in a Collection of Works by Several Authors:

Begin with the author and the title of the work you are citing, not with the name of the anthologist or the title of the anthology. The entry ends with the pages occupied by the selection you are citing:

```
Ng, Fae Myenne. "A Red Sweater." Charlie Chan Is Dead:
     An Anthology of Contemporary Asian American Fiction.
     Ed. Jessica Hagedorn. New York: Penguin, 1993. 358-
     68.

Porter, Katherine Anne. "The Jilting of Granny Weatherall."
     Literature for Composition. Ed. Sylvan Barnet, et al.
     3rd ed. New York: HarperCollins, 1992. 930-36.
```

Normally, you will give the title of the work you are citing (probably an essay, short story, or poem) in quotation marks. If you are referring to a book-length work (for instance, a novel or a full-length play), underline it to indicate italics. If the work is translated, after the period that follows the title, write "Trans." and give the name of the translator, followed by a period and the name of the anthology.

If the collection is a multivolume work and you are using only one volume, in Works Cited you will specify the volume, as in the example (page 334) of McPherson's essay. Because the list of Works Cited specifies the volume, your parenthetical documentary reference within your essay will specify (as mentioned earlier) only the page numbers, not the volume. Thus, although McPherson's essay appears on pages 2304–15 in the second volume of a two-volume work, a parenthetical citation will refer only to the page numbers because the citation in Works Cited specifies the volume.

Remember that the pages specified in the entry in your list of Works Cited are to the *entire selection,* not simply to pages you may happen to refer to within your paper.

If you are referring to a *reprint of a scholarly article,* give details of the original publication, as in the following example:

```
Mack, Maynard. "The World of Hamlet." Yale Review 41
     (1952): 502-23. Rpt. in Hamlet. By William
     Shakespeare. Ed. Edward Hubler. New York: New
     American Library, 1963. 234-56.
```

Two or More Works in an Anthology:

If you are referring to more than one work in an anthology in order to avoid repeating all the information about the anthology in each entry in Works Cited, under each author's name (in the appropriate alphabetical place) give the author and title of the work, then a period, two spaces, and the name of the anthologist, followed by the page numbers that the selection spans. Thus, a reference to Shakespeare's *Hamlet* would be followed only by

```
Barnet 407-512
```

rather than by a full citation of Barnet's anthology. This form requires that the anthology itself also be listed, under Barnet.

Two or More Works by the Same Author:

Notice that the works are given in alphabetical order (*Fables* precedes *Fools*) and that the author's name is not repeated but is represented by three hyphens followed by a period and two spaces. If the author is the translator or editor of a volume, the three hyphens are followed not by a period but by a comma, then a space, then the appropriate abbreviation (trans. or ed.), then (two spaces after the period) the title:

```
Frye, Northrop. Fables of Identity: Studies in Poetic
    Mythology. New York: Harcourt, 1963.
---. Fools of Time: Studies in Shakespearean Tragedy.
    Toronto:U of Toronto P, 1967.
```

A Translated Book:

```
Gogol, Nikolai. Dead Souls. Trans. Andrew McAndrew. New
    York: New American Library, 1961.
```

If you are discussing the translation itself, as opposed to the book, list the work under the translator's name. Then put a comma, a space, and "trans." After the period following "trans." skip two spaces, then give the title of the book, a period, two spaces, and then "By" and the author's name, first name first. Continue with information about the place of publication, publisher, and date, as in any entry to a book.

An Introduction, Foreword, or Afterword, or Other Editorial Apparatus:

```
Fromm, Erich. Afterword. 1984. By George Orwell. New
    American Library, 1961.
```

Usually a book with an introduction or some such comparable material is listed under the name of the author of the book rather than the name of the author of the editorial material (see the citation to Pope on p. 333). But if you are referring to the editor's apparatus rather than to the work itself, use the form just given.

Words such as *preface, introduction, afterword,* and *conclusion* are capitalized in the entry but are neither enclosed within quotation marks nor underlined.

A Book Review:
First, an example of a review that does not have a title:

Vendler, Helen. Rev. of <u>Essays on Style</u>. Ed. Roger
    Fowler. <u>Essays in Criticism</u> 16 (1966): 457-63.

If the review has a title, give the title after the period following the reviewer's name, before "Rev." If the review is unsigned, list it under the first word of the title, or the second word if the first word is *A, An,* or *The.* If an unsigned review has no title, begin the entry with "Rev. of" and alphabetize it under the title of the work being reviewed.

An Encyclopedia:
The first example is for a signed article, the second for an unsigned article:

Lang, Andrew. "Ballads." <u>Encyclopaedia Britannica</u>. 1910
    ed.
"Metaphor." <u>The New Encyclopaedia Britannica: Micropaedia</u>.
    1974 ed.

An Article in a Scholarly Journal:
Some journals are paginated consecutively; that is, the pagination of the second issue picks up where the first issue left off. Other journals begin each issue with a new page 1. The forms of the citations in Works Cited differ slightly.

First, the citation of *a journal that uses continuous pagination:*

Burbick, Joan. "Emily Dickinson and the Economics of
    Desire." <u>American Literature</u> 58 (1986): 361-78.

This article appeared in volume 58, which was published in 1986. (Notice that the volume number is followed by a space, then by the year, in parentheses, then by a colon, a space, and the page numbers of the entire article.) Although each volume consists of four issues, you do *not* specify the issue number when the journal is paginated continuously.

For a journal that paginates each issue separately (a quarterly journal will have four page 1's each year), give the issue number directly after the volume number and a period, with no spaces before or after the period:

Spillers, Hortense J. "Martin Luther King and the Style
    of the Black Sermon." <u>The Black Scholar</u> 3.1 (1971),
    14-27.

An Article in a Weekly, Biweekly, or Monthly Publication:

```
McCabe, Bernard. "Taking Dickens Seriously." Commonweal
     14 May 1965.
```

Notice that the volume number and the issue number are omitted for popular weeklies or monthlies such as *Time* and *Atlantic*.

An Article in a Newspaper:

Because newspapers usually consist of several sections, a section number may precede the page number. The example indicates that an article begins on page 1 of section 2 and is continued on a later page:

```
Wu, Jim. "Authors Praise New Forms." New York Times 8
     March 1987, Sec. 2:3 +.
```

You may also have occasion to cite something other than a printed source, for instance a lecture. Here are the forms for the chief nonprint sources.

An Interview:

```
Howard Saretta. Personal interview. 3 Nov. 1994.
```

A Lecture:

```
Seamus Heaney. Lecture. Tufts University. 15 Oct. 1994.
```

A Television or Radio Program:

```
Sixty Minutes. CBS. 30 Jan. 1994
```

A Film or Videotape:

```
Modern Times. Dir. Charles Chaplin. United Artists,
     1936.
```

A Recording:

```
Frost, Robert. "The Road Not Taken." Robert Frost Reads
     His Poetry. Caedmon, TC 1060, 1956.
```

A Performance:

```
The Cherry Orchard. By Anton Chekhov. Dir. Ron Daniels.
     American Repertory Theatre, Cambridge, Ma. 3 Feb.
     1994.
```

SAMPLE ESSAY WITH DOCUMENTATION: "THE WOMEN IN DEATH OF A SALESMAN"

Some research papers are largely concerned with the relation of a work to its original context. Several examples have been mentioned already, such as Elizabethan views of Julius Caesar, Charlotte Perkins Gilman's representation of medical treatment for women, and Orwell's use (in *1984*) of Zamyatin's *We*.

But of course there are other kinds of research papers. One kind is chiefly concerned with studying a critical problem, for instance with deciding among a variety of interpretations of a literary work. A paper of this sort necessarily involves a certain amount of summarizing, but it is much more than a summary of those interpretations, since it evaluates them and finally offers its own conclusions.

Two things motivated Ruth Katz, the author of the following paper, to choose the topic that she chose. The first was a classroom discussion, early in the semester, concerning the question of whether male authors necessarily represent females in certain ways. The second was a published essay that disparaged Linda, a character in Arthur Miller's *Death of a Salesman*.

Katz took notes on index cards, both from the play and from secondary sources, and she arranged and rearranged her notes as her topic and her thesis became clearer to her. Here we print the final version of her essay, prefaced with the rough outline that she prepared before she wrote her first draft.

```
Linda
    realistic
    encourages Willy  Both? Not so foolish; Knows how to calm
            → foolish? loving?                     him down
        prevented him from succeeding?
        doesn't understand W's needs? or nothing else to do?
        (quote some critics knocking Linda)
other women
    5 the Woman
    4 the two women in restaurant (Forsythe first, then Letta)
    3 Jenny
    2 W's mother (compare with father?)
            check to see exactly what the play says about her
    1 Howard's wife (and daughter?)
    6 discuss Linda last
titles?
    Linda Loman
    Women in Miller's Salesman
    Gender in . . .    Male and Female in Death . . .
    Men and Women: Arthur M's View
            Willy Loman's Women
```

Here is the final version of the essay.

Ruth Katz

The Women in <u>Death of a Salesman</u>

<u>Death of a Salesman</u>[1] is of course about a salesman,
but it is also about the American dream of success.
Somewhere in between the narrowest topic, the death of a
salesman, and the largest topic, the examination of
American values, is Miller's picture of the American
family. This paper will chiefly study one member of the
family, Willy's wife, Linda Loman, but before examining
Miller's depiction of her, it will look at Miller's
depiction of other women in the play in order to make
clear Linda's distinctive traits. We will see that
although her role in society is extremely limited, she
is an admirable figure, fulfilling the roles of wife and
mother with remarkable intelligence.

Linda is the only woman who is on stage much of the
time, but there are several other women in the play:
"the Woman" (the unnamed woman in Willy's hotel room),
Miss Forsythe and her friend Letta (the two women who
join the brothers in the restaurant), Jenny (Charley's
secretary), the various women that the brothers talk
about, and the voices of Howard's daughter and wife. We
also hear a little about Willy's mother.

We will look first at the least important (but not
utterly unimportant) of these, the voices of Howard's
daughter and wife on the wire recorder. Of Howard's
seven-year-old daughter we know only that she can
whistle "Roll Out the Barrel" and that according to
Howard she "is crazy about me." The other woman in
Howard's life is equally under his thumb. Here is the
dialogue that tells us about her--and her relation to
her husband.

> HOWARD'S VOICE. "Go on, say something."
> (*Pause.*) "Well, you gonna talk?"

---

[1]<u>Death of a Salesman</u> appears in Sylvan Barnet, Morton
Berman, and William Burto, <u>An Introduction to
Literature</u>, expanded. (New York: HarperCollins, 1994),
1034-98. References to the play are to this edition.

> HIS WIFE. "I can't think of anything."
> HOWARD'S VOICE. "Well, talk--it's turning."
> HIS WIFE (shyly, beaten). "Hello." (Silence.)
> "Oh, Howard, I can't talk into this . . . "
> HOWARD (snapping the machine off). That was my
> wife. (1067).

There is, in fact, a third woman in Howard's life, the maid. Howard says that if he can't be at home when the Jack Benny program comes on, he uses the wire recorder. He tells "the maid to turn the radio on when Jack Benny comes on, and this automatically goes on with the radio. . ." (1068). In short, the women in Howard's world exist to serve (and to worship) him.

Another woman who seems to have existed only to serve men is Willy Loman's mother. On one occasion, in speaking with Ben, Willy remembers being on her lap, and Ben, on learning that his mother is dead, utters a platitudinous description of her, "Fine specimen of a lady, Mother" (1053), but that's as much as we learn of her. Willy is chiefly interested in learning about his father, who left the family and went to Alaska. Ben characterizes the father as "a very great and a very wild-hearted man" (1054), but the fact that the father left his family and apparently had no further communication with his wife and children seems to mean nothing to Ben. Presumably the mother struggled alone to bring up the boys, but her efforts are unmentioned. Curiously, some writers defend the father's desertion of his family. Lois Gordon says, "The first generation (Willy's father) has been forced, in order to make a living, to break up the family" (103), but nothing in the play supports this assertion that the father was "forced" to break up the family.

Willy, like Ben, assumes that men are heroic and women are nothing except servants and sex machines. For instance, Willy says to Ben, "Please tell about Dad. I want my boys to hear. I want them to know the kind of stock they spring from" (1054). As Kay Stanton, a feminist critic says, Willy's words imply "an Edenic birth myth," a world "with all the Loman men springing directly from their father's side, with no commingling with a female" (69).

Another woman who, like Howard's maid and Willy's mother, apparently exists only to serve is Jenny, Charley's secretary. She is courteous, and she is treated courteously by Charley and by Charley's son, Bernard, but she has no identity other than that of a secretary. And, as a secretary--that is, as a nonentity in the eyes of at least some men--she can be addressed insensitively. Willy Loman makes off-color remarks to her:

> WILLY. . . . Jenny, Jenny, good to see you.
>   How're ya? Workin'? Or still honest?
>
> JENNY. Fine. How've you been feeling?
>
> WILLY. Not much any more, Jenny. Ha, ha!
>   (1073-74)

The first of these comments seems to suggest that a working woman is <u>not</u> honest--that is, is a prostitute or is engaged in some other sort of hanky panky, as is the Woman who in exchange for silk stockings and sex sends Willy directly into the buyer's office. The second of Willy's jokes, with its remark about not feeling much, also refers to sex. In short, though readers or viewers of the play see Jenny as a thoroughly respectable woman, they see her not so much as an individual but as a person engaged in routine work and as a person to whom Willy can speak crudely.

It is a little harder to be certain about the characters of Miss Forsythe and Letta, the two women in the scene in Stanley's restaurant. For Happy, Miss Forsythe is "strudel," an object for a man to consume, and for Stanley she and her friend Letta are "chippies," that is, prostitutes. But is it clear that they are prostitutes? When Happy tells Miss Forsythe that he is in the business of selling, he makes a dirty joke, saying, "You don't happen to sell, do you?" (1079). She replies, "No, I don't sell," and if we take this seriously and if we believe her, we can say that she is respectable and is rightly putting Happy in his place. Further, her friend Letta says, "I gotta get up very early tomorrow. I got jury duty" (1085), which implies that she is a responsible citizen. Still, the girls do not seem especially thoughtful. When Biff introduces Willy to the girls, Letta says, "Isn't he cute? Sit down with us, Pop" (1085), and when Willy breaks down in the restaurant, Miss Forsythe says, "Say, I don't like that temper of his" (1086). Perhaps we can say this: It is going too far--on the basis of what we see--to agree with Stanley that the women are "chippies," or with Happy, who assumes that every woman is available for sex, but Miss Forsythe and Letta do not seem to be especially responsible or even interesting people. That is, as Miller presents them, they are of little substance, simply figures introduced into the play in order to show how badly Happy and Biff behave.

The most important woman in the play, other than Linda, is "the Woman," who for money or stockings and perhaps for pleasure has sex with Willy, and who will use her influence as a receptionist or secretary in the office to send Willy directly on to the buyer, without his having to wait at the desk. But even though the Woman gets something out of the relationship, she knows that she is being used. When Biff appears in the hotel room, she asks him, "Are you football or baseball?" Biff replies, "Football," and the Woman, "angry, humiliated," says, "That's me too" (1088). We can admire her vigorous response, but, again, like the other women whom we have discussed, she is not really an impressive figure. We can say that, at best, in a society that assumes women are to be exploited by men, she holds her own.

So far, then--though we have not yet talked about Linda--the world of Death of a Salesman is not notable for its pictures of impressive women. True, most of the males in the play--Willy, Biff, Happy, Ben, and such

lesser characters as Stanley and Howard--are themselves
pretty sorry specimens, but Bernard and Charley are
exceptionally decent and successful people, people who
can well serve as role models. Can any female character
in the play serve as a role model?

Linda has evoked strongly contrasting reactions from
the critics. Some of them judge her very severely. For
instance, Lois Gordon says that Linda "encourages
Willy's dream, yet she will not let him leave her for
the New Continent, the only realm where the dream can be
fulfilled" (105). True, Linda urges Willy not to follow
Ben's advice of going to Alaska, but surely the
spectator of the play cannot believe that Willy is the
sort of man who can follow in Ben's footsteps and
violently make a fortune. And, in fact, Ben is so vile a
person (as when he trips Biff, threatens Biff's eye with
the point of his umbrella, and says, "Never fight fair
with a stranger, boy" (1054), that we would not want
Willy to take Ben's advice.

A second example of a harsh view of Linda is Brian
Parker's comment on "the essential stupidity of Linda's
behavior. Surely it is both stupid and immoral to
encourage the man you love in self-deceit and lies"
(54). Parker also says that Linda's speech at the end,
when she says she cannot understand why Willy killed
himself, "is not only pathetic, it is also an
explanation of the loneliness of Willy Loman which threw
him into other women's arms" (54). Nothing in the play
suggests that Linda was anything other than a highly
supportive wife. If Willy turned to other women, surely
it was not because Linda did not understand him.
Finally, one last example of the Linda-bashing school of
commentary: Guerin Bliquez speaks of "Linda's facility
for prodding Willy to his doom" (383).

Very briefly, the arguments against Linda are that
(1) she selfishly prevented Willy from going to Alaska,
(2) she stupidly encourages him in his self-deceptions,
and (3) she is materialistic, so that even at the end,
in the Requiem, when she says she has made the last

payment on the house, she is talking about money. But if we study the play we will see that all three of these charges are false. First, although Linda does indeed discourage Willy from taking Ben's advice and going to Alaska, she points out that there is no need for "everyone [to] conquer the world," and that Willy has "a beautiful job here" (1071), a job with excellent prospects. She may be mistaken in thinking that Willy has a good job--he may have misled her--but, given what seems to be the situation, her comment is entirely reasonable. So far as the second charge goes, that she encourages him in self-deception, there are two answers. First, on some matters she does not know that Willy has lied to her, and so her encouragement is reasonable and right. Second, on other matters she does know that Willy is not telling the truth, but she rightly thinks it is best not to let him know that she knows, since such a revelation would crush what little self-respect remains in him. Consider, for example, this portion of dialogue, early in the play, when Willy, deeply agitated about his failure to drive and about Biff, has to leave for good: she goes to Willy and says, "I think that's the best way, dear. 'Cause there's no use drawing it out, you'll just never get along" (1092). Linda is not the most forceful person alive, or the brightest, but she is decent and she sees more clearly than do any of the other Lomans.

There is nothing in the play to suggest that Arthur Miller was a feminist or was ahead of his time in his view of the role of women. On the contrary, the play seems to give a pre-feminist view, with women playing subordinate roles to men. The images of success of the best sort--not of Ben's ruthless sort--are Charley and Bernard, two males. Probably Miller, writing in the 1940s, could hardly conceive of a successful woman other than as a wife or mother. Notice, by the way, that Bernard--probably the most admirable male in the play-- is not only an important lawyer but the father of two sons, apparently a sign of his complete success as a man. Still, Miller's picture of Linda is by no means condescending. Linda may not be a genius, but she is the brightest and the most realistic of the Lomans. Things turn out badly, but not because of Linda. The viewer leaves the theater with profound respect for her patience, her strength, her sense of decency, and, yes, her intelligence and her competence in dealing with incompetent men.

[New page]

Works Cited

Bliquez, Guerin. "Linda's Role in Death of a Salesman." Modern Drama 10 (1968): 383-86.

Gordon, Lois. "Death of a Salesman: An Appreciation." The Forties: Fiction, Poetry, Drama. Ed. Warren French. Deland, Florida: Everett/Edwards, 1969. 273-83.

Koon, Helene Wickham, ed. Twentieth Century Interpretations of Death of a Salesman. Englewood Cliffs, New Jersey: Prentice-Hall, 1983.

Miller, Arthur. Death of a Salesman. An Introduction to Literature. Ed. Sylvan Barnet, Morton Berman, and William Burto. Expanded ed. New York: HarperCollins, 1994. 1034-98.

Parker, Brian. "Point of View in Arthur Miller's Death of a Salesman." University of Toronto Quarterly 35 (1966): 144-47. Rpt. in Koon. 41-55.

Stanton, Kay. "Women and the American Dream of Death of a Salesman." Feminist Readings of American Drama. Ed. Judith Schlueter. Rutherford, New Jersey: Fairleigh Dickinson UP, 1989. 67-102.

✓ A Checklist: Reading Drafts of Research Papers

1. Is the tentative title informative and focused?
2. Does the paper make a point, or does it just accumulate other people's ideas?
3. Does it reveal the thesis early?
4. Are generalizations supported by evidence?
5. Are quotations introduced adequately?

6. Are all of the long quotations necessary, or can some of them be effectively summarized?
7. Are quotations discussed adequately?
8. Are all sources given?
9. Does the paper advance in orderly stages? Can your imagined reader easily follow your thinking?
10. Is the documentation in the correct form?

16

Essay Examinations

WHAT EXAMINATIONS ARE

Chapters 9–13, on writing essays about nonfiction, fiction, drama, poetry, and film, discuss not only the job of writing essays but also the nature of the artistic forms themselves, on the assumption that writing an essay requires knowledge of the subject, as well as skill with language. Here a few words will be spent in discussing the nature of examinations; perhaps one can write better essay answers when one knows what examinations are.

An examination not only measures learning and thinking but stimulates them. Even so humble an examination as a short-answer quiz—chiefly a device to coerce students to do the assigned reading—is a sort of push designed to move students forward. Of course, internal motivation is far superior to external, but even such crude external motivation as a quiz can have a beneficial effect. Students know this; indeed, they often seek external compulsion, choosing a particular course "because I want to know something about . . . and I know that I won't do the reading on my own." (Teachers often teach a new course for the same reason; we want to become knowledgeable about, say, Asian-American literature, and we know that despite our lofty intentions we may not seriously confront the subject unless we are under the pressure of facing a class.)

In short, however ignoble it sounds, examinations force students to acquire learning and then to convert learning into thinking. Sometimes, it is not until preparing for the final examination that students—rereading the chief texts and classroom notes—see what the course was really about; until this late stage, the trees obscure the forest, but now, reviewing and sorting things out. A pattern emerges. The experience of reviewing and then of writing an examination, though fretful, can be highly exciting as connections are made and ideas take on life. Such discoveries about the whole subject matter of a course can almost never be made by writing critical essays on topics of one's own construction, for such topics rarely require a view of the whole. Further, we are more likely to make imaginative leaps when trying to answer questions that other people pose to us, rather than questions we pose to ourselves. (Again, every teacher knows that in the classroom questions are asked that stimulate the teacher to see things and to think thoughts that would otherwise have been neglected.) And although questions posed by others cause anxiety, when they have been confronted and responded to on an examination, the student often makes yet another discovery—a self-discovery, a sudden and satisfying awareness of powers one didn't know one had.

WRITING ESSAY ANSWERS

Let's assume that before the examination you have read the assigned material, marked the margins of your books, made summaries of the longer readings and of the classroom comments, reviewed all this material, and had a decent night's sleep. Now you are facing the examination sheet.

Here are seven obvious but important practical suggestions:

1. Take a moment to jot down, as a sort of outline or source of further inspiration, a few ideas that strike you after you have thought a little about the question. You may at the outset realize that, say, you want to make three points, and unless you jot these down—three key words will do—you may spend all the allotted time on one point.

2. Answer the question: If you are asked to compare two characters, compare them; don't just write two character sketches. Take seriously such words as *compare, summarize,* and especially *evaluate.*

3. You often can get a good start merely by turning the question into an affirmation, for example, by turning "In what ways does the poetry of Margaret Atwood resemble her fiction" into "Margaret Atwood's poetry resembles her fiction in at least . . . ways."

4. Don't waste time summarizing at length what you have read unless asked to do so—but, of course, you may have to give a brief summary in order to support a point. The instructor wants to see that you can *use* your reading, not merely that you have *done* the reading.

5. Budget your time. Do not spend more than the allotted time on a question.

6. Be concrete. Illustrate your arguments with facts—the names of authors, titles, dates, characters, details of plot, and quotations if possible.

7. Leave space for last-minute additions. If you are writing in an examination booklet either skip a page between essays, or write only on the right-hand pages so that on rereading you can add material at the appropriate place on the left-hand pages.

Beyond these general suggestions we can best talk about essay examinations by looking at the five commonest sorts of questions:

1. A passage to explicate
2. A historical question (for example, "Trace the influence of Maupassant on Kate Chopin")
3. A critical quotation to be evaluated
4. A wild question (such as "What would Virginia Woolf think of Amy Tan's *The Joy Luck Club*?"; "What would Macbeth do if he were in Hamlet's place?")
5. A comparison (for example, "Compare the dramatic monologues of Browning with those of T. S. Eliot")

A few remarks on each of these types may be helpful.

1. On explication, see pages 36–42 and pages 253–56. As a short rule, look carefully at the tone (speaker's attitude toward self, subject, and audience) and at the implications of the words (their connotations and associations), and see whether a pattern of imagery is evident. For example, religious language (*adore, saint*) in a secular love poem may precisely define the nature of the lover and of the beloved. Remember, *an explication is not a paraphrase* (a putting into other words) but an attempt to show the relations of the parts by calling attention to implications. Organization of such an essay is rarely a problem, since most explications begin with the first line and go on to the last.

2. A good essay on a historical question will offer a nice combination of argument and evidence; that is, the thesis will be supported by concrete details (names, dates, perhaps, even brief quotations). A discussion of Chopin's debt to Maupassant cannot be convincing if it does not specify certain works and certain characteristics. If you are asked to relate a writer or a body of work to an earlier writer or period, list the chief characteristics of the earlier writer or period, and then show *specifically* how the material you are discussing is related to these characteristics. If you quote some relevant lines from the works, your reader will feel that you know not only titles and stock phrases but also the works themselves.

3. If you are asked to evaluate a critical quotation, read it carefully, and in your answer take account of *all* the quotation. If, for example, the quoted

critic has said, "Alice Walker in her fiction always . . . but in her nonfiction rarely . . . ," you will have to write about fiction and nonfiction; it will not be enough to talk only about Alice Walker's novels or only about her essays (unless, of course, the instructions on the examination ask you to take only as much of the quotation as you wish). Watch especially for words like *always, for the most part, never;* that is, although the passage may on the whole approach the truth, you may feel that some important qualifications are needed. This is not being picky; true thinking involves making subtle distinctions, yielding assent only so far and no further. And (again) be sure to give concrete details, supporting your argument with evidence.

4. Curiously, a wild question, such as "What would Woolf think of *The Joy Luck Club*?" or "What would Macbeth do in Hamlet's place?" usually produces rather tame answers: A half-dozen ideas about Woolf or Macbeth are neatly applied to Vonnegut or Hamlet, and the gross incompatibilities are thus revealed. But, as the previous paragraph suggests, it may be necessary to do more than set up bold and obvious oppositions. The interest in such a question and in the answer to it may be largely in the degree to which superficially different figures resemble each other in some important ways. Remember that the wildness of the question does not mean that all answers are equally acceptable; as usual, any good answer will be supported by concrete detail.

5. On comparisons, see pages 47–50. Because comparisons are especially difficult to write, be sure to take a few moments to jot down a sort of outline so that you know where you will be going. A comparison of Browning's and Eliot's monologues might treat three poems by each, devoting alternate paragraphs to one author; or it might first treat one author's poems and then turn to the other's; but if it adopts this second strategy, the essay may break into two parts. You can guard against this weakness by announcing at the outset that you can treat one author first, then the other; by reminding your reader during your treatment of the first author that certain points will be picked up when you get to the second author; and by briefly reminding your reader during the treatment of the second author of certain points already made in the treatment of the first.

Appendix A

Two Stories

James Joyce
(1882–1941)

ARABY

North Richmond Street, being blind,[1] was a quiet street except at the hour when the Christian Brothers' School set the boys free. An uninhabited house of two stories stood at the blind end, detached from its neighbors in a square ground. The other houses of the street, conscious of decent lives within them, gazed at one another with brown imperturbable faces.

The former tenant of our house, a priest, had died in the back drawing-room. Air, musty from having long been enclosed, hung in all the rooms, and the waste room behind the kitchen was littered with old useless papers. Among these I found a few papercovered books, the pages of which were curled and damp: The *Abbot*, by Walter Scott, *The Devout Communicant* and *The Memoirs of Vidocq*.[2] I liked the last best because its leaves were yellow. The wild garden behind the house contained a central apple-tree and a few straggling bushes under one of which I found the late tenant's rusty bicycle-pump. He had been a very charitable priest; in his will he had left all his money to institutions and the furniture of his house to his sister.

When the short days of winter came dusk fell before we had well eaten our dinners. When we met in the street the houses had grown sombre. The space of sky above us was the colour of everchanging violet and towards it the lamps of the street lifted their feeble lanterns. The cold air stung us and we

---

[1]**blind** a dead-end street.

[2]*The Abbot* was one of Scott's popular historical romances. *The Devout Communicant* was a Catholic religious manual; *The Memoirs of Vidocq* were the memoirs of the chief of the French detective force.

played till our bodies glowed. Our shouts echoed in the silent street. The career of our play brought us through the dark muddy lanes behind the houses where we ran the gauntlet of the rough tribes from the cottages, to the back doors of the dark dripping gardens where odours arose from the ashpits, to the dark odorous stables where a coachman smoothed and combed the horse or shook music from the buckled harness. When we returned to the street light from the kitchen windows had filled the areas. If my uncle was seen turning the corner we hid in the shadow until we had seen him safely housed. Or if Mangan's sister came out on the doorstep to call her brother in to his tea we watched her from our shadow peer up and down the street. We waited to see whether she would remain or go in and, if she remained, we left our shadow and walked up to Mangan's steps resignedly. She was waiting for us, her figure defined by the light from the half-opened door. Her brother always teased her before he obeyed and I stood by the railings looking at her. Her dress swung as she moved her body and the soft rope of her hair tossed from side to side.

Every morning I lay on the floor in the front parlour watching her door. The blind was pulled down to within an inch of the sash so that I could not be seen. When she came out on the doorstep my heart leaped. I ran to the hall, seized my books and followed her. I kept her brown figure always in my eye and, when we came near the point at which our ways diverged, I quickened my pace and passed her. This happened morning after morning. I had never spoken to her, except for a few casual words, and yet her name was like a summons to all my foolish blood.

Her image accompanied me even in places the most hostile to romance. On Saturday evenings when my aunt went marketing I had to go to carry some of the parcels. We walked through the flaring streets, jostled by drunken men and bargaining women, amid the curses of labourers, the shrill litanies of shop-boys who stood on guard by the barrels of pigs' cheeks, the nasal chanting of street-singers, who sang a *come-all-you* about O'Donovan Rossa,[3] or a ballad about the troubles in our native land. These noises converged in a single sensation of life for me: I imagined that I bore my chalice safely through a throng of foes. Her name sprang to my lips at moments in strange prayers and praises which I myself did not understand. My eyes were often full of tears (I could not tell why) and at times a flood from my heart seemed to pour itself out into my bosom. I thought little of the future. I did not know whether I would ever speak to her or not or, if I spoke to her, how I could tell her of my confused adoration. But my body was like a harp and her words and gestures were like fingers running upon the wires.

One evening I went into the back drawing-room in which the priest had died. It was a dark rainy evening and there was no sound in the house. Through one of the broken panes I heard the rain impinge upon the earth, the

---

[3]Jeremiah O'Donovan (1831–1915), a popular Irish leader who was jailed by the British for advocating violent rebellion. A "come-all-you" was a topical song that began "Come all you gallant Irishmen."

fine incessant needles of water playing in the sodden beds. Some distant lamp or lighted window gleamed below me. I was thankful that I could see so little. All my senses seemed to desire to veil themselves and, feeling that I was about to slip from them, I pressed the palms of my hands together until they trembled, murmuring: *O love! O love!* many times.

At last she spoke to me. When she addressed the first words to me I was so confused that I did not know what to answer. She asked me was I going to Araby.

I forget whether I answered yes or no. It would be a splendid bazaar, she said; she would love to go.

—And why can't you? I asked.

While she spoke she turned a silver bracelet round and round her wrist. She could not go, she said, because there would be a retreat that week in her convent. Her brother and two other boys were fighting for their caps and I was alone at the railings. She held one of the spikes, bowing her head towards me. The light from the lamp opposite our door caught the white curve of her neck, lit up her hair that rested there and, falling, lit up the hand upon the railing. It fell over one side of her dress and caught the white border of a petticoat, just visible as she stood at ease.

—It's well for you, she said.

—If I go, I said, I will bring you something.

What innumerable follies laid waste my waking and sleeping thoughts after that evening! I wished to annihilate the tedious intervening days. I chafed against the work of school. At night in my bedroom and by day in the classroom her image came between me and the page I strove to read. The syllables of the word *Araby* were called to me through the silence in which my soul luxuriated and cast an Eastern enchantment over me. I asked for leave to go to the bazaar on Saturday night. My aunt was surprised and hoped it was not some Freemason[4] affair. I answered few questions in class, I watched my master's face pass from amiability to sternness; he hoped I was not beginning to idle. I could not call my wandering thoughts together. I had hardly any patience with the serious work of life which, now that it stood between me and my desire, seemed to me child's play, ugly monotonous child's play.

On Saturday morning I reminded my uncle that I wished to go to the bazaar in the evening. He was fussing at the hallstand, looking for the hatbrush, and answered me curtly:

—Yes, boy, I know.

As he was in the hall I could not go into the front parlour and lie at the window. I left the house in bad humour and walked slowly towards the school. The air was pitilessly raw and already my heart misgave me.

When I came home to dinner my uncle had not yet been home. Still it was early. I sat staring at the clock for some time and, when its ticking began to irritate me, I left the room. I mounted the staircase and gained the upper part of

[4]Irish Catholics viewed the Masons as their Protestant enemies.

the house. The high cold empty gloomy rooms liberated me and I went from room to room singing. From the front window I saw my companions playing below in the street. Their cries reached me weakened and indistinct and, leaning my forehead against the cool glass, I looked over at the dark house where she lived. I may have stood there for an hour, seeing nothing but the brown-clad figure cast by my imagination, touched discreetly by the lamplight at the curved neck, at the hand upon the railings and at the border below the dress.

When I came downstairs again I found Mrs Mercer sitting at the fire. She was an old garrulous woman, a pawnbroker's widow, who collected used stamps for some pious purpose. I had to endure the gossip of the tea-table. The meal was prolonged beyond an hour and still my uncle did not come. Mrs Mercer stood up to go: she was sorry she couldn't wait any longer, but it was after eight o'clock and she did not like to be out late, as the night air was bad for her. When she had gone I began to walk up and down the room, clenching my fists. My aunt said:

—I'm afraid you may put off your bazaar for this night of Our Lord.

At nine o'clock I heard my uncle's latchkey in the halldoor. I heard him talking to himself and heard the hallstand rocking when it had received the weight of his overcoat. I could interpret these signs. When he was midway through his dinner I asked him to give me the money to go to the bazaar. He had forgotten.

—The people are in bed and after their first sleep now, he said.

I did not smile. My aunt said to him energetically:

—Can't you give him the money and let him go? You've kept him late enough as it is.

My uncle said he was very sorry he had forgotten. He said he believed in the old saying: *All work and no play makes Jack a dull boy.* He asked me where I was going and, when I had told him a second time he asked me did I know *The Arab's Farewell to His Steed.*[5] When I left the kitchen he was about to recite the opening lines of the piece to my aunt.

I held a florin tightly in my hand as I strode down Buckingham Street towards the station. The sight of the streets thronged with buyers and glaring with gas recalled to me the purpose of my journey. I took my seat in a third-class carriage of a deserted train. After an intolerable delay the train moved out of the station slowly. It crept onward among ruinous houses and over the twinkling river. At Westland Row Station a crowd of people pressed to the carriage doors; but the porters moved them back, saying that it was a special train for the bazaar. I remained alone in the bare carriage. In a few minutes the train drew up beside an improvised wooden platform. I passed out on to the road and saw by the lighted dial of a clock that it was ten minutes to ten. In front of me was a large building which displayed the magical name.

[5]"The Arab to His Favorite Steed" was a popular sentimental poem by Caroline Norton (1808–77).

I could not find any sixpenny entrance and, fearing that the bazaar would be closed, I passed in quickly through a turnstile, handing a shilling to a weary-looking man. I found myself in a big hall girdled at half its height by a gallery. Nearly all the stalls were closed and the greater part of the hall was in darkness. I recognised a silence like that which pervades a church after a service. I walked into the center of the bazaar timidly. A few people were gathered about the stalls which were still open. Before a curtain, over which the words *Café Chantant* were written in coloured lamps, two men were counting money on a salver. I listened to the fall of the coins.

Remembering with difficulty why I had come I went over to one of the stalls and examined porcelain vases and flowered teasets. At the door of the stall a young lady was talking and laughing with two young gentlemen. I remarked their English accents and listened vaguely to their conversation.

—O, I never said such a thing!

—O, but you did!

—O, but I didn't!

—Didn't she say that?

—Yes! I heard her.

—O, there's a . . . fib!

Observing me the young lady came over and asked me did I wish to buy anything. The tone of her voice was not encouraging; she seemed to have spoken to me out of a sense of duty. I looked humbly at the great jars that stood like eastern guards at either side of the dark entrance to the stall and murmured:

—No, thank you.

The young lady changed the position of one of the vases and went back to the two young men. They began to talk of the same subject. Once or twice the young lady glanced at me over her shoulder.

I lingered before her stall, though I knew my stay was useless, to make my interest in her wares seem the more real. Then I turned away slowly and walked down the middle of the bazaar. I allowed the two pennies to fall against the sixpence in my pocket. I heard a voice call from one end of the gallery that the light was out. The upper part of the hall was now completely dark.

Gazing up into the darkness I saw myself as a creature driven and derided by vanity; and my eyes burned with anguish and anger.

Shirley Jackson
(1919–65)

THE LOTTERY

The morning of June 27th was clear and sunny, with the fresh warmth of a full-summer day; the flowers were blossoming profusely and the grass was richly green. The people of the village began to gather in the square, between the post office and the bank, around ten o'clock; in some towns there were so many people that the lottery took two days and had to be started on June 26th, but in this village, where there were only about three hundred people, the whole lottery took less than two hours, so it could begin at ten o'clock in the morning and still be through in time to allow the villagers to get home for noon dinner.

The children assembled first, of course. School was recently over for the summer, and the feeling of liberty sat uneasily on most of them; they tended to gather together quietly for a while before they broke into boisterous play, and their talk was still of the classroom and the teacher, of books and reprimands. Bobby Martin had already stuffed his pockets full of stones, and the other boys soon followed his example, selecting the smoothest and roundest stones; Bobby and Harry Jones and Dickie Delacroix—the villagers pronounced this name "Dellacroy"—eventually made a great pile of stones in one corner of the square and guarded it against the raids of the other boys. The girls stood aside, talking among themselves, looking over their shoulders at the boys, and the very small children rolled in the dust or clung to the hands of their older brothers or sisters.

Soon the men began to gather, surveying their own children, speaking of planting and rain, tractors and taxes. They stood together, away from the pile of stones in the corner, and their jokes were quiet and they smiled rather than laughed. The women, wearing faded house dresses and sweaters, came shortly after their menfolk. They greeted one another and exchanged bits of gossip as they went to join their husbands. Soon the women, standing by their husbands, began to call to their children, and the children came reluctantly, having to be called four or five times. Bobby Martin ducked under his mother's grasping hand and ran, laughing, back to the pile of stones. His father spoke up sharply, and Bobby came quickly and took his place between his father and his oldest brother.

The lottery was conducted—as were the square dances, the teenage club, the Halloween program—by Mr. Summers, who had time and energy to devote to civic activities. He was a round-faced, jovial man and he ran the coal business, and people were sorry for him, because he had no children and his wife was a scold. When he arrived in the square, carrying the black wooden box, there was a murmur of conversation among the villagers and he waved and called, "Little late today, folks." The postmaster, Mr. Graves, followed him, carrying a three-legged stool, and the stool was put in the center of the square and Mr. Summers set the black box down on it. The villagers kept their distance, leaving a space between themselves and the stool, and when Mr. Summers said, "Some of you fellows want to give me a hand?" there was a hesitation before two men, Mr. Martin and his oldest son, Baxter, came forward to hold the box steady on the stool while Mr. Summers stirred up the papers inside it.

The original paraphernalia for the lottery had been lost long ago, and the black box now resting on the stool had been put into use even before Old Man Warner, the oldest man in town, was born. Mr. Summers spoke frequently to the villagers about making a new box, but no one liked to upset even as much tradition as was represented by the black box. There was a story that the present box had been made with some pieces of the box that had preceded it, the one that had been constructed when the first people settled down to make a village here. Every year, after the lottery, Mr. Summers began talking again about a new box, but every year the subject was allowed to fade off without anything's being done. The black box grew shabbier each year; by now it was no longer completely black but splintered badly along one side to show the original wood color, and in some places faded or stained.

Mr. Martin and his oldest son, Baxter, held the black box securely on the stool until Mr. Summers had stirred the papers thoroughly with his hand. Because so much of the ritual had been forgotten or discarded, Mr. Summers had been successful in having slips of paper substituted for the chips of wood that had been used for generations. Chips of wood, Mr. Summers had argued, had been all very well when the village was tiny, but now that the population was more than three hundred and likely to keep on growing, it was necessary to use something that would fit more easily into the black box. The night before the lottery, Mr. Summers and Mr. Graves made up the slips of paper and put them in the box, and it was then taken to the safe of Mr. Summers's coal company and locked up until Mr. Summers was ready to take it to the square next morning. The rest of the year, the box was put away, sometimes one place, sometimes another; it had spent one year in Mr. Graves's barn and another year underfoot in the post office, and sometimes it was set on a shelf in the Martin grocery and left there.

There was a great deal of fussing to be done before Mr. Summers declared the lottery open. There were lists to make up—of heads of families, heads of households in each family, members of each household in each family. There was the proper swearing-in of Mr. Summers by the postmaster, as the official of the lottery; at one time, some people remembered, there had been a recital of some sort, performed by the official of the lottery, a perfunctory, tuneless chant that had been rattled off duly each year; some people believed that the official of the lottery used to stand just so when he said or sang it, others believed that he was supposed to walk among the people, but years and years ago this part of the ritual had been allowed to lapse. There had been, also, a ritual salute, which the official of the lottery had had to use in addressing each person who came up to draw from the box, but this also had changed with time, until now it was felt necessary only for the official to speak to each person approaching. Mr. Summers was very good at all this; in his clean white shirt and blue jeans, with one hand resting carelessly on the black box, he seemed very proper and important as he talked interminably to Mr. Graves and the Martins.

Just as Mr. Summers finally left off talking and turned to the assembled villagers, Mrs. Hutchinson came hurriedly along the path to the square, her sweater thrown over her shoulders, and slid into place in the back of the crowd. "Clean forgot what day it was," she said to Mrs. Delacroix, who stood next to her, and they both laughed softly. "Thought my old man was out back stacking wood," Mrs. Hutchinson went on, "and then I looked out the window and the kids were gone, and then I remembered it was the twenty-seventh and came a-running." She dried her hands on her apron, and Mrs. Delacroix said, "You're in time, though. They're still talking away up there."

Mrs. Hutchinson craned her neck to see through the crowd and found her husband and children standing near the front. She tapped Mrs. Delacroix on the arm as a farewell and began to make her way through the crowd. The people separated goodhumoredly to let her through; two or three people said, in voices just loud enough to be heard across the crowd, "Here comes your Missus, Hutchinson," and "Bill, she made it after all." Mrs. Hutchinson reached her husband, and Mr. Summers, who had been waiting, said cheerfully, "Thought we were going to have to get on without you, Tessie." Mrs. Hutchinson said, grinning, "Wouldn't have me leave m'dishes in the sink, now would you, Joe?," and soft laughter ran through the crowd as the people stirred back into position after Mrs. Hutchinson's arrival.

"Well, now," Mr. Summers said soberly, "guess we better get started, get this over with, so's we can go back to work. Anybody ain't here?"

"Dunbar," several people said. "Dunbar, Dunbar."

Mr. Summers consulted his list. "Clyde Dunbar," he said "That's right. He's broke his leg, hasn't he? Who's drawing for him?"

"Me, I guess," a woman said, and Mr. Summers turned to look at her. "Wife draws for her husband," Mr. Summers said. "Don't you have a grown boy to do it for you, Janey?" Although Mr. Summers and everyone else in the village knew the answer perfectly well, it was the business of the official of the lottery to ask such questions formally. Mr. Summers waited with an expression of polite interest while Mrs. Dunbar answered.

"Horace's not but sixteen yet," Mrs. Dunbar said regretfully. "Guess I gotta fill in for the old man this year."

"Right," Mr. Summers said. He made a note on the list he was holding. Then he asked, "Watson boy drawing this year?"

A tall boy in the crowd raised his hand. "Here," he said. "I'm drawing for m'mother and me." He blinked his eyes nervously and ducked his head as several voices in the crowd said things like "Good fellow, Jack," and "Glad to see your mother's got a man to do it."

"Well," Mr. Summers said, "guess that's everyone. Old Man Warner make it?"

"Here," a voice said, and Mr. Summers nodded.

A sudden hush fell on the crowd as Mr. Summers cleared his throat and looked at the list. "All ready?" he called. "Now, I'll read the names—heads of families first—and the men come up and take a paper out of the box. Keep the paper folded in your hand without looking at it until everyone has had a turn. Everything clear?"

The people had done it so many times that they only half listened to the directions, most of them were quiet, wetting their lips, not looking around. Then Mr. Summers raised one hand high and said, "Adams." A man disengaged himself from the crowd and came forward. "Hi, Steve," Mr. Summers said, and Mr. Adams said, "Hi, Joe." They grinned at one another humorlessly and nervously. Then Mr. Adams reached into the black box and took out a folded paper. He held it firmly by one corner as he turned and went hastily back to his place in the crowd, where he stood a little apart from his family, not looking down at his hand.

"Allen," Mr. Summers said. "Anderson. . . . Bentham."

"Seems like there's no time at all between lotteries any more." Mrs. Delacroix said to Mrs. Graves in the back row. "Seems like we got through with the last one only last week."

"Time sure goes fast," Mrs. Graves said.

"Clark. . . . Delacroix."

"There goes my old man," Mrs. Delacroix said. She held her breath while her husband went forward.

"Dunbar," Mr. Summers said, and Mrs. Dunbar went steadily to the box while one of the women said, "Go on, Janey," and another said, "There she goes."

"We're next," Mrs. Graves said. She watched while Mr. Graves came around from the side of the box, greeted Mr. Summers gravely, and selected a slip of paper from the box. By now, all through the crowd there were men holding the small folded papers in their large hands, turning them over and over nervously. Mrs. Dunbar and her two sons stood together, Mrs. Dunbar holding the slip of paper.

"Harburt. . . . Hutchinson."

"Get up there, Bill," Mrs. Hutchinson said, and the people near her laughed.

"Jones."

"They do say," Mr. Adams said to Old Man Warner, who stood next to him, "that over in the north village they're talking of giving up the lottery."

Old Man Warner snorted, "Pack of crazy fools," he said. "Listening to the young folks, nothing's good enough for *them*. Next thing you know, they'll be wanting to go back to living in caves, nobody work any more, live *that* way for a while. Used to be a saying about 'Lottery in June, corn be heavy soon.' First thing you know, we'd all be eating stewed chickweed and acorns. There's *always* been a lottery," he added petulantly. "Bad enough to see young Joe Summers up there joking with everybody."

"Some places have already quit lotteries," Mrs. Adams said.

"Nothing but trouble in *that*," Old Man Warner said stoutly. "Pack of young fools."

"Martin." And Bobby Martin watched his father go forward. "Overdyke. . . . Percy."

"I wish they'd hurry," Mrs. Dunbar said to her older son. "I wish they'd hurry."

"They're almost through," her son said.

"You get ready to run tell Dad," Mrs. Dunbar said.

Mr. Summers called his own name and then stepped forward precisely and selected a slip from the box. Then he called, "Warner."

"Seventy-seventh year I been in the lottery," Old Man Warner said as he went through the crowd. "Seventy-seventh time."

"Watson." The tall boy came awkwardly through the crowd. Someone said, "Don't be nervous, Jack," and Mr. Summers said, Take your time, son."

"Zanini."

After that, there was a long pause, a breathless pause, until Mr. Summers, holding his slip of paper in the air, said, "All right, fellows." For a minute, no one moved, and then all the slips of paper were opened. Suddenly, all women began to speak at once saying, "Who is it?," "Who's got it?," "Is it the Dunbars?," "Is it the Watsons?" Then the voices began to say, "It's Hutchinson. It's Bill." "Bill Hutchinson's got it."

"Go tell your father," Mrs. Dunbar said to her older son.

People began to look around to see the Hutchinsons. Bill Hutchinson was standing quiet, staring down at the paper in his hand. Suddenly, Tessie Hutchinson shouted to Mr. Summers "You didn't give him time enough to take any paper he wanted. I saw you. It wasn't fair!"

"Be a good sport, Tessie," Mrs. Delacroix called, and Mrs. Graves said, "All of us took the same chance."

"Shut up, Tessie," Bill Hutchinson said.

"Well, everyone," Mr. Summers said, "that was done pretty fast, and now we've got to be hurrying a little more to get done in time." He consulted his next list. "Bill," he said, "you draw for the Hutchinson family. You got any other households in the Hutchinsons?"

"There's Don and Eva," Mrs. Hutchinson yelled. "Make *them* take their chance!"

"Daughters draw with their husbands' families, Tessie," Mr. Summers said gently. "You know that as well as anyone else."

"It wasn't fair," Tessie said.

"I guess not, Joe," Bill Hutchinson said regretfully. "My daughter draws with her husband's family, that's only fair. And I've got no other family except the kids."

"Then, as far as drawing for families is concerned, it's you." Mr. Summers said in explanation, "and as far as drawing for households is concerned, that's you, too. Right?"

"Right," Bill Hutchinson said.

"How many kids, Bill?" Mr. Summers asked formally.

"Three," Bill Hutchinson said. "There's Bill, Jr., and Nancy, and little Dave. And Tessie and me."

"All right, then," Mr. Summers said. "Harry, you got their tickets back?"

Mr. Graves nodded and held up the slips of paper. "Put them in the box, then," Mr. Summers directed. "Take Bill's and put it in."

"I think we ought to start over," Mrs. Hutchinson said, as quietly as she could. "I tell you it wasn't *fair*. You didn't give him time enough to choose. *Every*body saw that."

Mr. Graves had selected the five slips and put them in the box, and he dropped all the papers but those onto the ground where the breeze caught them and lifted them off.

"Listen, everybody," Mrs. Hutchinson was saying to the people around her.

"Ready, Bill?" Mr. Summers asked, and Bill Hutchinson, with one quick glance around at his wife and children, nodded.

"Remember," Mr. Summers said, "take the slips and keep them folded until each person has taken one. Harry, you help little Dave." Mr. Graves took the hand of the little boy, who came willingly with him up to the box. "Take a paper out of the box, Davy," Mr. Summers said. Davy put his hand into the box and laughed. "Take just *one* paper," Mr. Summers said. "Harry, you hold it for him." Mr. Graves took the child's hand and removed the folded paper from the tight fist and held it while little Dave stood next to him and looked up at him wonderingly.

"Nancy next," Mr. Summers said. Nancy was twelve, and her school friends breathed heavily as she went forward, switching her skirt, and took a slip daintily from the box. "Bill, Jr.," Mr. Summers said, and Billy, his face red and his feet over-large, nearly knocked the box over as he got a paper out. "Tessie," Mr. Summers said. She hesitated for a minute, looking around defiantly, and then set her lips and went up to the box. She snatched a paper out and held it behind her.

"Bill," Mr. Summers said, and Bill Hutchinson reached into the box and felt around, bringing his hand out at last with the slip of paper in it.

The crowd was quiet. A girl whispered, "I hope it's not Nancy," and the sound of the whisper reached the edges of the crowd.

"It's not the way it used to be," Old Man Warner said clearly. "People ain't the way they used to be."

"All right," Mr. Summers said. "Open the papers. Harry, you open little Dave's."

Mr. Graves opened the slip of paper and there was a general sigh through the crowd as he held it up and everyone could see that it was blank. Nancy and Bill, Jr., opened theirs at the same time, and both beamed and laughed, turning around to the crowd and holding their slips of paper above their heads.

"Tessie," Mr. Summers said. There was a pause, and then Mr. Summers looked at Bill Hutchinson, and Bill unfolded his paper and showed it. It was blank.

"It's Tessie," Mr. Summers said, and his voice was hushed. "Show us her paper, Bill."

Bill Hutchinson went over to his wife and forced the slip of paper out of her hand. It had a black spot on it, the black spot Mr. Summers had made the night before with the heavy pencil in the coal-company office. Bill Hutchinson held it up, and there was a stir in the crowd.

"All right, folks," Mr. Summers said, "let's finish quickly." Although the villagers had forgotten the ritual and lost the original black box, they still remembered to use stones. The pile of stones the boys had made earlier was ready; there were stones on the ground with the blowing scraps of paper that had come out of the box. Mrs. Delacroix selected a stone so large she had to pick it up with both hands and turned to Mrs. Dunbar. "Come on," she said. "Hurry up."

Mrs. Dunbar had small stones in both hands, and she said, gasping for breath, "I can't run at all. You'll have to go ahead and I'll catch up with you."

The children had stones already, and someone gave little Davy Hutchinson a few pebbles.

Tessie Hutchinson was in the center of a cleared space by now, and she held her hands out desperately as the villagers moved in on her. "It isn't fair," she said. A stone hit her on the side of the head.

Old Man Warner was saying, "Come on, come on, everyone." Steve Adams was in the front of the crowd of villagers, with Mrs. Graves beside him.

"It isn't fair, it isn't right," Mrs. Hutchinson screamed, and then they were upon her.

Appendix B

Glossary of Literary Terms

The terms briefly defined here are for the most part more fully defined earlier in the text. Hence many of the entries below are followed by page references to the earlier discussions.

Absurd, Theater of the   plays, especially written in the 1950s and 1960s, that call attention to the incoherence of character and of action, the inability of people to communicate, and the apparent purposelessness of existence

accent   stress given to a syllable (258)

act   a major division of a play

action   (1) the happenings in a narrative or drama, usually physical events (*B* marries *C*, *D* kills *E*), but also mental changes (*F* moves from innocence to experience); in short, the answer to the question, "What happens?" (2) less commonly, the theme or underlying idea of a work (217–18)

allegory   a work in which concrete elements (for instance, a pilgrim, a road, a splendid city) stand for abstractions (humanity, life, salvation), usually in an unambiguous, one-to-one relationship. The literal items (the pilgrim, and so on) thus convey a meaning, which is usually moral, religious, or political. To take a nonliterary example: The Statue of Liberty holds a torch (enlightenment, showing the rest of the world the way to freedom), and at her feet are broken chains (tyranny overcome). A caution: Not all of the details in an allegorical work are meant to be interpreted. For example, the hollowness of the Statue of Liberty does not stand for the insubstantiality or emptiness of liberty.

alliteration   repetition of consonant sounds, especially at the beginnings of words (*f*ree, *f*orm, *ph*antom) (262)

allusion   an indirect reference; thus when Lincoln spoke of "a nation dedicated to the proposition that all men are created equal," he was making an allusion to the Declaration of Independence.

ambiguity   multiplicity of meaning, often deliberate, that leaves the reader uncertain about the intended significance

anagnorisis a recognition or discovery, especially in tragedy—for example, when the hero understands the reason for his or her fall (212)

analysis an examination, which usually proceeds by separating the object of study into parts (42–47)

anapest a metrical foot consisting of two unaccented syllables followed by an accented one. Example, showing three anapests: "As I came / to the edge / of the wood"(259)

anecdote a short narrative, usually reporting an amusing event in the life of an important person

antagonist a character or force that opposes (literally, "wrestles") the protagonist (the main character). Thus, in *Hamlet* the antagonist is King Claudius, the protagonist is Hamlet; in Antigone, the antagonist is Creon, the protagonist Antigone.

antecedent action happenings (especially in a play) that occurred before the present action (220)

apostrophe address to an absent figure or to a thing as if it were present and could listen. Example: "O rose, thou art sick!" (242)

approximate rhyme only the final consonant-sounds are the same, as in *crown/alone,* or *pail/fall*

archetype a theme, image, motive, or pattern that occurs so often in literary works it seems to be universal. Examples: a dark forest (for mental confusion), the sun (for illumination)

aside in the theater, words spoken by a character in the presence of other characters, but directed to the spectators, i.e. understood by the audience to be inaudible to the other characters

assonance repetition of similar vowel sounds in stressed syllables. Example: *light/bride* (262)

atmosphere the emotional tone (for instance, joy, or horror) in a work, most often established by the setting

ballad a short narrative poem, especially one that is sung or recited, often in a stanza of four lines, with 8, 6, 8, 6 syllables, with the second and fourth lines rhyming. A **popular ballad** is a narrative song that has been transmitted orally by what used to be called "the folk"; a **literary ballad** is a conscious imitation (without music) of such a work, often with complex symbolism.

blank verse unrhymed iambic pentameter, that is, unrhymed lines of ten syllables, with every second syllable stressed (264)

cacophony an unpleasant combination of sounds

caesura a strong pause within a line of verse (260)

canon a term originally used to refer to those books accepted as Holy Scripture by the Christian church. The term has come to be applied to literary works thought to have a special merit by a given culture, for instance the body of literature traditionally taught in colleges and universities. Such works are sometimes called "classics" and their authors are "major authors." As conceived in the United States until recently, the canon consisted chiefly of works by dead white European and American males—partly, of course, because middle class and upper class white males were in fact the people who did most of the writing in the Western Hemisphere, but also because white males (for instance, college professors) were the people who chiefly established the canon. Not surprisingly the canon-makers valued (or valorized or "privileged") writings that revealed, asserted, or reinforced the canon-makers' own values. From about the 1960s feminists and Marxists and others argued that these works had been regarded as central not because they were inherently better than other works but because they reflected the interests of the dominant culture, and that other work, such as slave narratives and the diaries of women, had been "marginalized."

In fact, the literary canon has never been static (in contrast to the Biblical canon, which has not changed for more than a thousand years), but it is true that certain authors, such as Homer, Chaucer, and Shakespeare have been permanent fixtures. Why? Partly because they do indeed support the values of those who in large measure control the high cultural purse strings, and perhaps partly because these books are rich enough to invite constant reinterpretation from age to age, that is, to allow each generation to find its needs and its values in them. (85–87)

catastrophe   the concluding action, especially in a tragedy

catharsis   Aristotle's term for the purgation or purification of the pity and terror supposedly experienced while witnessing a tragedy

character   (1) a person in a literary work (Romeo); (2) the personality of such a figure (sentimental lover, or whatever). Characters (in the first sense) are sometimes classified as either "flat" (one-dimensional) or "round" (fully realized, complex). (162–68, 223–24)

characterization   the presentation of a character, whether by direct description, by showing the character in action, or by the presentation of other characters who help to define each other

cliché   an expression that through overuse has ceased to be effective. Examples: acid test, sigh of relief, the proud possessor

climax   the culmination of a conflict; a turning point, often the point of greatest tension in a plot (161, 219)

comedy   a literary work, especially a play, characterized by humor and by a happy ending (213–15)

comparison and contrast   to compare is strictly to note similarities; to contrast is to note differences. But *compare* is now often used for both activities. (47–50)

complication   an entanglement in a narrative or dramatic work that causes a conflict

conflict   a struggle between a character and some obstacle (for example, another character or fate) or between internal forces, such as divided loyalties (161, 220)

connotation   the associations (suggestions, overtones) of a word or expression. Thus *seventy* and *three score and ten* both mean "one more than sixty-nine," but because *three score and ten* is a biblical expression, it has an association of holiness; see *denotation*. (296–297)

consistency building   the process engaged in during the act of reading, of reevaluating the details that one has just read in order to make them consistent with the new information that the text is providing (6)

consonance   repetition of consonant sounds, especially in stressed syllables. Also called half rhyme or slant rhyme. Example: *arouse/doze* (262)

convention   a pattern (for instance, the 14-line poem, or sonnet) or motif (for instance, the bumbling police officer in detective fiction) or other device occurring so often that it is taken for granted. Thus it is a convention that actors in a performance of *Julius Caesar* are understood to be speaking Latin, though in fact they are speaking English. Similarly, the soliloquy (a character alone on the stage speaks his or her thoughts aloud) is a convention, for in real life sane people do not talk aloud to themselves.

couplet   a pair of lines of verse, usually rhyming (263)

crisis   a high point in the conflict that leads to the turning point (161, 219)

criticism   the analysis or evaluation of a literary work (36–47, 90–145)

cultural materialism   criticism that sets literature in a social context, often of economics or politics or gender. Borrowing some of the methods of anthropology, cultural materialism usually extends the canon to include popular material, for instance comic books and soap operas (77)

dactyl   a metrical foot consisting of a stressed syllable followed by two unstressed syllables. Example: *underwear* (259)

deconstruction   a critical approach that assumes language is unstable and ambiguous and is therefore inherently contradictory. Because authors cannot control their language, texts reveal more than their authors are aware of. For instance, texts (like such institutions as the law, the churches, and the schools) are likely, when closely scrutinized, to reveal connections to a society's economic system, even though the authors may have believed they were outside of the system. (122–24, 143)

denotation   the dictionary meaning of a word. Thus *soap opera* and *daytime serial* have the same denotation, but the connotations (associations, emotional overtones) of *soap opera* are less favorable. (296)

dénouement   the resolution or the outcome (literally, the "unknotting") of a plot (161, 219)

deus ex machina   literally, "a god out of a machine"; any unexpected and artificial way of resolving the plot—for example, by introducing a rich uncle, thought to be dead, who arrives on the scene and pays the debts that otherwise would overwhelm the young hero

dialogue   exchange of words between characters; speech

diction   the choice of vocabulary and of sentence structure. There is a difference in diction between "One never knows" and "You never can tell." (150–52, 234)

didactic   pertaining to teaching; having a moral purpose

dimeter   a line of poetry containing two feet (260)

discovery   see *anagnorisis*

drama   (1) a play; (2) conflict or tension, as in "The story lacks drama" (203–31)

dramatic irony   see *irony*

dramatic monologue   a poem spoken entirely by one character but addressed to one or more other characters whose presence is strongly felt

effaced narrator   a narrator who reports but who does not editorialize or enter into the minds of any of the characters in the story

elegy   a lyric poem, usually a meditation on a death

elision   omission (usually of a vowel or unstressed syllable), as in *o'er* (for *over*) and in "Th' inevitable hour"

end rhyme   identical sounds at the ends of lines of poetry (262)

end-stopped line   a line of poetry that ends with a pause (usually marked by a comma, semicolon, or period) because the grammatical structure and the sense reach (at least to some degree) completion. It is contrasted with a *run-on line*. (261)

English (or Shakespearean) sonnet   a poem of 14 lines (three quatrains and a couplet), rhyming *abab cdcd efef gg* (263)

enjambment   a line of poetry in which the grammatical and logical sense run on, without pause, into the next line or lines (261)

epic   a long narrative, especially in verse, that usually records heroic material in an elevated style

epigram   a brief, witty poem or saying

epigraph   a quotation at the beginning of the work, just after the title, often giving a clue to the theme

epiphany   a "showing forth," as when an action reveals a character with particular clarity

episode   an incident or scene that has unity in itself but is also a part of a larger action

epistle   a letter, in prose or verse

essay   a work, usually in prose and usually fairly short, that purports to be true and that treats its subject tentatively. In most literary essays the reader's interest is as much in the speaker's personality as in any argument that is offered.

euphony   literally, "good sound," a pleasant combination of sounds

explication   a line-by-line unfolding of the meaning of a text (36–42, 253–56)

exposition   a setting-forth of information. In fiction and drama, introductory material introducing characters and the situation; in an essay, the presentation of information, as opposed to the telling of a story or the setting forth of an argument (220)

eye-rhyme   words that look as though they rhyme, but do not rhyme when pronounced. Example: *come/home* (262)

fable   a short story (often involving speaking animals) with an easily grasped moral

farce   comedy based not on clever language or on subtleties of characters but on broadly humorous situations (for instance, a man mistakenly enters the ladies' locker room)

feminine rhyme   a rhyme of two or more syllables, with the stress falling on a syllable other than the last. Examples: *fatter/batter; tenderly/slenderly* (262)

feminist criticism   an approach especially concerned with analyzing the depiction of women in literature—what images do male authors present of female characters?—and also with the reappraisal of work by female authors (134–36, 144)

fiction   an imaginative work, usually a prose narrative (novel, short story), that reports incidents that did not in fact occur. The term may include all works that
invent a world, such as a lyric poem or a play.

figurative language   words intended to be understood in a way that is other than
literal. Thus *lemon* used literally refers to a citrus fruit, but *lemon* used figuratively refers to a defective machine, especially a defective automobile. Other
examples: "He's a beast," "She's a witch," "A sea of troubles." Literally, such expressions are nonsense, but writers use them to express meanings inexpress-
ible in literal speech. Among the commonest kinds of figures of speech are
apostrophe, metaphor, and *simile* (see the discussions of these words in this
glossary). (238–43)

flashback   an interruption in a narrative that presents an earlier episode

flat character   a one-dimensional character (for instance, the figure who is only
and always the jealous husband or the flirtatious wife) as opposed to a round or
many-sided character.

fly-on-the-wall narrator   a narrator who never editorializes and never enters a
character's mind but reports only what is said and done

foil   a character who makes a contrast with another, especially a minor character
who helps to set off a major character

foot   a metrical unit, consisting of two or three syllables, with a specified arrangement of the stressed syllable or syllables. Thus the iambic foot consists of an
unstressed syllable followed by a stressed syllable. (258–60)

foreshadowing   suggestions of what is to come (168–71, 220)

formalist criticism   analysis that assumes a work of art is a constructed object
with a stable meaning that can be ascertained by studying the relationships between the elements of the work. Thus, a poem is like a chair; a chair *can* of
course be stood on, or used for firewood, but it was created with a specific purpose that was evident and remains evident to all viewers. (120–22, 143)

free verse   poetry in lines of irregular length, usually unrhymed (264)

gap   a term from reader-response criticism, referring to a reader's perception that
something is unstated in the text, requiring the reader to fill in the material—
for instance, to draw a conclusion as to why a character behaves as she does.
Filling in the gaps is a matter of "consistency-building." Different readers of
course may fill the gaps differently, and readers may even differ as to whether
a gap exists at a particular point in the text.

gender criticism   criticism concerned especially with alleged differences in the
ways that males and females read and write, and also with the representations
of gender in literature (134–40, 144)

genre   kind or type, roughly analogous to the biological term *species*. The four
chief literary genres are nonfiction, fiction, poetry, and drama, but these can
be subdivided into further genres. Thus fiction obviously can be divided into
the short story and the novel, and drama obviously can be divided into tragedy
and comedy. But these can be still further divided—for instance, tragedy into
heroic tragedy and bourgeois tragedy, comedy into romantic comedy and satir-
ical comedy.

gesture   physical movement, especially in a play (226)

half-rhyme   repetition in accented syllables of the final consonant sound but without identity in the preceding vowel sound; words of similar but not identical sound. Also called near rhyme, slant rhyme, approximate rhyme, and off-rhyme. See *consonance*. Examples: *light/bet; affirm/perform* (262)

hamartia   a flaw in the tragic hero, or an error made by the tragic hero (212)

heptameter   a metrical line of seven feet (260)

hero, heroine   the main character (not necessarily heroic or even admirable) in a work; cf. *protagonist*

heroic couplet   an end-stopped pair of rhyming lines of iambic pentameter (263)

hexameter   a metrical line of six feet (260)

historical criticism   the attempt to illuminate a literary work by placing it in its historical context (129)

hubris, hybris   a Greek word, usually translated as "overweening pride," "arrogance," "excessive ambition," and often said to be characteristic of tragic figures (210)

hyperbole   figurative language using overstatement, as in "He died a thousand deaths" (252)

iamb, iambic   a poetic foot consisting of an unaccented syllable followed by an accented one. Example: *alone* (259)

image, imagery   imagery is established by language that appeals to the senses, especially sight ("deep blue sea") but also other senses ("tinkling bells," "perfumes of Arabia") (243–45)

indeterminacy   a passage that careful readers agree is open to more than one interpretation. According to some poststructural critics, because language is unstable and because contexts can never be objectively viewed, all texts are indeterminate (6)

innocent eye   a naive narrator in whose narration the reader sees more than the narrator sees (181–82)

internal rhyme   rhyme within a line (262)

interpretation   the assignment of meaning to a text (90–96)

intertextuality   all works show the influence of other works. If an author writes (say) a short story, no matter how original she thinks she is, she inevitably brings to her own story a knowledge of other stories, for example, a conception of what a short story is, and, speaking more generally, an idea of what a story (long or short, written or oral) is. In opposition to formalist critics, who see a literary work as an independent whole containing a fixed meaning, some contemporary critics emphasize the work's *intertextuality*, that is, its connections with a vast context of writings and indeed of all aspects of culture, and in part depending also on what the reader brings to the work. Because different readers bring different things, meaning is thus ever-changing. In this view, then, no text is self-sufficient, and no writer fully controls the meaning of the text. Because we are talking about connections of which the writer is unaware, and because "meaning" is in part the creation of the reader, the author is by no means an authority. Thus, the critic should see a novel (for instance) in connection not only with other novels, past and present, but also in connection with other kinds of narratives, such as TV dramas and films, even though the author of the book lived before the age of film and TV. See Jay Clayton and Eric Rothstein, eds., *Influences and Intertextuality in Literary History* (1991).

irony   a contrast of some sort. For instance, in **verbal irony** or **Socratic irony** (211) the contrast is between what is said and what is meant ("You're a great guy," meant bitterly). In **dramatic irony** or **Sophoclean irony** (211) the contrast is between what is intended and what is accomplished (Macbeth usurps the throne, thinking he will then be happy, but the action leads him to misery), or between what the audience knows (a murderer waits in the bedroom) and what a character says (the victim enters the bedroom, innocently saying, "I think I'll have a long sleep")

Italian (or Petrarchan) sonnet   a poem of 14 lines, consisting of an octave (rhyming *abbaabba*) and a sestet (usually *cdecde* or *cdccdc*) (263)

litotes   a form of understatement in which an affirmation is made by means of a negation; thus "He was not underweight," meaning "He was grossly overweight"

lyric poem   a short poem, often songlike, with the emphasis not on narrative but on the speaker's emotion or reverie

Marxist criticism   the study of literature in the light of Karl Marx's view that economic forces, controlled by the dominant class, shape the literature (as well as the law, philosophy, religion, etc.) of a society (129–30, 144)

masculine rhyme   rhyme of one-syllable words (*lies/cries*) or, if more than one syllable, words ending with accented syllables (*behold/foretold*) (262)

mask   a term used to designate the speaker of a poem, equivalent to *persona* or *voice* (232–36)

meaning   critics seek to interpret "meaning," variously defined as what the writer intended the work to say about the world and human experience, or as what the work says to the reader irrespective of the writer's intention. Both versions imply that a literary work is a nut to be cracked, with a kernel that is to be extracted. Because few critics today hold that meaning is clear and unchanging, the tendency now is to say that a critic offers "an interpretation" or "a reading" rather than a "statement of the meaning of a work." Many critics today would say that an alleged interpretation is really a creation of meaning (90–96)

melodrama   a narrative, usually in dramatic form, involving threatening situations but ending happily. The characters are usually stock figures (virtuous heroine, villainous landlord).

metaphor   a kind of figurative language equating one thing with another: "This novel is garbage" (a book is equated with discarded and probably inedible food), "a piercing cry" (a cry is equated with a spear or other sharp instrument) (239)

meter   a pattern of stressed and unstressed syllables (258–60, 265–69)

metonymy   a kind of figurative language in which a word or phrase stands not for itself but for something closely related to it: *saber-rattling* means "militaristic talk or action" (241)

monologue   a relatively long, uninterrupted speech by a character

monometer   a metrical line consisting of only one foot (260)

montage   in film, quick cutting (279); in fiction, quick shifts

mood   the atmosphere, usually created by descriptions of the settings and characters

motif   a recurrent theme within a work, or a theme common to many works

motivation   grounds for a character's action (223)

myth   (1) a traditional story reflecting primitive beliefs, especially explaining the mysteries of the natural world (why it rains, or the origin of mountains); (2) a body of belief, not necessarily false, especially as set forth by a writer. Thus one may speak of Yeats and Alice Walker as myth-makers, referring to the visions of reality that they set forth in their works.

narrative, narrator   a narrative is a story (an anecdote, a novel); a narrator is one who tells a story (not the author, but the invented speaker of the story). On kinds of narrators, see *point of view*. (178–86)

New Criticism   a mid-twentieth-century movement (also called formalist criticism) that regarded a literary work as an independent, carefully constructed object, hence it made little or no use of the author's biography or of historical context and it relied chiefly on explication (120–22, 143)

New Historicism   a school of criticism holding that the past cannot be known objectively. According to this view, because historians project their own "narrative"—their own invention or "construction"—on the happenings of the past, historical writings are not objective but are, at bottom, political statements (130–31, 144)

novel   a long work of prose fiction, especially one that is relatively realistic

novella   a work of prose fiction longer than a short story but shorter than a novel, say about 40 to 80 pages

objective point of view   a narrator reports but does not editorialize or enter into the minds of any of the characters in the story (180)

octave, octet   an eight-line stanza, or the first eight lines of a sonnet, especially of an Italian sonnet (263)

octosyllabic couplet   a pair of rhyming lines, each line with four iambic feet

ode   a lyric exalting someone (for instance, a hero) or something (for instance, a season)

omniscient narrator   a speaker who knows the thoughts of all of the characters in the narrative (179)

onomatopoeia   words (or the use of words) that sound like what they mean. Examples: *buzz, whirr* (262)

open form   poetry whose form seems spontaneous rather than highly patterned (265)

oxymoron   a compact paradox, as in "a mute cry," "a pleasing pain," "proud humility"

parable   a short narrative that is at least in part allegorical and that illustrates a moral or spiritual lesson

paradox   an apparent contradiction, as in Jesus' words: "Whosoever will save his life shall lose it; but whosoever will lose his life for my sake, the same shall save it" (252)

paraphrase   a restatement that sets forth an idea in diction other than that of the original (61–63, 79, 321)

parody   a humorous imitation of a literary work, especially of its style

pathos   pity, sadness

pentameter   a line of verse containing five feet (260)

peripeteia   a reversal in the action (212)

persona   literally, a mask; the "I" or speaker of a work, sometimes identified with the author but usually better regarded as the voice or mouthpiece created by the author (150–51, 232–34)

personification   a kind of figurative language in which an inanimate object, animal, or other nonhuman is given human traits. Examples: "the creeping tide" (the tide is imagined as having feet), "the cruel sea" (the sea is imagined as having moral qualities) (241)

plot   the episodes in a narrative or dramatic work—that is, what happens. (But even a lyric poem can be said to have a plot; for instance, the speaker's mood changes from anger to resignation.) Sometimes *plot* is defined as the author's particular arrangement (sequence) of these episodes, and *story* is the episodes in their chronological sequence. Until recently it was widely believed that a good plot had a logical structure: *A* caused *B* (*B* did not simply happen to follow *A*), but in the last few decades some critics have argued that such a concept merely represents the white male's view of experience. (161, 218–23)

poem   an imaginative work in meter or in free verse, usually employing figurative language

point of view   the perspective from which a story is told—for example, by a major character or a minor character or a fly on the wall; see also *narrative, narrator, omniscient narrator* (178–86)

Post-Modernism   the term came into prominence in the 1960s, to distinguish the contemporary experimental writing of such authors as Samuel Beckett and Jorge Luis Borges from such early twentieth-century classics of modernism as James Joyce's *Ulysses* (1922) and T. S. Eliot's *The Waste Land* (1922). Although the classic modernists had been thought to be revolutionary in their day, after World War II they seemed to be conservative, and their works seemed remote from today's society with its new interests in such things as feminism, gay and lesbian rights, and pop culture. Postmodernist literature, though widely varied and not always clearly distinct from modernist literature, usually is more politically concerned, more playful—it is given to parody and pastiche—and more closely related to the art forms of popular culture than is modernist literature.

prosody   the principles of versification (256–65)

protagonist   the chief actor in any literary work. The term is usually preferable to *hero* and *heroine* because it can include characters—for example, villainous or weak ones—who are not aptly called heroes or heroines.

psychological criticism a form of analysis especially concerned both with the ways in which authors unconsciously leave traces of their inner lives in their works and with the ways in which readers respond, consciously and unconsciously, to works.

pyrrhic foot in poetry, a foot consisting of two unstressed syllables (260)

quatrain a stanza of four lines (263)

realism presentation of plausible characters (usually middle class) in plausible (usually everyday) circumstances, as opposed, for example, to heroic characters engaged in improbable adventures. Realism in literature seeks to give the illusion of reality.

reader-response criticism criticism emphasizing the idea that various readers respond in various ways and therefore that readers as well as authors "create" meaning (124–27, 143)

recognition see *anagnorisis* (212)

refrain a repeated phrase, line, or group of lines in a poem, especially in a ballad

resolution the dénouement or untying of the complication of the plot

reversal a change in fortune, often an ironic twist (212)

rhetorical question a question to which no answer is expected or to which only one answer is plausible. Example: "Do you think I am unaware of your goings-on?"

rhyme similarity or identity of accented sounds in corresponding positions, as, for example, at the ends of lines: *love/dove; tender/slender* (261–62)

rhythm in poetry, a pattern of stressed and unstressed sounds; in prose, some sort of recurrence (for example, of a motif) at approximately identical intervals (256–61)

rising action in a story or play, the events that lead up to the climax

rising meter a foot (for example, iambic or anapestic) ending with a stressed syllable

romance narrative fiction, usually characterized by improbable adventures and love

round character a many-sided character, one who does not always act predictably, as opposed to a "flat" or one-dimensional, unchanging character

run-on line a line of verse whose syntax and meaning require the reader to go on, without a pause, to the next line; an enjambed line (261)

sarcasm crudely mocking or contemptuous language; heavy verbal irony

satire literature that entertainingly attacks folly or vice; amusingly abusive writing

scansion description of rhythm in poetry; metrical analysis (256–64)

scene (1) a unit of a play, in which the setting is unchanged and the time continuous; (2) the setting (locale, and time of the action); (3) in fiction, a dramatic passage, as opposed to a passage of description or of summary

selective omniscience a point of view in which the author enters the mind of one character and for the most part sees the other characters only from the outside. (179–80)

sentimentality excessive emotion, especially excessive pity, treated as appropriate rather than as disproportionate

sequence   a group of related scenes in a film (277)

sestet   a six-line stanza, or the last six lines of an Italian sonnet (263)

sestina   a poem with six stanzas of six lines each and a concluding stanza of three lines. The last word of each line in the first stanza appears as the last word of a line in each of the next five stanzas but in a different order. In the final (three-line) stanza, each line ends with one of these six words, and each line includes in the middle of the line one of the other three words.

setting   the time and place of a story, play, or poem (for instance, a Texas town in winter, about 1900) (171–72, 227–28)

short story   a fictional narrative, usually in prose, rarely longer than 30 pages and often much briefer

shot   in film, what is recorded between the time the camera starts and the time it stops (275–77)

simile   a kind of figurative language explicitly making a comparison—for example, by using *as, like,* or a verb such as *seems* (239)

soliloquy   a speech in a play, in which a character alone on the stage speaks his or her thoughts aloud

sonnet   a lyric poem of 14 lines; see *English sonnet, Italian sonnet* (263–64)

speaker   see *persona*

spondee   a metrical foot consisting of two stressed syllables (259)

stage direction   a playwright's indication to the actors or readers—for example, offering information about how an actor is to speak a line

stanza   a group of lines forming a unit that is repeated in a poem (262–64)

stereotype   a simplified conception, especially an oversimplification—for example, a stock character such as the heartless landlord, the kindly old teacher, the prostitute with a heart of gold. Such a character usually has only one personality trait, and this is boldly exaggerated.

stream of consciousness   the presentation of a character's unrestricted flow of thought, often with free associations, and often without punctuation

stress   relative emphasis on one syllable as compared with another (257)

structuralism   a critical theory holding that a literary work consists of conventional elements that, taken together by a reader familiar with the conventions, give the work its meaning. Thus, just as a spectator must know the rules of a game (e.g., three strikes and you're out) in order to enjoy the game, so a reader must know the rules of, say, a novel (coherent, realistic, adequately motivated characters, a plausible plot, for instance *The Color Purple*) or of a satire (caricatures of contemptible figures in amusing situations that need not be at all plausible, for instance *Gulliver's Travels*). Structuralists normally have no interest in the origins of a work (i.e., in the historical background, or in the author's biography), and no interest in the degree to which a work of art seems to correspond to reality. The interest normally is in the work as a self-sufficient construction. Consult Robert Scholes, *Structuralism in Literature: An Introduction,* and two books by Jonathan Culler, *Structuralist Poetics* (1976) and (for the critical shift from structuralism to poststructuralism) *On Deconstruction* (1982).

structure   the organization of a work, the relationship between the chief parts, the large-scale pattern—for instance, a rising action or complication followed by a crisis and then a resolution

style   the manner of expression, evident not only in the choice of certain words (for instance, colloquial language) but in the choice of certain kinds of sentence structure, characters, settings, and themes (152–59, 295–309)

subplot   a sequence of events often paralleling or in some way resembling the main story

summary   a synopsis or condensation

symbol   a person, object, action, or situation that, charged with meaning, suggests another thing (for example, a dark forest may suggest confusion, or perhaps evil), though usually with less specificity and more ambiguity than an allegory. A symbol usually differs from a metaphor in that a symbol is expanded or repeated and works by accumulating associations. (174–78, 243–45, 283–87)

synecdoche   a kind of figurative language in which the whole stands for a part ("the law," for a police officer), or a part ("all hands on deck," for all persons) stands for the whole (241)

tale   a short narrative, usually less realistic and more romantic than a short story; a yarn

tercet   a unit of three lines of verse (263)

tetrameter   a verse line of four feet (260)

theme   what the work is about; an underlying idea of a work; a conception of human experience suggested by the concrete details. Thus the theme of *Macbeth* is often said to be that "Vaulting ambition o'erleaps itself." (187–88, 216, 280–82)

thesis   the point or argument that a writer announces and develops. A thesis differs from a *topic* by making an assertion. "The fall of Oedipus" is a topic, but "Oedipus falls because he is impetuous" is a thesis, as is "Oedipus is impetuous, but his impetuosity has nothing to do with his fall." (21–22, 316–17)

thesis sentence   a sentence summarizing, as specifically as possible, the writer's chief point (argument and perhaps purpose) (21–22)

third-person narrator   the teller of a story who does not participate in the happenings (179–81)

tone   the prevailing attitude (for instance, ironic, genial, objective) as perceived by the reader. Notice that a reader may feel that the tone of the persona of the work is genial while the tone of the author of the same work is ironic. (151–52, 181, 234)

topic   a subject, such as "Hamlet's relation to Horatio." A topic becomes a *thesis* when a predicate is added to this subject, thus: "Hamlet's relation to Horatio helps to define Hamlet." (316–17)

tragedy   a serious play showing the protagonist moving from good fortune to bad and ending in death or a deathlike state (210–13)

tragic flaw   a supposed weakness (for example, arrogance) in the tragic protagonist. If the tragedy results from an intellectual error rather than from a moral weakness, it is better to speak of "a tragic error." (212)

tragicomedy   a mixture of tragedy and comedy, usually a play with serious happenings that expose the characters to the threat of death but that ends happily

transition   a connection between one passage and the next

trimeter   a verse line with three feet (260)

triplet   a group of three lines of verse, usually rhyming (263)

trochee   a metrical foot consisting of a stressed syllable followed by an unstressed
   syllable. Example: garden (259)

understatement   a figure of speech in which the speaker says less than what he
   or she means; an ironic minimizing, as in "You've done fairly well for yourself"
   said to the winner of a multimillion-dollar lottery (252)

unity   harmony and coherence of parts, absence of irrelevance

unreliable narrator   a narrator whose report a reader cannot accept at face
   value, perhaps because the narrator is naive or is too deeply implicated in the
   action to report it objectively (182)

verse   (1) a line of poetry; (2) a stanza of a poem

vers libre   free verse, unrhymed poetry (264)

villanelle   a poem with five stanzas of three lines rhyming *aba,* and a concluding
   stanza of four lines, rhyming *abaa.* The first and third lines of the first stanza
   rhyme. The entire first line is repeated as the third line of the second and
   fourth stanzas; the entire third line is repeated as the third line of the third and
   fifth stanzas. These two lines form the final two lines of the last (four-line)
   stanza.

voice   see *persona, style,* and *tone* (151–52, 232–34)

Appendix C

A Checklist: Writing with a Word Processor

Pre-writing
1. Take notes. Brainstorm; try listing, then linking and clustering your ideas. Use an outline if you find it helpful.
2. Check that your transcriptions are accurate if you quote.
3. Keep your notes together in one file.
4. Organize your sources in a bibliography.
5. *Always back up your material.*
6. Printout your notes.

Preparing a First Draft
1. Use your notes—move them around in blocks. Expand your idea.
2. Incorporate notes to yourself in your first draft.
3. Read your draft on screen to check for errors.
4. Print out a copy of your first draft.

Working with Your Draft
1. Revise your printed draft with pen or pencil. Incorporate these changes into your computer file.
2. Read your corrected draft on the screen; then print out a fresh copy.
3. Repeat these steps as many times as necessary.

Responding to Peer Review
1. Give a copy to a peer for comments and suggestions.
2. Respond appropriately to your reviewer, making changes in your computer file.
3. Print out your revised version and reread it.

Preparing a Final Copy
1. If there are only a few changes, make them on your printed copy. Otherwise, incorporate your changes in your computer file and print out your final copy.

Credits

Brooks, Gwendolyn, "We Real Cool" from *Blacks* by Gwendolyn Brooks. Reprinted by permission of the author.

Didion, Joan, "Los Angeles Notebook" from *Slouching Towards Bethlehem* by Joan Didion. Copyright © 1965, 1966, 1967, 1968 by Joan Didion. Reprinted by permission of Farrar, Straus and Giroux, Inc.

Eliot, T. S., Excerpt from "Little Gidding" in *Four Quartets*. Copyright 1943 by T. S. Eliot and renewed 1971 by Esme Valerie Eliot. Reprinted by permission of Harcourt Brace & Company. Also from *Collected Poems* by T. S. Eliot, reprinted by permission of Faber and Faber Ltd.

Frost, Robert, "The Span of Life" from *Robert Frost Collected Poems*. "The Telephone" from *The Poetry of Robert Frost* edited by Edward Connery Lathem. Copyright 1916, © 1969 by Holt, Rinehart and Winston. Copyright 1944 by Robert Frost. Reprinted by permission of Henry Holt and Company.

Housman, A. E., "Eight O'Clock" from *The Collected Poems of A. E. Houseman* from *Last Poems*, copyright 1922 by Holt, Rinehart and Winston. Copyright 1950 by Barclays Bank Ltd. Reprinted by permission of Henry Holt and Company, Inc.

Hughes, Langston, "Dream Deferred" ("Harlem") from *The Panther and the Lash* by Langston Hughes. Copyright 1951 by Langston Hughes. Reprinted by permission of Alfred A. Knopf, Inc.

Jackson, Shirley, "The Lottery" from *The Lottery* by Shirley Jackson. Copyright © 1948, 1949 by Shirley Jackson. Renewal copyright © 1976, 1977 by Lawrence Hyman, Barry Hyman, Mrs. Sarah Webster and Mrs. Joanne Schnurer. Reprinted by permission of Farrar, Strauss and Giroux, Inc.

Kennedy, X. J., "Little Elegy" by X. J. Kennedy from *Nude Descending a Staircase*. Reprinted by permission of the publisher.

Mora, Pat, "Immigrants" from *Borders* by Pat Mora. Reprinted by permission of Arte Publico Publishers.

Watterson, *Calvin and Hobbes*, copyright © 1993 by Watterson. Dist. by Universal Press Syndicate. Reprinted with permission. All rights reserved.

Yeats, W. B., "The Friends that Have It" from *Collected Works in Verse and Prose* by W. B. Yeats. "The Balloon of the Mind" from *The Poems of W. B. Yeats: A New Edition* edited by Richard J. Finneran.

Index of Authors, Titles, and First Lines of Poems

Index of Terms